The Neuropsychology of the Unconscious

The Norton Series on Interpersonal Neurobiology
Louis Cozolino, PhD, Series Editor
Allan N. Schore, PhD, Series Editor, 2007–2014
Daniel J. Siegel, MD, Founding Editor

The field of mental health is in a tremendously exciting period of growth and conceptual reorganization. Independent findings from a variety of scientific endeavors are converging in an interdisciplinary view of the mind and mental well-being. An interpersonal neurobiology of human development enables us to understand that the structure and function of the mind and brain are shaped by experiences, especially those involving emotional relationships.

The Norton Series on Interpersonal Neurobiology provides cutting-edge, multidisciplinary views that further our understanding of the complex neurobiology of the human mind. By drawing on a wide range of traditionally independent fields of research—such as neurobiology, genetics, memory, attachment, complex systems, anthropology, and evolutionary psychology—these texts offer mental health professionals a review and synthesis of scientific findings often inaccessible to clinicians. The books advance our understanding of human experience by finding the unity of knowledge, or consilience, that emerges with the translation of findings from numerous domains of study into a common language and conceptual framework. The series integrates the best of modern science with the healing art of psychotherapy.

A NORTON PROFESSIONAL BOOK

The Neuropsychology of the Unconscious

Integrating Brain and Mind in Psychotherapy

Efrat Ginot

FOREWORD BY ALLAN N. SCHORE

W. W. NORTON & COMPANY
New York • London

For information about permission to reproduce
selections from this book, write to Permissions,
W. W. Norton & Company, Inc.,
500 Fifth Avenue, New York, NY 10110

For information about special discounts for bulk
purchases, please contact W. W. Norton Special Sales
at specialsales@wwnorton.com or 800-233-4830

Manufacturing by Courier Westford
Production manager: Christine Critelli

ISBN: 978-0-393-70901-8

W. W. Norton & Company, Inc.
500 Fifth Avenue, New York, N.Y. 10110
www.wwnorton.com

W. W. Norton & Company Ltd.
Castle House, 75/76 Wells Street, London W1T 3QT

1 2 3 4 5 6 7 8 9 0

To my beloved family: My husband Prem,
my daughters Ariel and Talya Ramchandani

CONTENTS

ACKNOWLEDGMENTS

First and foremost, I would like to express my deep appreciation to all my patients and supervisees, past and present, who have taught me so much of what I know. This book could not have been conceived of without the rich clinical experiences provided by the countless long-term therapeutic and supervisory interactions in which I have been privileged to participate over the years. The persistent spirit of optimism in the face of emotional suffering and stubborn repetitions I have witnessed in both patients and therapists has profoundly touched me. Being a part of my patients' all-too-human struggles has enlightened me to the ever-shifting balance between despair and the promise of change, between the power of the unconscious and the capacity for reflective awareness.

I want to express special thanks to Dr. Allan Schore, a most generous and open-minded mentor to many clinicians, who has been a significant intellectual influence in my journey to integrate brain and mind. I am greatly indebted to Allan Schore for believing in me and for suggesting I write a book for the Norton Series on Interpersonal Neurobiology. His wisdom and support will always be appreciated.

The help I received from the editorial staff of Norton made writing this book a very gratifying process. I would like to thank Deborah Malmud, my editor at Norton Professional Books, for her belief in the project, patience, unfailing editorial judgment, and helpful guidance. I knew I could always turn to her with any questions or doubts. I would like to extend many thanks to Kathryn Moyer for her consistent editorial guidance and support. In her, I found another source of calm when I felt somewhat destabilized. I would also like to thank Laura Poole for her editorial work on the manuscript.

I would like to extend special thanks to Lois Refkin, who read the manuscript with an expert editorial eye and provided many helpful suggestions.

This project would have been much harder to pursue without the support of my dear friends and colleagues, who repeatedly expressed belief in the book and in my ability to complete it. Special appreciation goes to Dr. Leanne Domash and Dr. Irit Felsen for their help and encouragement. Similarly, I want to thank Sara Lavner, Meryl Messineo, Marci Soutin Levin, and Judy Kotick for their continued ability to listen and provide reassurance. The loving support of my sister, Bilha Neufeld, is also greatly appreciated.

Finally, I want to thank my husband, Prem, for his unwavering support. In particular, I would like to acknowledge his crucial assistance whenever I inevitably encountered difficulties and minor calamities stemming from an uncooperative computer. Similarly, I want to thank my daughter Ariel for her keen understanding of the subject matter of this book and her editorial help early on, when it was still an idea to develop. Her continued support has been very meaningful to me. Many thanks go to my younger daughter Talya—who is on her way to becoming a psychologist herself—for helping me in all things technological, especially during the last stages of preparing the manuscript. Her knowledge of the workings of the Word program was, and still is, a big help.

FOREWORD

ALLAN N. SCHORE, PHD

The construct of the unconscious, in psychoanalysis, psychology, philosophy, and even neuroscience, has its origins in the late 19th century. For most of the ensuing 20th century these models remained unchanged, and somewhat static. But in the last quarter of that century emerging relational and intersubjective clinical psychoanalytic models triggered a significant transformation in Freud's major contribution to human knowledge: a deeper explication of the human unconscious in all aspects of human functioning. As a result, psychoanalysis, the science of unconscious processes, is at this point in the 21st century undergoing a substantial reformulation. In parallel, scientific studies of essential "implicit" functions have shifted focus from a "cognitive unconscious" to an "affective unconscious." As the reader will soon appreciate, a substantial driver of this transformation continues to be the integration of neuroscience with psychoanalysis. In this important volume, Efrat Ginot takes on the challenge of integrating psychoanalysis and neuroscience in order to continue this deeper exploration of the human unconscious. I believe she makes a substantial contribution in that effort.

Freud's monumental contribution to science was his discovery of the critical role of the dynamic unconscious in everyday life (1901), and in his works he created a theoretical perspective that could bring into focus the unconscious, subjective internal world that is instrumental in guiding the individual's moment-to-moment interactions with the external environment. Drawing upon his early experience as a neurologist, over the course of his prolific later writings as a psychoanalyst all of his investigations represented attempts to elucidate the realms of the mind beneath conscious awareness. Although throughout his career he attempted to reformulate his ideas with the structural and topographic theories, his classic concept of the dynamic unconscious remained unchanged—that the self-regulatory functions of the unconscious system operate via the process of repression in order to bar access of sexual and aggressive wishes into consciousness. In this manner, consciously experienced painful negative emotions are repressed and thereby denied entrance into conscious awareness. Clinical technique is thus aimed at "making the unconscious conscious."

It is now clear that Freud was correct in positing that the unconscious mind develops before the conscious, and that the early development of the unconscious is equivalent to the genesis of a self-regulating system that operates beneath conscious, verbal levels for the rest of the life span. However, the idea that the unconscious solely represents material that is repressed and banned from consciousness has been disproven. Psychoanalytic theoreticians are now describing "implicit memory and unrepressed unconscious" (Mancia, 2006). It is now established that implicit memory systems mature before explicit memory systems, and that the right brain matures in the first two years, before the left (see Schore, 2012). I have therefore suggested that the later-onset repression results from the growth of left prefrontal callosal axons over to the right. Levin (1991) points out that callosal transmission begins at 3 and 1/2 years of age, a period of intense interest to Freud:

> Thus, the beginning of the Oedipal phase, a psychological and neuro-anatomical watershed in development, coincides with the onset of the ability (or inability) of the hemispheres to integrate their activities (p. 21)...The development of this defensive function, which Freud called the repression barrier, is accomplished by the increasing and reversible dominance of the left over the right hemisphere, which is known to occur during brain maturation (p. 194).

Basch (1983) also proposes that "in repression it is the path from episodic to semantic memory, from right to left [brain], that is blocked" (p. 151).

Recent discoveries about implicit functions and the right brain (Hugdahl, 1995) have thus been a major force in upending Freud's equivalence of repression with the unconscious (Schore, 2003a). In recent years neuroscience, especially brain imaging research, is actively exploring the implicit (unconscious) processing of cognitions, but even more importantly, affect and affect regulation. Thus the processing of both negative *and* positive emotions occurs at unconscious levels, not because they are repressed, but because *bodily based affects are expressed rapidly and spontaneously, so rapidly that they occur beneath levels of conscious awareness*. Moreover, neuroscience has also confirmed that not only cognitions but also affects can be unconscious, indeed dissociated, and therefore the unconscious also contains not only repressed but dissociated affects.

Due to the fact that all of these implicit emotional functions are in turn expressions of the "emotional" right brain, I have proposed that

Freud's seminal model of a continuously active unconscious mind describes the adaptive moment-to-moment operations of a hierarchical, self-organizing regulatory system that is located in the cortical and subcortical areas of the right brain. Regarding this transformation in Freud's unconscious I have suggested, "Instead of a repository of archaic untamed passions and destructive wishes, it is now seen as a cohesive, active mental structure that continuously appraises life's experiences and responds according to its scheme of interpretation" (2003a, p. xvi).

Another significant alteration of Freud's model is expressed in the concept of a "relational unconscious" whereby one unconscious mind communicates with and interactively regulates another unconscious mind. Due to the fact that affects are communicated within relational transactions via right brain-to-right brain emotional transactions, implicit relational knowledge and internal working models of relationships operate at unconscious levels. Thus adaptive self-regulating processes of the brain-mind-body that occur at levels beneath awareness occur in two modes, (a) autoregulation, via the processes of a "one-person psychology" of an intrapsychic unconscious, or (b) interactive regulation, under the operations of a "two-person psychology" and a relational unconscious. These conceptual alterations have in turn had significant impacts on clinical practice. Ultimately, the most powerful theoretical and clinical models of both psychoanalysis and neuroscience must incorporate aspects of both the one-person psychology of an autoregulating isolated brain and the two-person psychology of an interactively regulating brain.

Indeed, that integrative goal is a major focus of this groundbreaking book. In the following pages, Ginot concludes, "the centrality of the dynamic unconscious—the one created by the rejection of unwanted material—as the foundation of everyday pathology can no longer be accepted without doubts." She observes, "Far from serving a defensive function and being the container for unwanted experiences, unconscious processes are ever present and widespread and in essence are the neuropsychological force behind most of our mental and behavioral operations." Throughout the book, she blends theory and clinical practice with the pragmatic dictum, "the more we learn about our unconscious forces, the better equipped we are to better understand and treat the emotional and behavioral predicaments we encounter in our patients and in ourselves."

And so she sets to the task of utilizing an interdisciplinary perspective in order to offer a neurobiologically informed model not only of unconscious processes, but also of the relationship between unconscious and conscious systems, as well as the unique roles of the right and left hemispheres in what she calls "the conscious-unconscious continuum." Over the following chapters the reader is presented with very recent neurobiological research, which Ginot in turn integrates into more complex models of essential functions of the human mind, both implicit and explicit. These data are extracted from a number of different sources—the laterality literature, including right and left cortical and subcortical regions, the involvement of the amygdala in unconscious fear detection, the role of cortico-striatal basal ganglia and cortico-cerebellar systems in procedural learning, the default system and self-referential functions, and the mirror neuron system and self-narratives and language development. Much of this material may be new to the reader.

In addition to a masterful overview of the rapidly expanding body of studies on the neuropsychology of the unconscious, the author also presents a creative integration of clinical and neurobiological data to formulate a clinically relevant model, illustrated by numerous case vignettes. Indeed, along the way she uses an interpersonal neurobiological model of the unconscious to explicate the underlying mechanisms of a wide variety of clinical phenomena, including affect regulation, intersubjectivity, early attachment and emotional development, trauma, defense patterns of unconscious repetitions and resistance, narcissistic dynamics, transference-countertransference interactions, unconscious and conscious therapeutic change mechanisms, and especially the expression of unconscious aspects of the patient and therapist in clinical enactments, a significant contribution of her earlier works. Her explorations on the neurobiological underpinnings of narratives and reflective awareness are original and provocative.

With respect to the current surge in studies of brain lateralization, throughout this book Ginot discusses the relevance of my work on the right brain (as well as the work of others on the right hemispheric portion of the mirror neuron system, e.g., Cattaneo & Rizzolatti, 2009; Uddin et al., 2007) as a scientific foundation for more complex neuropsychological models of the unconscious. My ongoing studies in developmental neuropsychoanalysis models the early development of the unconscious (vs. the later-forming conscious) mind and the implicit subjective self. Throughout the life span, implicit emotional communication and psychobiological regulation, operating at nonconscious levels, supports the survival functions of the right brain, what I have termed as the biological substrate of the human unconscious (Schore, 1994, 2003a, 2012). Consonant with this proposal, Tucker and Moller (2007) assert, "The right hemisphere's specialization for emotional communication through nonverbal channels seems to suggest a domain of the mind that is close to the motivationally charged psychoanalytic unconscious" (p. 91).

Indeed, a growing body of studies document that unconscious processing of emotional information is mainly subsumed by a right hemisphere subcortical route (Gainotti, 2012), that unconscious emotional memories are stored in the right hemisphere (Gainotti 2006), and that this hemisphere is centrally involved in unconscious functions (Joseph, 1992) associated with maintaining a coherent, continuous, and unified sense of self (Devinsky, 2000; McGilchrist, 2008). From infancy through all later stages of development, right-lateralized, rapidly acting emotional processes are dominant for enabling the organism to cope with stresses and challenges, and thus for emotional resilience and well-being. These right brain-to-right brain communications, operating at levels beneath conscious awareness, allow for the ongoing maturation and development of the human unconscious mind across the lifespan. The relational nature of the psychotherapeutic context is thus a seminal matrix for the evolution of more complex unconscious structure and function.

In light of the fact that in the upcoming chapters the author repeatedly refers to and elaborates upon my studies, in the next part of this foreword I will briefly offer the reader some very recent neuroscience data on the unique roles of the right brain, as well as updates of my ongoing studies on the application of this research to clinical phenomena. I will specifically address three matters: the central role of the right brain in attachment communications within the therapeutic alliance, in transference-countertransference communications within mutual enactments, and in relational mechanisms of therapeutic change. And then I shall invite the reader forward into the creative mind of Efrat Ginot.

RIGHT BRAIN ATTACHMENT COMMUNICATIONS WITHIN THE THERAPEUTIC ALLIANCE

In my writings in modern attachment theory I have attempted to describe the interpersonal neurobiological origins of the life-sustaining emotional bond between the infant and the mother. Grounded in both developmental psychoanalysis and developmental neuroscience, my overarching regulatory theory posits the long-held principle that the first relational contact is between the unconscious of the mother and the unconscious of the infant (J.R. Schore, 2012). During attachment episodes of right-lateralized visual-facial, auditory-prosodic, and tactile-gestural nonverbal communications the primary caregiver regulates the infant's burgeoning positive and negative bodily based affective states. At the most fundamental level, the right brain attachment mechanism is expressed as interactive regulation of affective-autonomic arousal, and thereby the interpersonal regulation of biological synchronicity between and within organisms. In this co-created dialogue, the "good enough" mother and her infant co-construct multiple cycles of both "affect syn-chrony" that up-regulates positive affect (e.g., joy-elation, interest-excite-ment) and "rupture and repair" that down-regulates negative affect (e.g., fear-terror, sadness-depression, shame).

Furthermore, the theory posits that the hardwiring of the infant's developing right brain, which is dominant for the emotional sense of self, is influenced by nonconscious (implicit) right brain-to-right brain affect-communicating and -regulating transactions with the mother. Internal representations of attachment experiences are imprinted in right-lateralized implicit-procedural memory as an internal working model that encodes nonconscious strategies of affect regulation. In this manner, the evolutionary mechanism of early attachment bonding is central to all later aspects of human development, especially adaptive right brain social-emotional functions essential for survival.

These earliest dyadic social-emotional experiences may be predominantly either regulated or dysregulated, imprinting secure or insecure attachments. In marked contrast to an optimal growth-facilitating secure attachment scenario, in a relational growth-inhibiting early environment of insecure attachment the caregiver is either emotionally inaccessible or emotionally intrusive, and poor at receiving and regulating the infant's negative and positive affective states. In the most problematic early scenario of attachment trauma ("relational trauma" of abuse and/or neglect) the primary caregiver of an insecure disorganized-disoriented infant induces traumatic states of enduring negative affect in the child (Schore, 2001, 2003b).

A large body of research now highlights the central role of insecure attachments in the psychoneuropathogenesis of all psychiatric disorders (Schore, 2003a,b, 2012, 2013, 2014). During early critical periods, frequent dysregulated and unrepaired organized and disorganized-disoriented insecure attachment histories are "affectively burnt in" the infant's early developing right brain. Not only traumatic experiences but also the defense against overwhelming trauma, dissociation, is stored in implicit-procedural memory (Schore, 2009a). In this manner attachment trauma is imprinted into right cortical-subcortical systems, encoding insecure internal working models that are nonconsciously accessed at later points of interpersonal emotional stress. These insecure working models are a central focus of affectively-focused psychotherapy of early forming self pathologies and personality disorders.

In light of the commonality of nonverbal, intersubjective, implicit right brain-to-right brain emotion-transacting and -regulating mechanisms in the caregiver-infant and the therapist-patient relationship, developmental attachment studies have direct relevance to the treatment process. From the first point of intersubjective contact, the empathically immersed clinician is attuned to the continuous flow and shifts in the patient's feelings and experiences. Her oscillating attentiveness is focused on barely perceptible cues that signal a change in state, in both patient and therapist, and on nonverbal behaviors and shifts in affects. The therapist must be experienced as being in a state of vitalizing attunement to the patient; that is, the crescendos and decrescendos of the patient's autonomic arousal and affective state must be in resonance with similar states of crescendo and decrescendo, cross-modally, of the therapist. In this manner, the psychobiologically attuned clinician tracks not only the verbal content but also the nonverbal, moment-to-moment bodily based rhythmic structures of the patient's internal states, and flexibly and fluidly modifies his/her own behavior to synchronize with that structure, thereby co-creating with the patient a growth-facilitating context for the organization of the therapeutic alliance.

In accord with a relational model of psychotherapy, right brain processes that are reciprocally activated on both sides of the therapeutic alliance lie at the core of the psychotherapeutic change process. These implicit clinical dialogues convey much more essential organismic information than left brain explicit, verbal information. Rather, right brain interactions "beneath the words" nonverbally communicate essential nonconscious bodily based affective relational information about the inner world of the patient (and the therapist). Rapid communications between the right-lateralized "emotional brain" of each member of the therapeutic alliance allow for moment-to-moment "self-state sharing," a co-created, organized, dynamically changing dialogue of mutual influence. In this relational matrix, both partners match the dynamic contours of different emotional-motivational self-states, and simultaneously adjust their social attention, stimulation, and accelerating/decelerating arousal in response to the partner's signals.

At all stages of the life span, "The neural substrates of the perception of voices, faces, gestures, smells, and pheromones, as evidenced by modern neuroimaging techniques, are characterized by a general pattern of right-hemispheric functional asymmetry" (Brancucci et al., 2009, p. 895). More so than conscious left brain verbalizations, right brain-to-right brain visual-facial, auditory-prosodic, and tactile-gestural subliminal communications reveal the deeper aspects of the personality of the patient, as well as the personality of the therapist (see Schore 2003a for a right brain-to-right brain model of projective identification, a fundamental process of implicit communication between the relational unconscious systems of patient and therapist). This reciprocal communication between the relational unconscious of both members of the therapeutic alliance is described by Casement (1985): "It is usual for therapists to see themselves as trying to understand the unconscious of the patient. What is not always acknowledged is that the patient also reads the unconscious of the therapist, knowingly or unknowingly" (p. 3).

Hammer (1990) describes the state of mind the therapist enters into in order to facilitate right brain-to-right brain communications with the patient:

> My mental posture, like my physical posture, is not one of leaning forward to catch the clues, but of leaning back to let the mood, the atmosphere, come to me—to hear the meaning between the lines, to listen for the music behind the words. As one gives oneself to being carried along by the affective cadence of the patient's session, one may sense its tone and subtleties. By being more open, in this manner, to resonating to the patient, I find pictures forming in my creative zones; an image crystallizes, reflecting the patient's experience. I have had the sense, at such times, that at the moments when I would pick up some image of the patient's experience, he was particularly ripe for receiving my perceptions, just as I was for receiving his. An empathic channel appeared to be established which carried his state or emotion my way via a kind of affective "wireless." This channel, in turn, carried my image back to him, as he stood open in a special kind of receptivity. (pp. 99-100)

In order to receive and monitor the patient's nonverbal bodily based attachment communications the affectively attuned clinician must shift from constricted left hemispheric attention that focuses on local detail to more widely expanded right hemispheric attention that focuses on global detail (Derryberry & Tucker, 1994), a characterization that fits with Freud's (1912) description of the importance of the clinician's "evenly suspended attention." In the session, the empathic therapist is consciously, explicitly attending to the patient's verbalizations in order to objectively diagnose and rationalize the patient's dysregulating symptomatology. However, she is also listening and interacting at another level, an experience-near subjective level, one that implicitly processes moment-to-moment attachment communications and self states at levels beneath awareness. Bromberg (2011) concludes, "Allan Schore writes about a right brain-to-right brain channel of affective communication - a channel that he sees as 'an organized dialogue' comprised of 'dynamically fluctuating moment-to-moment state sharing.' I believe it to be this process of state sharing that ...allows...'a good psychoanalytic match'" (p. 169). Writing in the psychiatry literature, Meares (2012) describes "a form of therapeutic conversation that can be conceived...as a dynamic interplay between two right hemispheres."

On the matter of the verbal content, the words in psychotherapy—it has long been assumed in the psychotherapeutic literature that all forms of language reflect left hemispheric functioning of the conscious mind. Current neuroscience now indicates this is incorrect. In an overarching review Ross and Monnot (2008) conclude, "Thus, the traditional concept that language is a dominant and lateralized function of the left hemisphere is no longer tenable" (p. 51).

> Over the last three decades, there has been growing realization that the right hemisphere is essential for language and communication competency and psychological well-being through its ability to modulate affective prosody and gestural behavior, decode connotative (non-standard) word meanings, make thematic inferences, and process metaphor, complex linguistic relationships, and non-literal (idiomatic) types of expressions. (p. 51)

Other studies reveal that the right hemisphere is dominant for the processing of specifically emotional words (Kuchinke et al., 2006), especially attachment words associated with positive interpersonal relationships (Mohr, Rowe, & Crawford, 2007). These data suggest that the early responding right brain, which is more "physiological" than the later-responding left, is involved in rapid bodily based intersubjective communications within the therapeutic alliance.

RIGHT BRAIN TRANSFERENCE-COUNTERTRANSFERENCE COMMUNICATIONS WITHIN MUTUAL ENACTMENTS

There is now a growing consensus that despite the existence of a number of distinct theoretical perspectives in clinical work, Freud's concepts of transference and countertransference have now been expanded and (re-) incorporated into all forms of psychotherapy. Transference-countertransference affective transactions are currently seen as an essential relational element in the treatment of all patients, but especially the early forming severe psychopathologies.

In such cases implicit right brain-to-right brain nonverbal communications (facial expressions, prosody-tone of voice, gesture) convey unconscious transference-countertransference affective transactions, which revive earlier attachment memories, especially of intensely dysregulated affective states. Gainotti (2006) observes, "the right hemisphere may be crucially involved in those emotional memories which must be reactivated and reworked during the psychoanalytical treatment" (p. 167). In discussing the role of the right hemisphere as "the seat of implicit memory," Mancia (2006) notes: "The discovery of the implicit memory has extended the concept of the unconscious and supports the hypothesis that this is where the emotional and affective— sometimes traumatic—presymbolic and preverbal experiences of the primary mother-infant relations are stored" (p. 83). Transference has been described as an expression of the patient's implicit memories. These memories are expressed in "heightened affective moments" as transferential right brain-to-right brain nonverbal communications of fast-acting, automatic, dysregulated bodily based states of intensely stressful emotional arousal (e.g., fear-terror, aggression-rage, depression-hopeless despair, shame, disgust). Right-lateralized implicit-procedural emotional memory also encodes the dissociative defense against re-experiencing relational trauma, and thereby generates dissociated (unconscious) affects. Other research now indicates that the right hemisphere is fundamentally involved in autobiographical memory (Markowitsch et al., 2000).

As the empathic clinician implicitly monitors the patient's nonverbal transferential communications, her psychobiologically attuned right brain, which is dominant for emotional arousal (MacNeilage et al., 2005), tracks, at a preconscious level, the patterns of arousal rhythms and flows of the patient's affective states. Clinicians are now asserting "transference is distinctive in that it depends on early patterns of emotional attachment with caregivers" (Pincus et al., 2007, p. 636) and describing the clinical importance of "making conscious the organizing patterns of affect" (Mohaupt et al., 2006, p. 243). Converging evidence from neuroscience now indicates, "Simply stated, the left hemisphere specializes in analyzing sequences, while the right hemisphere gives evidence of superiority in processing patterns" (van Lancker & Cummings, 1999, p. 95). Even more specifically, "Pattern recognition and comprehension of several types of stimuli, such as faces, chords, complex pitch, graphic images, and voices, has been described as superior in the normal right hemisphere" (van Lancker & Sidtis, 2006, p. 233).

But in addition, the therapist is implicitly tracking her own countertransferential responses to the patient's transferential communications, patterns of her own somatic, interoceptive, bodily based affective responses to the patient's right brain implicit facial, prosodic, and gestural communications. Via these right brain mechanisms, the intuitive, psychobiologically attuned therapist, on a moment-to-moment basis, nonconsciously focuses her right brain countertransferential broad attentional processes upon patterns of rhythmic crescendos / decrescendos of the patient's regulated and dysregulated states of affective autonomic arousal. Freud's (1915) dictum, "It is a very remarkable thing that the *Ucs* of one human being can react upon that of another, without passing through the *Cs*" (p. 194) is thus neuropsychoanalytically understood as a right brain-to-right brain communication from one relational unconscious to another. In this manner, "The right hemisphere, in fact, truly interprets the mental state not only of its own brain, but the brains (and minds) of others" (Keenan et al., 2005, p. 702).

Right brain-to-right brain transferential-countertransferential unconscious communications between the patient's and therapist's "internal worlds" represent an essential relational matrix for the therapeutic expression of dissociated affects associated with early attachment trauma and thereby "subjectively unconscious danger" (Carretie et al., 2005) and "unconscious emotion" (Sato & Aoki, 2006). These affective communications of traumatized self states were neither intersubjectively shared nor interactively regulated by the original attachment object in the historical context, but now the patient has the possibility of a reparative relational experience. According to Borgogno and Vigna-Taglianti (2008):

> In patients whose psychic suffering originates in…preverbal trauma… transference occurs mostly at a more primitive level of expression that involves in an unconscious way…not only the patient but also the analyst…These more archaic forms of the transference-countertransference issue—which frequently set aside verbal contents—take shape in the analytical setting through actual mutual enactments (p. 314).

Right brain bodily based dialogues between the relational unconscious of the patient and the relational unconscious of the affectively-sensitive empathic therapist are activated and enhanced in the "heightened affective moments" of re-enactments of early relational trauma. Enactments are now seen as powerful manifestations of the intersubjective process and expressions of complex, though largely unconscious, self-states and relational patterns (see Schore, 2012, for an extensive interpersonal neurobiological model of working in clinical enactments).

The relational mechanism of mutual enactments represents an interaction between the patient's emotional vulnerability and the clinician's emotional availability (the ability to "take" the transference). It is most fully operational during (inevitable) ruptures of the therapeutic alliance, described by Aspland et al. (2008) as "points of emotional disconnections between client and therapist that create a negative shift in the quality of the alliance" (p. 699), that act as "episodes of covert or overt behavior that trap both participants in negative complementary interactions" (p. 700). Although such ruptures of the alliance are the most stressful moments of the treatment, these "collisions" of the therapist's and patient's subjectivities also represent an intersubjective context of potential "collaboration" between their subjectivities, and thereby a context of interactive repair, a fundamental mechanism of therapeutic change. This co-created emergent relational structure within the therapeutic alliance contains a more efficient feedback communication system of not only right brain communications but also right brain interactive regulations of intensely dysregulated affective states associated with early relational trauma.

Indeed, the essential biological homeostatic functions of affective, bodily based, intersubjective attachment communications in all human interactions, including those embedded in the psychobiological core of the therapeutic alliance, are involved in the regulation of right brain/mind/body states. The importance of this right limbic-autonomic connection is stressed by Whitehead (2006): "Every time we make therapeutic contact with our patients we are engaging profound processes that tap into essential life forces in our selves and in those we work with...*Emotions are deepened in intensity and sustained in time when they are intersubjectively shared*. This occurs at moments of *deep contact*" (p. 624, author's italics). At moments of deep contact, intersubjective psychobiological "limbic resonance" between the patient's and clinician's relational unconscious generates an interactively regulated amplification of arousal and affect, and so unconscious affects are deepened in intensity and sustained in time. This increase of emotional intensity (energetic arousal) allows dissociated affects beneath levels of awareness to emerge into consciousness in both members of the therapeutic dyad.

deepening
the work

"Heightened affective moments" of the treatment afford opportunities for right brain interactive affect regulation, the core of the attachment process. In a seminal article in the clinical psychology literature, Greenberg (2007) describes a "self-control" form of emotion regulation involving higher levels of cognitive executive function, which allows individuals "to change the way they feel by consciously changing the way they think" (p. 415). He proposes that this explicit form of affect regulation is performed by the verbal left hemisphere, and unconscious bodily based emotion is usually not addressed. This regulatory mechanism is at the core of verbal-analytic understanding and controlled reasoning, and is heavily emphasized in models of cognitive behavioral therapy. In contrast to this conscious emotion regulation system, Greenberg describes a second, more fundamental implicit affect regulatory process, performed by the right hemisphere, that rapidly and automatically processes facial expression, vocal quality, and eye contact in a relational context. This type of therapy attempts not control but the "acceptance or facilitation of particular emotions," including "previously avoided emotion," in order to allow the patient to tolerate and transform them into "adaptive emotions" (2007). More recently he concludes:

of
CBT

vs

> Problems in vulnerable personalities arise most from deficits in the more implicit forms of regulation of emotion and emotional intensity. Although deliberate behavioral and cognitive forms of regulation—more left hemispheric processes—are useful for people who feel out of control to help them cope, over time, it is the building of implicit or automatic emotion regulation capacities that is important

to achieve transformation for highly fragile, personality disordered clients (Schore, 2003). (Greenberg, 2014, p. 351)

RIGHT BRAIN RELATIONAL MECHANISMS OF THERAPEUTIC CHANGE

In cases of early attachment maturational failures, especially histories of relational trauma, deep emotional contact and implicit interactive affect regulation are central mechanisms of right brain psychotherapy change processes. Indeed the hallmark of trauma is damage to the relational life. The repair and resolution of relational trauma therefore must occur in a therapeutic relational context. In this challenging work, more so than detached cognitive understanding, emotional relational factors lie at the core of the change mechanism.

The clinical work involved in traumatic re-enactments involves a profound commitment by both participants in the therapeutic dyad and a deep emotional involvement on the part of the therapist. These types of cases, difficult as they may be, represent valuable learning experiences for the therapist, and they call for expert skills (Schore, 2012). Ultimately, effective psychotherapeutic treatment of early evolving self pathologies (including personality disorders) can facilitate neuroplastic changes in the right brain, which is dominant for attachment functions throughout the life span. This interpersonal neurobiological mechanism allows optimal longer-term treatment to potentially transform insecure disorganized-disoriented attachments into "earned secure" attachments. That said, the developing right brain system ("right mind," Ornstein, 1997) is relationally impacted in all attachment histories, including insecure organized and secure attachments.

Changes mediated by affectively-focused, relationally oriented psychotherapy are imprinted into the right brain, which is dominant for the nonverbal, implicit, holistic processing of emotional information and social interactions (Decety & Lamm, 2007; Hecht, 2014; Schore, 2012; Semrud-Clikeman, 2011). The right brain is centrally involved in implicit (vs. explicit) affectivity, defined as "individual differences in the automatic activation of cognitive representations of emotions that do not result from self-reflection" (Quirin, Kazen, Rohrmann, & Kuhl, 2009, p. 401-402). It also predominates over the left for coping with and assimilating novel situations, and also for emotional resilience (see Schore, 2012). These adaptive functions are mobilized in the change processes of psychotherapy.

The growth-facilitating relational environment of a deeper therapeutic exploration of the relational-emotional unconscious mind can induce plasticity in both the cortical and the subcortical systems of the patient's right brain. This increased connectivity in turn generates more complex development of the right-lateralized biological substrate of the human unconscious, including alterations of the patient's nonconscious internal working model, which encodes more effective coping strategies of implicit affect regulation, and thereby adaptive, flexible switching of self-states in different relational contexts. Thus, long-term psychotherapy may increase the patient's capacity for right brain "social intelligence." In a very recent, comprehensive overview of laterality research, Hecht (2014) states:

> Mounting evidence suggests that the right hemisphere has a relative advantage over the left hemisphere in mediating social intelligence—identifying social stimuli, understanding the intentions of other people, awareness of the dynamics in social relationships, and successful handling of social interactions. (p. 1)

Long-term psychotherapy may also induce structural changes in white matter tracts in the right hemisphere, which underlie increased "interpersonal competence,'" defined as "the capacity to interact and communicate with others, to share personal views, to understand the emotions and opinions of others, and to cooperate with others or resolve conflict should it occur" (De Pisapia et al., 2014, p. 1262). Their diffusion tensor imaging shows that right lateralization in white matter integrity is associated with interpersonal competence. They conclude,

> The finding may have implications for theories claiming that the right hemisphere plays a major role in modulating emotion and nonverbal communication during the first interpersonal relationship that every human being experiences, namely the infant-mother relationship (Schore, 1997, 2000, 2009b). According to this line of research, the development of emotions and social intelligence in the individual—from childhood to adulthood—depends on the quality of their relationship with a principal caregiver and those socioemotional competencies heavily rely on right brain function. Our results support this hypothesis, highlighting the association between white matter in the right hemisphere and interpersonal competence. (p. 1262)

In his masterly review of brain laterality research, Iain McGilchrist (2009) asserts:

> If what one means by consciousness is the part of the mind that brings the world into focus, makes it explicit, allows it to be formulated in language, and is aware of its own awareness, it is reasonable to link the conscious mind to activity almost all of which lies ultimately in the left hemisphere. (p. 188)

On the other hand:

> The right hemisphere, by contrast, yields a world of individual, chang-
> ing, evolving, interconnected, implicit, incarnate, living beings within
> the context of the lived world, but in the nature of things never fully
> graspable, always imperfectly known—and to this world it exists in a
> relationship of care. (p. 174)

Psychotherapy, "a relationship of care," can alter more than the left-lat-
eralized conscious mind; it also can influence the growth and development of the unconscious "right mind." It is undoubtedly true that both
brain hemispheres contribute to effective therapeutic treatment, but in
light of the current relational trend that emphasizes "the primacy of
affect," the right brain, the "social," "emotional" brain, is dominant in all
forms of psychotherapy.

This lateralization conception of dual brains brings us back to my
earlier thoughts about the relationship between the right and left
brains, and what Ginot calls "the conscious-unconscious continuum."
In upcoming pages she will assert, "What a neuropsychological
understanding of the *relationship between the unconscious and the
conscious realms* can offer us is an opportunity to expand how we help
patients alter old patterns that no longer work for them and maintain
such emotional and behavioral changes over time." Psychotherapy
right brain change mechanisms are activated in moments of intense
emotional arousal and relational intersubjective contact, but left brain
change mechanisms such as conscious reflective awareness are activated
in quiet moments of moderate arousal, whether the patient is in the
presence of the therapist or alone.

Earlier I proposed that the most powerful theoretical and clinical
models of both psychoanalysis and neuroscience must incorporate aspects
of both the one-person psychology of an autonomous, autoregulating,
isolated brain and the two-person psychology of an interactively regulating
relational brain. Very recent models of brain laterality now offer research
demonstrating that throughout adulthood the right hemisphere continues
to be dominant for affiliation, while the left supports power motivation,
competition, and autonomy (Kuhl & Kazen, 2008; McGilchrist, 2009;
Quirin et al., 2013). Indeed, Hecht (2014) now concludes:

> As biological creatures that depend on their environment and its
> resources for survival and well-being, the human existential condi-
> tion is such that a person needs power and autonomy that will enable
> carrying one's (own) weight, i.e. meeting one's individual needs suffi-
> ciently and independently. In addition, human beings have an innate
> psychobiological need for affiliation and social connection, which is
> necessary for both emotion-regulation and personal growth. Part of

the human challenge is to achieve equilibrium between opposite and conflicting needs and desires; the need to be part of a social group and the need for independence, the longing for intimacy and closeness with significant others and the desire for some privacy and occasional solitude. (p. 14)

This clearly suggests that left brain changes can also occur as a result of psychotherapy, i.e., via reflective awareness, mentalization, the construction of a verbal narrative, and cognitive re-appraisal. The neuropsychology of these more conscious clinical phenomena is is a primary focus of the upcoming chapters.

I close this foreword by returning to where I began, with the assertion that, due to continuing advances in a number of scientific and clinical domains, the fundamental construct of the human unconscious is now being reformulated and indeed transformed. Unconscious processes are no longer thought of as solely the expression of the mind, but of the mind/brain/body. Efrat Ginot is optimally positioned for the task, both as a psychoanalyst who has studied the unconscious close up in both her patients and herself, and as a neurobiologically informed psychotherapist with a deep knowledge of neuroscience. As the reader will soon discover, this highly informative book is timely, creative, provocative, and as any paradigm-changing effort must be, even controversial.

REFERENCES

Aspland, H., Llewelyn, S., Hardy, G.E., Barkham, M., & Stiles, W. (2008). Alliance rupture resolution in cognitive-behavior therapy: a preliminary task analysis. *Psychotherapy Research, 18*, 699-710.

Basch, M.F. (1983). The perception of reality and the disavowal of meaning. *Annual of Psychoanalysis, 11*, 125-154.

Borgogno, F., & Vigna-Taglianti, M. (2008). Role-reversal: a somewhat neglected mirror of heritages of the past. *American Journal of Psychoanalysis, 68*, 313-328.

Brancucci, A., Lucci, G., Mazzatenta, A., & Tommasi, L. (2009). Asymmetries of the human social brain in the visual, auditory and chemical modalities. *Philosophical Transactions of the Royal Society of London Biological Sciences, 364*, 895-914.

Bromberg, P.M. (2011). *The shadow of the tsunami and the growth of the relational mind*. New York: Routledge.

Carretie, L., Hinojosa, J.A., Mercado, F., & Tapia, M. (2005). Cortical response to subjectively unconscious danger. *NeuroImage, 24*, 615-623.

Casement, P. (1985). *Learning from the patient*. New York: Guilford Press.

Cattaneo, L., & Rizzolatti, G. (2009). The mirror neuron system. *Archives of Neurology, 66,* 557-560.

De Pisapia, N., Serra, M., Rigo, P., Jager, J., Papinutto, N., Esposito, G., Venuti, P., & Bornstein, M.H. (2014). Interpersonal Competence in young adulthood and right laterality in white matter. *Journal of Cognitive Neuroscience, 26,* 1257-1265.

Decety J., & Lamm, C. (2007). The role of the right temporoparietal junction in social interaction: How low-level computational processes contribute to meta-cognition. *The Neuroscientist, 13,* 580-593.

Derryberry, D., & Tucker, D.M. (1994). Motivating the focus of attention. In P.M. Niedenthal & S. Kiyayama (Eds.), *The heart's eye: Emotional influences in perception and attention* (pp. 167-196). San Diego: Academic Press.

Devinsky, O. (2000). Right cerebral hemisphere dominance for a sense of corporeal and emotional self. *Epilepsy & Behavior, 1,* 60-73.

Freud, S. (1901). The psychopathology of everyday life. *Standard Edition,* 6. London, Hogarth Press, 1960.

——— (1912). Recommendations to physicians practicing psycho-analysis. *Standard Edition,* Vol. 12. London, Hogarth Press, 1957.

——— (1915). The unconscious. *Standard Edition,* Vol. 14. London, Hogarth Press, 1957.

Gainotti G. (2006a). Unconscious emotional memories and the right hemisphere. In M. Mancia (Ed.), *Psychoanalysis and neuroscience* (pp. 151-173). Milan: Springer Milan.

——— (2012). Unconscious processing of emotions and the right hemisphere. *Neuropsychologia, 50,* 205-218.

Greenberg, L.S. (2007). Emotion coming of age. *Clinical Psychology Science and Practice, 14,* 414-421.

——— (2014). The therapeutic relationship in emotion-focused therapy. *Psychotherapy, 51,* 350-357.

Hammer, E. (1990). *Reaching the affect: Style in the psychodynamic therapies.* Northvale, NJ: Jason Aronson.

Hecht, D. (2014). Cerebral lateralization of pro- and anti-social tendencies. *Experimental Neurobiology, 23,* 1-27.

Hugdahl, K. (1995). Classical conditioning and implicit learning: The right hemisphere hypothesis. In R.J. Davidson & K. Hugdahl (Eds.), *Brain Asymmetry* (pp. 235-267). Cambridge, MA: MIT Press.

Keenan, J.P., Rubio, J., Racioppi, C., Johnson, A., & Barnacz, A. (2005). The right hemisphere and the dark side of consciousness. *Cortex, 41,* 695-704.

Kuchinke, L., Jacobs, A.M., Vo, M.L.H., Conrad, M., Grubich, C., & Herrmann, M. (2006). Modulation of prefrontal cortex by emotional words in recognition memory. *NeuroReport, 17,* 1037-1041.

Kuhl, J., & Kazen, M. (2008). Motivation, affect, and hemispheric asymmetry: power versus affiliation. *Journal of Personality and Social Psychology, 95,* 456-469.

Levin, F. (1991). *Mapping the Mind.* Mahweh, NJ: Analytic Press.

MacNeilage, P. F., Rogers, L., & Vallortigara, G. (2009). Origins of the left and right brain. *Scientific American, 301,* 160-167.

Mancia, M. (2006). Implicit memory and unrepressed unconscious: How they surface in the transference and in the dream. In M. Mancia (Ed.), *Psychoanalysis and neuroscience* (pp. 97-123). Milan: Springer.

Markowitsch, H. J., Reinkemeier, A., Kessler, J., Koyuncu, A., & Heiss, W. D. (2000). Right amygdalar and temperofrontal activation during autobiographical, but not fictitious memory retrieval. *Behavioral Neurology, 12,* 181-19.

McGilchrist, I. (2009). *The master and his emissary.* New Haven, CT: Yale University Press. *reviews brain laterality research*

Meares, R. (2012). *A dissociation model of borderline personality disorder.* New York: W.W. Norton.

Mohr, C., Rowe, Rowe, A.C., & Crawford, M.T. (2007). Hemispheric differences in the processing of attachment words. *Journal of Clinical and Experimental Neuropsychology, 1,* 1-10.

Mohaupt, H., Holgersen, H., Binder, P-E, & Nielsen, G.H. (2006). Affect consciousness or mentalization? A comparison of two concepts with regard to affect development and affect regulation. *Scandinavian Journal of Psychology, 47,* 237-244.

Ornstein, R. (1997). *The Right Mind: Making Sense of the Hemispheres.* New York: Harcourt Brace.

Pincus, D., Freeman, W., & Modell, A. (2007). A neurobiological model of perception: Considerations for transference. *Psychoanalytic Psychology, 24,* 623-640.

Quirin, M., Kazen, M., Rohrmann, S., & Kuhl, J. (2009). Implicit but not explicit affectivity predicts circadian and reactive cortisol: Using the implicit positive and negative affect test. *Journal of Personality, 77,* 401-425.

———, Gruber, T., Kuhl, J., & Dusing, R. (2013). Is love right? Prefrontal resting brain asymmetry is related to the affiliation motive. *Frontiers in Human Neuroscience, 7,* 1-11.

Ross, E.D., & Monnot, M. (2008). Neurology of affective prosody and its functional-anatomic organization in right hemisphere. *Brain and Language, 104,* 51-74.

Sato, W., & Aoki, S. (2006). Right hemisphere dominance in processing unconscious emotion. *Brain and Cognition, 62,* 261-266.

Schore, A. N. (1994). *Affect regulation and the origin of the self.* Mahweh, NJ: Erlbaum.

——— (1997). Earlier organization of the nonlinear right brain and development of a predisposition to psychiatric disorders. *Development & Psychopathology, 9,* 595-631.

——— (2000). Attachment and the regulation of the right brain. *Attachment & Human Development, 2,* 23-47.

——— (2001). The effects of relational trauma on right brain development, affect regulation, and infant mental health. *Infant Mental Health Journal, 22,* 201-269.

——— (2003a). *Affect regulation and the repair of the self.* New York: W.W. Norton.

——— (2003b). *Affect dysregulation and disorders of the self.* New York: W.W. Norton.

——— (2009a). Attachment trauma and the developing right brain: Origins of pathological dissociation. In P.F. Dell, & J.A. O'Neil (Eds.), *Dissociation and the dissociative disorders: DSM-V and beyond* (pp. 107-141). New York: Routledge.

——— (2009b). Relational trauma and the developing right brain: An interface of psychoanalytic self psychology and neuroscience. *Annals of the New York Academy of Sciences, 1159,* 189-203.

——— (2012). *The science of the art of psychotherapy.* New York: W.W. Norton.

——— (2013). Regulation theory and the early assessment of attachment and autistic spectrum disorders: A response to Voran's clinical case. *Journal of Infant, Child, and Adolescent Psychotherapy, 12,* 164-189.

——— (2014). Early interpersonal neurobiological assessment of attachmentand autistic spectrum disorders. *Frontiers in Psychology, 5, Article 1049.* doi: 10.3389/fpsyg.2014.01049.

Schore, J.R. (2012). Using concepts from interpersonal neurobiology in revisiting psychodynamic theory. *Smith College Studies in Social Work, 82,* 90-111.

Semrud-Klikeman, M., Fine, J. G., & Zhu, D. C. (2011). The role of the right hemisphere for processing of social interactions in normal adults using functional magnetic resonance imaging. *Neuropsychobiology, 64,* 47-51.

Tucker, D. M., & Moller, L. (2007). The metamorphosis. Individuation of the adolescent brain. In D. Romer & E. F. Walker (Eds.), *Adolescent psychopathology and the developing brain.* (pp. 85-102). Oxford, UK: Oxford University Press.

Uddin, L.Q., Iacoboni, M., Lange, C., & Keenan, J.P. (2007). The self and social cognition: The role of cortical midline structures and the mirror system. *Trends in Cognitive Sciences, 11,* 153-157.

van Lancker, D., & Cummings, J.L. (1999). Expletives: neurolinguistic and neurobehavioral perspectives on swearing. *Brain Research Reviews, 31,* 83-104.

van Lancker Sidtis, D. (2006). Where in the brain is nonliteral language? *Metaphor and Symbol, 21*, 213-244.

Whitehead, C.C. (2006). Neo-psychoanalysis: A paradigm for the 21st century. *Journal of the Academy of Psychoanalysis and Dynamic Psychiatry, 34*, 603-627.

Tackling the Unconscious:
Questions with No Easy Answers

EXPLORING THE NEUROPSYCHOLOGY OF UNCONSCIOUS processes is an effort intended to reframe some current ideas of the unconscious. Such efforts, although still in their early stages, may also hold an important key into our psychological functioning and its drawbacks. This book has grown out of more than 30 years of clinical and supervisory experience. Over the years, even as my clinical knowledge and confidence grew, intriguing questions about the psychotherapeutic process have remained. Why are emotional and behavioral difficulties so pernicious, enduring, stubborn, and repetitive even when we gain insight and are determined to change them? I became increasingly curious as to why people continue to engage in behaviors and interactions that cause them misery. Similarly, I wondered why our minds, with all of their magnificent consciousness, sense of agency, and certitude of mastery, cannot make sure we do not reexperience dysregulated self-states or repeat destructive behaviors.

As it became exceedingly clear that it is not easy for most patients to stop and think before acting, adopting new patterns of perceiving feeling and acting, I looked for possible explanations. The interpretations suggesting that a powerful resistance is at play did not offer the reassurance that we truly grasp the underlying reason for such impediments to change. Indeed, as will be discussed in the following chapters, unconscious systems are resistant to change, but not because of defensive reasons or a volitional adherence to old self-object representations; the resistance is built into the machinery of the brain/mind.

It seemed to me then and now that as long as explanations of human behavior did not account for their embeddedness within our bodily properties, our brain/mind processes, something significant was missing. Obviously, as part of the therapeutic process, various psychodynamically based interpretations could be offered in an attempt to address some patients' difficulties to pursue more adaptive behaviors. Although such analysis, especially of transference–countertransference interactions, clearly benefited some patients, for others the difficulties of achieving their therapeutic goals remained, and together we tried to understand the source of stubborn repetitions. Issues regarding the possibility, quality, and range of therapeutic change increasingly appeared to be entwined with implicit processes and internal structures that seemed to have a life of their own.

Over time I realized that the problems involved in lasting changes to one's moods, typical ways of perceiving, feeling, and acting, seem to stem from the tenacious properties of the brain/mind. What has made it even clearer is the often experienced phenomenon of old affects and behaviors, even those thought to have been transformed, reasserting themselves in states of dysregulation. After delving into the neuropsychological literature, it became clear that the answers to these dilemmas (and to others that will be raised in the various chapters) may indeed be found in the way the human brain/mind works. Predisposed to operate in the service of life management in the most energy-saving and efficient ways (Damasio, 2010), and "valuing" past reinforced learning above all else, unconscious brain/mind systems automatically enact what they already know (Koziol, 2014). As the scope of my research has widened, it has also become evident that the more we learn about our unconscious forces, the better equipped we are to better understand and treat the emotional and behavioral predicaments we encounter in our patients and in ourselves.

Without a doubt, no other development has opened the door to a new understanding of what generates and sustains emotional difficulties and destructive repetitions than the aggregate of neuropsychological findings about unconscious processes. In spite of its neuroscientific underpinnings, this book is not about neuroscience per se. It mostly aims to use neuropsychology to better answer some of the more nagging questions: some relating to the power of unconscious systems to repeat and enact established patterns, others seeking those therapeutic processes that most proficiently enhance enduring changes. The following chapters seek to anchor the understanding of our dynamic life—with all its complexities and pitfalls—in the context of the broad and ever-present processes of the unconscious. As so much of our mental and behavioral functions occur out of awareness and even seem to possess unconscious control processes (Hassin, 2007), the adaptive and the maladaptive functions of the unconscious need to be better explained (Wilson, 2003).

The book, then, strives to expand the theoretical and clinical prism through which we understand the unconscious, its neuropsychological foundations, its pervasive influence, and the resulting implications for clinical practice. Drawing from diverse therapeutic material, affect theory, research in cognitive neuroscience, and other neuropsychological findings, the book presents an expanded picture of unconscious processes—one that depicts the unconscious as giving expression to whole patterns of feeling, thinking, and behaving, patterns that are so integrated and entrenched as to make them our personality traits. In particular, it attempts to explore the hidden foundations of the clinical manifestations of repeated self-destructive patterns, resistance to change, and the tendency to experience compromised affect regulation even in the face of seemingly knowing better.

THE CENTRALITY OF THE UNCONSCIOUS

There is no concept as central to psychoanalysis and many other psychotherapeutic approaches as that of the unconscious. Before presenting a new neuropsychological model of unconscious processes, we need to examine why there is a need for an updated understanding based on the latest neuropsychological findings. Following Sigmund Freud's matchless contributions, deciphering the role of unconscious forces in our emotional and interpersonal difficulties has become a cornerstone in clinical work. It is almost inconceivable not to look for unconscious impulses, defenses, conflicts, and motivations as the underlying factors responsible for many patients' persistent struggles. Despite the importance we assign to the unconscious, some of the prevalent assumptions about its attributes are being challenged by fast-growing neuropsychological data.

For instance, the terms *repression* and more recently *dissociation* have come to most commonly describe the defensive functions of the dynamic unconscious. Painful memories, traumatic experiences, intolerable affects, and conflicts—or other experiences that do not fit the conscious sense of self—are rejected from consciousness and relegated to the unconscious domain. In clinical practice, we often use the concepts of repression and dissociation with the confidence that they actually convey a psychological reality about how our minds operate. We assume that when we do not recall events from our childhood we forget them for a reason and that we tend to disavow and reject traumatic and painful experiences that are rejected by our conscious ideas of who we are.

Consequently, since the early days of psychoanalysis, and during much of the continued development of the psychotherapeutic field, the views of how unconscious processes work have implied a purposeful or intentional selection of what is consigned to the unknown. This defensive function characterizes both Freudian concepts emphasizing a dynamic repression of threatening id material and the more contemporary move to understand unconscious processes in terms of defensive dissociation of unacceptable self-other representations. Although dissociative processes are considered inevitable and a natural part of our psychological functioning (e.g., Bromberg, 1998, 2006; Dalenberg and Paulson, 2009; Fairbairn, 1996; Stern, 2010; Sullivan, 1948), they are often understood mainly through their defensive functions, especially in regard to what is perceived to be too emotionally overwhelming to one's sense of self. Consequently, repression as well as dissociation assume motivational intentions. In both models the unconscious is the container for the defended-against painful experiences that cannot coexist with one's conscious sense of self. Until we make active attempts to get in touch with dissociated self-states, unacceptable memories or affects—a therapeutic goal—unconscious processes control what gets remembered or forgotten, what stays hidden, and what is allowed to become conscious and integrated (Bromberg, 2006, 2011; Solms and Zellner, 2012b; Stern, 2010).

Other accepted notions that are similarly being challenged by neuropsychology are the assumed unconscious causes underlying evident difficulties to change. Recurrent struggles to overcome entrenched emotional and behavioral patterns, to choose what we really want rather than what we "unconsciously know," have also been understood as driven by unconscious motivation. Repeated patterns that no longer help individuals attain what they consciously wish for are seen as determined by unresolved conflicts, the patient's loyalty to internalized attachment figures, or an unconscious "need" to repeat such behaviors as a way to maintain self-objects connections that engender a sense of well-being (see Fosshage, 2005, 2011). Under this reasoning, if a behavior keeps occurring in spite of therapeutic insight, there must be an unconscious motivation for this repetition. Secondary gains, fearing change—again implying some kind of defensive motivation—offer other accounts for such repetitions.

It seems, however, that these psychodynamic explanations are based on evidence presented by the behavior itself: if emotional and behavioral patterns are repeated, they must be motivated by a sense of gratification, even if we do not really know what it might be and merely assume its nature. If we do not remember events it is because something in us, out of self-protection, actively does not wish to. This type of circular thinking does not really provide a satisfactory elucidation, but encourages assumptions about hidden motivations that often imply a willful intent embedded in a wish to remain unaware of intolerable experiences.

As the various chapters demonstrate, willful intentions, conscious or unconscious, do not guide our tendency to repeat familiar patterns. Instead, complex brain processes do. Neuropsychological data are making clear that the defensive functions of the unconscious need to be reevaluated and elucidated. Through various topics, the book explores automatic and innate defensive maneuvers as well as their repeated enaction (a term borrowed from Stewart, 2010; Varela et al., 1991 and others). This exploration is done in the context of the ongoing vital commitment of brain/mind processes to the essential but inaccessible functions of life maintenance. These processes seek and reinforce the best positive adaptation to any encountered situation, internal as well as external (Damasio, 2010; LeDoux, 2002, 2014).

Such processes are the foundation for our unconscious, rendering its functions entirely adaptive or "normative" (Fosshage, 2005, 2011; Stoycheva et al., 2014; Wilson, 2003). Consequently, the centrality of the dynamic unconscious—the one containing repudiated material—as the foundation of everyday pathology can no longer be accepted without doubts. For example, many unconscious learning processes and memory systems are dedicated to various defenses against threats to one's homeostasis and sense of well-being. These adaptive defense mechanisms are essential for life management; in this discussion, however, their origin, purpose, and function are cast in a different light. In effect, from the very beginning, defenses become part of the fabric of all unconscious processes, but they are recruited and repeatedly and indiscriminately employed entirely out of awareness against a wide range of potential threats or, conversely, positive experiences as well (Koziol and Budding, 2010; LeDoux, 2014; Lewis and Todd, 2007).

Indeed, it has been strongly suggested that there is not one unconscious or conscious "central director" in charge of how the self perceives and experiences the environment. Rather, our subjective experiences and awareness (or lack thereof) depend on numerous regions and their synchronized activity or inhibition. In a similar way, once a pattern of action has been reinforced, there is no conscious or unconscious volition or motivation involved in its enactment beyond the brain/mind's automatic and innate purpose to restore equilibrium (Cozolino, 2002; Damasio, 1999, 2010; Koziol, 2014; Koziol and Budding, 2009; LeDoux, 2002, 2014; Panksepp and Biven, 2012).

In recent years, an increasing number of clinical researchers and thinkers have recognized the need to reassess some of our theoretical and practical knowledge through the integration of neuroscience. Cozolino (2002, 2006), Fonagy (2008), Fosshage (2011), Mancia (2006, 2007), Fotopoulou (2012), Schore (1994, 2011, 2012), Siegel (1999, 2007), and Solms and Zellner (2012a, 2012b) are a few that come to mind. In spite of the quickly accumulating body of neuropsychological findings questioning some of our accepted notions as to how the unconscious realm works, this information has not yet been sufficiently incorporated into existing theoretical or psychotherapeutic models.

A NEW MODEL OF THE UNCONSCIOUS
IN THE CONTEXT OF OLD CONCEPTS

The all-encompassing characteristics of the unconscious realm—emphasizing enacted complex self-systems—still stimulate an examination of their relationship to the more established concepts of the unconscious. This evaluation is especially interesting in regard to some of the long-held theories that have seen the unconscious as a distinct domain. The unconscious realm is supposed to contain experiences that have been defensively detached from conscious awareness. As a result of dissociation, self-states that are unacceptable to the conscious self are hidden from consciousness.

In Freud's views, unacceptable impulses are rejected from consciousness and then replaced by fantasies that become disconnected from the original experiences that gave rise to them (Freud, 1915). The rejected or transformed impulses, desires, and unfulfilled needs and subsequent conflicts come to occupy a space that is irrational, timeless, and resistant to contradictory input from external reality. Unconscious processes also typically employ what has been called primary processes or sub-symbolic thinking (Bucci, 2007a, 2007b, 2011; Curtis, 2009). Intolerable self-other representations and traumatic experiences are also relegated to oblivion in the more current understanding of dissociative processes. As in the Freudian model, they are hidden and become known through interpersonal enactments, especially in the therapeutic environment (Bromberg, 1998, 2006; Stern, 2010).

In spite of the emphasis on therapeutic enactments, these models do not sufficiently stress the ongoing reciprocal exchange between the concious and unconcious realms (Damasio, 2010; Schore, 2012). Unconscious processes are not separate from conscious ones; there is a dynamic relationship between the two, affecting and influencing each other. Hidden networks and systems find expression through all aspects of our functioning and not just through enactment of dissociated traumatic experiences (Stewart, 2010). In effect, the interaction between the conscious and the unconscious realms speaks to the very efforts of therapy. If one of its goals is structural change, we can say that without this interrelationship therapy could never be effective.

In other respects, some of the assumptions we have taken for granted regarding the volitional defensive functions of the unconscious are not supported. The first obvious problem questions whether the threats emanating from unacceptable impulses or self-other interactions are consciously felt. The usual assumption is that once felt or articulated—again, we are not clear about the subjective parameters of a threat felt—they are then deemed dangerous or too painful. But if such experiences are volitionally "forgotten," they are not dissociated but merely suppressed—intentionally chosen not to be reflected on. Does such an act of disavowal constitute unconscious repression?

Another possibility is that some threats to our well-being are unconscious and can happen entirely under the radar. Indeed, as the various chapters indicate, much of what we react to occurs out of awareness and without our intentional volition (Bargh, 2007, 2014; Hassin, 2007; LeDoux, 2014; Panksepp and Biven, 2012; Schore, 2012, among others). This is especially true when we consider unconscious perceptions of and defensive reactions to anxiety-bound situations. Automatic defenses, such as avoidance, will be employed against the perceived danger out of awareness. Moreover, those defensive maneuvers—simple in nature or complex and sophisticated—that proved effective in the past will be used and enacted again and again.

THE DYNAMIC AND NONDYNAMIC UNCONSCIOUS

We know now that a large part of the unconscious does not simply contain delineated repressed memories or unacceptable self-states, but mostly intertwined neural networks of innate affects, the conditioned learning they induced, myriad automatic defenses, and the innumerable associations to them (Damasio, 2010; Koziol and Budding, 2010; LeDoux, 2002, 2014; LeDoux and Doyere, 2011; Panksepp and Biven, 2012; Schore, 2012). The significance of early implicit memory networks, the "nondynamic unconscious" (Mancia, 2006) or the normative unconscious (Stoycheva et al., 2014), and their enduring effects on further emotional and cognitive development (Schore, 1994, 2012), has only underscored the nondynamic and nondissociated aspects of the unconscious. Formed before the memory system is mature enough to encode explicit memories, early experiences and the implicit emotional and attachment knowing they create continue to shape internal and external patterns. As a child grows, some memory clusters and associations disappear from explicit recall as they are displaced by newer memories. The "forgotten" or weakened memories, however, may still become a part of an unconscious system that goes on to influence mental functioning and behaviors (Dudai, 2011; Fernyhough, 2013). The procedural aspect of implicit memory clearly shifts what unconscious processes compose; they are not only a container for discarded and rejected experiences, but the underpinning for our conscious being. It is a dynamic amalgam of synchronized processes and learned blueprints that repeat themselves, and less a hiding place for dynamically rejected experiences.

Freud's ideas, however, are still relevant and in some agreement with findings in neuropsychology, a field not available to him at the time.

When Freud calls the unconscious "the true psychic reality," one that obeys different rules (1900, 612), he clearly describes the power of the unconscious. This unconscious reality can modify perception of reality and affects one's sense of self and relationships (Ansermet and Magistretti, 2004; Curtis, 2009; Wilson, 2003, 2011). Similarly, Freud's belief that fantasies are the result of fusion and distortion that falsify and change an infantile experience speaks to the many associative links constructing unconscious maps. As the various subjects discussed herein will demonstrate, early associative links are the fundamental building blocks of unconscious systems.

Freud also thought of the unconscious as the domain where childhood fantasies—competing with one's father for mother's love and the fear of castration, for example—are created for particular purposes (1905, 1915). These fantasies are constructed not of memories or procedural learning, as demonstrated in today's research. Rather, in Freud's model they are composed of rearranged associations that create new, drive-guided unconscious fictional scenarios, defensively masking the original troubling impulses bound with sexuality and aggression. Eventually fantasies become more and more removed from both internal and external realities and are formed by imagination alone.

The existence of prevalent sexual or libidinal complications in our love life is a good example of how the new model of unconscious forces both resembles and differs from the more traditional one. As repeated bodily, emotional, cognitive, and behavioral experiences and the many associations to them take place out of awareness; as fear conditioning is linked to contextual external and internal stimuli, there are many opportunities for unconcious sexual hitches. Remember that all learning experiences are intertwined throughout the brain/mind; unconscious associations between sexual feelings and specific contexts of emotional and interpersonal interactions may compromise a healthy progression of libido and sexual joy. Sexuality may be linked to states of fear or aggression, for example, suffusing it with inhibitions and unconscious anxiety. Sexuality can also become ingrained into a perceived need for interpersonal or actual power over others, or used as means of seduction, all without awareness of the true need for connection behind sexual exploits. The body as the seat of sexuality is entirely intertwined with our affects, fantasies and cognitions.

Learning processes and the interpersonal and internal events that give rise to them determine the character of one's sexual development. It is not that sexual impulses do not exist; on the contrary, such drives stemming from primordial emotions systems play a fundamental role in the development of the human psyche (Panksepp and Biven, 2012). But it is not simply that such impulses are rejected because they are not accepted by the individual's conscious self; they become an unconscious part of the many learned associations that make up our unconscious enacted maps. The unconscious qualities of sexual urges exist out of awareness, underpinned by the learning and self-regulating processes of the brain/mind. Potential sexual complications are particularly susceptible to unconscious learning processes because of the integrated processes of body, affect, and cognition. Throughout the book, this integration will show how unconscious brain/mind processes are the result of learned experiences rather than conflictual drives, which tend to be manifested in more of a conscious nature. In addition, we now know that a distinct "self" as one entity does not exist. "Self-organization means auto-organization, without the necessity of some central agency like a self" (Lewis and Todd, 2007, 408). All we can discuss is the subjective experience of a self or selves (Bromberg, 1998) and their many levels of consciousness, underpinned by layers of self-organizing networks (Damasio, 1999, 2010).

Similarly, in more contemporary views of dissociative processes, it is no longer id impulses and the conflicts they create that are being defended against. Rather, what become dissociated are self-other representations, interpersonally derived traumas, and whole or fragmented self-states that are too overwhelming or entirely do not fit with the existing sense of self. Such intolerable states need to be removed from the conscious awareness for one to emotionally and psychically survive (see Bromberg, 1998, 2006; Curtis, 2011; Fairbairn, 1952; D. B. Stern, 2010; D. N. Stern, 2004; Sullivan, 1956). This unconscious does reflect real memories and events, especially interpersonal and traumatic ones, and thus acknowledges more reality-bound memories. But here as well, the notion of the unconscious is almost entirely wrapped around the need to defend oneself from unpleasant experiences, and then store the rejected memories out of awareness.

THE GOAL OF INTEGRATION

Although the emphasis on the underlying neuroscience may appear to some to be reductionist in nature and more mechanical than the dynamic models we are used to, the integration of brain and mind and the understanding of how they are entirely one and the same is the only way to move forward in our attempts to help others (Kandel, 1999, 2001). At this early stage of neuropsychological research, we are limited in most of the distinct conclusions we can draw. What we can do is follow the most salient and repeated findings and make use of them to broaden our knowledge and enhance our ability to help patients.

The objective of this book is to improve our clinical understanding by presenting a new model of the unconscious, one that is continuing to emerge from the integration of neuropsychological research with clinical experience. As many such findings suggest, the unconscious realm is first and foremost a dynamic amalgam of processes that give rise to all of our conscious experiences. As each following chapter demonstrates, the characteristics of the unconscious explored in this book point to brain/mind functions that considerably expand the scope of unconscious processes. Far from serving a defensive function and being the container for unwanted experiences, unconscious processes are ever present and widespread and in essence are the neuropsychological force behind most of our mental and behavioral operations.

Not surprisingly, as much as we understand that unconscious processes exert their influence on who we are and on how we react to our environment, we still tend to underestimate their pervasiveness. We "forget" that much of our perceptions, decisions, thoughts, emotional reactions, and behaviors are automatically enacted and executed away from awareness. The fact that even very complex patterns—usually embodying an inseparable combination of emotions, motivations, cognitions, and attachments—are unconsciously enacted as well is particularly difficult to grasp (Bargh, 2014; Churchland, 2013; Fosshage, 2011; Hassin, 2010; Stewart, 2010). This is especially so because we tend to consciously feel as if each and every action we undertake is volitionally directed.

A central aspect of unconscious brain/mind processes (a term borrowed from Panksepp and Biven, 2012) is that much of what takes place within the neural underpinning of all our mental functioning is out of our conscious control. What's more, in light of what Damasio (2010) calls "the vast unconscious," we get to consciously experience only a small sliver of such neural activity (Koziol, 2014). What gives this vast unconscious away is the fast and automatic reaction patterns to emotional, personal, social, and cognitive stimuli (Churchland, 2013; Damasio, 2010; Hassin et al., 2007; Mancia, 2006; Panksepp, 2012; Stewart, 2010). Much of the unconscious content is hidden and inaccessible, but its footprints can be found in all our emotional, cognitive, and behavioral enactions (Cozolino, 2002; Damasio, 2010; Koziol, 2014; Stewart, 2010; Wallim, 2007). In this process, although it may seem counterintuitive and in contrast to the picture of the unconscious as a seething cauldron of dangerous impulses (Freud, 1915), our unconscious is the reliable and persistent feature that gives us the sense of stability and continuity.

Throughout the book I use the adjectives *unconscious* and *implicit* interchangeably. In addition, I have borrowed a few terms that I think help explicate complicated matters. From Damasio and Koziol and Budding I have taken the term *maps* or *models*; from Panksepp, his use of the term *mind/brain*, mostly used here as *brain/mind* to connote their unity; and from Schore I have borrowed the centrality of affect regulation as a process under the guidance of unconscious forces. Throughout the various chapters, however, to emphasize the sense of the dynamic qualities inherent in our unconscious, I have chosen to refer to unconscious maps or models as unconscious self-systems. Such unconscious self-systems are the ones that underpin and guide the more consciously experienced self-states.

Conceptually and clinically, Bromberg's (1998, 2006) work delineating how different self-states coexist within one psyche with various degrees of "familiarity" among them is an important guiding principle in further understanding how unconscious self-systems come to be and function. As we now know, when unconscious self-systems reach levels of consciousness through neural activity, they are experienced as self-states (Baars, 1989; Bromberg, 1998, 2006; Churchland, 2013; Damasio, 2010). At times, the connection among self-states is severed as well, giving rise to an increased level of unconscious rigidity (Bromberg, 2006; Koziol and Budding, 2010). Unconscious self-systems are an amalgam of encoded visceral sensations, affects, cognitive styles, behaviors, and action tendencies, all intertwined into units we cannot access directly but become aware of through their automatic enaction (for the psychoanalytic view of self-states, see Bromberg's seminal contribution, 1998, 2006).

In addition, there is growing evidence that affect and cognition are much more integrated than we have traditionally held. Throughout the book, although the words *affect, emotion, cognition,* and *behaviors* are often used separately for the convenience of the discussion, these choices are in no way meant to convey that they are separate entities. The opposite seems to be the case, a view that will be elaborated in the ensuing chapters.

We can proceed now to the very exciting task of trying to integrate neuropsychology into our understanding of the unconscious and its pervasiveness in our psychic functioning. This integration is not seamless; much of what has been found points to the need to change, tweak, and reframe how we view some of what we know about unconscious processes. As a result, some of our long-accepted therapeutic processes need to be reexamined as well, always with the important goal of becoming better clinicians.

What a neuropsychological understanding of the relationship between the unconscious and the conscious realms can offer us is an opportunity to expand how we help patients alter old patterns that no longer work for them and maintain such emotional and behavioral changes over time. As we better understand the stubborn and repetitive nature of brain/mind functions, we also need to realize that just talking about them and gaining verbal insight as to their source may not be enough to induce transformation.

A great deal of nonverbal, implicit learning takes place in the therapeutic relationship (Aron, 1996; Bromberg, 1998, 2006; Fosshage, 2005,

2011; Renn, 2012; Schore, 2012; Stern et al., 1998), as well as growth experiences stimulated by enactments (Bromberg, 2006; Chused, 1998; Pizer, 2003; Stern, 2010). More recently, the power of mentalization and reflective awareness on emotional states in real time has been consistently found to be an effective therapeutic approach (Bateman and Fonagy, 2004, 2012; Jurist, 2008). In addition to such established processes, psychodynamic psychotherapy as well as psychoanalysis will gain a great deal by incorporating more active techniques that are effective in engaging and changing dysregulated states. Focusing on the inseparable links between affect and body (Ogden et al., 2006), between dysregulation and negative self-narratives (Ginot, 2012), or on the reactivation of emotional memories to alter their impact through reconsolidation (Ecker et al., 2012; Lane et al., 2014) are all examples of therapeutic practices that tackle the neuropsychological underpinning of entrenched patterns. The emphasis in such approaches, as well as others such as cognitive-behavioral therapy (Beck, 1979), is also on employing reflective awareness practices and homework meant to reinforce different ways of regulating affect and tie contextualizing past experiences.

The field of trauma studies and the therapeutic approaches it has advanced, for example, have greatly benefited from neuroscience (Shapiro, 2002; van der Kolk, 1994; Yehuda et al., 1996, 2005, 2008). As we will see throughout the various chapters, a fresher understanding of unconscious processes can expand our theoretical understanding of and our particular approaches to what ails our patients. An understanding of the mechanisms of repetition and entrenchment also changes how we think about therapeutic phenomena such as resistance and defense. It highlights the effects of early development and the role of emotional systems in the creation of unconscious self-systems. As the following chapters demonstrate, the neuropsychological model of unconscious processes inevitably redefines such central aspects of the therapeutic process, leading to potential new ways of addressing old problems.

There has been a noticeable proliferation of therapeutic modalities in recent years, developed and practiced in an effort to overcome the obstacles inherent in the therapeutic endeavor, especially with so-called difficult patients. The multiplicity of modalities may in itself be a covert recognition that any potential solution will not be found in a therapeutic technique per se but in a deeper understanding of how brain/mind processes, unconscious as well as conscious ones, affect emotional and behavioral well-being. Thus, combining clinical observations with neuropsychological research can enhance our understanding of the home of the unconscious processes that are at the roots of our repeated and automatically enacted emotional and behavioral patterns. At the same time, such expanding knowledge will open the way for more effective therapeutic approaches.

The Neuropsychology
of the Unconscious

CHAPTER 1

"My Unconscious Made Me Do It": An Excuse or an Accurate State of Affairs?

G OING THROUGH LIFE AND ENCOUNTERING its countless challenges, most of us take for granted the ubiquitous and familiar sense of being in control and entirely conscious. We are certain that we know why we do certain things and not others, why we pursue particular goals or people, and what our reasons are for important decisions. We are aware of our bodily and mental engagement with the environment, external as well as internal, and can easily give verbal expression to various feelings, sensations, and thoughts. Yet in parallel with the importance of consciousness to our effortless functioning, the unconscious realm is always in action, guiding our feelings, thoughts, and behaviors.

The recognition that our behaviors, thoughts, and feelings are not entirely conscious, carefully planned, or intentional has been, of course, a keystone of psychoanalysis and psychotherapy, paving the way to a more comprehensive understanding of human nature. In effect, in spite of the multiplicity of therapeutic approaches, the influences of unconscious processes are often the common denominator. Conceptual changes have already occurred in how we view the unconscious, in particular the move away from the centrality of repression as a way to defend against id material and impulses. The unconscious is no longer thought of as the container to fantasies that are the distorted derivatives of the original forbidden impulses. With the contemporary emphasis on the dissociation of self-other representations or self-states, the concept of the unconscious has become more inclusive, reflecting the current importance given to defensively dissociated relational trauma (See Bromberg, 1998).

In addition, prevalent ideas regarding the unconscious have largely assumed that the dissociated material, be it interpersonal memories, self-other states, or associations linked to drives and arousal states (see Ansermett and Magistretti, 2004; Solms and Zellner, 2012a, 2012b), can be reliably unearthed in therapy. According to this model, therapeutic explorations and free associations can unmask the purpose of unconscious defenses and the defended-against content. As a result, unconscious material can become conscious and integrated, losing its dynamic grip on one's functioning. But in a departure from the almost exclusive focus on the defensive functions assigned to the unconscious in both these models—either repression or dissociation—a new picture of unconscious processes is rapidly emerging.

In effect, unconscious processes are large-scale brain/mind functions that are pervasive and generally much more influential than we usually consider them to be. At the same time, as inaccessible as unconscious processes are, they are constantly enacted in every mental and behavioral manifestation and in all relationships, including the therapeutic one. For example, a great deal of our perception and the processing of internal and environmental stimuli occur out of awareness (Tsuchia and Adolphs, 2007). We are aware of neither the stimuli nor how we perceive, categorize, or interpret them. Such ongoing processes underpin many of the interpersonal processes in psychotherapy; the way to enactments, for instance, does not only depend on dissociated or unconscious "content" but on the very process of unconscious perception and interpretation.

Key modifications to Freud's concepts of the unconscious and subsequent notions of dissociation stem from the recognition that unconscious processes, always humming in the background, are not separate from our broader mental and social functioning; rather, they are an inextricable part of them (Churchland, 2013; Curtis, 2009; Damasio, 2010; Koziol and Budding, 2010). Rather than containing distinct memories, relational traumas, conflicts, or instinctual wishes defensively repressed or dissociated, the unconscious realm seems to be totally inclusive and comprehensive in nature. Via clusters of neural networks integrating all aspects of brain/mind functioning—sensory, emotional, cognitive, and behavioral—the unconscious is always being generated in present feelings, thoughts, and actions (Colombetti, 2010; Stewart, 2010). Although far from being a simple repetition of past representations, interactions with our internal and external environment stimulate and enact existing response models that have been tested and reinforced in the past (Bargh, 2007, 2014; Damasio, 2010; Di Paolo et al., 2010; Wegner, 2007; Koziol and Budding, 2010; Westen, 1999, 2006).

UNCONSCIOUS PROCESSES: THE SILENT BUT CONSTANT ENGINES BEHIND MOST OF OUR PSYCHOLOGICAL FUNCTIONS

These new insights are supplanting more traditional ideas that regard the unconscious as a static container of discrete memories and emotions buried deep and waiting to be discovered. Such views, developed without the framework of neuroscience, have assumed a delineated border between conscious and unconscious states. They have also considered forgotten childhood memories as defensively motivated and therefore capable of being accurately and reliably recalled. Without the knowledge gleaned from neuropsychology, the clinically based understanding of the unconscious could not consider its wider aspects—the many networks and neural maps that underpin and direct all facets of experience. Although in our therapeutic work we presume that verbal accounts of newly uncovered memories or free associations are true reflections of the unconscious, such systems are inaccessible to words and are more faithfully implied through enaction, or the typical ways of relating to oneself and to others (Bromberg, 2006; Churchland, 2013; Curtis, 2009; Engel, 2010; Koziol, 2014; Schore, 2012).

In light of neuropsychological research, the subject of threat-driven defensive dissociation comes under scrutiny as well. Many forces are innately set in place to preserve the sense of well-being and successfully adapt to danger, but the assumption that there is a self-agency that unconsciously determines what is allowed to stay conscious or what is not unacceptable to one's sense of self has proven problematic (Horga and Maia, 2012; Lewis and Todd, 2007; Wegner, 2007). It is not a single central self-agency, conscious or unconscious, that intervenes or controls defensive activity. Ingrained defensive reactions are the result of a concerted synchronized automatic reaction to environmental interactions that threaten adaptation. Once they achieve their goal, particular neural and chemical links will be activated again in response to contextual cues that have already been deemed as threatening. In addition, as memory research indicates, in the absence of retrieval (explicit memory reactivation), long-term memories are susceptible to amnesic inhibitory enzymes (Dudai, 2011). These findings raise further questions as to an unconscious drive to forget, guided by a single self-agency.

Defenses such as avoidance are automatically guided and implemented by the emotional systems (Panksepp and Biven, 2012) and the amygdala (LeDoux, 2002, 2014) in response to unpleasant physioaffective conditions and hyper- or hypo-states of arousal (Schore, 2012).

These and other reservations about prior views of the unconscious do not originate from new conceptual or clinical reevaluation. They are the result of a major shift in our understanding of how the brain/mind works. As the following sections of this chapter show, what inspires the need to reframe the nature, scope, and function modes of the unconscious are advances in neuroscience. On their own, neuropsychological findings and conclusions are not enough. They need to be tested and become relevant out of the lab as well—most important, in the way we comprehend and work with our patients. We need to recognize what neuropsychology identifies as unconscious brain processes in our patients and ourselves. Doing so will enable research findings to cross the line from the abstract and piecemeal to the knowable and concrete. As part of integrated theoretical and clinical models, neuropsychological insights, then, can truly advance our understanding and therapeutic abilities. Specifically in this book, the integration of neuropsychology into our clinical experience has many implications for how we comprehend the unconscious, and consequently to a host of therapeutic issues intimately intertwined with such expanded knowledge.

WHAT LIES UNDERNEATH: THE UNCONSCIOUS BRAIN/MIND

One of the exciting developments in our understanding of the unconscious involves the much-expanded picture of its scope of action and influence. Libet (1985) and Libet et al. (1967) conducted experiments showing that brain activity preceded seemingly conscious decisions of subjects instructed, for example, to raise their fingers at will. Since then, it has become very clear that unconscious processes are involved even when we feel we make deliberate choices. As neuroscience continues to demonstrate, the unconscious is in essence an instrumental system that actively relates to the external world and learns through perceptions, priming, and actions (Bargh, 2007, 2014; Damasio, 2010; Dijksterthuis et al., 2007; Glaser and Kihlstrom, 2007; Hassin et al., 2007; Koziol and Budding, 2010; Wegner, 2007).

At the heart of unconscious systems is the brain's efficiency in acquiring implicit skills and patterns that involve all aspects of our perceptual, visceral, emotional, and cognitive functioning. Such capacities are developed as necessary and indispensable tools that ensure the important task of survival, adaptation, and life management. From the very beginning of life, learning experiences are encoded implicitly and retained for future adaptation and on the maintenance of physical and emotional well-being. With an increasing amount of associations to these original learning experiences and memories, implicit lessons create dynamic systems that continue to scan the environment for further cues, challenges, and threats.

These experiences coalesce into emotional, cognitive, and behavioral procedural lessons that do not demand conscious attention when a certain reaction is called for. As development continues, new experiences are fitted into existing representations and neural maps, further strengthening specific adaptational organizations and complex patterns of response to both conscious and unconscious, external and internal stimuli (Damasio, 2010; Engel, 2010; Hassin, 2010; Koziol, 2014; Koziol and Budding, 2010; LeDoux, 2002; Lewis, 2005; Stewart, 2010; Wegner, 2007). Such complex patterns can pursue goals with apparent motivation and determination, but without conscious will or plan (Bargh, 2007, 2014). In effect, conscious awareness is not necessary for the execution of many of our emotional and interpersonal needs.

Within the all-important purpose of adaptation there was evolutionary pressure to develop a survival system that could act quickly and without deliberation and still efficiently. Automatically enacted, out-of-awareness patterns became very effective at executing most life management tasks, without having to rely on any deliberation in the face of environmental challenges. With time, another system—one that is slower, more deliberate, and therefore more flexible—developed as well, leading to slower thoughtful functions, and adaptive abilities that depend on planning and mindful attention (Damasio, 2010; Koziol and Budding, 2010; LeDoux, 2002; Lewis and Todd, 2007; among many others). What is becoming clear is that despite the more (relatively) recent development of conscious processes, the unconscious ones are still very much in the picture, and furthermore are the center of our functioning. Being ontologically older and much better equipped to quickly respond to familiar situations, the unconscious realm became the essential mode of functioning. In effect, there is ample evidence from social, psychological, and economic studies that unconscious processes monitor, control, and guide the way we pursue goals and desires as well as our adaptive approaches to changes in the environment (Bargh, 2007, 2014; Churchland, 2013; Glaser and Kihlstrom, 2007; Eitam et al., 2008; Wilson, 2003). Although considered within the field of consumer behavior, Kahneman's (2011) conceptualizations regarding the slow—more reflective—and the fast implicit mental systems are such clear examples. Similarly, a popular book, *The Power of Habit* (Duhigg, 2012), also ties our propensity to develop unshakable habits to neural circuits and reinforced patterns.

Underpinning unconscious processes are neural connections across all brain regions that use synchronized activation and inhibition to establish maps, models, or schemas that give rise to conscious experiences or conscious self-states (Bromberg, 1998; Bucci, 2007a, 2007b; Damasio, 1999, 2000, 2010; Koziol and Budding, 2010). The unconscious system as a whole, then, is actively engaged with the world outside and inside of us, and although operating out of awareness, it is an active and constant participant in our responses to all stimuli coming from the internal and external environments. Brain, body, and environment are inextricably linked at all times, from the perception, feelings, and interpretation of all incoming stimuli to the many unconsciously encoded associations that follow. The particular ways all these processes entwine, persist, and are enacted give unconscious self-systems their unique characteristics (Colombetti, 2010; Di Paolo et al., 2010).

OUR IMPLICIT MAPS/SELVES: THE CASE OF HENRY

After weeks of preparations for his wife's 40th birthday, Henry presented the few presents he had thoughtfully put together. As Ruth eagerly opened each one, she was visibly delighted. Excitedly, Henry asked her to open the wrappings of the last package. He was sure she would really appreciate that last one—a new smartphone. Upon opening the package, however, Ruth's facial expression showed distinct disappointment. "Oh, I was really hoping for the latest version, don't you remember? I told you about it two weeks ago. Oh, I don't know . . . do you think you can exchange it?" Henry was immediately and deeply hurt by his wife's unexpected reaction. In reaction, he hastily left the room and refused to interact with Ruth for the rest of the night. What was to be her birthday celebration became an unpleasant feud.

As Henry later reported in therapy, that hurt feeling was very familiar to him: an unpleasant pressure in his chest, followed by thoughts of being mocked and rejected by others, especially those close to him. Convinced that Ruth disregarded his good intentions, he felt unappreciated, his judgment and thoughtfulness questioned. At that moment, Henry's emotional world collapsed into that humiliating sensation. Dimly he thought that he might be overreacting, but he could not avoid drowning in the state he was in—painful feelings of being slighted and unappreciated and thoughts of failing his wife became the only internal reality he was fully aware of. The anger that followed also seemed to him entirely justified. How could she not appreciate all these presents, the effort he put into selecting them? Why couldn't she be satisfied with what he had got?

Henry was also certain that his sense of indignation was really about his wife's reaction, and in quick succession, similar experiences from their past came up with the same urgency. It had happened before, he accused his wife. "As a matter of fact," he said, "every time I try to do something nice, you find fault with it, you find the one thing that is wrong." Henry felt the need to fight back, to explain and defend his choice, and the inevitable fight spoiled the intimate time they had just shared.

During the next therapy session, Henry realized that throughout that emotional event he "forgot" that his wife's disappointment had nothing to do with him, that her spontaneous reaction only expressed a genuine disappointment about what she desired in a phone, an important item for her. He could not see at the moment that her expressed wishes were not statements about his competence but about her own preference.

"How could that happen?" Henry asked in therapy. How could he lose sight of what was really going on and as a result ruin their evening? He was particularly upset with himself, because he hated to upset Ruth, hated to lose sight of how good they are together and how caring and appreciative she is.

Our understanding of Henry's emotional reaction and behavior can be greatly explicated through the following model of unconscious processes. As therapy progressed, Henry was increasingly able to trace some of his implicit self-systems to his childhood home, his parent's marriage, and their relationship with him and his brother. This vignette, like the neuropsychological findings that follow, clearly illustrates the power of internal maps to become activated and enacted in a familiar emotional context that triggers unconscious systems.

The brain's predisposition for map making underpins our physiological, emotional, cognitive, and behavioral maps or unconscious self-systems. The metaphor of the map used by Damasio (2010) describes a neural organization characterized by different patterns of synchronized neural and chemical activity. Clusters of neurons or regions can fire together or stay quiet in response to external or internal stimulation. The potentially endless combinations of on-and-off firing of neuron clusters create particular patterns, images, or maps associated with specific emotional, behavioral, or interpersonal situations (Churchland, 2013; Cozolino, 2002, 2006; Damasio, 2010).

Mapping takes place within all of our sensory perceptions, body structures, and mental functions. The brain maps external and internal experiences; physiological, emotional, cognitive, and behavioral expressions; memories, beliefs, wishes, and future plans. The process of mapping helps us hold on to our perceptions and, on a more conscious level, connect images to words. Damasio suggests that the signals relaying the conditions of body states and emotion—experiences that constitute a core self-system—are in the form of images as well. Although the vast amount of maps are entirely out of awareness and therefore not accessible to consciousness, when maps important for life maintenance become part of the conscious realm, they are committed to working memory and can be recalled at will. These constitute our conscious self-states and the basis for potential reflective awareness. Recently, the concept of working memory has been found to operate unconsciously, as well as consciously, illustrating the capacity of the implicit systems to function just as well as explicit working memory. Both conscious and unconscious working memory systems are essential to early development and to the establishment of adaptive behaviors and patterns; they generate rules, extract patterns and expectations, and underpin procedural learning essential for optimal development (Gilhooley, 2008; Hassin, 2007; Koziol, 2014; Lewis, 2005; Lewis and Todd, 2007; Paul and Ashby, 2013).

These maps or models—in this psychodynamic model they are mostly referred to as implicit or unconscious self-systems—place perceptions and reactions under the influence of unconscious "know-how" and response tendency. Brain maps, the particular ways neural activities are distributed and synchronized, dynamically shift in response to stimuli, thus reflecting the firing patterns of the neurons that feed them. What makes these maps unconscious is not only the images or memory traces embedded in them—early attachment experiences, emotional memories, identification patterns, defenses, and self-narratives—but also the ongoing process of continuously re-creating them. Automatically and out of awareness this process of re-creation happens whenever we interact with and respond to the external environment and to signals arising from within us. Consequently, past-encoded self-systems are always being resurrected in the present time, blending the past and the present, the conscious and the unconscious (Chartrand et al., 2007; Churchland, 2013; Damasio, 2010; Gendlin, 2012; Horga and Maia, 2012).

Furthermore, neural systems interacting with the environment are always engaged in a fast and automatic selection of relevant information in the context of potential action (Hutto, 2012; Stewart, 2010). This manner of processing of stimuli is an important characteristic of the brain/mind. It involves constant unconscious predictions about forthcoming sensory events and reactions to them. This perceptual processing, so dynamic and highly selective in nature, becomes increasingly dependent on already established neural patterns. The observations that the interpretive and behavioral systems overlap means that perception leads to action, but action leads to reinterpretations as well (Chartrand et al., 2007; Wegner, 2007). The propensity to enact existing patterns unconsciously and automatically is a main feature of our implicit self-systems, underscoring the view of the unconscious as a dynamic global system always in action (Cappuccio and Wheeler, 2012; Sheets-Johnstone, 2010). These characteristics illustrate the blurry boundaries between unconscious self-systems and their enacted manifestations in our conscious self-states. All levels of mental functioning, including internal and social language, are connected to bodily senses and perceptions and are considered a form of action (Borghi and Cimatti, 2010). Interestingly, similar ideas of unconscious automaticity and repetition that were articulated by Janet (1913) and Freud and Breuer (1895) have recently received contemporary support from neuropsychology. Similarly, Melanie Klein's conceptualization of the enactive nature of unconscious properties and their inevitable projection onto and shaping of reality fits this model as well (see Shapira, 2013).

The implications of these unconscious neural maps for how we can better understand patients' difficulties are manifold. Maps or self-systems are especially central to the formation and maintenance of defenses that are instinctively marshaled to deal with physical and emotional discomforts. Such homeostatic pressures demand repeated responses that lead to relief or reward—to a state of resolution—even if these responses are only good temporarily but are not adaptive in the long run (Koziol, 2014). Helpless rage in the face of misattunement and the avoidance of close relationships as a result, fearful behaviors (LeDoux, 2002) that once conditioned become irrationally generalized to many situations, the inability to regulate hyperaroused affects (Panksepp and Biven, 2012; Schore, 1994, 2003, 2009, 2012), and recurrent negative interpretations about one's self-worth (Ginot, 2012) for example, will all become part of one's developing map.

NEW DIRECTION: THE ROLE OF SUBCORTICAL REGIONS

Underpinning the expanded knowledge of unconscious processes are neuropsychological findings linking the unconscious neural maps just described to particular brain regions, especially the subcortical ones. The neural connections from the more primitive parts of the brain to the most advanced precortical ones, the neuraxis, pass through four main levels: the brain stem, the diencephalon (thalamus and hypothalamus), the limbic structures (such as the hippocampus and the amygdala), and basal ganglia, and finally the cerebral cortex. Deliberate control is mediated by corticolimbic connections, whereas more automatic patterns and states of action readiness are underpinned by brain stem regions and the hypothalamus (Frijda, 1986; Izzard, 1993; Lewis and Todd, 2007).

Connected to cortical areas through distinct loops in an ongoing process, these vertically organized brain systems have a part in all our bodily mental and behavioral functions (Damasio, 2010; Koziol, 2014; Koziol and Budding, 2010; Lewis and Todd, 2007; Panksepp and Biven, 2012; Siegel, 2007; Toates, 2006). The structures that appear to encode, mediate, and underpin the sensory-motor manifestations of the encoded maps are subcortical. As Pollack, Watt, and Panksepp note: "The brain stem areas are absolutely essential to consciousness" (2000, p. 81), and do not merely serve as arousal switches. Significantly, Schore (1994, 2011, 2012) has long considered the subcortical regions of the right hemisphere as the seat of the unconscious and the root of procedural mutual attunement and regulation. His neuro-interpersonal model further illuminates the inevitable relevance of unconscious processes to our emotional and interpersonal lives. Significantly, Panksepp's research into innate, subcortical affective systems and their on-going influence on all levels of consciousness charts a clear role for the periaqueductal gray (PAG) in our self-systems and our more conscious self-states (Panksepp and Biven, 2012). Similarly, Lewis and Todd (2007) emphasize the role of the limbic system in the development of emotional and cognitive functions. At this point, and based on neuropsychological knowledge, the discussion of the unconscious model focuses on two subcortical areas: the basal ganglia and the cerebellum.

The Basal Ganglia: Building Blocks of Procedural Learning

In particular, the cortico-striatal system—comprising loops between cortical areas and the basal ganglia—mediates habits and procedural leaning networks, largely governed by reward. A wide range of primary, secondary, and imagined rewards underpin all types of interactional "know-how." The ability to acquire procedural knowledge, emotional as well as behavioral, affords the individual the enduring benefits of learning and practice. These conclusions further highlight how the unconscious realm functions as an instrumental system that learns by being engaged with the environment. Its "lessons" are easily reinforced, and their activation within contextual cues bypass conscious control (Bargh, 2007). Procedural learning is so important that we have two systems mediating it: the cortico-striatal or basal ganglia and the cortico-cerebellar (Doyon and Ungerleider, 2002; Kozial, 2014).

The organization of the cortex includes a number of connections with the basal ganglia—bilateral subcortical nuclei that select or inhibit behaviors based on their instrumental reward outcome (Koziol, 2014). The basal ganglia are involved in a wide range of learning functions: emotional, cognitive, and behavioral (Arsalidou et al., 2013). Because of their numerous links to areas such as the prefrontal cortex, motor and sensory cortices, areas in the brain stem, and importantly the amygdala and hippocampus, these nuclei play a central integrative role. Through the process of selective disinhibition and inhibition, the basal ganglia guide the most adaptive or appropriate responses to a given situation; emotional, cognitive, or interpersonal responses are released or inhibited. The basis for the basal ganglia's dynamic selective activity is the reward system that underpins their reinforcement dependent instrumental learning (Cockburn and Frank, 2011).

Once emotional, cognitive, and behavioral habits are established with the help of the basal ganglia, they are best executed without conscious mediation. Such unconscious functioning answers the need for efficient and repetitive modes of executing habits. The quick and automatic implementation of all habits, from the perceptual/emotional to complex social interactions, illustrates the adaptive strength of procedural learning or instrumental knowledge. This procedural knowledge identifies what actions in the past led to favorable or unfavorable results. Such instrumental learning is essential for smooth functioning in everyday life. Much of our acquired learned habits and their sensitivity to familiar context and situations are dopamine-dependent and under the control of the basal ganglia (Awh and Vogel, 2008; Koziol, 2014; Koziol and Budding, 2010; Moustafa et al., 2008). In this way, based on the physical or emotional value inherent in various interactional situations, the cortico-striatal loops are entirely involved in the release or the inhibition of appropriate responses—approach or avoidance. As we will see, throughout development, we respond to and acquire a wide range of dopamine-dependent responses, all designed to minimize pain and increase pleasure and well-being. Many of these unconscious responses are necessary defenses that run the gamut from interactional avoidance or a cautious approach to all relationships and emotional engagements to the need to alleviate pain through substance abuse.

The dopamine reward system that governs the connections between the basal ganglia and the prefrontal cortex (PFC) plays a major role in selecting and encoding behaviors that preserve well-being (Damasio, 2010; Frank and Claus; 2006; Koziol and Budding, 2010). The highest dopamine concentration is found within the basal ganglia and the PFC, so these regions constitute a critical reward circuitry. It is suggested that the signals from the orbitofrontal cortex are involved in the subcortical decisions of what behavior to pursue, based on its reward value or result (Doll and Frank, 2009). Once a behavior is learned and represented in the cortex, a similar situation can release this behavior out of awareness. In other words, a top-down decision about a certain reaction involves a bottom-up participation of the basal ganglia illustrating the bidirectional relationship between the conscious and unconscious realms.

Activities within different dopaminergic pathways lead to the release or inhibition of particular reactions. A surge in dopamine accompanies positive rewards and will reinforce specific behaviors. Once a context of positive conditions is established, the basal ganglia receive information regarding its motivational significance. Such positively reinforced behaviors are not always emotionally useful in the long run. Attachment experiences that reinforce the child's emotional dependence on a parent are an example of positive reinforcement of a problematic pattern. In response to the parent's unconscious communications, the child may excessively comply with the parent's emotional needs for closeness, comfort, and caretaking. Such instrumental leaning based on dopamine release will severely limit the infant's, the child's, and then the adolescent's capacity to develop an independent sense of personal agency.

In contrast, dips in dopaminergic activity result in negative reinforcement and avoidant responses (Niv, 2007). Activity within other pathways leads to negative outcomes and avoidance of the behaviors tried. This unconscious avoidance is associated with a dip or decrease in dopaminergic activity (Koziol, 2014). As a result of a plunge in dopamine in response to painful affects or hurtful intersubjective experiences, reaching-out behaviors become inactive, causing what become ingrained avoidant defenses. Similarly, anxiety-inducing situations will be accompanied by a dopamine dip and an inactivation of specific emotional and relational responsiveness. Consequently, more appropriate, integrated, or trusting patterns, for example, are suppressed. As we often see in patients, it seems as if more active, reaching-out behaviors slipped away, never to gain strength and validation, thereby disappearing from one's repertoire (Heekeren et al., 2007; Pizzagalli et al., 2008). This effect may lead to an elaborate but totally unconscious system of avoidant reactions that within one's daily pursuits are seldom perceived as such. As part of the unconscious map they are "who we are." Such avoidant behaviors are totally out of awareness, so much so that they are executed seamlessly and inevitably, as if there is no other alternative.

Importantly, this dopamine-dependent system is thought to regulate different sets of mental functions, ranging from the control of movement to the modulation of desire, motivation, affect, and cognitive styles (Sillitoe and Vogel, 2008). It also mediates attention, moods, and appetite urges, all elements of complex unconscious self-systems or maps. We can see how wide-ranging the influence of such self-systems is, especially when they override the more deliberate and reflexive conscious system. As Koziol and Budding (2010) maintain, dopaminergic pathways are also involved in higher-order instrumental learning, such as the orbitofrontal and medial circuits, affecting an even wider swath of personality traits. Important among them are emotional, interpersonal, and motivational learning, reinforced or discouraged by dopamine dips or surges (see also Lewis and Todd, 2007; Panksepp and Biven, 2012). These become our emotional and behavioral tendencies; they reside in our unconscious maps, but find enacted expressions in our more conscious self-states.

Within the various self-systems, the perceptual, emotional, cognitive, and behavioral tendencies are embedded in a particular affective valence: negative or positive and all shades in between. (Recall that these functions are intertwined in the brain/mind but are mentioned separately for clarity.) It is interesting to speculate on the clinical relevance of such conclusions. Beyond the obvious importance of avoidant defenses so prevalent in our functioning, what seem to underpin irrational repetitive behaviors, even those that essentially work against one's well-being, are these entrenched, action-oriented self-systems. We saw this clearly in Henry's case. Similarly, when we try to understand a patient's poor choice of a mate, for example—a choice that clearly leads to more heartache than satisfaction—what may unconsciously drive it is paradoxically the dopamine-dependent reward system. In this case, the reward is not simply positive affect but the incentive of familiarity—out of awareness and through learned emotional and interpersonal habits reengaging in old and familiar intersubjective interactions.

Although we may not be aware of the triggering elements embedded in a situation, the unconscious repetition of a particular response pattern is experienced with a known emotional and interpersonal certainty. The intensity of the repeated response echoes the original one, as well as the cognitive, affective, and behavioral associations that gave rise to it. Until one becomes more aware of such patterns (usually in therapy) there is little or no comprehension as to what is being repeated and why. Janice, for example, who watched her overworked mother being "pushed around" by her father, showed in her own marriage an exquisite sensitivity to her husband's behaviors and verbal communications. Automatically and without understanding why, she reacted with a great deal of anger whenever she perceived him as trying to take advantage of her. At those moments, her outrage was experienced as intensely as the raw emotions and relational patterns she implicitly absorbed during her childhood. Her mother's simmering rage and her own network of emotional memories came alive each time she reacted with the activated self-system that perceived her present life through past experiences.

The Cerebellum:
Where the Unconscious Action Is

Although our knowledge of the full array of functions linked to the cerebellum is incomplete, based on recent findings, neuropsychologists suggest that the cerebellum mediates autonomic, sensory, motor, affective, and cognitive functioning—in other words, a large part of our mental life (Koziol, 2014; Koziol and Budding, 2010). The cerebellum forms distinct circular loops with every region of the cortex (with the exception of the inferotemporal cortex). As a result, the cerebellum seems to adjust our responses by regulating neural signals in most regions. Through these links the cerebellum can influence what information gets through to the cortical area (Andreasen and Pierson, 2008) and thus play an important role in regulating behavior, cognition, and affect. For example, within the emotional circuit, studies show that stimulating various regions of the cerebellum in different intensities results in either an exaggerated emotional response, such as heightened temper, or in blunted emotional reactions (A. N. Schmahmann et al., 2007; J. Schmahmann, 2004). Again, we need to remember that all of these processes occur out of awareness and determine behavioral and emotional outputs. Upon enaction, they transform the unconscious map into post hoc consciously perceived behaviors and states.

The cerebellum's function is embodied in its capacity to bypass the more deliberate brain/mind functions and allow for fast, automated behaviors across contexts (Koziol, 2014). Based on past experiences, it learns to predict and anticipate the outcome of any behavior or response. The cerebellum essentially serves as a predictor or anticipator of sensory and motor feedback, allowing us to unconsciously generate fast, implicit, and automatic behaviors. In effect, these mechanisms constitute internal models (Ito, 2011). Based on past internalized experience as well as on current sensory information, the cerebellum predicts how a behavior should unfold or develop (Ito, 2008). In the process it exerts influence on sensory perceptions, as well as on affective, cognitive, and intentional systems. This influence extends to learning processes, imitative processes, verbal working memory, perceptions the cortex experiences, and the behaviors it releases (Horga and Maia, 2012; Koziol, 2014; Lewis, 2005; Petrosini, 2007). In this way the cerebellum underpins and guides what neural maps or self-systems are selected to be expressed. The cortex alone cannot fulfill these functions, because doing so will prove too slow, leading Koziol and Budding (2010) to conclude that to accomplish its predictive function, the cerebellum itself contains behavioral models.

The cortico-cerebellar circuitry "allows the cerebellum to copy the contents of cortical 'working memory,' or what the brain intends to do" (Koziol, 2014, p. 51), which is essentially the process of constructing internal models. These are composed of the intertwined aspects of all our mental and behavioral functions, and they influence higher cortical areas. In its function as an anticipatory regulator, the cerebellum informs the cortex about the predicted outcome of a response, allowing it to execute behaviors in real time, out of awareness. Therefore, the cortico-cerebellar pathways project the most efficient behavioral outputs, including affects and thoughts (Ito, 2005). Consequently, the cerebro-cerebellar loops also teach the prefrontal cortices to anticipate outcomes of behaviors, affects, and relational responses and think fast ahead (Ito, 2008; Pally, 2007). This contributes to unconscious thought processes because the cerebellum's activity occurs outside of awareness. Similarly, Thach (2014) suggests that the cerebellum can initiate movement and purposeful activity out of awareness. This observation clearly supports the fact that a wide range of information, including cognitive, is stored in the cerebellum, constituting unconscious self-states. By helping the brain learn procedures through repeated interaction with the environment, cortico-cerebellar loops encourage intuitive "knowledge" (Koziol, 2014;

Pezzulo and Dindo, 2011) that can be either adaptive and appropriate or the opposite, inappropriate and even self-destructive.

Our Automatic Selves: Why We Repeat

Inappropriate patterns repeat themselves when the cerebellum's influence is imbalanced or compromised. In that case, its neural messages may bias the cortex to interpret perceptions in an inflexible way. Within an interpersonal situation, for example, when an anticipation is biased toward a painful outcome, what will be released are old behaviors that successfully relieved anxiety, regardless of their adaptability to the current situation. Perceptions embedded within specific emotional exchanges will be rigidly linked only to past associations and experiences, without being corrected or refined by the cerebellum. As a result, the predictions regarding the unfolding perception or behavior may be entirely based on an internal model alone—not taking into account aspects of current reality. In this case, the cerebellum fails to correct the released responses and adapt them to what is called for. These faulty predictive processes may lead to the repetition of behaviors and defenses that no longer work for the individual (Pally, 2000, 2007). We need to remember that these complex series of brain/mind processes occur out of awareness.

The evolutionary expanded pathways between conscious and unconscious functioning—the subcortical output—extend, as we saw, to the main planning areas of the brain, the PFC and its various executive functions (Donald, 2001). These links explain the control unconscious processes have over higher executive functions; they also lead to the automatic and out-of-awareness implementation of complex courses of action, belief systems, and goal pursuit, sometimes occurring over long periods of time (Bargh, 2007, 2014). This continuous tug depicts how unconscious patterns seem to have a life of their own, and often win over conscious intention and deliberate wishes. Unless mindful efforts are exerted, the quick and automatic activation of subcortical areas overrides the slower, reflective function (Damasio, 2010; Lane, 2000; Lane et al., 2014; LeDoux and Doyere, 2011; Ochsner and Gross, 2005).

The unconscious action of the subcortical and other regions indicate that the brain/mind favors automaticity. An automated response is one occurring without conscious participation, biasing the PFC to release old patterns in a rigid and repetitive way. Automatic behaviors demand less effort and show less activation; decrease in activation during learning indicates that representations within the brain have become more efficient as automaticity has taken hold (Damasio, 2010; Koziol and Budding, 2010). Important for mediating and performing tasks automatically, the basal ganglia also mediate repetition of emotional cognitive and

behavioral patterns. Together, the interacting and merging cortico-cerebellar and cortico-striatal systems manipulate and guide response patterns that "know" what to do and how to react, repeating past patterns
entirely out of awareness (Koziol, 2014; Koziol and Budding, 2010).

Since reinforced neural processes coalesce into efficient unconscious
maps or self-systems in response to adaptational pressures, as development proceeds the encoded systems react to a wide range of stimuli
as if they were the same—as if they all represented the same level of
threat or challenge (Phelps, 2009). The overall purpose of these leveling
processes is to maximize fast and automatic response patterns. Consequently, novel conditions may be perceived and interpreted within the
existing "knowledge" of a core system, subsuming new situations into an
existing unconscious system. This characteristic explains what is often
witnessed in people: the tendency to feel, behave, and interpret the
world in very familiar and predictable ways, even when circumstances
differ and these guiding systems work against us. As we'll see in the
next section, what determines the severity of automaticity and repetition
is the degree of flexibility possessed by a particular self-system. The
following sections tackle the issue of automatic repetitions of behaviors,
even in the face of concrete proof as to their lack of appropriateness.

THE FIRST CONTINUUM: RIGIDITY VERSUS FLEXIBILITY

An important continuum that characterizes the nature of the unconscious, the rigidity–flexibility continuum, is the result of the coexistence
and interaction between two adaptational systems. The first—the fast
and automatic one residing deep in subcortical circuits—takes shortcuts
to perception and response. In the process, this system tends to lead
to the enactment of old patterns whether or not they are adaptive to
present stimuli. Let's recall that repeated unconscious behaviors are in
essence patterned, organized, and directed toward accomplishing goals,
conscious and unconscious alike. One important goal is the successful reduction of hyperaroused or hypoaroused affects and the return
of well-being, even in the short term (Damasio, 2010; LeDoux, 2014;
Schore, 2012). Behaviors, emotions, and cognitive process that were successful at achieving this goal remain part of the system, generally bound
in a particular interpersonal context.

In an environment that presents constant novelty and change (as we
could easily describe our daily existence), what is required is flexibility
in choosing and implementing behaviors that can achieve one's goals in
light of shifting circumstances. What enables this flexibility is the participation of the second system, the prefrontal cortical one. Slower and
more deliberate, it can examine new situations with less perceptual dis-

tortion and fewer automatic response tendencies, thereby offering new solutions when old ones do not prove successful.

As Koziol and Budding (2010) note, the interplay between cortical and subcortical regions can be envisioned as a movement back and forth between more controlled and reflective responses and automatic responses based solely on models that are stimulus-bound. The loops between subcortical areas and the cortex have evolved so that both automatic and higher-order control can coexist and interact. This interaction renders behavioral patterns adaptive and efficient. If only the slower and more deliberate nature of the prefrontal area or only the subcortical automatic system were to operate, there would be no flexible adjustments and all behaviors would inevitably prove inappropriate.

Successful behaviors and adaptations are based on alternating between and combining these two modes of functioning. Less adaptive behaviors—the ones that don't change even when conditions do—rely on the forward, unconscious models, without being corrected by the cerebellum or reflected on by the PFC. Significantly, affect regulation may be partly couched in the continuous tension between automaticity and the need for novel and flexible responses that can frame the new situation without the influence of the old emotions, convictions, and behaviors. Old systems that are not flexible enough compromise our ability to tolerate the ambiguities and differences inherent in new situations. Entirely out of awareness, without any sense that this is taking place, any perceived newness is interpreted as a threat to one's sense of well-being. For example, unconsciously experiencing any intimacy as controlling or suffocating compromises one's ability to tolerate and regulate these feelings. In effect, one is not aware that his or her complicated attempts to avoid intimacy reflect such a threat; one only experiences a familiar discomfort and a need to get away or fight.

Occurring out of awareness, this old sense of being emotionally controlled or intruded on, regardless of the interactional reality, stems from an internal predictive model that will respond in anger or distorted convictions about the other person, prompting incessant strife. In this case, the person's affect regulation is victim to biased anticipations of the other's intentions. Often such expectations also express a narrow projected understanding as to the meaning of the other person's words or actions. The ensuing responses are guided by entrenched feelings and behaviors, mediated by the cerebellum and the basal ganglia. The felt short-lived sense of relief at "successfully" (and unconsciously) avoiding a painful experience by reacting fast with old coping mechanisms only reinforces the automatically enacted patterns. The automatically recruited pattern in this contextual situation prevents a new and fresh confrontation with the contextually different aspects of the interaction; the other person does not really intend to control or intrude, and often his or her behavior is not directed at the aggrieved person at all. Consequently, no new learning is taking place. This inability to learn from reality characterizes the more rigid poles of this continuum, perpetuating and even reinforcing a closed system that perceives all interpersonal interchanges, for example, only through old self-systems.

Koziol (2014) recently emphasized the novelty–routinization dimension of brain/mind processes. The left hemisphere tends to "prefer" procedural knowledge, while the right hemisphere is sensitive to novelty. The hemispheres work in tandem to apply routinized responses or new ones when either is appropriate. For obvious reasons, this continuum may be the significant variable that determines how patients respond to therapy. Importantly, we need to understand and refine what modalities can be most effective with more rigid patients, and with entrenched repetitions in general. The two interacting systems will be further discussed in regard to the therapeutic concepts of repetition and resistance.

THE SECOND CONTINUUM: GRADATIONS OF CONSCIOUSNESS

So far we have seen that the implicit realm is not only a storage place for stable representations, but part of an active and dynamic present, always expressed through unconscious expectations, predictions, and a wide range of reaction to internal and external events. The present, however, does not simply repeat old representations. As was illustrated through the reciprocal loop between subcortical and cortical regions, it regenerates past memories and experiences, in the process merging old practiced patterns with current input. Present functioning, then, is entirely rooted in one's particular past, humming implicitly in the background. Past experiences as well as innate affects hover at the periphery, directly inaccessible and yet at the border of our consciousness, resurrected with each mental activity (Churchland, 2013; Damasio, 2010; Panksepp and Biven, 2012; Pollack et al., 2000). Although at times we partly sense the unconscious nature of the actions or dynamics we are engaged in (Sheets-Johnstone, 2012), we may still not fully understand how or why we find ourselves in particular situations.

The conscious realm has not replaced the unconscious one; they coexist. To illustrate the relationship between the conscious and unconscious realms, Damasio (2010) describes two interacting brain functions. Similar to Koziol (2014) and Panksepp (2012), Damasio's model underscores the continuous bilateral interaction between the unconscious and the conscious, cortical and subcortical areas. The explicit realm constructs explicit maps of people, objects, and events during the perception process and then reconstructs them during recall. The other holds dispositions—potentially relevant images—rather than full-fledged neural maps. This is the implicit sphere, where it is determined if and how maps will be reconstructed in the image space, and the one that gives rise to conscious experiences.

Like other researchers (Horga and Maia, 2012; Koziol, 2014; Koziol and Budding, 2010; Panksepp, 2012; Schore, 2012; Wegner, 2007), Damasio sees these brain functions as reflecting different evolutionary ages. The dispositional or the vast unconscious domain (subcortical) is an effective guide for repetitive patterns and learned behaviors. Because conscious image space is limited, only a small number of images can be accessed at any given time. To deal with the enormous number of images stored out of consciousness, a strategy has developed for managing them automatically from the bottom up. This strategy was most likely established prior to consciousness. In that archaic scheme, images that were selected to enter awareness were those most valuable for survival and what Damasio calls life management. Later on, consciousness most likely developed for an added dimension of efficiency.

In similar models, consciousness rises out of the global interconnectivity among brain regions (Baars, 1989; Churchland, 2013). The transition from the unconscious to consciousness occurs as a result of global ignition, involving stimulation that moves from the posterior areas of the brain to the anterior ones. We become conscious of our internal and external surroundings when groups of neurons are activated in a synchronized but transient fashion in response to a stimulus. The connections among neural groups supply the context to what we experience, but at the same time the context itself is left out of awareness (Churchland, 2013; Damasio, 2010; Dehaene et al., 2006; Dudai, 2011; Mancia, 2006, 2007). This provides a coherent conscious experience. Based on their findings, Horga and Maia also suggest a graded view in which conscious and unconscious processes rely on the same neural substrates and are engaged in the same neural processing. The difference between the conscious and the unconscious realms, according to them, is a function of the strength of the representation and the strength of the firing regarding any particular one.

In effect, consciousness possesses an important role as to what gets enacted. Although the basal ganglia and the cerebellum are involved in selecting the appropriate response, habit, or emotional reaction, their involvement does not necessarily mean a behavioral output, since the frontal cortex is also receiving information from other cortical regions. The additional input of stimuli from the current situation can and often should override the automaticity of subcortical regions and lead to more adaptive responses to new conditions (Koziol and Budding, 2010). It is also widely accepted (e.g., Craig, 2002; Damasio, 1999, 2000, 2010; Panksepp and Biven, 2012; Tsuchiya and Adolphs, 2007) that emotions— as experienced via bodily interoceptive information—are essential to the formation of what Damasio calls the "core Self." This physio/ emotional core self in turn grounds our continuous sense of self as well as our autobiographical self. The brain regions thought to mediate these self-representations range from the brain stem nuclei through the thalamus to the cortex (Tsuchiya and Adolphs, 2007).

It seems, then, impossible to delineate a clear line between implicit processes and their more conscious products. The body of neuropsychological evidence so far points to a continuous bidirectional influence between neural systems integrating affect, cognition, and behavior encoded in deeper regions of the brain and the PFC regions that mediate execution. Significantly for the clinical process and therapeutic change, as the cerebral cortex interacts with lower levels, it can alter unconscious processes and thereby exert adaptive control over behavior. As will be discussed in Chapter 8, which delineates the importance of reflective awareness, conscious efforts can be used to strengthen deliberate functions that sidestep automatic, stimulus-bound response. At the same time, however, the recruitment of top-down reflection may not be enough to successfully influence internal self-systems guided by the subcortical regions. These dynamic but unconscious regions need to be engaged as well (Koziol, 2014; Paul and Ashby, 2013; Schore, 2012) to achieve enduring change. Without a doubt, many unconscious and nonverbal aspects of the therapeutic encounter affect and alter unconscious self-systems as well. As such systems were largely acquired and practiced intersubjectively, their transformation can happen within the new context of the therapeutic relationship.

The integration between conscious and unconscious processes creates a continuum of consciousness (Horga and Maia, 2012; Laub and Auerhahn, 1993; Pally, 2007) that spans the gamut from total inaccessibility to conscious awareness of a felt and enacted self-state. Some early representations, memories, and experiential interactions will never become conscious—the encoded content embodied in the maps will always remain out of recollection or verbal reach (Damasio, 2010). This nondynamic unconscious (Mancia, 2006), which gets laid down via early memories and experiences, cannot be recalled due to the immaturity of the hippocampus and language abilities during early childhood.

An important implication to the emerging view of consciousness as a continuum is the growing realization that we cannot speak of a conscious self without the underlying unconscious processes that are always actively at work informing it (Churchland, 2013). Even if we may not know the full story of an unconscious system, it leaves fingerprints on every pattern of our mental existence. Chapter 3, discussing the unconscious in action, will illustrate how the hidden has no choice but to become known through the various manifestations of the vast unconscious.

INTEGRATION OF AFFECT AND COGNITION

Just as separating brain processes from their function is artificial (Koziol, 2014), so is the utter differentiation between affect, cognition, and action. In the course of development, subcortical maps increasingly integrate physio/affective reactions with a wide range of cognitive functions. As cognition develops, it inevitably becomes affected by and fused with emotional experiences. By being embedded within affective states, thought patterns and cognitive defenses become part of unconscious patterns as well (Bucci, 2007a, 2007b; Curtis, 2009; Damasio, 1999, 2010; Gazzaniga, 2008; Lewis and Todd, 2007; Panksepp, 2012; Schore, 2012; Wilson, 2002, 2003, 2011). Felt emotions are usually accompanied by and intertwined with thoughts that give emotions their familiar shape and meaning. Some of these thoughts are components of the various emotion programs, unfolding during development (Panksepp and Biven, 2010; Sergerie and Armony, 2006). Others are later cognitive responses to the emotion under way (Damasio, 2010). Gazzaniga's (2008) model stresses the function of the left brain, whose role is to decode, explain, interpret, and make sense of the emotional right hemisphere.

As we see, our cognitive awareness and thought processes are entirely intertwined with the affective systems and the experiences they give rise to. All aspects of an experience—its sensory/emotional intensity, its personal meaning, and the language used to make sense of it and incorporate it into already existing templates of perception and understanding—become part of a map or a pattern (Gazzaniga, 2008; Lewis and Todd, 2007; Panksepp, 2012; Schore, 2012; Sergerie and Armony, 2006). As Tsuchiya and Adolphs (2007) note, the more conceptual, cognitive, and interpretive aspects of emotions are mediated by the more anterior sectors of PFC, such as the cingulate and insular cortex. In Damasio's words: "the images evoked by these reactions end up being a part of the feeling percept along with the representations of the object that caused the emotion in the first place, the cognitive component of the emotion program, and the perceptual readout of the body state" (2010, p. 127).

As part of a more conscious self-state, feelings and the cognitions entwined with them are often experienced seamlessly and in an integrated way that is usually not questioned. Affects and the words that go with them seem to be part of a unitary experience or state (Panksepp and Biven, 2012). For example, think of how we express fears regarding specific objects, how one might describe anxieties about efficacy or self-worth, or how feelings of rage and despair cannot be differentiated from negative thoughts. The integration of affect and cognition in effect gives any self-state its characteristic flavor. But whereas a felt self-state conveys the fusion of affects with their cognitive components, what remains unconscious is the underlying meaning conveyed through this integration. A repetitive and familiar negative approach to challenges, a sensitivity to criticism and the ensuing self-protective defensiveness, an automatic tendency to see oneself as a victim or as the guilty party at any interaction, are instances of automatic expressions of deeper personal meaning that express both the sensory/affective as well as the cognitive aspects of a particular situation.

As Lewis and Todd state (2007), in every part of the brain it is impossible to assign either cognitive or emotional functions to any particular structure. Many structures do both. For example, the amygdala mediates both cognitive appraisal of threats as well as emotions of fear and rage. Even areas considered to be involved in cognitive tasks, such as the PFC or the hippocampus, are coupled with wider subcortical areas such as the limbic system, the basal ganglia, and cerebellum. The brainstem nuclei and the PAG, as we saw before, are closely intertwined with cortical areas mediating perceptions and cognitive appraisals (Koziol and Budding, 2010: Panksepp and Biven, 2012). Affect and cognition always work together, although at times, most likely due to the prominence of a defensive system, the strength of one modality overrides the other. In such cases, the development of an adaptive integration of affect and cognition is an important goal.

Our primordial or innately generated emotions are active, providing direct experience of one's body and emotion. They are the foundation for more complex levels of self-systems that continue to develop and further expand to include verbal and cognitive components (Damasio, 2010) and, in Panksepp's (Panksepp and Biven, 2012) model, our secondary and tertiary learning processes. Negative emotions or dysregulated states lead to negative memories and negative narratives. The opposite is true of positive emotions. The emotion-feeling-cognition loop starts with the multilayered perceptions of specific situations and their sensory, bodily, and emotional significance to the individual (Damasio, 2010; Panksepp and Biven, 2012; Schore, 2012). That meaning, conscious or not, is embedded in the child's cognitive developments, embodying affect and cognition. The dynamic and therapeutic implications of this integration are elaborated in Chapter 4, which considers self-narratives as an expression of dysregulated affective states.

BORN TO ACT: THE CENTRALITY OF ENACTION TO MENTAL AND BEHAVIORAL FUNCTIONING

The accumulated evidence that the unconscious is always being enacted in the present, interacting with conscious self-states, is also steering our views away from seeing the unconscious as a static system containing buried memories waiting to be unearthed in therapy. Instead we recognize that the propensity to action is guided by the motor functions of the brain (Gendlin, 2012; Koziol and Budding, 2010; Sheets-Johnstone, 2010) and its intertwined links to all other mental functions. Because guidance of action is a dominant function of the brain, neural responses in sensory regions are closely connected to and depend on action context. As we saw in the previous sections, the cerebellum and the basal ganglia are important to the acquisition and the enaction of instrumental knowledge.

Consequently, this tendency to act lies at the heart of the body/brain/mind's continual expression of implicit self-systems. This is especially true in the tendency to enact responses that worked in the past and were encoded as part of a brain/mind map. According to Gendlin (2012), the brain/mind directly acts on the environment, and the environment directly happens to the body in an ongoing interactional loop. Internal beliefs and expectations change the conscious perceptions of present events just as external events affect the unconscious body/mind perceptions of them. In many imperceptible ways to us, the two realms of relating to our internal and external experiences, the conscious and the unconscious, affect and transform each other. This is a process of inextricable interaction between the brain/mind and the physical environment, between perception and action. In this way, embodied cognition is continually tied to its enacted relationship with the external surroundings. As some have observed, mental and physiological activities are inseparable from conscious and unconscious functions and from bodily experiences that interact with our surroundings (Borghi and Cimatti, 2010; Sheets-Johnstone, 2010, 1012; Stewart, 2010; Varela et al., 1991).

In an important way, the brain/mind's tendency to put into action conscious and unconscious systems alike incorporates all of the aspects that have been previously discussed. What are constantly enacted are the particular maps, habits, and entrenched learning that make up an unconscious self-system; in other words, we exist in action (or in an active inaction) (Gendlin, 2012; Pollack et al., 2000; Varela et al., 1991). We need to remember that a disinhibition of a behavior—avoidant or cautious defenses that cause a person to withdraw, for an example—is part of the cortical-subcortical loops as well, only in this case, what gets to be experienced in a conscious self-state is the lack of action. As we saw, this enactment is not only determined by the automatic forces of subcortical areas but is also under the influence of the PFC, which can exert reflectiveness and slowed action. The balance between rigidity and flexibility as well as the degree of reflective awareness greatly affects the nature and level of unconsciousness of any enactment.

Most significant, this tendency to act reveals a great deal about what we consider hidden. Unconscious systems have no choice but to reveal themselves in all aspects of our mental and behavioral functioning. It is not necessarily the content of the map or self-system that is unearthed; what becomes significant is an identified pattern of being and relating to oneself and others. More often than not, such a pattern has been in action long before a patient started therapy. One might have been aware of a negative experience, but the full scope and meaning of an emotional and relational pattern may not become conscious until therapy. By being activated often and without deliberate thought, enacted patterns have the unique ability to educate therapist and patient as to what lies beneath, the forces guiding him to behaviors that ultimately are not "on his side."

The fact that the unconscious is constantly influencing our actions, especially the automatic implementation of rigid systems, has particular implications to the therapeutic process. For it is in the transference–countertransference entanglements and their possible culmination in enactments that unconscious self-systems of patient and therapist get to be expressed and fully experienced. Enactments and their resolution add a direct and unmediated way to enter an unconscious system as they show up in the therapeutic relationship. Other sources for identifying the patient's maladaptive patterns stem, of course, from the patient's life difficulties, obstacles that echo the unconscious underlying map by repeating themselves in a rigid and unreflective way. This propensity to be enacted places unconscious self-systems front and center, playing multiple roles in every level of our functioning and our psychotherapeutic engagements with patients.

WHAT THE BRAIN DOES BEST: LEARNING PROCESSES

As determined by evolution, the brain's default position is to learn, especially in the service of adaptation and survival. It is not that psychological theories have not acknowledged the centrality of learning processes, especially during childhood. With new neuropsychological information, however, we can refine and expand our understanding. It is important to note that the current data on how the brain learns, and the relevance of this information to practicing therapists, are very different from the early, simplistic emphasis on stimulus-response pairing.

For example, attachment studies consistently demonstrate that different parenting styles lead to distinct attachment styles (Hesse and Main, 2000, 2006; Fonagy, 2008). In longitudinal studies, dysregulated attachment observed in toddlers led to borderline disorders at age 19 (Lyons-Ruth, 2003). Similarly, many have shown that being subjected to attunement failures in infancy and childhood may result in subsequent emotional and interpersonal difficulties (Beebe, 2010; Beebe and Lachmann, 2002; Cozolino, 2002, 2006; Schore, 2012; Siegel; 2007; Stern, 1985; Tronick, 2007; Wallin, 2007).

Indeed, early interactions directly affect the neural structure of the brain and the connections it creates, especially the earlier maturing right brain. As we saw in the previous sections, the brain's propensity to learn quickly and efficiently and file the acquired lessons in unconscious maps is a key to our implicit mental life. From early on this learning process is one of the most complicated brain/mind phenomena, largely driven by our ongoing innate emotions. When early learning links behaviors with concepts and emotions, the process does not include conscious reflection or choice. Only later does a child reach some level of formulated wishes and intentions. But the original, early learning of the emotional, cognitive, and behavioral concepts remains as compelling in its influence on later behaviors (Bargh, 2007).

The result is an automatic, unconscious connection between behavioral representations, their emotional roots, and their corresponding conditions and motor representations. If a situation has an acute personal significance and thus generates intense emotions, the brain will proceed to integrate all the aspects of the situation: sensory, emotional, behavioral, and cognitive. It then generates the composite in response to cues or in response to appropriate stimuli. As Bounomano observes: "Much of what we learn is absorbed unconsciously as a result of the brain's tendency to link concepts that occur together" (2011, p. 183), especially events that are experienced together. Seemingly effective mental and behavioral actions to internal and external stress—mostly quick and instinctive—will be unconsciously learned and activated. Reactive rage, thoughts that justify the source of hurt in order to minimize the sense of not being loved, and narratives of externalization are all examples of innate coping behaviors. From instinctive and imperceptible avoidance through projective identification to sophisticated mental maneuvers such as rationalization and self-aggrandizing, such unconsciously enacted and reinforced ways to restore homeostasis become effective and then entrenched.

This learning is not linear or entirely stimuli-determined. First, it is subjected to epigenetic influences inherent in the interaction between one's innate temperamental qualities and the environment. In addition, the brain/mind's tendency to employ shortcuts in perceptual and reactive processes, while enabling quick learning, may also reinforce old lessons at the expense of new ones. This reliance on already existing maps for quick assumptions and responses, recruiting old associations in the service of new learning, may prevent us from acquiring new experiences. This is often the case when unconscious self-systems clearly operate independently from what the situation demands; they do not learn from reality. A tendency to feel victimized or unworthy, for example, will not take into account what the current situation actually presents.

As we'll see in Chapters 2 and 4, which discuss aspects of the developmental underpinning of unconscious patterns, many characteristics of unconscious processes do have very early roots. The complex neural activities underlying all facets of learning—especially those occurring within early relationships—clearly form our unconscious core systems. Along the way, learning, memories, and implicit systems are inextricably intertwined.

The power of learning to shape unconscious systems opens the window to reexamine some concepts central to our theoretical models of the mind and to clinical work. How can we best address the experiential "realness" of unconscious convictions, feelings, and defenses, for example? As mentioned, the brain does not have a central agency deciding what gets to be unconscious or unacceptable to the conscious self. Consequently, we need to be able to decode as best we can some of the past roads that created the particular unconscious terrain and its current enacted manifestations. When encountering difficulties in resolving a conscious conflict, or when a patient is unable to make decisions and move forward in an active, self-affirming way, more traditional interpretations assume the existence of an unconscious conflict holding one back. It may be more accurate to explain such paralysis in terms of opposing learned patterns, both encoded in the presence of specific intersubjective settings. The activation of different self-systems that were created and reinforced within dissimilar intersubjective environments seems more related to how the brain/mind works. Different environmental conditions will result in the activation of the particular unconscious self-system, enacting into consciousness its experiential lessons.

MEMORY LANE: HOW RELIABLE IS IT?

Another important development directing the emerging view of the unconscious is the very prolific field of memory research (Kandel, 2001). As noted by Fernyhough (2013), Churchland (2013), and others, the issues of forgetfulness, repression, and dissociation cannot be understood as simply directed by an unconscious force trying to avoid the pain of trauma or feelings that are not perceived as part of one's sense of self. Our memory systems and the maps they create occur without a central "supervisor" (Churchland, 2013; Damasio, 2010; Gendlin, 2012; Koziol, 2014; Rolls, 2011). There is no full understanding of why some memories endure explicitly and others do not. We know that there is a continuous process of memories being constructed and eliminated, and that memories are a composite of traces emanating from many sensory/motor interactions (Dudai, 2011; Fernyhough, 2013; McClelland, 2011). With implicit memories as well as all other learning, the associative connections may determine what memories stay and which ones fade away. The CA3 part of the hippocampus, for example, may serve as an association center that links together (arbitrarily as far as we know) co-occurrences of input. The associative process includes inputs about emotional memories that reach the cortex from subcortical emotion centers, such as the amygdala (Rolls, 2011).

Out of awareness, the unconscious selection of traces and images is also affected by the need to maintain one's well-being, current mood, and self-state. This is also the case where explicit memories are concerned (Churchland, 2013; Damasio, 2010; Panksepp and Biven, 2012). It is well established that memory recall is similarly dependent and colored by our mood (Damasio, 2010; Rolls, 2011). Again, when trying to deconstruct the creation of an unconscious-conscious self-system, a child besieged by negative interactions and resulting sad moods will encode and then remember negatively tinged experiences. At the same time, it is also very possible that a child with a genetic predisposition for depression or anxiety will tend to encode more negative memories. Emotional states, then, affect both storage and recall of memories, both conscious and unconscious (Rolls, 2011). In addition, frequent recall strengthens memories (Fernyhough, 2013; Rolls, 2011). As we think of the default network system that operates when the brain is at rest and engaged in inward rumination (see the following section), the focus on negative memories and experiences may strengthen them at the expense of more varied and positive ones.

This neural process opens the door to a great deal of biased memory construction and recall. As Dudai says, "a key memory system in the brain is specifically structured to extract from experience unconscious rules and abstractions that allow organisms to deal with the ever-changing world that surrounds them in an expedient and self-serving manner" (2011, p. 42). Furthermore, memories are constructed, shaped, and reshaped by the act of remembering itself. Memories are actually altered a bit with each recall (Nader and Einarsson, 2010). Each time a memory is recalled, it becomes labile, as different processes affect the content and the form in which it is reconsolidated (Dudai, 2011; Fernyhough, 2013; LeDoux and Doyere, 2011; Nadel and Hardt, 2011). As will be discussed in Chapter 8, this process in effect holds great promise for therapeutic techniques capable of helping patients experience past emotional memories while reflecting and recontextualizing them (Ecker et al., 2012; Jurist, 2008).

Neuropsychological findings regarding the nature of memory have also revealed that consciously recalled memories are not an exact replica of events or experiences. As Dudai (2011) maintains, memories as a tool for survival are not about accuracy. Consequently, on entering consciousness, memories do not re-create events faithfully. Memories are constructions: made in the present moment of an ensemble of perceptions and traces of images, they engage many brain regions, integrating circuits from the medial temporal lobe and the control systems in the PFC. Within this integration, sensory, emotional, and behavioral memories are fused with past representations, including how they already were experienced and interpreted. This complex process of reassembling different parts of experience renders memories vulnerable to various degrees of distortions not only at the time of encoding but at the time of recall as well (Churchland, 2013; Damasio, 2010; Dudai, 2011; Fernyhough, 2013, p. 102). In essence, unreliable memories are the result of the intricate and multiple neuropsychological and chemical processes occurring on all levels of the neural system. It is easy to see how memory imperfection may result from the many potential problems inherent in such a complex system (Dudai, 2011; Fernyhough, 2013).

In addition, although the explicit images making up the autobiographical self are stored in the cerebral cortex, they still need to interact with the proto-self machinery. These systems are located in the brain's subcortical regions: the dispositional sphere that constructs maps (Damasio, 2010), in the PAG region, the source of the core emotions (Panksepp, 2012), and the cerebellum and basal ganglia (Koziol, 2014), which encode, control, and release implicit patterns. Similarly to processes involved in all memory functions, the construction of the autobiographical self calls for complex coordination between various brain regions and functions. In this process of constructing our core self and its memories, the veracity of recalled memories has as much to do with who we are today, our entrenched internal maps, and our current mood as with the original event, time, and context when the specific memory occurred. When responding to an interaction, the memories that are newly created are already influenced by past memory composites, affecting the present interaction as well as the memory of it.

Most important, there is no neuropsychological evidence for distinct repressive forces within the brain. By the same token, there is no evidence that memory of traumatic events operates in special ways (Churchland, 2013; Fernyhough, 2013). What traumatic memories seem to do is emphasize certain aspects of the event, an emotional and imagistic property that becomes part of any unconscious-conscious system. As we saw, processes of memory and forgetfulness are the result of wide-scale cooperation among diverse brain regions and the consequence of neurochemical events, many still unknown. There is evidence, however, for conscious successful effort of suppression (Anderson and Green, 2001; Anderson and Levy, 2009). People can willfully choose not to think about painful events, but according to these researchers, there's no special mechanism that deals with traumatic events. On the contrary, traumas can be recalled more readily because of their emotional intensity and its subsequent effects on encoding (Damasio, 2010; Fernyhough, 2013; van der Kolk, 1994).

Of course, memories are not just explicit. Most memories are encoded without our awareness, but their emotional component can be readily activated (Cortina and Liotti, 2007; Mancia, 2006, 2007). As a matter of fact, it is especially the inaccessible memories and the numerous unconscious links and associations attached to them that influence our behaviors as they coalesce into a stable unconscious self-system. Out-of-awareness memories include those encoded before we develop the capacity for episodic/autobiographical memory. The early immaturity and instability of the memory system render autobiographical memories even more fragile. Upon later recall, they may be greatly influenced by the present context and affect, making them even less reliable as accurate representations of real events.

It has been recently underscored that although early memories may seem vivid and convincing, they are unreliable; early memories are especially susceptible to other people's stories, photos, and repeated accounts of family members (Fernyhough, 2013; Loftus, 1996). Such fragile memories, based on interactions with others rather than actual events, also become part of stable implicit self-systems. Colored by negative affects or the quick activation of the amygdala, implicit memories can become excessively distorted, giving prominence to negative affects and cognitions of particular events—in other words, a negative spin to positive or even affectively neutral events.

When we try to deconstruct the nature and scope of unconscious self-systems, the emotional convictions and the narratives and behavior tendencies that are embedded within them and the influence of the emotional system on cognition and memory (Lewis and Todd, 2007; Panksepp, 2012) cannot be overstated. Considering the emotional pull of negative moods, anxiety, and intense fear and the way they shape memory, the prevalence of negative self-systems and their consciously felt self-states is entirely understandable. As Damasio (2010) observed, negative moods give rise to negative memories, possibly distorted, and negative emotional states will also result in encoded, negative memories.

Memory research emphasizes the need to refine our approach to how we construct our conscious and unconscious sense of who we are. If memories are biased because they embody composites of many sensory/motor interactions, how do we approach the autobiographical core self, or, more accurately, core selves? It seems more and more likely that in therapeutic work, the effort to re-create reality as it was and trust it is less important than our patients' internal experience. Here again, neuroscience is only confirming what we know clinically. But the confirmed knowledge frees us to deal with this internal experience and, most important, its meaning. This realization leads to new ways to address internal experiences through their enacted manifestations and not necessarily via their remembered content (Badenoch, 2008; Bromberg, 1998, 2006, 2011; Ogden, 1986, 2004; Schore, 2012).

THE DEFAULT SYSTEM: A SELF-REFERENTIAL FUNCTION

This brief discussion of the default system also sheds light on how unconscious bodily, emotional, and cognitive integrated self-systems are created and maintained. The default mode network—brain regions such as the medial PFC, the medial temporal lobes, the lateral parietal cortex, and posterior cingulate cortex—has been found to be active when we are at rest, not physically active but internally engaged in thinking, imagining, daydreaming, and fantasizing (Gusnard et al., 2001; Raichle et al., 2001). The function of this circuitry, demanding a great deal of metabolic effort—as has been shown on functional magnetic resonance images—is seen by these researchers as underpinning self-referential processing, thinking about a current situation or future goals. These researchers further hypothesize that the high metabolic nature of this neural mode ensures that we are in touch and have a sense of what is going on internally and externally.

The default system has been found to be the most active when people are away from external stimuli, but inwardly focused on self-reflective thoughts and attempts to make sense of emotional events and interpersonal interactions. At these moments our minds tend to wander and drift off, absorbed in a mélange of fantasies, affects, and interpretations as they relate to internal as well as external experiences. The default network is connected to the medial temporal lobe memory system, so the past is often present in these self-referential ruminating mental activities (Gazzaniga et al., 2014).

Additional findings have shown that the default network is also activated by autobiographical memories, imagining the self in future locations, and tasks that engage individuals in moral dilemmas. Furthermore, similar brain regions are activated when we think about emotional beliefs and the states of mind of other people. These observed processes indicate that the default system is not just engaged in self-referential ruminations (Gazzaniga et al., 2014). What is common to these interlinked processes is the system's activation; when at rest, we ruminate self-referentially or imagine ourselves in relation to others (Buckner and Carroll, 2007; Mitchell et al., 2005). It has been suggested (Tamir and Mitchell, 2011, 2013) that the high resting activity measured in the default system may demonstrate that our brain/mind tends toward a simulated, imagined reality, valuing it more than external reality. According to these researchers, such virtual scenarios may function to help us navigate and understand the real world around us. But the moment we reengage with purposeful activities, the default mode recedes and becomes deactivated, allowing us to seamlessly participate in the actual requirements of our environment (Mitchell, 2009).

As we think about the components of unconscious self-systems and their placement on the conscious-unconscious continuum, the default network may hold some clues to the creation and execution of unconscious systems. Self-referential ruminations, judgments, and interpretations of emotional and interpersonal events may hold the key to many encoded false interpretations and convictions as they relate to dysregulated emotional states.

A growing child, for example, trying to make sense of hurtful interactions might come to the conclusion that she is to blame. The emotional and cognitive products stemming from her imagination, fantasies, and self-directed blame also become part of unconscious self-systems. Her "conclusions" regarding her self-worth may not be consciously acknowledged, but they still join a previous system of similar feelings and thoughts. In the attempt at sense making, the self-referential interpretations offered by the ruminative processes are most likely influenced by existing unconscious maps. Similarly, perceiving the other's state of mind, interpreting parental angry or abusive behavior, may also become a part of a self-blaming and victimized system. The result is an intensification of negative, depressed self-systems or a self-blaming tendency. Although such self-directed interpretations of difficult emotional interactions may recede from one's attention, they still hover in the background of our conscious awareness, lurking and resurfacing during times of dysregulation. As will be discussed in Chapter 4, this process is particularly present in the negative self-narratives that are almost always a part of dysregulated affective states.

A NEUROPSYCHOLOGICAL MODEL OF THE UNCONSCIOUS WITHIN EXISTING CLINICAL KNOWLEDGE

In many important ways, the neuropsychological model of the unconscious echoes the efforts of some clinicians to explicate how and why repeated core patterns are such a prominent part of psychopathology. For example, Bucci's multiple code theory suggests the existence of three systems, the subsymbolic, symbolic nonverbal, and symbolic verbal (2007a, 2007b). Emotional schemas—the affective core, consisting of subsymbolic somatic and sensory-motor representations—are the building blocks of memory and underlie one's sense of self and the relational self. Bucci's ideas about the subsymbolic affective core and emotional schemas correspond to Fosshage's emphasis on the implicit realm and its persistent organized patterns (2005, 2011). In Fosshage's model, procedural knowledge and relational know-how are encoded through images that can become verbally accessible through the therapeutic process. The necessity to combine both implicit and explicit therapeutic approaches, emphasized by Fosshage, is discussed further in Chapter 8. Like Bucci, Fosshage sees both affective and cognitive processing as part of the implicit realm. In contrast to Bucci, who sees dissociated schemas as the subsymbolic negation of experiences employed defensively, Fosshage's view of dissociation is closer to the model presented here: learned implicit patterns, symbolically or imagistically encoded, are activated in response to a particular situation and may or may not serve a defensive purpose.

As research keeps revealing new information about the brain/mind, the exploration of the neuropsychological underpinnings of unconscious processes can never be complete (certainly not in this volume). But beyond the temptation to address such limitations, I think that therapists can consider the knowledge that is already available to us, so we can better understand our patients' brain/minds. One significant implication from the inextricable connections between affect and cognition, conscious and unconscious processes, stems from the fact the PFC developed to alter the direct stimulus response loop (Lewis and Todd, 2007; Luu et al., 2007).

The fact that emotional responses and their potential distorted appraisals can be examined and then slowed down has certainly been a cornerstone in most therapeutic approaches. In particular this capacity has been recruited to improve affect regulation. Within the self-regulation activities of the brain/mind, we can not establish whether affect regulates cognition or vice versa, so therapists need to recruit all functions to bring about change. Brain regions become regulated and regulating by being synchronized with each other (Lewis and Todd, 2007). Consequently, when trying to help patients overcome unconscious entrenched systems, affect, cognition, and the implementation of new behaviors and practices are needed to create and sustain change, a topic that is developed in the following chapters.

DREAMS AS THE VOICE OF THE UNCONSCIOUS

Another enacted manifestation of the unconscious fusions of emotions, experiences, and memories can be found in our dream lives. Dreams have long been thought to carry within them communications from unknown realms, thus conveying some hidden conflicts, struggles, and wishes. Freud's ideas, and later Jung (see Jung, 1957), codified this connection and provided psychoanalysts and psychotherapists with essential symbols and metaphors as a way of getting a glimpse into the unconscious (Freud, 1900). Although dreams and the unconscious seem to be intertwined, especially within the therapeutic community, the way dreams accurately represent the unconscious is far from being known. As we understand it today, dreams give expression to emotional self-states, inchoate early memories, and the often distorted associations that accompany them.

Because the topic of this book is the nature of the unconscious, dreams are discussed here only in terms of their ability to reflect some unconscious and conscious preoccupations. (Unfortunately this very limited space can only offer an extremely limited discussion of how significant dreams can be as an enacted expression of unconscious processes.) But dreams as the long presumed "royal road" into the unconscious have also been the subject of conceptual changes, driven by questions as to the function of dreaming and by recent neuroscientific findings.

For example, seeing dreams as expressions of repressed wishes and unresolved instincts has come into question, and so has the existence of a censuring self that hides their true meaning (Hobson, 1988). Rather, a new understanding of dreams as resulting from spontaneous brain activity has emerged. As dreams are released from the cognitive influence of the PFC, their role in unconscious learning and in memory consolidation and reconsolidation has been emphasized (Stickgold et al., 2001). Hobson and Stickgold (1995) have demonstrated that dream states are accompanied by a reactivation of old memories, taking them from a consolidated state to a fragile and labile state. As is later discussed (in the context of how affective experiences during therapy enhance new brain/mind connections), dreams can also lead to new associations among pre-existing memories (see Nalbantian, 2011), and produce new learning.

Converging neuropsychological evidence has shown the role of sleep and REM and non-REM dreaming states in the consolidation of learning and memory tasks. During REM sleep in particular, the brain is engaged more with processing associative memories than simple consolidation of recent memories. This enhanced associative activity is the result of the lower activity of the dorsolateral PFC, the increased activity in the anterior cingulate cortex and the amygdala, and the decreased blood flow from the hippocampus to the neocortex (Stickgold et al., 2001).

Dreams, then, can give voice to some unconscious memories and their associative processes. Dream content, however, is not determined by a censuring agency but by the nature of the neural and chemical activity that gives rise to affects and the many associations embedded in them.

As Stickgold and colleagues (2001) have found, emotions may play a crucial role in REM sleep. Greater amygdala activity during REM sleep adds to the deactivation of higher cognitive processing. The brain's bias toward emotional processing, especially when under the influence of the amygdala, is prevalent in our dream lives. Dreams suffused with fear and anxiety scenarios are quite common, expressing one's unique reservoir of affect, emotional memories, and the many associations attached to them. The role of fear and anxiety in shaping unconscious self-systems is discussed in Chapter 2.

Emotional memories are more saliently present and processed than other types of mental activities. Significantly, depression or presleep viewing of distressing films resulted in reports of negative emotion in early night REM states (Stickgold et al., 2001). Other limbic system regions are activated during REM sleep, and their relatively cognition-free associations help explain some of the bizarre imagery encountered in dreams. Although REM dreams occur in the absence of focused cortical attention, the activated remaining cortical areas still try to make some sense of the limbic productions, providing whatever narrative they can come up with (Stickgold et al., 2001). According to these authors, our remembered dreams reflect the dreaming brain/mind's hypersensitivity to emotions. This sensitivity is combined with the brain's attempts to "identify and evaluate novel cortical associations in the light of emotions mediated by limbic structures activated during REM" (Stickgold et al., 2001, p. 1056).

As with many of the therapeutic concepts explored in this book— ideas newly framed by neuropsychological progress—the emerging models of our dreaming lives strengthen their clinical relevance. Dreams can no longer be thought of as simply carrying repressed or dissociated memories or as a defense against unpleasant instincts. As part of always active brain/mind processes, they allow us, however strangely, to peek into unconscious processes as interpreted, recalled, and retold by our conscious self. In this way dreams can be placed on the rigid–flexible and on the conscious-unconscious continuums as well.

Moreover, the realization that dreams are partly the product of limbic activity, reactivated emotional memories, and the compromised cognitive sense imposed on them offers great therapeutic opportunities. Very often, more than the remembered content, the affect resurrected in dreams is significant for the possibility of change. As often experienced in treatment, the intense emotions that are revealed in dreams seem to provide one of the most direct accesses to what lies underneath; the emotional glue that holds a self-system together. Although we cannot witness the underlying neural substrate of dreams, we can still become aware of some of our emotional preoccupations, emotional struggles, and fears. As with the discussed necessity to simultaneously

combine emotional experience with reflective awareness (further elucidated in Chapter 8), the emotions in dreams reflect existing, subcortically mapped (Damasio, 2010) self-systems.

The specific ways emotional events affect dreams as well as the process of meaning-making of the emotional associations are still obscure;
the information afforded to us about the unique and personal meanings found in dreams is less so. This book emphasizes the ongoing
interactions between subcortical and cortical areas, and dreams are part
of this relationship. They arise in the deep unconscious but find their
way into meaning and consciousness. Just as with enacted emotions,
cognitions, and behaviors, dreams can also be seen as enacted manifestations of unconscious emotional memories and self-systems. Whether
dreams have any role in shaping unconscious systems is not known at
this point. What we do know about dreams and how we use them in
clinical practice has greatly expanded, providing us with an important
glimpse into unconscious systems and more conscious self-states. Some
of the cases described in this book are aided by their dreams. Dreams
may have more of a role in making the unconscious conscious, after all,
through the endless ways they surface and find their way into our conscious awareness.

What we do know about dreams so far and how to use them in our
clinical work has greatly expanded. In some ways, shifting emphasis
from assumed symbols as representing the unconscious to a focus on
the raw affects experienced in them provides us with further valuable
information about the emotional glue of a particular system. Similarly,
viewing all parts of a dream as echoing different self-systems can also
give us an important glimpse into the patient's different unconscious
systems and how they relate to each other or how internally split they
are. Together with all other enacted manifestations of unconscious processes, dreams open a window into what is hidden but still expressed.

CHAPTER 2

The Lasting Power of Anxiety: The Developmental Building Blocks of Self-Systems

O F THE SEVEN PRIMARY AFFECTIVE systems identified by Panksepp and Biven (2012)—seeking/expectancy, fear/anxiety, rage/anger, lust/sexual excitement, care/nurturance, panic/grief/sadness, and play/ social joy—the fear system seems to exert the strongest effect on a wide range of aversive experiences, both conscious and unconscious, and on the autonomic need to use defenses to modulate them. Although fear responses and fear-infused memories are an inevitable part of development, it can be especially devastating when fears induced by early ongoing traumatic experiences become part of one's implicit system. Fear memories trigger the acquisition of new fear responses, an associative process that occurs automatically and involuntary in subcortical circuitry (Hamann, 2009; LeDoux, 2000, 2002, 2014). As a result they are key aspects in our emotional development and in shaping the emotional and defensive characteristics of unconscious self-systems.

As any clinician can attest, the pervasiveness of fear and anxiety in our mental lives is considerable and often debilitating. Beyond the clearer cases of phobias or panic attacks, chronic nonspecific and persistent anxious worries or ruminations seem to be part of many people's conscious and unconscious dynamic makeup. Because of how unpleasant fear and anxiety feel, both in body and mind, these emotions are at the root of many of our dysregulated states. They also underpin the autonomic defensive efforts mobilized to regain a sense of well-being. This interaction between affect and defense, between the dysregulation brought about by a noxious unbearable state and the natural need to regain homeostasis, to a large degree forms many of our personality traits. The expanded and more complex definition of the unconscious suggested here is reflected in the significant role the fear system has both in forming unconscious processes as well as in driving their unconscious enactment.   •

Affective systems, each with distinct neural pathways and neuromodulators, are the engine driving all other mental processes. As such they are both the foundation and the glue holding together the many innate and learned aspects of our brain/mind self-systems: the stored images, memories, associative connections, physiological components, and cognitive interpretations. Unconditioned emotions generated in response to the environment are essential for further emotional learning and for the many nuanced configurations of blended affects, cognitions, and behaviors. In the process of learning, an emotional response (e.g., fear) is also acquired in reaction to a previously neutral experience coupled with unconditioned fear. The retention of these responses over time constructs emotional memories and many learned associations to them that then coalesce into an unconscious map or self-system (Damasio, 2010; LeDoux, 2002, LeDoux and Doyere, 2011; Panksepp and Biven, 2012).

As Panksepp and Biven (2012, p. 36) write: "The FEAR system generates a negative affective state from which all people and animals wish to escape." Fear is accompanied by autonomic arousal, including increased heartbeat, higher blood pressure, and extreme, unpleasant sensations of unreality or imminent danger. It releases arousal chemicals, such as epinephrine, norepinephrine, and glutamate, that mobilize the signals of unconditioned fear and activate the sympathetic system. In turn these processes generate fight-or-flight responses. All emotions, fear and generalized anxiety included, start early, arouse automatically, and are set by our genome (Damasio, 2010; LeDoux, 2014; Panksepp, 2008; Panksepp and Biven, 2012). Together with environmental pressures, epigenetic interactions account for individual differences in the experience, tolerance, and regulation of fear. Although this is an important fact to remember when working with patients, we still need to focus on the experiential consequences of such interactions between nature and nurture. Understanding the influence of one's temperament can certainly help, but essentially what needs tending in therapy is the scope and strength of currently maladaptive fear systems, and the defenses erected against them.

THE NEUROPSYCHOLOGICAL ESSENCE OF FEAR AND ANXIETY

Any discussion of the universal emotions of fear and anxiety inevitably raises a question: what can we add to what we already know from the many theories about anxiety, especially Freud's? Although what we know so far to a large extend rests on psychoanalytic concepts, and more recently cognitive-behavioral therapy approaches, when we examine the relevant neuropsychological findings we realize that they shed a new light on how we see the source of fears and their enduring effects. In a divergence from older views that regarded anxiety as the result of unresolved conflicts or repressed wishes and fantasies (Freud, 1926), neuroscience is showing that fear and anxiety are innate, universal physiological states that are activated by internal and environmental stresses. Most significantly, the physioaffective experience of anxiety in response to invisible stimuli can occur entirely out of awareness (see Ohman, 2009; Ohman et al., 2000).

The roots of fear and anxiety, then, are found in the integrated processes of brain, mind, and body; as such they affect many conditioned responses and learned associations. Within a particular unconscious system they can become intertwined with internal and interpersonal difficulties and conflicts, but only after being conditioned so. As clinical experiences clearly indicate, fears and anxieties are behind many embedded patterns of distorted perceptions and defensive responses, often in the context of neutral stimuli or benign interpersonal situations. These response patterns can be complex, sophisticated, or fully rationalized, but they are still the automatic response to stimuli that rouses what has become irrational fear and anxiety. In these instances, what informs one's feelings and behaviors are not the real aspects of the internal or external environment but the unconscious system with its own emotionally determined convictions.

Neuropsychological research, then, can illuminate the far-reaching effects that early fears have on developing and sustaining negative emotional states and the myriad defenses and self-narratives associated with them. This is particularly true for fears embedded in the early intersubjective environment. The renewed examination of the roots and effects of the FEAR system and its main executor, the amygdala, will further illuminate our human vulnerability to dysregulating emotions and their pervasive effects. It will also explicate the internal workings of an unconscious self-system in which the building blocks of fear go on to develop maladaptive perceptions and defenses.

SELF-SYSTEMS AND FEAR

From the beginning, our brains possess the innate capacity for specific or free-floating fear, the latter usually called *anxiety*. The FEAR system, like all other affective systems, is essentially "objectless" (Panksepp and Biven, 2012, p. 176). Like the other affective systems, through conditioned and associative learning, fear becomes linked to actual objects, interactions, experiences, cognitive processes, and unconditioned situations

(LeDoux, 2014). Repeated fearful or anxiety-suffused experiences will often result in fearful memories and associations. In turn, the emotional and behavioral patterns these memories coalesce into will be triggered by more generalized and neutral stimuli, both internal and external.

Through evolutionary necessity, fears, innate to all species, developed to serve as an important guide to behaviors important to survival and to the maintenance of life tasks. Learning and memories guided by raw fear have been effective ways to avoid danger, and learning occurring in the context of high arousal tends to be remembered more efficiently (Damasio, 2010; Hamann, 2009; Koziol and Budding, 2010 LeDoux, 2002; Panksepp and Biven, 2012). In the attempts to understand how the fear system operates and what pathways it uses, numerous studies have established the amygdala as the center of the fear system (LeDoux, 2002; LeDoux and Doyere, 2009; Ohman, 2009; Phelps, 2009).

The Seat of Fear and Anxiety: The Amygdala

As part of the limbic system, the amygdala (there is one in each hemisphere) belongs to the older regions of the brain. The amygdala is a center for information or association in the service of controlling emotional responses. It receives input from all internal and external sensory modalities as well as from connections linked to higher-order processing structures such as the prefrontal cortex and the hippocampal region. Importantly, it has connections to brain stem areas involved in controlling fight-or-flight reactions and physiological homeostasis (the autonomic nervous system and stress hormones). Primordial, innate emotional response circuits, mediating systems such as fear, rage, lust, and attachment needs are active within the periaqueductal gray (PAG) and the hypothalamus, largely driven by associations and unconscious assessments sent by the amygdala. Through their interaction with the amygdala, these innate circuits also influence cortical processes, including perceptions, interpretations, and action tendencies that reach consciousness (LeDoux, 2002; Lewis and Todd, 2007; Panksepp and Biven, 2012).

Significantly, the amygdala directs the perception of sensory information at the posterior cortex (LeDoux, 2002, 2014), and affects self-monitoring in the anterior cingulate cortex as well as attention. Pathways from the amygdala also reach the basal ganglia, enhancing the activation of this important learning system (Koziol, 2014). Amygdala activation has been seen in almost all the imaging studies that have explored fear, anxiety, and negative feelings (Hamann, 2009; LeDoux and Schiller, 2009; Phelps, 2007, 2009). Just anticipating a shock or watching a wide range of negative stimuli (LeDoux and Schiller, 2009; Vuilleumier, 2009) increased amygdala activation in animal and human subjects, and damage to the amygdala impairs the learning of implicit physiological fear emotions but leaves cognitive awareness intact (Buchanan, et al., 2009; Canli, 2009).

The basolateral amygdaloid complex serves as the conduit relaying fear to the central nucleus of the amygdala. Two pathways of fear perception and processing have been identified (LeDoux, 2002). The "low and dirty" pathway goes directly to the amygdala, where an emotion of fear is being generated, thereby bypassing the cortex. When activated, the amygdala releases neuromodulators that spread throughout the forebrain area (LeDoux, 2002; LeDoux and Schiller, 2009). The second pathway, "the high road," goes trough the cortex and is available to conscious awareness of fear. Both modes affect each other and work in a coordinated way. Internal connections allow the amygdala to integrate converging sensory and higher-order information, internally process it within its networks, and then generate outputs that affect behavioral and physiological responses to threatening situations. Receiving both the unconditioned stimulus (such as a shock in animals, or a frightened state of arousal embedded in an interaction with a parent) and conditioned stimulus (a tone presented at the same time, or internal thoughts and self-blaming associations happening at the same time) the amygdala converges them into associative learning (LeDoux and Doyere, 2011). Fear conditioning, then, is a form of learning that occurs out of awareness and is independent of it. In effect, unconscious patterns embodying emotional, cognitive, and behavioral patterns based on fear responses accurately reflect the nature of conditioned fear and the innate ways of coping with them.

LeDoux's recent (2014) contribution further underscores the unconscious nature of conditioned fear and the unconscious defenses recruited against it. The mechanisms that unconsciously detect and respond to fear are entirely separate from the conscious feeling or awareness of fear, according to LeDoux. Fear conditioning is effective because it exploits the process of associative learning underpinned by innate neural circuits. The plasticity determined by neural and chemical attributes increases the synaptic connections between stimuli, events, or feelings. "As such, fear conditioning is explained solely in terms of associations created and stored via cellular, synaptic, and molecular plasticity mechanisms in amygdala circuits" (LeDoux, 2014, p. 4). Conditioned fear responses, in animals and humans, do not require any consciousness, and implicit memories created by fear conditioning are distinct in their mechanism from declarative fear memories. These findings have obvious implications for our everyday, hidden developmental hazards. Associative learning linking states of fear arousal can be prevalent and unintended, yet create unconscious fearful associations and systems.

Surprisingly, fMRI in both humans and animals have shown activation of the amygdala in response to stimuli associated with positive and negative emotions. Such studies also indicate that the amygdala mediates positive emotions (LeDoux and Schiller, 2009; Phelps, 2007). By being involved in assessing and updating the current value of stimuli, the amygdala may be critical to certain aspects of appetitive or reward learning (LeDoux and Doyere, 2011; LeDoux and Schiller, 2009).

Deep Subcortical Regions'
Role in Fear Activation

Further attempts to pinpoint the underlying machinery of conditioned fears and their ensuing anxious behaviors, Panksepp and Biven (2012) argue that there is a bottom-up programming of the amygdala to react to fear. For example, electrical stimulation administered to deep subcortical regions (which all mammals share) generates innate fear responses even when there is no outside danger. The circuitry responsible for the fear system is important for sustained anxious feelings and fear learning. As was already noted, we learn best in the context of emotional arousal, generated externally or internally—memories tend to be encoded and better recalled (Damasio, 2010; Fernyhough, 2013; Lewis and Todd, 2007; Panksepp and Biven, 2012).

A discussion of the amygdala has to emphasize its deep subcortical connections (Koziol, 2014; Panksepp and Biven, 2012), as well as its influence on the prefrontal cortex. These neural links explain the findings that a wide range of conditioned fear responses occur automatically and implicitly (Hamann, 2009; LeDoux and Doyere, 2011; Ohman, 2009; Panksepp and Biven, 2012). In tandem, subcortical regions and the amygdala control the emotional flavor of implicit memories and the associations to them in higher cortical areas. In addition, the amygdala and its related connections influence explicit memories encoded by the hippocampus. This temporal region, essential for explicit memories, records the links among the many aspects of a fear-conditioning situation. Both types of learning, the implicit and the explicit, are under the domain of the larger emotion system, and specifically the amygdala.

THE AMYGDALA'S CENTRAL ROLE IN SHAPING DEVELOPMENT

The evolutionary success of the fear system, enabling humans to remember danger, also has darker, more knotty facets. An enhanced neuropsychological sensitivity to real and imagined threats has all but guaranteed a heightened susceptibility to fear-infused memories and conditioned learning. When we recall that the basic role of the amygdala is mediating vigilance and effective learning (Whelan et al., 2009), we can start to grasp the many opportunities for negative emotional memories that inevitably are part of any infant and child's experiences.

As part of the FEAR system the amygdala is a relevance detector (Phelps, 2009) that informs us about what is important to survival but also activates other neural systems to be especially attuned to information deemed important to wellbeing. The fear system can become hypersensitized when it encounters extreme or chronic negative situations or interactions and as a result widen the range of internal and external cues eliciting anxiety (Panksepp and Biven, 2012, p. 176; Schore, 2012). This is particularly relevant to early development: we should think of infants and children exposed to chaotic, noisy, and traumatic conditions. The fear-inducing and negative aspects of such situations, even those deemed benign by a parent, may still arouse innate fearful reactions in infants and children and will leave indelible and unconscious fear-suffused memories.

Pain, physioaffective distress, loud noises, and sudden movements, all signaling danger, arouse fear in the PAG in animals and humans (Panksepp and Biven, 2012). This indicates again the many opportunities for the activation of innate fear responses. These can easily transform into a free-floating, generalized anxiety. Infants become anxious, for example, when they are not being attuned to and can experience extreme hyperaroused dysregulation when their raw affects are not being modulated internally or by a parent. In response, innate physiological defensive states such as detachment, avoidance, rage, or panic on the one hand, and a depressed, helpless dissociation on the other, will be automatically and unconsciously employed (LeDoux, 2014; Schore, 2012; Tronick, 2007).

In an interesting imaging study, pictures of fearful and angry faces were found to activate the amygdalas of children and adolescents, but neutral faces did not. The amygdalas of infants, however, reacted to neutral, expressionless faces and not to aggressive or scary ones (Phelps, 2009; Phelps and LeDoux, 2005). These results may explain the prevalence of fear-based emotional, cognitive, and behavioral patterns and the quick activation of avoidant behaviors on one hand and negative thinking on the other. Countless experiences encountered by infants and children daily, especially fears embedded in the relational environment, may give rise to conditioned fear responses, associations, and defenses.

We need to consider the depressed mother, for instance, who finds it impossible to summon expressions of joy and validation, staring at her infant flatly in spite of her best intentions. In infancy, such neutral facial expressions can have devastating effects. Years later, an unconscious self-system will automatically experience interpersonal interactions through this early associative learning. A less benign but similarly damaging is the hurried, constantly busy mother. Well meaning as she may be, her matter-of-factness or lack of expression may still be emotionally distressing (Schore, 2012; Tronick, 2007). In these cases, as well as in many seemingly benign situations, the vigilant amygdala will give rise to a state of arousal and fear that automatically becomes associated with a wide range of internal and external experiences, behaviors, and personal meaning.

The amygdala will react then, even when the cues in others people's faces are subtle, as in the case of nearly imperceptible facial changes or dilated pupils (Hamann, 2009). Because the amygdala is active from birth, emotional discomfort and arousal states inevitably become embedded in some of the endless number of the interpersonal encounters carried out during childhood. Such fear-inducing interactions and memories will coalesce into an unconscious self-system associated with particular interpersonal cues. In this way the amygdala contributes to unconscious decisions as to what is relevant for the person and how the person should act. It is a self-organizing process in which perception, action, and the amygdala modulate each other in the service of survival (Gazzaniga et al., 2014). Due to the amygdala's sensitivity, then, the presence of an unconscious self-system glued together with fears, vulnerability, and automatic defenses against them is a given in all of us. If the amygdala's sensitivity is exaggerated, even relatively benign and inevitable intersubjective failure at attunement tolerated by some infants will be more dysregulating to others.

As part of an unconscious self-system the amygdala also influences subcortical brain-mapping areas. As we already saw in the previous chapter, areas such as the basal ganglia and the cerebellum have a central role in encoding and executing patterns of perception, emotion, and behavior. Consequently, whole neuropsychological tendencies will be enacted unconsciously, regardless of what is called for in new situations (Gendlin, 2012; Koziol, 2014; LeDoux and Schiller, 2009; Radman, 2012; Stewart, 2010). These dynamics underlie subjective interpretations and reactions, such as projection, perceptual distortions, and automatic repetitions of defensive behaviors. Here again, we come to appreciate the far-reaching amygdala's influence on our conscious-unconscious continuum of functioning throughout life.

THE FEAR SYSTEM AND THE AMYGDALA: EFFECTIVE TEACHERS

All children must learn to navigate, adapt, and make sense of their emotional environment and endure an immature emotional system high on reactivity and arousal and low on innate regulation (Beebe and Lachman, 2002; Schore, 2012; Tronick, 2007). It is not far off to assume that the emotional conditioning mediated by the amygdala lies at the heart of the unconscious, its emotional memories, the emotionally laden cognitive ruminations and worries, and finally automatic and unconscious defensive patterns. The conditioning model expanded on by LeDoux (2002, 2014; LeDoux and Doyere, 2011; Phelps and LeDoux, 2005) and others have enabled us to better understand emotional learning experiences during childhood and adolescence (Tottenham et al., 2009).

Echoing psychotherapeutic models, neuroscience emphatically shows as well that the periods of infancy, childhood, and adolescence are especially fraught with the potential for situations that may enhance the state of fear. What we have examined so far presents this argument with more convincing specificity. It may be that the importance of the amygdala is especially pronounced during the developmental period when learning is at the center of all developmental processes, especially those that encode the meaning of relevant social and intersubjective stimuli, such as facial expressions (Siegel, 1999, 2007). As suggested by Tottenham et al. (2009), the amygdala may be less critical once all the associations have been formed, most likely some time during young adulthood, although its influence as threat detector is still noticeable.

Fear conditioning during adolescence has effectively generated new fearful associations. Pairing, for example, a neutral cue with an air blast or puffs to the larynx (an anxiety-inducing stimulus) has demonstrated that this age group can learn to associate neutral stimuli with negative ones. This learning process was accompanied by greater amygdala activity in response to the previously neutral stimulus. Even among adults a noticeable similar activity in response to an acquired fear has been detected. In studies exploring the effects of safety cues, the amygdala surprisingly was recruited to signal safety as well as danger (Tottenham et al., 2009). Learning that certain cues are not linked to aversive puffs of air to the eye (safe condition) also showed amygdala involvement.

As Monk et al. (2003a, 2003b) have also shown, throughout childhood and adolescence, neural processes in the amygdala mediate the learned significance of positive and negative stimuli. These findings suggest again the extent of the amygdala's involvement in detecting and encoding the emotional significance of incoming stimuli, even the mildly aversive ones or those not deemed threatening on a conscious level. Throughout childhood and adolescence, as well as in adulthood, then, it is the quality of the interpersonal environment, the duration and intensity of both positive and negative emotional environments, that will determine much of our unconscious memories and associations, the self-systems they coalesce into, and in turn the felt self-states they give rise to.

When trying to better understand the various developmental forces that shape who we are, it seems important to consider childhood and young adulthood experiences as impactful and crucial as early infancy. Chaotic, threatening conditions, humiliating and injurious interactions diminishing to one's sense of self, and overwhelming painful feelings in response to perceived or real rejection, for example, all activate the amygdala and result in anxious/painful memories and associative links that become just as convincing as the original experiences.

When we also take the default network into account, the brain/mind's attempts at rest to make sense or ruminate on past emotional and inter-personal situations (Gusnard et al., 2001; Raichle et al., 2001; see Chapter 1), the amygdala's role in shaping one's self-referential and self-other ruminations also seems substantial. The degree to which a child's, an adolescent's, or an adult's attention, thoughts and affects are already unconsciously attuned to threats and negative feelings will affect the end result of default system processing. Self-referential and self-other ruminations trying to re-create a hurtful situation; imagining unacted on alternatives or attempting to understand the meaning of an emotional experience will also be suffused with negativity and self-blame. The FEAR system and its executor, the amygdala, has many tentacles influ-encing one's unconscious as well as conscious subjective sense of self, as well as many learning experiences.

The anxiety-linked "lessons" residing within a particular self-system becomes "practical knowledge" (Fosshage, 2005, 2011; Gallagher, 2012), the developing blueprint for how we perceive, understand, and behav-iorally navigate the endless number of individual challenges and inter-personal demands. Throughout life, if there is no attempt to modulate these unconscious emotional patterns, an entrenched self-system will automatically color all further interpersonal encounters with old anxiet-ies and defenses. The developing unconscious systems affected by fears are unique to each individual. They are based on specific memories and experiences, on the emotional values of these experiences, and on the many learned and conditioned associations that have amassed around them. These learned patterns are not accessible to consciousness but they still determine much of our interactions with others and our own sense of self, our courage, intentions, risk taking, and avoidance. The background, as Radman observes, is always potentially enacted, a tool of potentiality (Radman, 2012). Consequently, the background uncon-scious makes up our core self (Damasio, 2010) and emotional schemas (Bucci, 2007a, 2007b). It influences who we are not in a dormant abstract fashion but in an alive and enactive way, always expressing conditioned fears and the many anxious situations attached to them.

WHAT YOU DON'T KNOW CAN HURT YOU: EMBEDDED FEARS AS PART OF UNCONSCIOUS SELF-SYSTEMS

Much of what the brain learns occurs without awareness and without the help of the neocortex (Koziol and Budding, 2010; LeDoux, 2014). The cues that provoke these learned associations are often imperceptible or entirely out of awareness. Such cues can re-create past fearful experiences without current justification. For many types of emotional memories, the acquisition of new fear responses is automatic and involuntary, especially during infancy, childhood, and adolescence. As we know, although those memories encoded before the capacity for episodic-autobiographical memory matures (Mancia, 2006, 2007) rarely, if ever, become explicit, they still carry enduring affective meaning and behavioral consequences (Damasio, 2010; Fernyhough, 2012).

As discussed in Chapter 4, the mirror neuron system may underlie much of our interpersonal learning. Mediating a neuropsychological link between subjectivities that observe and relate to each other, the mirror neuron system seems to be involved in mutual action understanding, imitation, and empathy—interpersonal processes that also constitute the building blocks of attachment (Gallese, 2006; Iacoboni, 2008; Rizzolatti et al., 2002). Parents' sensitivity to their infants' distress may be facilitated by the activation of the mirror neuron system.

For example, in a study employing fMRI imaging, Lenzi et al. (2008) have demonstrated the extent of the shared emotional communication between infants and their mothers. When observing and imitating images of their babies' expressions, the mothers' mirror neuron system (their insula as well as their amygdalas) became activated. This activation was stronger when the mothers viewed emotional expressions as opposed to neutral ones. Interestingly, the level of activation was correlated with the mothers' level of reflectiveness as measured by the Adult Attachment Interview. Imitating the babies' expressions resulted in greater activation than observing alone. Taken together with findings that an activated mirror neuron system reaches the limbic system and the amygdala through the insula (Carr et al., 2003), one can see the significance of the parent's regulating response and level of attunement. Mothers' unconscious reactions to their babies in the form of facial expressions have been shown to find an echo in the babies' mirror neuron system and limbic system (Ohman, 2009; Pfeifer et al., 2008; Phelps, 2009; Tottenham et al., 2009; Whalen et al., 2009).

The amygdala's fast-acting automaticity will detect and in some cases amplify (most likely determined by a genetic predisposition toward anxiety) perceived threats to a secure sense of well-being posed by misattunement. The amygdala's activation in response to such a wide range of distressing situations, even to seemingly benign but repeated experiences that "miss the mark" in terms of attunement, can coalesce into unconscious painful lessons against which defenses need to be marshaled. Such learning experiences can center on states of arousal eventually leading to empty feelings of not being seen and validated. These initially inchoate sensations will prime the amygdala to continually seek and identify similar threats or emotional patterns in all interpersonal interactions. Depressed moods, states of hyper-arousal and thoughts doubting or severely denigrating one's self-worth in relation to others have indeed been found to correlate to amygdalar activity (Sharpley, 2010).

In situations of potential danger, real or imagined, feedback from the amygdala enhances the perceptions of such stimuli in subcortical maps (Surgulladze et al., 2003) inducing defensive responses. Out of awareness the whole system gives rise to automatic defensive reactions such as avoidance, attack, passivity, rationalization, or addictive cravings—defenses that proved themselves efficient in controlling fears and anxieties and thus became part of the self-system (Gainotti, 2006; Grawe, 2007; Hamann, 2009; Koziol and Budding, 2009; LeDoux, 2002, 2014; Lewis and Todd, 2004, 2007; Phelps, 2007, 2009).

As we saw in the last chapter, for the sake of efficiency, the brain will always take short-cuts and respond with well-established patterns (Bargh, 2007; Bounomano, 2011; Damasio, 2010; Koziol and Budding, 2010; Wegner, 2007). We are not aware of internal instructions to react with fear or with generalized anxiety to particular interpersonal situations or to reenter a familiar loop of negative ruminations in response to a familiar emotional challenge. Nor are we aware of the tendency to experience stimuli and react to them as if they truly threaten and endanger our well-being. Similarly, we are not aware of the original events that made us experience fear arousal in the first place or practice a certain defense against it. Many of these learning processes occur before explicit memories come on line, and even then they continue to occur out of awareness. As these learned fear-induced perceptions and responses continue to further generate anxious associations, although we may feel the anxiety itself, we do not understand what is taking place or why.

During states of hyperarousal we involuntarily and unconsciously reactivate old fears and treat them as current. The stimuli that activate emotional responses may be entirely unknown or possess various degrees of perceptual awareness. But even with some awareness regarding the environmental signals, old fear responses and the entrenched defenses against them may still be carried out automatically and take over (Hamann, 2009; Murray et al., 2006; Ohman, 2009). As we saw before, the quick and automatic reactions to perceived fearful situations, entirely based on past associative learning, are not just isolated behaviors but underpin complex emotional, cognitive, and behavioral patterns. They become the inevitable part of any intersubjective encounter. Imperceptible cues, signaling real or imagined danger, interpersonal discomfort, and painful experiences embedded in early interactions will color relationships, including the psychotherapeutic one.

Most important, a direct, out-of-awareness route to the amygdala promotes defensive patterns to even weak sensory or perceptual stimuli (Ohman, 2009). These systems affect all aspects of our adult emotional life, behaviors, and social interactions. We feel things, interpret events, and act in certain ways, but we don't know why. The emotional program is executed even in the face of willpower. Feelings tend to take over and become the dominating experience. This is one of the underlying explanations for the automatic repetition of attachment difficulties, defensive behaviors, and compromised affect regulation—all are determined by unconscious forces that can overcome conscious intent.

Significantly, if unconscious fear is guided by different neural mechanisms than consciously felt fear (LeDoux, 2014) we can conclude that the destructive effects of unconscious fears can be more pernicious than those of consciously felt fear. At least when we feel fear we can attempt to deal with it; when we don't have enough of an awareness of unconscious fear and the avoidant defenses it automatically recruits, we have less of a chance of dealing with it well. In this context, the psychotherapeutic process provides one of the few opportunities to better identify such a system. The resultant better understanding of unconscious fears and defenses can rarely be achieved through narratives, autobiographical stories and memories, or free associations. Unconscious material is mostly inaccessible to any verbal articulation that can faithfully give it expression. What makes such anxiety-related patterns knowable are the wide-range, blunt and more subtle, emotional and behavioral manifestations continually enacted. The unconscious presence of anxiety can also be "detected" by the therapist's emotional reactions. Often, as we know, we come to inhabit and experience affects that the patient is unaware of (or only marginally so). Unconscious patterns also become an inevitable part of therapeutic enactments, again giving therapists and patients the chance to better identify, understand, and work through them (Bromberg, 2006, 2011; Cozolino, 2002, 2006; Fosshage, 2005, 2011, Renn, 2012; Wallin, 2007, among many others).

THE BEST DEFENSE IS DOING NOTHING: THE CASE OF RON

Ron, a 31-year-old man, sought therapy after a long period of time in which he felt frustrated and unhappy with his job as a teacher in a large high school. He claimed that the school principal "had it out for him," and as a result he tried to make himself "invisible, stay under the radar, and just get by." He saw the reasons for his unhappiness in a "bad work situation that did not encourage or push him, but tended to be pressured and critical." He felt unappreciated. As a result of his ability to coast, Ron saw himself as the "smart one" and was proud of his tendency to be slow, postpone things, and in general not drive himself "crazy like some of the other teachers." In spite of this expressed pride, he was not satisfied with himself, and yearned to feel more energetic and more effective with his students. On the one hand, he wanted to do more; on the other hand, he said, he did not know how to begin.

Ron described a similar way of being with the women he dated as well. He tended to be passive, indecisive, and "not all there." At a certain point, when they started to expect things of him, he wanted to leave. What was notable and even startling about his initial presentation was his lack of awareness about his internal life, his clear patterns of complex and sophisticated avoidant behaviors both at work and in his love life—difficulties that quickly emerged in therapy. It became exceedingly clear that during much of the time, Ron was mired in a state of anxiety: a state of physical stress, fear, and negative predictions. This was especially true when he had to make decisions that involved some risks or when his work was going to be evaluated by people above him. Such evaluations happened periodically, and each time Ron felt "sick to his stomach."

Though Ron was aware of a generalized discomfort, he was not aware of the extent that anxiety permeated much of his thinking and decisions. He was eager to understand the source of his difficulties, to unravel what was so hard for him to grasp and articulate before. With some trepidation, feeling he was being disloyal to the parents he felt close to, Ron slowly began to get the full picture of his childhood. The older brother to two siblings, he started to describe an angry, complicated, and short-tempered father and a mother who tended to be more passive, silently suffering at home and at the office where she worked. As Ron remembers, his father was often frustrated with his own perceived failure in life and would occasionally come home angry and impatient. Although his father was also a kind and loving man, when it came to his son he couldn't tolerate his childlike limitations or what he perceived to be a failure. Over time Ron realized how much he feared his father's anger, temper, and criticism, and how disappointed he felt not to be helped by his passive mother.

Although we do not have direct access to the innumerable emotional memories and learned behaviors associated with anxiety states— these happened out of awareness and were controlled by amygdala activation—Ron's repeated self-defeating behaviors around performance and potential judgment spoke of an unconscious state. In this unconscious system, fear of his father's criticism and the humiliating shame that followed taught Ron to be very cautions and avoidant of almost any task that involved an authority figure, who in his perception sat in judgment of him. Some of Ron's earliest memories reflected a pervasive anxiety of not doing things right. In the face of his father's frustrations and lashing out, Ron's instinctive tendencies to avoid being judged became a

behavioral pattern that largely controlled his life. Passivity, procrastina-
tion, and the rationalization of these actions became a central dynamic
in his conscious self-states; in a trade-off against anxiety, passivity
became an almost acceptable defense. He knew something was wrong
in the way he approached work and relationships, but was unconscious
about the actual nature and extent of the amalgam of fear and defenses.

As is sometimes the case when unconscious systems are enacted,
Ron experienced physical, emotional, and cognitive manifestations of
the underlying affects: physical markers of anxiety and fear together
with the certainty of failure and humiliation. These were activated
when he needed to make decisions that could be second-guessed,
when he was expected to actively pursue a new educational initiative
at school, or when he was asked to do something out of the ordinary for the school community. A nascent anxiety was then triggered,
and with it a host of emotional reactions, convictions, and negative
ruminations—the manifestations of internal processes. What he was
unaware of was how paralyzed he was by his fear of being judged and
found wanting. Fear shaped his decisions and determined most of his
moves in many interpersonal interactions. Not only did he avoid taking
chances at work, he frequently tormented himself about the quality of
the work he did. Similarly, when dating a woman, he needed closeness
but that feeling was tangled with the unconscious fears embedded in
every relationship; having to "submit" to the woman he felt close to,
thus "giving up" on his own psychic autonomy and making her too
important in his life. From that position of power, he came to see, a
woman would control him and criticize his flaws. Fears of being controlled by the other were mingled with intense fears of failing and
disappointing them.

Ron's feelings were often enacted with me as well. He would express
doubt about his "performances" as a patient, ruminate on how "boring or interesting" his story was, and obsessively second-guess much
of what he said. Through identifying his many diverse behaviors with
me, at work, and with his girlfriends, Ron steadily gained a much better
picture of the anxiety, the many learned associations it created, and the
defenses that were unconsciously driving him. The more he was able to
experience anxious and fearful feelings and tolerate them and the negative predictions they engender, the better he was able to consciously
prevent himself from enacting them.

THE AMYGDALA'S CONTROL OF COGNITION

The amygdala doesn't just detect and encode emotionally relevant experiences. Having extensive connectivity with cortical areas, it is also

involved in the regulation or modulation of a wide range of cognitive functions. Among them are attention, perception, and working and explicit memory (LeDoux and Schiller, 2009). Because it also projects to higher-order association areas in the temporal and frontal lobes, it affects how emotional and cognitive stimuli are processed in higher cortical areas. Conversely, some of the prefrontal regions involved in higher cognitive functions, such as working memory, planning, and executive control, have more limited or no projections back into the amygdala (Canli, 2009; Hamann, 2009; Ohman, 2009; Phelps, 2009).

Considering the implications of this biological topography (LeDoux and Schiller, 2009), it is important to note that the amygdala's influence on our cognitive functioning is generally greater than the other way around. Taken together, these links explain how emotional self-states arising from implicit self-systems can take over one's conscious experience, shutting out reflection, judgment, and perspective. We can see how the amygdala is a major determining part of any implicit system; it modulates emotional memories, links them to neutral situations, and serves as a controlling narrow lens through which incoming stimuli are perceived, interpreted, and processed.

The amygdala's impact on perception and course of action are particularly felt when there's a great deal of demand for one's attention: in this case, the incoming information will be altered quickly and automatically without any chance for reflective correction (Vuilleumier, 2009). Again, the implication for childhood experiences is clear; fear-suffused situations or even those deemed by the amygdala to be like loud noise or states of physiological stress will have greater effect on stored memories. Later, the amygdala's control of attention will direct the individual's perception to similar situations, focusing on the anxiety-producing aspects.

Throughout life this primacy of emotional processing directed by the amygdala and its subcortical links ensures that emotional experiences are more likely to get our brain/mind's full attention. This process will often be at the expense of cognitive processes, such as current perspective and assessment, resulting in affect dysregulation. Again we see how easily negative self-systems can become the only experiential state available at a given time; emotions and their narratives take over.

Fear Systems and Other Emotions

The vigilance and anxiety generated by the fear system rarely function in isolation: almost all interactions and internal states of emotional arousal embody a range of affects. The infant or child subjected to unattuned caregiving will encode a host of physioaffective memories that reflect the many negative and positive aspects embedded in and stemming from the countless interactions with caregivers and then with one's peers. Inevitably, the fear system interacts with other emotion systems, resulting in unconscious memories that bind fears to other affective experiences. Attachment needs, lust and sexuality, the ease of interacting with others, and social joy can all be tainted by anxiety. At times, it is actually impossible to view the various emotional memories and their learned associations as distinct and separate entities.

The panic/grief system, for example, inducing intense dread of being abandoned, neglected, and not taken care of, will become more sensitive and reactive because of the amygdala's vigilance. These emotion systems can also interact with the rage system, resulting in a core self that integrates angry thoughts and feelings interchangeably turned against the caregivers and the self. Emotions and/or narratives expressing nonconscious needs to punish others or be punished may ensue (Panksepp and Biven, 2012).

A dysregulated self-system associated with an enmeshed relationship with a parent can also be traced to the amygdala's vigilance for relational rewards or for what works best in the intersubjective realm. Children will often develop emotional and behavioral patterns unconsciously designed to maintain whatever resonance and validation they can receive, whatever semblance of affection, recognition, or emotional stability. Within such an interactional system they cannot develop their own sense of agency, so they submit to the parental one. Narratives of self-denigration demonstrating the enormous power others have, the exaggerated importance of others, and the need to help others at one's expanse are some of the prevalent narratives among these patients.

Clinically, we often see patients who display an exquisite ability to scan other people's faces, get their affect, and endlessly strive to please them, all to maintain the relationship. Patients can surprise us in how well they can read our affects and even predict them and how preoccupied they can be with the perceived judgment of others. This preoccupation, rooted in vigilance about the parent, is the best they could do to maintain their sense of well-being.

Damasio (2010) hypothesized that neurons in areas mediating emotions, such as the mirror neuron system at the premotor-prefrontal region or systems linked to the amygdala, would also activate areas that habitually map the state of the body and move it into action. In humans these include somatomotor regions. All of these regions have dual functions: they perform a sensory role, holding a map of the body, and they also generate and participate in action. These processes, as we saw before, have been supported by studies and imaging studies (Damasio, 2010; Koziol and Budding, 2009). Adding to these regions is the mirror neuron system, which is also involved in early emotional and procedural learning embedded in early development and its intersubjective emotional world (Gallese et al., 2007; Gazzaniga, 2008; Ramachandran,

2011). Studies have shown that the right brain amygdala, reacting to real or perceived threats to physical or emotional survival, determines the subjective quality of the emotional engagement.

Mediated by the mirror neuron systems, emotional stimuli were found to reach the amygdala through the insula (Carr et al., 2003), again affecting other brain regions encoding memories, defenses, and action plans. These visceral and affective traces are mostly distributed in the right brain, essentially forming our unconscious or implicit selves (Schore 1994, 2003) and the blueprints for future conscious and nonconscious interpretations of all new experiences. It's not just that the brain creates memories that coalesce into enduring implicit systems; due to the ease, quickness, and prevalence of fear conditioning, much of what gets laid down is of negative and anxiety-producing nature (Edelman and Tononi, 2002; Hanson and Mendius, 2009; LeDoux, 2002; LeDoux and Doyere, 2011; Linden, 2008).

The amygdala's quick reaction and automatic call for defensive actions affect some self-systems more than others. This depends on a particular amalgam of memory traces held together by specific and repeated intersubjective interactions that induced fear or terror in the child's world. In this context, we can understand how the amygdala and the fear system can create a fearful, anxious, or avoidant self-system in all of us, coexisting with more adaptive and less fearful self-states. The individual self-systems are on a continuum of severity, but in an almost universal way the fear function encourages the development of an unconscious island of anxiety, felt more consciously as an insecure, hesitant, confused, or altogether avoidant self-state. The ease with which fears get aroused and the automaticity with which whole patterns of behaviors are activated in response to perceived threat eventually acquire a stubborn strength.

This model of the brain/mind, emphasizing early emotional learning as guiding behavior, seems to tweak the notion of unconscious conflicts as emotional obstacles to adaptive functioning. Taking into account the effect of unconscious systems and their inevitable enaction, it is not difficult to see how whole patterns of behaviors are determined by emotional learning and avoidant defenses rather than an unconscious conflict. Having said that, however, the experience of consciously felt fears and anxiety—the common expressions of unconscious memories—will lead to conscious conflicts and hesitation, passivity, and other defenses, as we saw in Ron's case. In effect, conflicts can be viewed in the context of the constant, unconsciously shifting self-systems and hence in felt self-states. These internally or externally triggered shifts often present us with opposing desires and behaviors; we want to engage, to become close to others, and yet old fears, entrenched guardedness, and defenses take over. Although we know certain actions are important to our professional life, for example, without realizing it we still avoid them and even rationalize the reasons for doing so. It is only when we become aware of such shifting states and their enormous pull that we can start to resolve a conflict. As Bromberg observed (1998), a conscious conflict is an achievement over activated unconscious self-states.

IS THERE HOPE IN REFLECTION?

There are many implications for psychotherapy in the connections between the amygdala and the medial prefrontal cortex. This link provides a path for cortical reflective control over the amygdala's tendency to overreact to perceived danger (Glaser and Kihlstrom, 2007). The finding that the amygdala's activation can come under the influence of reflective assessment (Ochsner and Barrett, 2001; Phelps, 2007, 2009) indicates that there is always the potential for affect regulation. An additional interesting clue that may help in fostering affect regulation is the finding that explicit and implicit learning of fear and fear inhibition may be processed by different neural mechanisms. This finding suggests that awareness of safety and lack of the fearful stimulus may be necessary to inhibit a fearful response (Koziol and Budding, 2010; LeDoux, 2002; LeDoux and Doyere, 2011; Panksepp and Biven, 2012).

In a relevant and unexpected finding, the amygdala itself has been found to detect and learn cues of safety coming from the environment (Tottenham et al., 2009). In this case it seems that the emotional context of safety affected the emotion system positively, allowing the fear system to be overridden by positive affects (Panksepp and Biven, 2012). The significance of such a model of the brain/mind is clear. Within the safety of the psychotherapeutic process, it may be possible for the reflective system to develop and undercut the effects of the fear system. The process, which is discussed in detail in Chapter 8, is one simultaneously recruiting the underlying emotional structure, the defenses against it, as well as more conscious and deliberate processes that can derail an automatic expression of an unconscious fear-suffused self-system. Equally important, if not more so, is the fact that the therapeutic relationship and its emotional depth can promote a great deal of implicit learning. Through imitative and internalizing processes, with the help of the therapist's empathy and the nonjudgmental quest for an honest self-understanding, new ways of seeing oneself and others are developed and reinforced (Fosshage, 2005, 2011; Schore, 2012). Imperceptibly at first, old fears and defenses weaken and recede as new ones take their place.

CHAPTER 3

The Unknowable in Action

As WE HAVE SEEN SO far, neuropsychological findings support the assertions that unconscious processes monitor, control, and guide our behavior, pursue goals and desires, and automatically react to changes in the environment. The complexity of the predictive mechanisms of the brain is such that some in the field question the notion of free will altogether (Bargh, 2007, 2014; Wegner, 2002, 2007). Although it is impossible for us to have introspective access to the causal connections between neural activity and its behavioral outcomes, we still want to gain a clearer picture of these unconscious processes. More specifically, in spite of the structural dissociation between conscious intention and the behavioral (motor) systems in the brain—rendering most of the processes that guide action opaque to conscious access (Bargh, 2007; Prinz, 2003)—we still need to better understand how unconscious influences manifest themselves. For therapists who repeatedly witness the dual facets of the therapeutic process—its struggles and its victories—such a quest is particularly important. Although we cannot directly access those guiding neural processes, nor would we want to, we need to better understand their telltale signs in our patients and ourselves.

In fact, the inaccessible workings of the brain/mind notwithstanding, we still recognize unconscious patterns and motivation, actions carried out of awareness, at times at great cost to one's well-being. How do we reconcile this contradiction, and proceed to conclude that we "know" one's unconscious? The answer is provided by the dynamic relationship and resulting continuum between hidden neural processes and their enacted expressions in bodily sensations, feelings, thoughts, and behaviors—often inextricably entwined. This active and ongoing interchange between the unconscious and the conscious realms enables us to identify the unique self-systems that make up neural patterns. Paradoxically, this reciprocal relationship between the conscious and the unconscious makes our understanding of unconscious processes and repetitions at once more complex and more accurate and could lead us toward better psychological treatment.

Some of the more traditional conceptualizations of the unconscious have viewed it as a separate entity containing well-delineated memories or traumatic experiences that were made unconscious because they could not be tolerated by the conscious sense of self. Consequently, such approaches assumed that uncovering repressed—or in the more contemporary parlance, dissociated—memories would make the unconscious conscious and thus enable psychic integration. As we have learned, however, the immense unconscious system does not conform to this view; the widespread networks that always hum in the background and give rise to our conscious states cannot be reduced to specific events, memories, and content. This unconscious background is composed of many fused perceptions, memories, and emotions, many of them created before conscious memory is viable, others the result of unconscious associative learning processes.

Understandably, the importance of recognizing the unconscious has always been an inseparable aspect of dynamically oriented psychotherapy, and recently mindful awareness is considered a necessary precursor to affect regulation and integration (Cozolino, 2002; 2006; Siegel, 1999, 2007; Wallin, 2007). But views as to how we recognize the unconscious, its effects, and its manifestations are rapidly changing. Slips of the tongue and free associations, for example, have long been thought to get to what is hidden and give us clues about out of awareness wishes, conflicts, or motivation. Because physioaffective, cognitive, and behavioral processes are all enmeshed within brain/mind processes and structures, the words uttered as slips of the tongue or free associations, uncensored as they might be, are too limited to get to the heart of the unconscious. Words cannot actually convey the complexity of the intertwined neural/mental procedures embodying an unconscious self-system with widespread characteristics (Churchland, 2013, p. 224). Although words alone may indeed fall short at revealing our unconscious properties, what is becoming exceedingly clear is that enacted affects, thoughts, and behaviors can.

THE ENACTED UNCONSCIOUS

As neuropsychological data indicate, unconscious processes can only be inferred and glimpsed, mostly through the endless ways we actively experience and negotiate our internal and external environment. Although our mental patterns reflect a very narrow slice of the engine underneath, the brain's tendency to enact unconscious systems automatically and without deliberation underlies our ability to recognize and identify some of the unconscious influences at play. This is what the brain does well: automatically and out of awareness implementing past experiential lessons so that we do not have to relearn things each time anew. The repeated enaction (a very useful term coined Varela et al., 1991) of neural/self-systems gives expression to learned perceptual biases, emotional patterns, automatic cognitive interpretations, successful actions, and defenses. These authors, like many others after them, actually stress the embodied properties of the mind, aspects we often experience in the therapeutic process.

Interestingly, evidence that action tendencies motivate most mental processes—conscious and nonconscious alike—is put forward by the two poles of neuropsychological research. While cognitive neuroscience underscores enacted cognition (Colombetti, 2010; Engel, 2010; Koziol, and Budding, 2000; Sheets-Johnstone, 2010). Panksepp, a leading voice in affective neuroscience, also emphasizes the motor or action tendencies underpinning consciousness. In his words: "There is considerable evidence that our actions continually guide and focus our attentional and perceptual resources, for one end—the generation of effective behavior to help us survive" (Panksepp, 2003, p. 204). In other words, any understanding of how unconscious maps influence perception and behavior has to take into account the active motor connection to facets of functioning. Both the cognitive and the affective fields of study agree that unconscious self-systems "know" what to do and how to react, and thus create a pattern that repeats itself entirely out of awareness (see also Fosshage, 2005, 2011). Moreover, novel conditions are perceived and interpreted within the existing "knowledge" of the core system, ensuring a familiar reaction (Koziol, 2014).

On the other hand, higher-order control provides autonomy from automatic reactions, but the more deliberate system also functions slowly, having to reassess the nature of an appropriate response anew each time. Because such a process is a drawback to quick adaptation based on past learning, repeated and automatic self-systems have remained a major part of adaptational demands (Damasio, 2010; Koziol, 2014; Lewis and Todd, 2007). In the case of unintended slips of the tongue and free associations, it is possible that they may indeed reflect a lack of guardedness, as spontaneous utterances that essentially give voice to what is already "half there," a self-state that is not fully recognized yet, but can still be identified through enacted behaviors. Bollas's (1987) "unthought known" comes to mind. When discussing the unconscious, then, it seems much more accurate to speak of unconscious processes rather than well-delineated memories (Churchland, 2013; Damasio, 2010).

What Is Being Revealed

As we saw, the unconscious gives rise to our behaviors through enacted models and maps (Damasio, 2010; Koziol and Budding, 2010; Panksepp `and Biven, 2012) that are put into action in response to internal and environmental stimuli (Gendlin, 2012; Sheets-Johnstone, 2010, 2012). The processes that control the execution of many of our actions are usually mentioned in regard to skills, but they are present in the automatic execution of bodily, emotional, perceptual, cognitive, and action-oriented responses. In line with our awareness of a continuum of unconsciousness, the more under the influence of the lower brain regions and their experience-dependent maps, the more these patterns are automated (Bargh, 2014; Koziol and Budding, 2009). Consequently, we can state that implicit self-systems are always expressing themselves in enacted interpersonal and intrapersonal actions, and therefore they become knowable and treatable. These enacted unconscious maps become part of our more conscious self-states, comprising felt self-states, or conscious mind (Churchland, 2013; Damasio, 2010).

Enacted mental functions are context-based, automatically responding to stimuli and situations reminiscent of those that already left their neural, chemical, and psychological marks. These functions are carried out by the cerebellum, the neocerebellum, and the basal ganglia that link representations of specific behavioral contexts with the relevant motor tendencies. The PAG is considered by Panksepp and Biven (2012) to underpin emotional systems. In this way, complex behaviors can be mapped onto specific environmental features and contexts. Eventually, these behavioral patterns, encompassing multiple brain regions, are being guided automatically by the relevant contextual input. This process bypasses conscious control (Hassin 2007; Koziol and Budding, 2009; Panksepp, 2003, 2008; Panksepp and Biven, 2012; Thach, 1996, 2014).

The map-making neurochemical networks favor what already worked; what proved successful to the organism in the past should work again, given a similarity of stimuli characteristics. Similar internal and external conditions will produce responses that alleviated discomfort in the past, internal or external maneuvers that helped relieve the unpleasant or even terrifying sensations associated with a dip in dopamine. Similarly, in the case of dopaminergic surge linked to a particular situation or behavior, what follows is an increase in the cortico-striatal synapses that are activated and strengthened together (see Chapter 1). The result is a particular pattern of linked perception and enaction, linked motor tendencies with bodily sensations, emotions, and cognitions. That set of neurons is likely to be activated in similar situations, and the same behavior (or defensive mechanism) is likely to be executed.

Two often witnessed consequences of enacted unconscious systems or patterns are their distorted qualities and the power they wield over reality. The unconscious as background to present experiences, however, is not a simple, exact repetition of past representations or a totally new rearrangement of them. In interacting with our environment, we regenerate existing action models, acting on the environment with behavioral patterns that were tested in the past (Colombetti, 2010; Koziol and Budding, 2010; Panksepp and Biven, 2012; Sheya and Smith, 2010). If our unconscious models are not overly rigid, this encounter with the environment can change them a bit, educate them as to more effective internal and external reactions, as well as more appropriate reactions that work best for the situation. As we see in Chapter 6, however, a rigid system will only enact what it knows and not learn from changing circumstances. This interaction between unconscious maps and their effects on our functioning enable therapists to identify unconscious self-systems.

The Connection Between Perception and Action

Neural patterns involved in unconscious systems do not carry images of the external world or descriptions of objects and experiences. What they do support are sets of procedural know-hows about possible viable actions. These connections constitute a dynamic process with an active, enacted aspect that is an inseparable part of the encoded representations as well as the interaction with the world. What is interesting about this realization is that the ways our brain/mind is organized lead to action-oriented representations or directives, automatically prescribing patterns of action (Colombetti, 2010; Engel, 2010). These actions, spanning the range from adaptive to highly defensive and maladaptive, are based on past learning and reinforcement. Because perception, processing, and response are all intertwined, our unconscious self-systems and more conscious self-states are action-ready and action-related. The enactments of our internal mind are already embedded in its very existence.

Such action-oriented patterns include aspects of bodily dynamics, that is, biophysical properties of the hormonal, chemical, and skeletal systems. They also include emotions and cognitive styles, as well as tendencies to perceive, interpret, and think about particular situations, such as interpersonal encounters. Automatic enaction will guarantee the required quick responses to relevant information and sensorimotor exchange. Engel (2010) describes them as patterns of dynamic interaction that span the entire cognitive system. The fact that response patterns become quick and automatic does not, of course, ensure their capacity to respond in a current appropriate way, only that a response is selected and executed. We often see such unconscious enaction of self-damaging emotional and behavioral patterns in our patients' behaviors and repetitions.

Because representations are intertwined with action selection, Engel retermed them with the more action-oriented word: *directives* (2010, p. 229), stressing their active qualities. When such enactive representations are triggered, they control prospective courses of action. As in Damasio's (2010) model delineating the links between the conscious and unconscious realms, directives correspond to dispositions for meaningful actions. These reach consciousness and behavioral manifestations through the global activity of brain networks and the ability of some to rise the surface of consciousness (Baars, 1989; Churchland, 2013). In this way, directives construe our unconscious ways of "knowing" how to do things or how to respond to environmental demands (Engel, 2010). Engel further speculates that "these dynamic patterns actually implement procedural knowledge of sensorimotor contingencies" (2010, p. 237).

These processes explain our fast and automatic response patterns, from simple skills to sophisticated intersubjective interactions, from automatic unconscious avoidance to subtle, cognitive, and highly rationalized defenses. Consequently, all our felt self-states with their typical moods, defenses, and cognitive interpretations can be seen as rooted in unconscious processes.

If we recall that Damasio (2010), Koziol and Budding (2009) as well as Panksepp (see Pollack, Watt and Panksepp, 2000) and Lewis (2005), all emphasize the existence of internal maps or models in subcortical regions, an action-oriented view of representations predicts that traces of expectancy should appear in motor regions even if the expectations themselves concern perceptual events and stay out of awareness. This is indeed the case. Synchrony between sensory and motor assemblies happens specifically during tasks that require the coupling of perception and movements (Engel, 2010; Thach, 1996). The links between perception and action suffuse the brain/mind with inherent predictive qualities whereby expectations color perceptions and interpretations and prescribe a course of action, all out of awareness (Koziol, 2014; Pally, 2000, 2007).

THERAPEUTIC IMPLICATIONS

This state of affairs has great relevance to the emotional and behavioral difficulties we encounter in our clinical work. The automatic, unconscious connections between contextual stimuli and their corresponding motor representations can be generalized to all self-states and repeated patterns. Perani et al. (1999) showed that merely hearing action verbs activates implicit motor representations as well as working memory structures such as the dorsolateral PFC, the anterior cingulate cortex, and premotor and parietal cortexes. Similarly, the visual presentation of a meaningful action activates the same areas, as does the generation of action verbs or the retrieval of verbs from memory.

As we often witness the therapeutic process, emotions, defenses against them, memory assemblies and their potential distorted meaning, dysregulated affect, and the narratives that accompany them are all "action-ready." In fact, the function of unconscious patterns as guiding action is what determines the "meaning" of internal states (Engel, 2010; Panksepp and Biven, 2012). In other words, the action itself embodies the specific meaning of a particular unconscious self-system and how it negotiates the environment via the more conscious self-states. This observation explains the fast shifts in self-states we often see in ourselves and in patients and the ease with which an emotional/cognitive state takes over to become the only felt experience.

When we further consider Perani et al.'s findings, as well as the effective priming effects shown by Bargh (2007) and Bargh et al. (2001; Bargh and Morsella, 2008) we can fully appreciate how fast both patient and therapist can activate each other's unconscious systems. If verbs can activate motor areas, the effects of speech alone may be substantial, working quickly and out of awareness, leading to enactments. (Therapeutic enactments will be discussed in the following chapter.)

Repetition Compulsion as Meaning Making

Understanding the brain/mind's tendency to perceive and act at the same time according to encoded patterns expands our understanding of how unconscious maps or self-systems express themselves through enacted feelings, behaviors, and cognitions. In addition, the fast and automatic enactment of mental patterns sheds light on the important phenomenon of repetition compulsion. Repetition of maladaptive defenses, addictive patterns, and dysregulated affective states is at the core of many human difficulties, often raising the obvious question as to why they continue even in the face of being so hurtful and damaging. As mentioned before, the answers are found less in the need to suffer (or in any other motivational aspects that assume volitional intent) and more in the brain architecture. Throughout the brain, wiring and connectivity is carried out via widespread circuitry, allowing stored information to instantly inform incoming information, assess it, and interpret it according to what already exists. Hence the frequent predictions and projections we all engage in, the "filling in the story" that occurs automatically (Churchland, 2013).

We can look at repetition compulsion—our tendency to repeatedly engage in behaviors regardless of their adaptability to current situational demands—as an expression of such brain/mind organization. We also know that procedural learning is just as important to adaptation as higher-order cognitive controls, creating from very early on vast neural connections informing all levels of affective and cognitive functioning. Procedural and automatic repertoires constitute patterns of organized perceptions and behaviors that accomplish various predictable goals very efficiently. Procedural learning systems and repertoires, however, are not processed in a cortico-centered model of cognition but occur in a fast and automatic way without reflection. It's not that we are unaware of what we are doing at any point, but that we are not aware of the underlying perceptions, affects, motivations, and cognitions that go together with such a self-state. A more pragmatic, less motivational view of the unconscious sees it as rooted in the inevitable enaction of unconscious self-systems.

In any environmental context, whether responding to internal fears or to external challenges, the most appropriate response or coping mechanism is selected based on past experience. In an ongoing fashion and entirely out of our awareness, the brain stem with the help of the emotional brain and possibly the mirror neuron system (Damasio, 2010; Gazzaniga et al., 2014; Pfeifer and Dapretto, 2011; Watson and Greenberg, 2011) determines without our conscious participation how much any given situation should matter to us. The assigned value then affects the neural signals and the degree of emotional and behavioral responses to a particular situation (Koziol and Budding, 2009, p. 49). The striatum is the region sensitive to the context that generates the behavior. As such it biases the PFC with information about the most appropriate behavior given the current emotional, cognitive, and perceptual patterns it detects (Koziol and Budding, 2009). These complex neuropsychological processes explain why we have such limited awareness and control over affective states in real time and automatically enact whole patterns of perceptions and behaviors.

The enacting tendencies of unconscious systems do not only result in automatic repetitions; if powerful and rigid enough, such systems often recreate the very same experiences by projecting them into a situation or by unconsciously seeking an environment that will mirror and trigger them. The old cliché stating the influence of self-fulfilling prophecies is not far from the mark, and for good reason. Intuitively, observing people's tendency to repeat behaviors and seek situations that fit into their expectations, a mechanism that guides this was already assumed. And indeed, the neuropsychological model of the unconscious supports this old understanding of human nature. As we "happen" onto the environment and the environment "happens" to us (Gendlin, 2012), our unconscious often chooses a fit between a particular environment and our internal predictions, expectations, beliefs, and procedural knowhow.

This process is not a passive one; unconsciously driven, it is rather an active search for a fit, a search that without more adaptive forces frequently ends with more misery. It is not that a patient willfully wishes to suffer; John, the clinical case in this chapter, did not consciously seek to hurt himself or his wife. However, unaware of the self-system cued to excited unpredictability and a confused hyperarousal state, he engaged in affairs that corresponded to an internal composite of emotional memories.

It is interesting to contemplate in this context how seemingly conscious choices are made, and how only in hindsight such choices strongly confirm the contours and nature of an unconscious system. When we consciously decide on how much risk to take in a career, for example, or when we rationally weigh all the aspects of a situation and deem it not important enough to participate in, or when we are totally sure that the person we met is the only one for us, how much is still determined by unconscious forces such as anxiety, avoidance, and an entrenched relational map? This question is certainly at the core of many therapeutic processes, and the delineation of what might no longer be adaptable, and therefore should not color our choices, is an important part of the therapy.

In the course of self-understanding and identifying enacted behaviors, the patient's picture of how the brain/mind works frequently contributes to a profound sense of hope and the possibility of change. Once comprehended, the dynamic of the brain/mind unconscious processes can be tackled and changed. The mutual therapeutic appreciation of the propensity for automatic enaction underscores dual therapeutic needs: empathy for one's difficulties on the road to self-actualization and the continued emphasis on working through and reexamining old damaging patterns of behaviors and relationships in light of the past and in the context of the different present.

Repetition compulsion is carried out in the context of acting on the environment, whether internal or external; it is the end result of an unconscious map or self-system responding to stimuli that demand attention. The embodied nature of such responses reflects the out-of-awareness meaning given to a particular situation once internal pressures or interpersonal conditions are reminiscent of previous ones. If we recall that the emotional and cognitive core is making sense of the environment, this meaning cannot be but embodied. As a result, the highly selective and active perceptual processing dictates what patterns get expressed. Repetition compulsion, then, can be seen as the essence of enacted unconscious processes, expressing entrenched emotional, cognitive, and behavioral habits. This view, however, does not erase many of the complexities embodied in such repetitions. An out-of-awareness response readiness is not a simple stimulus-response mechanism; it is intertwined with the many affects and convictions that underlie every emotional system. As previously mentioned, all actions in response to the environment are about making meaning of that environment—of the pain, despair, or reward it holds for us. In a rigid system this meaning-making process is entirely embodied in the automatic expectation and interpretation already there. A more flexible system may deliberately consider the nature of the current context, especially if new information is presented. When the result of this automatic process is only based on past meaning, an emotion, interpretation, or reaction that has not readapted to a new situation, the repetition expresses greater degrees of unconsciousness. Because of the unconscious nature of such an enaction, its unfitness to the present situation is not perceived, and instead what is experienced is a natural conviction that only one response is possible.

AN UNACKNOWLEDGED TURBULENT CHILDHOOD: THE CASE OF JOHN.

Persistent repetitions of unconscious self-systems can occur even when one is entirely sure as to the "real" causes of a particular pattern of behavior. John, for example, sought therapy after being caught by his wife having one more affair. This was not the first time she became aware of his "insignificant flings," as he put it, but this time she could not forgive him anymore and left the house, taking their two young children with her. At the very first session, he described these affairs as meaningless and casual. He insisted that his frequent travelling for work presented him with wonderful opportunities he could not resist, but added that they had nothing to do with his marriage or how he felt about his wife. He loved his family life.

But John also felt devastated and wrecked with sorrow and guilt for hurting his wife. He continually said he still loved her and did not want to break up the marriage. Repeatedly, he said that he did not know why he had embarked on these short affairs. John's feelings, both his love for his wife and his remorse, seemed genuine and deeply felt.

When trying to understand why he cheated, more times than his wife ever knew, John clearly swung between two states: the conviction that he was justified in "experiencing some excitement" in his life, and a loving appreciation for his family life. On the one hand, he recognized how important his wife's stable love was for him, but on the other, he claimed that he needed something new in his life; that married life was too monotonous and predictable. Even his wife's love was seen as "weak and unsatisfying" at times.

Initially John could not bring himself to contemplate that the reasons for his affairs might not be clear-cut and reality-bound; after all, he repeatedly chose to stay with his wife and also felt love and appreciation for her. His conviction that these affairs did not mean much and that "they had nothing to do with his childhood" were also strong and unshakable for a while. It was only when he realized that unless he "got his act together" and convinced his wife that he could do better, that his therapeutic work started.

As John came to realize, his repetitious affairs were unconscious enactments of an unconscious part of him that was not fully acknowledged. John clearly remembered his childhood and even said that he fully understood its effects on him as an adult. As an example, he said that he was determined to be a better father than the one he had, and indeed he was. He was also determined to never become an alcoholic as his mother was, and had not touched alcohol since college.

With her alcoholic binges, John's mother had created a family life rife with unpredictability and turmoil. A few times a week, upon becoming drunk, her behavior would become emotional and often irrational; she would engage her sons in the same old jokes and long stories and demanded their full participation in whatever activity she was involved in. She would laugh and cry interchangeably, and the two boys were never sure what to expect. She often tried to pick noisy fights with their father, but at those times he would quickly retreat into his home office. John and his brother knew she was different from other mothers, but they still could not understand the source of their discomfort and humiliation when watching her. They did not talk about it to friends or teachers.

John's father spent as much time as he could out of the house or in his office, and he did not help the boys deal with their mother's erratic behavior, nor did he explain to them what her behavior meant. The word "alcoholism" was not uttered, even when they grew older and she got worse. After college, when John met his wife, he knew he had found the love of his life. Consciously, he realized that she was "together, stable and predictable," all the things his mother was not. She made him feel loved, valued, and safe. But a couple of years after the wedding, John started to feel and say to himself that something was missing, some excitement in the face of the predictable dynamics of their relationship. The birth of their first child only intensified his cravings for "something more" in his life.

John's first affair and the secret excitement around it convinced him that "meaningless affairs were the solution." If he felt less restless as a result, he would not be resentful and would have a better life at home, or so he rationalized to himself. John did not fall in love with any of the women, but he loved the sense of secrecy, unpredictability, and even the fear of being caught. These experiences felt just as real as enjoying his married life and the children that followed.

As therapy continued, John himself slowly realized that what was enacted in his affairs was that self-state associated with his mother and her unpredictable emotions. Such high levels of excitatory states—scary, confusing, or humiliating as they might have been—were neurochemically learned and reinforced as a major relational pattern. As much as part of him sought stability, the other self-system, known but unconscious as the same time, could not help but become enacted as well. In spite of his "knowing better" and the conscious conflict and guilty feelings the affairs created, John could not resist pursuing them. "The promise of new dates, the danger they contained, the risk taking, and having to lie to his wife," was intoxicating to him.

Obviously, John's behavior was not an exact replica of the content of his old experiences and the memories of his mother's behavior. What he was unconsciously enacting was the sense of unpredictability and heightened emotionality. The settled-down predictability involved in married life was far from satisfying on its own. As his other self-system embodying all these other emotions was triggered by the fantasy of excitement, John was literally swept away, helplessly, but with a great deal of heightened anticipation.

HOW MUCH CAN WE "LEARN" FROM REALITY?

John's example illustrates how an unconscious self-system that developed in response to an unpredictable mother is enacted out of awareness, thereby revealing a great deal about an internal and persistent unconscious pattern. As an active self-system on the lookout for what was familiar, it perceived any disagreement as provocation to be defended against and fought off. Current reality was enfolded into old structures, triggering old relational and internal experiences. John's unconscious should be understood not just in terms of implicit memories or experiences that were not remembered; what makes the system unconscious are the distorted and enacted qualities that his early patterns wielded on reality.

John's unconscious as background to his present experiences guided his interactions in his intimate relationship, resurrecting the intense drama of growing up with an alcoholic mother. What is so intriguing about the repetition of maladaptive patterns is their stubborn enactments even in the face of repeated failures to achieve a "positive" outcome. In spite of his exciting affairs, John became exceedingly miserable, feeling he was losing control over his life. Patients who repeatedly engage in subtle but well-rationalized avoidance behaviors, for example, do not just seek the pain of failure for its own sake; as in Ron's case from Chapter 2, something in the current situation presents a very specific meaning to the unconscious system. John unconsciously associated the excitement of his affairs with the familiar sense of unpredictability and heightened emotionality from his mother. The contextual meanings embedded in their situations—for Ron a fear of risking judgment by an authority figure, for John a yearning for unpredictability and heightened emotionality in his relationships—gave rise to their enacted patterns. This process explains another puzzling aspect of unconscious systems: left to their own devices, they do not "learn" from reality. In spite of his cognitive abilities, for example, John could not see that he was not reacting to the present but to shadows of his past.

ENACTED SELF-STATES: RELATIONAL EMBODIMENT

As in John's case, there is neuropsychological evidence for the notion of unconscious guidance of higher mental processes, such as interpersonal perceptions and behaviors, as well as sophisticated goal pursuit (Bargh, 2007, 2014). Dissociation between conscious awareness and intention on the one hand, and the operation of complex motor and goal representations on the other (Prinz, 2003), further illuminates the prevalence of unconscious enaction of emotional and behavioral patterns. As we saw, developmental processes bring about the mapping of unconscious representations mediated by the cerebellum and the basal ganglia and their links with the PFC. Schore's model also clearly explicates this process (1994, 2003, 2005, 2009, 2012). Emphasizing early mutual attunement, Schore sees relational and regulatory patterns encoded in the right brain as the blueprint for both relational patterns and affect regulation.

Within an intersubjective interaction, each relational self is linked to a mental representation of a significant other. These clusters of representations are then reactivated in social encounters and intersubjective interactions. As we often experience through therapeutic work, enacted physical-sexual, emotional, and behavioral patterns are especially sensitive to contextual activation within intimate relationships. Couples and the therapeutic relationships are particularly vulnerable to repetitious activation of interlocking interpersonal dynamics.

Presenting evidence that self-other representations or directives are automatically activated, Andersen et al. (2007), Schore (2012), as well as Bargh (2007, 2014) among others, maintain that the activation of significant self-other representations and the relational self in general are unconscious. The inevitable activation of affects within the therapeutic relationship, and with them the range of the automatic self-other representation, is behind the mechanism of transference, according to these authors. Directives suffused with old traumatic relational experiences will lead to projections and, in the case of an interpersonal entangle-ment, to projective identification. When self-other representations get activated by interpersonal contextual cues—unconsciously reminding a particular self-system of old relational experiences and the many asso-ciations they accrued—they spread to other self-other-linked represen-tations. In the process, they activate those aspects in the self-system related to the self-concept. In this way, representations of the self that started as being fused with the other eventually become linked with one's own feelings and thoughts about oneself (Andersen and Chen, 2002; Andersen et al., 2007).

Indeed, most often the repetition of relational patterns does not express only one system of representational know-hows. A patient might engage in a relationship where he may switch from perceiving himself as a victim to being a victimizer. Either of these enacted self-states con-tributes to an interactional environment rife with conflict, either one causing pain and self-sabotage. The switch between self-states often experienced in psychotherapy is in effect the embodiment of complex developmental forces. The infant and the child will always identify with and internalize both sides of the interaction. The memories that are associated with these internal physioaffective states will form distinct unconscious self-systems, as will memories linked to the parent. Both aspects of the repeated interactions—the victim and the victimizer—will be activated at different times within a relationship (Benjamin, 1995, 2004) and will simultaneously include the span of representations about the other and about the self as a subjectivity.

One important implication for clinical work is the realization that unconscious processes are not stable, distinct entities waiting to be revealed, but are always in touch with and inform and activate our men-tal and behavioral functions. Even if the content of particular neural maps is not accessible, the enacted affective, somatic, behavioral, and cognitive expectations—habits or patterns—give them voice and expose their particular characteristics. In the therapeutic process, the presence of autobiographical narratives, explicit memories, and the verbal mean-ings of one's emotions and behaviors can cause us to overlook auto-matic, mindless repetitions. These enacted repetitions, blunt and subtle, relational and conveying one's relationship to oneself, are the manifes-tations of implicit self-systems. This is especially true in the intersubjec-tive realm, where we tend to perceive and react to others through old entrenched systems (Bargh, 2014), laying the foundations for transfer-ence-countertransference entanglements.

Transference, then, is not simply unconsciously relating to the ther-apist as if he or she were the patient's parent. Rather, it reflects the patient's typical ways of being with others, and in a larger sense, the patient's way of being in the world. What is embodied in transference are perceptual, emotional, and behavioral systems that from early on coalesced into an enacted relational pattern. The question of whether a patient will bring the same relational pattern to every potential therapist is interesting. It is not so much about the actual similarities between a therapist and a parent (such similarities are largely improbable) but about how the patient perceives his here-and-now experiences with the therapist and the extent to which old patterns affect current perceptions. Because the therapist is susceptible to the same unconscious enacted processes (just like in all intimate relationships), enactments often ensue.

Within the therapeutic intersubjective environment, the activation of transference is not the result of an accurate one-to-one representation; those seldom exist. Using the context of relational theories as a model (Aron, 1996; Benjamin, 1995; Bromberg, 2006; Mitchell, 1993, 1997, 2000), we have come to understand that transference and countertransference embody self-other representations that come to life within the unique characteristics of the therapist–patient match. The therapist's interpersonal and unconscious contribution is just as important to the mutually activated relational systems. Through conscious and unconscious communication, the therapist's input, personality traits, and behaviors will activate the patient's relational system, become generalized, and invoke early directives. At the same time, her own self-system will be activated by the patient's emotional and behavioral input. When these significant self-other representations are activated out of awareness in both participants, which is inevitable, a prolonged enactment can develop. The next chapter discusses therapeutic enactments further. The flexibility/rigidity continuum is helpful for deciphering the differences we see in the nature of transference among patients and therapists. A more flexible, open unconscious system will most likely result in less transferential distortions than an unconscious relational system that sees all others through a rigid lens.

UNINTENDED BEHAVIORS IN THE PURSUIT OF GOALS

Goals and motivation can also be triggered by the environment without conscious awareness, choice, or intention, and then be executed entirely unconsciously. Along the way, unconscious emotions, beliefs, and defenses are expressed. Automatic goal pursuit involves perceptually monitoring the environment and unconsciously guiding a prolonged course of action. Because consciousness is not necessary for checking and controlling behavior, the implicit systems guide complex interactions with the environment and with others. Enabling this split between consciousness and goal pursuit is the fact that within the brain/mind, working memory and consciously held intentions are stored in different locations and structures from the representations used to guide action and behavior. This dissociation is the basis for implicit systems that underpin emotional and relational patterns that seem independent of intentional will or cognitive understanding. Interestingly, this dissociation does not prevent the enactment of the unconscious aspects relating to goal pursuit and wishes; although not accessible to consciousness in terms of their content, their telltale signs are expressed in behaviors that are unconsciously guided.

Like many processes discussed in these chapters, the unconscious guidance of our behavioral "choices" does not fall into a simple dichotomy of black and white or conscious and unconscious. As some researchers suggest, the brain/mind has unconscious vigilance over its own automatic, unconscious processes (Glaser and Kihlstrom, 2007). Subjects have been found to unconsciously monitor and correct for bias in judgments, just as they might do consciously. Also, as Bargh et al. (2001; Bargh and Morsella, 2008) demonstrated, unconscious motivation, especially goal pursuit, possesses qualities similar to those deemed fundamental in conscious motivation: action toward goal satisfaction, persistence, and resumption after disruption. Consequently, these researchers see an unconscious correction for unintended thoughts and biases.

These findings may point toward the existence of unconscious meta-cognition processing goals that seek accuracy and are achieved through self-monitoring. Under certain conditions this system will unconsciously compensate for anticipated threats to the attainment of these goals. The notion of a purpose-guided unconscious and the findings supporting it illuminate unconscious processes as "aware" in their own way, with "insights" that operate out of conscious awareness. Like implicit learning, such knowledge operates unconsciously, can be unintentional, and is manifested in one's behaviors (Glaser and Kihlstrom, 2007). Such findings and observations clearly support a model of a vast unconscious, with a life of its own, giving rise to our experiences. In addition, the idea that the unconscious monitors, enacts, and corrects behavior reinforces the notion that although unconscious systems are inaccessible in neural processes and representations, they are still knowable and recognizable when enacted in feelings, thoughts, and behaviors.

FROM UNCONSCIOUS TO CONSCIOUS: THERAPEUTIC SIGNIFICANCE

To round out the discussion on the brain's tendency to favor automaticity, we also need to briefly address the question of how such enacted systems become conscious. At this time, this question is very far from being answered. However, a leading hypothesis about this process views the process of consciousness as dependent on the ongoing complex networks always humming in the background—a process Baars (1989) called the global workplace. As Damasio (1999, 2010) and others observe (i.e., Churchland, 2013; Koziol, 2014; Panksepp and Biven, 2012), consciousness is a product of ignited representations "kept" not as ready-made images but as dispositions spread out among subcortical networks that find their way into consciousness due to particular reinforced patterns. Consciousness, then, is the product of the constant communication and interaction between the two realms (see Changeux, 2011; Dehaene et al., 2006; Dehaene and Changeux, 2011).

What is relevant to therapists at this point is the growing understanding that when this interactional process between the conscious and unconscious realms ceases to be flexible enough, the lower level can exert a much stronger control over enacted patterns. This can be particularly debilitating to patients whose more reflective functioning can become compromised during dysregulation. Often, a wide-range of emotional and physical abuse deprives children of the ease and flexibility dependent on an unhampered development of prefrontal functions. As we saw in John's case, the self-system that mapped the frequent, tortured, but at the same time exciting encounters with his mother precluded a reflective awareness. John simply could not understand what was going on as he was forced to resonate with his mother's emotional states.

As an adult married man, although one part of him knew he was endangering his marriage, these reflections were not helpful when his unconscious familiarity with the tangle of specific emotional experiences connected with his mother was triggered and enacted. In spite of the need for enacted excitatory states, John's affairs were not necessarily a forgone conclusion. He happened to find such heightened states of emotional engagement with women, but it could have been a risk-taking hobby or sport as well. But because John was not aware of that particular self-system, no further understanding, contexualization or sublimation could take place.

At that time, the only available mental state was one of justified enaction. This activated self-system was in essence a dysregulated and unprocessed one, and thus had a much larger emotional sway than his sporadic willful decision not to become engaged with any further affairs. As therapy proceeded, the balance tilted, and John was able to recruit reflective awareness as the excitement seeking self-state was activated, and consequently make different decisions. What most likely contributes to the strength of unconscious maps and their embedded elements of emotional memories, negativity, and defense is the default system.

Because it is intertwined with so many other processes, the default network system will most likely consolidate this inward preoccupation, leading to entrenched convictions and behaviors. Consequently, the necessity to be immersed in and cope with emotions such as fear, panic, grief, and gross inattunement, for example, and with the innately enacted defenses against them, may tilt development toward the prominence of unconscious processes. This is especially so when repeated bruising experiences leave their indelible mark on the rapidly created unconscious self-systems maps. Within such emotional turmoil reflective abilities suffer (Fonagy et al., 2002). The prominence of inflexible emotional/defensive systems that are not modulated by prefrontal functions gives the lower levels full control over unconscious execution of behavior (Koziol and Budding, 2010). In such cases, the bottom-up activation will grab our attention without the realization that we are reacting or, conversely, avoiding a response.

As will be discussed in the following chapter, understanding the brain/mind's propensity to enact internal systems, especially in times of dysregulation, can inform therapists of the power of such unconscious processes. More significantly, enacted patterns—a blend of embodied and action-ready perceptions, emotions, cognitions, and behaviors—are the culmination of all these subcortical–cortical interactions. In this way, although not providing us with exact replicas, unconsciously enacted patterns may be the only indirect representatives of what lies beneath.

After all, we are conscious of our actions; we "know" what we are doing, what we want, and our intentional goals. We are aware or sentient of our bodily and mental engagement with the environment and with our internal life. By paying attention to all these enacted manifestations, therapists can also become aware of those inaccessible self-systems—neural hubs that hum in the background, giving expression to stored memories, associations, and personal preferences (Bromberg, 2006; Ginot, 2007, 2009, 2012). What we cannot be aware of are the many networks and models that direct behaviors and in turn are directed by them.

Again we see that the unconscious background is not a separate entity of our mental functioning, but is generated in present feelings, thoughts, and actions (Churchland, 2013; Gendlin, 2012). The background functions implicitly, generating elements of the past in the present, generally not with a mechanical repetition but with different levels of nuance and flexibility. The level of adaptability to new situations and to the need to change one's old responses is fully dependent on the balance between rigidity and flexibility. A more flexible system—more under the control of higher cortical regions and less under the influence of the more rigid subcortical ones—will take into account new demands. In this case, the unconscious system itself can "learn" from a new environment and change.

The realization that perceptions in themselves cannot be differentiated from action tendencies of the brain has led to a perspective describing the unconscious as a function of the brain/mind that is continuously
involved in perceiving, interpreting, and acting on the world. It can
be said that all of our links, with our internal sense of self as well as
our environment, are suffused and affected by unconscious processes
embedded in subcortical regions (Churchland, 2013; Damasio, 2010;
Koziol and Budding, 2009; Panksepp and Biven, 2012). These regions
constantly inform our conscious perceptions, affects, beliefs, cognitions,
and actions—all aspects of our dynamic conscious mental life. Far from
being considered as distinct and unknown on all levels, the unconscious
can be perceived as inhabiting a continuum from total neural inaccessibility to enacted visibility through our mental and behavioral patterns.
This view of the unconscious as a system always in action and interaction with the environment, both internal and external, is at the root of
our ability to recognize the unknown. Such recognition, when assisted
by a developing reflective awareness and the embrace of the unknown,
will help patients live out the unconscious in a very different way; with
less fear, confusion, and self-destruction.

TOO TIMID TO TAKE CARE OF HERSELF: THE CASE OF ANNA

Anna's case exemplifies an enaction of a self-system containing all facets
of cognitive, emotional, and behavioral functioning. A strong relational
and emotional pattern was also accompanied by thoughts, beliefs, and
automatic behaviors. A timid and second-guessing pattern of relating to
others, to the environment, and to herself became Anna's central conscious self-identity.

Anna was a post-college young woman when she started therapy due
to feeling intensely confused and upset about her parents' reactions to
her coming out as a lesbian. They did not reject her, but at the same
time could not hide their disapproval and disappointment. In addition to
their projected fears for her future, they were very fearful about never
becoming grandparents. (Anna is an only child.) Anna "felt their pain"
and felt very guilty for hurting them. She needed tools to deal with them
and with her own guilt, she said.

As Anna's therapeutic journey began, she revealed a recurrent tendency to give up on her own desires and thoughts. Since she could
remember, she was always a "people pleaser" who tried to avoid conflict
at all cost. At the slightest intimation, real or imagined, that somebody
was angry with her, Anna felt truly frightened and even devastated.
The thought that somebody disapproved of her was too much to bear;
it made her all "clammy and uncomfortable," she repeated many times.

This familiar discomfort was at its height when her parents were unhappy with her sexual orientation. She simply wished to fold, she said with tears, give up on her real sexual desires and follow her parents' plans for her.

Anna's parents indeed seemed to have had a great deal of sway over her, making her choices for her, and in the name of parental caring, discouraging any move that might be "too risky," according to them. They forbade her to be friends with girls who they thought were not "smart or ambitious enough," and they convinced her that studying art was not going to lead her to a good professional life. They also pushed her towards a college that they thought would best advance her future.

Throughout her childhood, Anna felt consciously happy and content. She sensed that her parents loved her very much and that in many ways she was the center of their emotional world. Far from feeling discomfort, she felt entirely entwined with her parents' wishes and ideas, and it did not occur to her to question them. She fully trusted them and did not see any problem in her automatic tendency to agree with them and justify their point of view. She always thought they did everything out of love for her. Being an only child only exacerbated these feelings. Most of all, she seldom fought with them; accepting their way of being with her, their intrusion and control, felt like the most natural thing to do.

Anna's relationship with her parents became the blueprint for all her relationships and life choices. She had a very difficult time making decisions on her own and would incessantly consult her parents or her friends. Any forced decision was accompanied by a great deal of anxiety and insecurity, and she was left with a great deal of second guessing and deep regret after having made a decision. In other areas as well, Anna tended to doubt her own thoughts and wishes, and frequently she automatically assumed the other person she interacted with was right and knew better than her.

Up to the point when Anna's sexual awakening revealed to her that she was gay, the need to hold on to what was emanating from her did not assert itself. But now, as therapy started, she realized that she must either fight for her psychic survival or literally lose all hope for happiness. This was the first time Anna had to confront a previously unquestioned way of being. Once recognizing this important struggle, and over a couple of years, Anna was able to identify the shape and form of her psychic entanglement with her parents and the powerful repetitions of the self-system that it created. She slowly got to see and understand the incalculable damage to her emotional and autonomous growth. Beyond not taking responsibility for her own decisions and relying on others for them, Anna was most unsettled and disturbed by her unacknowledged emotional timidity, by the previous conviction that only her parents knew what was good for her.

As is often the case, Anna's progress toward self-agency was not smooth, but rather characterized by the resurfaced system of submission to the other at her own expense. In her first serious relationship, one that lasted about four years, she often enacted her timidity and lack of conviction in her own strength and rightness. This happened often enough to annoy her girlfriend, who perceived her timidity and inability to know what she wanted as a sign of "weakness and lack of character." The girlfriend's criticism frequently hurt Anna, but again and again she found herself putting her girlfriend's needs first. As this relational pattern was repeatedly enacted with me as well, Anna courageously continued to examine how an early submission to her parents' desires and needs continued to define her later on. She understood that her adaptation to their powerful convictions was inevitable; they were her world as well, and being submerged in it, she had no chance to see herself. Anna came to see them as very fallible people, who while being convinced that they knew what was best for her crushed her own subjectivity.

CHAPTER 4

Therapeutic Enactments: Unconscious Processes and Self-Systems Revealed

FOLLOWING LAST CHAPTER'S DISCUSSION OF the inevitability of enacted self-systems, this chapter further examines how therapeutic enactments in particular can reveal unconscious aspects of the patient and the therapist. As we already have seen, enacted unconscious relational styles are interpersonal manifestations of unconscious self-systems. Within the therapeutic intersubjective interaction, enactments reveal the participants' implicit relational and emotional patterns that inevitably come alive within the analytic dyad. It is suggested here that the analyst's eventual self-awareness of her own participation, followed by self-disclosure of her experience, promotes a conscious, verbally articulated encounter with the patient's unconscious relational styles, creating opportunities for enhanced mentalized affectivity and integration.

The focus on enactments as communicators of unconscious affective and relational patterns also reflects a growing realization that explicit content, verbal interpretations, and the mere act of uncovering memories are insufficient venues for understanding patients. Schore (2003, 2005, 2009, 2012) has emphasized this paradigm shift from verbal and interpretive ways of relating to and understanding the other to unmediated emotional responsiveness. Integrating clinical experience with a vast body of neuropsychological research, Schore has articulated the centrality of empathetic attunement in affect regulation as well as the role of the right brain in affective unconscious communication. The therapeutic dyad, according to Schore, intensifies the patient's (as well as the therapist's) experience of dysregulated emotions and defensive adaptations. As they become part of an enmeshed interaction within the intersubjective field, they constitute a powerful mode of unconscious communication; through the analyst's affect tolerance, they also become an important means toward affect regulation. Similarly, Gallese (2006, 2008) and Iacoboni (2006, 2007, 2008) have researched the role of the mirror neuron system in generating automatic and prereflexive empathetic reactions and have shown the brain's propensity to respond to others by activating corresponding neural networks.

As intense manifestations of transference–countertransference entanglements, enactments seem to generate a wide range of interpersonal and internal reactions, spanning the awareness continuum. Expressed and revealed through enactments are implicit early representations and relational patterns with all their affects, defensive adaptations, and behavioral manifestations. By setting the stage for direct and nonverbal access to the patient's representational world, enactments take us beyond transference and interpretations and provide us with a new appreciation of what it means to know the other.

Enactments can be described as mutually reactivated self-systems or entangled implicit relational schemas of both patient and analyst and as such they serve as a gateway to the patient's unconscious relational system. To further understand the enacted qualities of our unconscious, this chapter explores what enactments convey, what possible mechanisms they use, and how the therapist's use of his or her own experience in the dyad contributes to the patient's self-awareness and growth.

Often described as relational impasses, enactments can create an intersubjective field in which both patient and analyst find themselves in an ongoing emotional entanglement that temporarily diminishes the likelihood of meaningful reflection (Bromberg, 2006, 2011; Chused, 1998; Mann, 2009; Maroda, 1991; D. B. Stern, 2010; D. N. Stern, 2004). What was a conscious collaborative effort can seem in danger of collapsing under the weight of difficult, threatening, and seemingly inexplicable feelings and behaviors in patient and analyst. At their most extreme, enactments can threaten to halt the analytic process altogether or get out of control. Whether sudden or insidious, early or late in analysis, or long or short in duration, enactments are almost always a surprise. Resulting from a patient's raw transferential feelings and projected perceptions that find conscious and unconscious emotional echoes in the analyst or from a pervasive, deadened atmosphere of being stuck and not moving, enactments indicate that something is out of sync. This "something" and its remarkable implications for clinical practice are another facet of the unconscious enacted.

A THERAPEUTIC IMPASSE: THE CASE OF TINA, PART 1

The following vignette, which depicts an experience that took place about two years into therapy, highlights how unconscious intersubjective processes embody and reveal early relational styles, and introduces the important role of the analyst's self-disclosure.

A professional, middle-aged woman who was married with two children, Tina had been in analysis before and, according to her, learned a great deal about herself and her relationship with her deceased parents, who came to this country as refugees from the political turmoil in their country of origin. Explaining her wish to begin analysis again, Tina said that she was aware of some recurring behaviors she wanted to change. She did not like how oppositional she was and how easily argumentative she became in many situations. She suspected that her automatic opposition to others' opinions was really hurting her ability to achieve more and have easier relationships. She also wanted to further understand her "constant resistance to needing others," a lifelong problem she attributed to her experience of caring for her emotionally devastated mother, trying to "cure" her of grief and sadness. Tina could take care of herself.

She related all of this information with an earnest, optimistic demeanor, interspersed with cynicism and self-deprecating humor. She would give this process a trial, she said, adding that maybe what was behind her opposition "is something so dark and scary that we would not be able to deal with it." This was not said with a warning tone or with hostility. It did not even feel like a challenge, but like a neutral, matter-of-fact statement. "In any case," she said, "Not to worry, I'll be a good patient." Listening to her, I was surprised to find myself feeling both optimism and dread, reacting to what was said, but more so to some unuttered and unidentified feelings as well. I felt worried about future clashes and at the same time was aware of a wish to provide her with the opportunity to safely encounter what was clearly hidden and only enacted through feelings, thoughts, and actual behavior.

Tina indeed started as a "good" patient. She easily talked about her past treatment, her overprotected and yet emotionally demanding upbringing, and her problematic relationship with her husband. Rather quickly, it became apparent that she was well rehearsed in telling her story. Her words did not resonate or lack affect; she expressed feelings of anxiety and sadness, especially when recalling how miserable and grief-stricken her parents often appeared. What seemed stale was Tina's assured way of presenting her feelings and thoughts. It was as if she was not curious at all about any new possibilities or discovering something fresh about herself.

ENACTMENTS AS COMMUNICATORS OF RELATIONAL SYSTEMS

Bromberg (Chefetz and Bromberg, 2004) speaks of enactment as the patient's effort to negotiate dissociated self-states that, owing to traumatic experiences, are not verbally symbolized. Similarly, D. B. Stern (2010) as well as Maroda (1991) view enactment as the interpersonal manifestations of unformulated dissociated self-states that are not allowed to conflict with conscious ones. Their views, steeped in clinical encounters and experience, are fully in sync with the view of the unconscious as brain/mind processes in action. In Bromberg's view, dissociated self-states have "no choice" but to engage with others and reveal themselves. In effect, as was discussed in Chapter 3, such an understanding parallels recent data describing neuropsychological processes that inevitably generate the enactment of unconscious maps.

Noting the unavoidable relational impasses that accompany enactments, Bromberg sees them as venues for communication whose real message to the analyst is to get engaged with the patient truly and authentically. Such an engagement, guided by the analyst's countertransference, can help one recognize and resolve painful attachment patterns that, left unidentified and reflected on, are doomed to repeat themselves (Bucci, 2011; Chefetz and Bromberg, 2004; Chused, 1998; Ginot, 2009; Jacobs, 1991, 2005; Pizer, 2003; Renik, 1998). By embodying the replications of early learned emotional and defensive patterns, enactments are in essence an expression of the repetition compulsion process. In the current view explicated here, the repetition of unconscious maps is an unavoidable aspect of brain/mind processes and indeed has no choice but to be activated in response to the environment.

What Is Being Communicated: Implicit Affective and Relational Patterns

What enactments seem to communicate in such gripping and indirect ways are those implicit patterns formed before verbal memory was fully developed and those defensively dissociated later on by an emotionally overwhelmed sense of self (Bromberg, 1998, 2006, 2011; Bucci, 2007a, 2007b, 2011; Mancia, 2006, 2007; Pally, 2000, 2007; Stern, 2010). As Schore (2003) and others have shown, early attunement and attachment patterns between infants and caretakers create lasting neural imprints in the brain's network, resulting in implicit, enduring, and repetitive relational modes of being that ultimately influence one's capacity for affect regulation and integration. (Beebe and Lachmann, 2002; Cozolino, 2002, 2006; LeDoux, 2002; Siegel, 1999, 2007; Wallin, 2007). Early experiences also shape the nature of the infant's internal states of arousal, directly affecting the prevalence and rigidity of either hyperaroused or hypoaroused dissociated autonomic states, each characterized by a different emotional tone and forms of defensiveness (Schore, 2012).

An environment suffused with emotional stress and compromised soothing in early childhood will result in frequent activation of the fear system and automatic defenses meant to minimize the viscerally experienced stress (see Chapter 2). Such an environment skews the developing neural systems toward nonconscious self-states that tend to experience heightened interpersonal difficulties and poor regulation (Cozolino, 2006; LeDoux, 2002; Schore, 2003; Watt, 2003, 2005). The degree of neural dissociation or integration between these representational networks determines which attachment state will be most often activated and repeated, thereby affecting the quality of one's relationships throughout life (Bucci, 2007a, 2007b; Cozolino, 2002, 2006; Ginot, 2007, 2009; Lyons-Ruth, 1999, 2003; Wallin, 2007). Emphasizing the importance of neural integration to the sense of well-being, Siegel (2007) has concluded that early relational experiences are directly related to the quality of self-regulation embedded within various regions of the prefrontal cortex.

As we saw in Chapter 2, the amygdala and its related circuits have been of particular importance in how implicit patterns are created and stored out of awareness. Fear conditioning mediated by the amygdala occurs from the very beginning of life, without conscious awareness and with long-lasting neural impact (Grawe, 2007; LeDoux, 2002; Mancia, 2006). Besides storing implicit memories pertaining to perceived threat and danger, the amygdala modulates the formation of explicit memories in the circuits of the hippocampus.

Later in life the amygdala's automatic anxious reactions, even when deemed out of place and irrational, will result in increased levels of stress hormones and other physiological reactions. More significant, we may not be aware altogether of our conditioned interpersonal anxiety and its reactivation in specific situations. Fearful reactions within a relationship, for example, can be activated when we are unaware of the triggering stimuli and even when our conscious attention is not directly or intentionally focused on them (Grawe, 2007; LeDoux, 2002; Mancia, 2006, 2007). These encoded emotional and interpersonal representations constitute, in Lyons-Ruth's words, "enactive representations that are developed in infancy before the explicit memory system associated with consciously recalled images or symbols is available" (2003, p. 88). Throughout adulthood, regardless of the actual situation but cuing into individual meaning, the amygdala and its related circuits continue to nonconsciously focus on and react in repetitive ways to perceived interpersonal threats and discomfort.

The early maturing right hemisphere has also been shown to be involved in implicit emotional learning that precedes verbal development and as such "represents the biological substrate of the dynamic unconscious" (Schore, 2005, p. 831). Whereas the slower-maturing left brain is associated with verbal and conceptual processing, including that of emotional information, the right brain involves the subjective experience of emotions; most important, it is the site of nonconscious emotional conditioning and autobiographical memories (Schore, 2012). Wittling and Roschmann (1993), for example, found that in subjects viewing emotional films, the right hemisphere indicated stronger affective reactions. Similarly, lateral visual presentations of facial emotional expression coupled with painful stimuli were harder to extinguish in the right hemisphere than in the left.

Morris et al. (1998) showed that the masked presentations of emotional facial expressions—visual stimuli transmitted below conscious perception—generated a strong neural response in the right hemisphere amygdala, but not in the left. Conversely, conscious unmasked presentations of the same stimuli enhanced neural activity in the left, but not in the right amygdala. In another study Morris et al. (1999) demonstrated that emotionally loaded stimuli can be detected, learned, and processed out of the subject's awareness by the right hemisphere's subcortical pathways, establishing implicit memories and learning schemas.

The implications of these findings to early emotional development, later relational patterns, and clinical work are significant. Before the fully developed PFC, especially the dorsolateral area, and before the slower-to-mature reasoning left hemisphere are ready to provide contextual cognitive and affective regulation, the emotional brain is susceptible to amygdala-driven fearful assaults generated by situations of misattuned and stressful interactions. Furthermore, the slower growth of the left hemisphere, the "interpreter" (Gazzaniga, 2008; Gazzaniga et al., 2014), may result in affectively rooted and highly distorted representations of self and others, generated by immature, self-blaming "explanations" for painful situations. The "negative bias" of the early maturing right brain and its propensity to encode for negatively charged affects could also affect the emotional tone of the encoded patterns within it (Gazzaniga, 2008; Hanson and Mendius, 2009; Schore, 2003, 2005, 2012; Siegel, 2007) (see Chapter 5). Dawson et al. (1999) showed that infants of severely depressed mothers were found to have a significant shift of dominance to the right brain, a shift that persisted into their childhood, not surprisingly reflecting their mothers' right-brain dominance. In light of these and other inherent potential emotional and cognitive pitfalls embodied in the human brain, the intersubjective quality of early attachment patterns seem more significant than ever (Braten, 2007; Cozolino, 2006; Schore, 1994, 2003, 2012; Siegel, 1999, 2007).

Indeed, attachment studies have demonstrated strong connections between interactional patterns during infancy and subsequent styles of

secure, avoidant, anxious-ambivalent, and disorganized attachment (Diamond, 2004; Fonagy, 2001, 2008; Fonagy et al., 2002; Hess and Main,
2000; Siegel, 1999). Longitudinal studies have revealed that behaviors of
disorganized attachment style endured as dissociative affective patterns
through age 19 (Lyons-Ruth, 2003). Echoing LeDoux's (2002) emphasis on amygdala fear conditioning and automatic defensive reactions
such as withdrawal, aggression, and submission, as well as Gainotti's
(2006) and Schore's (2003, 2012) descriptions of the preverbal development of implicit self representations in the right brain, Lyons-Ruth
(2003) concludes that attachment strategies are early defensive adaptations designed to deal with the caretaker's failure to provide soothing
responses in the face of overwhelming fear or stress.

Both clinical and neuropsychological findings indicate that each
unconscious relational self-system is linked to a mental representation
of a significant other, and these clusters of representations are then
reactivated in social encounters (Andersen et al., 2007). These self-other
representations, the associations they engender, and the relational self
get enacted on the basis of automatic processes, solidifying and maintaining the underlying roots of one's unconscious reactions. Although
established representations are activated out of awareness based on real
or projected characteristics of the other, the reactions themselves are
felt and experienced, though not understood or reflected on. As in the
activation of any unconscious cluster of representations, when self-with-
significant-other representations get activated by interpersonal contextual cues they spread to other self-linked representations. These include
associations related to those aspects in the unconscious self-system that
are related to the self-concept or self-worth.

The relevance of these and many other findings to a further understanding of what is being communicated during transference-countertransference enactments is obvious. Residing within the implicit maps
of the right hemisphere are early emotional conditioning (remember
the role of the amygdala) and preverbal memories. These memories,
mostly sensory-motor and affective, generate many unconscious associations and further conditioned defenses and adaptational maneuvers.
Over time all of these coalesce into nonconscious relational self-systems,
with various degrees of integration among them (Bucci, 2007a, 2007b;
Gainotti, 2006; Happaney et al., 2004; Miller, et al. 2001; Schore, 2003,
2009). What gets to be known through enactments, then, are relational
patterns and self-representations that can never be articulated through
verbal interchanges alone. As has been discussed, the neural nature of
unconscious maps has no conscious access, but it does have an enacted
quality. Indeed, noting the inevitable relational impasses characterizing transference–countertransference interactions, Bromberg sees enactments as unconscious messages to the analyst to get engaged directly

and emotionally with unsymbolized self-states that cannot be otherwise expressed (Bromberg, 2006).

THE CASE OF TINA: PART 2

With time, Tina settled into a challenging and bantering way of relating, interspersed with being compliant and seeking recognition for it. When she was argumentative, she was not openly hostile or contemptuous, but playfully thwarting, needing to be smart, to be right, and to have the last word. At other times, she seemed eager to please, agreeing with me and complimenting me for my interventions. Her compliments and compliance made me feel uneasy and anxious. I was vaguely aware of fearing retaliation, devaluation, and a pending attack. At the same time, I had the odd feeling that her flattering words were not really directed at me; they felt more like a generic, well-practiced brush-off to keep me at bay. Even when she agreed with me, she really did not; she somehow molded and shaped any intervention to suit her own known frame of reference. When feeling frustrated and irritated, I would ask myself whether unconsciously I was somehow contributing to the growing staleness of our sessions.

When I discussed my experience with Tina, she quickly agreed with me. She said that she was again reverting to her "old habit of being in control" of herself and of the situation. She acknowledged how guarded she was of letting anyone help her; it was "too unfamiliar" for her, and she did not really know how to do it. Tracing her behavior to her depressed parents, Tina felt that there was very little room in any relationship, including her marriage, for her to be overtly needy. Being self-sufficient and feisty was most comfortable and natural for her. Her caretaking role as a child with her anxious and sad parents again moved to the forefront. However, these discussions would also quickly drift to known territories and, rather than opening up the inquiries to additional emotional memories and experiences, seemed to close them off.

As time went by, I realized that the core of our interaction was construed around a dance that Tina performed with great expertise. Somehow, using her abilities to analyze, explain, joke, and thwart, she exerted unwavering control over her emotional responses and the emotional atmosphere of our interaction. My various interventions were heard, examined, and then subtly dismissed. Tina, it seemed, simply could not take much from me in any meaningful way. Although I understood and could even empathize with her need to be self-sufficient, I still felt superfluous, diminished, and unimportant. What she seemingly sought from me was an ongoing validation of her insights and conclusions. Often I would catch myself drifting away, too reluctant to reengage, preferring my own private world, feeling that putting any real stamp on the process was at best difficult and at worst mostly useless.

What I was not aware of yet was my growing inner rebellion against being so often thwarted and pushed away. Consequently, our interactions mostly reflected largely unconscious mutual communications that could not yet be reflected on and understood—in essence, an entanglement of implicit relational patterns emanating from us. Unaware, I became more active and verbal than ever before, repeatedly attempting to direct our interaction, in essence trying to wrest some control away from Tina. Over a period of a few sessions, I relentlessly challenged her expressed feelings and explanations, deeming them too intellectual, too rehearsed, and too defensive. My interventions were not dynamically incorrect; some of these interpretations and observations had been discussed before. Rather, the emotional context of these interventions, my lack of felt empathy, my feelings of suffocation, and my overly active and controlling behaviors should all have alerted me to the fact that I was deeply involved in an enactment. At the time, however, although uncomfortable and anxious about feeling suffocated and rendered useless, I was not aware of my actions.

After these sessions, Tina would leave the office angry, defiant, and visibly distressed. But when she described her feelings and reactions during the next session, what I heard was not her vulnerability but more of the same: an unreflected-on, consuming need to fight me and thwart my attempts to help her. All through these few weeks, my feelings of deadness became more palpable, lodging themselves in my body, which at times felt paralyzed and listless.

The "How" of Enactments: Shared
Unconscious Communication

It is no coincidence that neuropsychological findings regarding unconscious communication have paralleled the growing realization in psychoanalytic writings that some aspects of countertransference present us with an opportunity for direct emotional knowing. But what actually takes place in an enactment? How can two people communicate unconsciously with each other, and even more intriguingly, transmit a great deal of information about implicit and dissociated schemas? As an increasing body of research and clinical experience indicates, explicitly and implicitly exchanged communications activate unconscious self-systems if they touch the embedded particular meaning they contain.

When we remember the findings reported by Perani et al. (1999) and by Bargh (2007) and Bargh et al. (2001; Bargh and Morsella, 2008) for example, we again realize how fast and out of awareness old patterns jump into action. Action words as well as priming stimuli, perceived consciously or unconsciously, activated motor regions in the brain in the first case and resulted in the unconscious execution of behaviors in the second. The interchange of specific words between patient and therapist, for example, may activate the emotional, cognitive, and behavioral associations and meaning connected with a particular word. It is not that all mutual interpersonal communications are delivered on an explicit level; the contrary is true. After all, therapy uses facial expressions and other easily perceived physical manifestations that convey a great deal of emotional messages. What remains unconscious is the act of perception itself, the personal and hidden meanings that the perception carries and activates, and the action-ready interpretations, emotions, and defenses embedded within the particular self-system that comes on line.

In a similar vain, and echoing Gallese and Lakoff's (2005) suggested connection between the mirror neuron system and the development of language, Borghi and Cimatti (2010) consider language a form of action as well, strongly connected to the body. In their view, language contributes to a unitary sense of our body/self and helps shape the way we implicitly perceive our body. The integrated sense of our bodies underpinned by language extends and pushes the anatomical boundaries between others and us. Language connects us not only on a pure verbal level but also in more implicit ways that transcend physical boundaries.

Our brains/minds, then, are evolutionarily primed to receive and impart a great deal of intersubjective information, particularly of an emotional and visceral nature (Miller, 2008; Schore, 2003, 2012). Consequently, similar neuropsychological processes and mechanisms underpin direct nonverbal communication between parents and children as well as between patients and analysts, setting the stage for reciprocal nonconscious emotional give and take. What we communicate goes far beyond what we consciously intend to, and much of it is involuntary and out of our awareness. Facial expressions, gestures, gaze, and vocal qualities have all been shown to accurately convey the participants' emotional and relational states (Beebe and Lachman, 2002; Diamond, 2004; Fonagy et al. 2002; Gallese et al., 2007; Iacoboni, 2006, 2007; Lyons-Ruth, 2003; Mancia, 2006, 2007; Pally, 2006; Schore, 1994, 2005, 2007; Siegel, 1999).

Schore's writings in particular have emphasized the role of the right brain in nonconscious communication processes between self-states of parents and children and between patients and therapists. Extensively connected to the limbic system and thus sensitive to interactional communication, conscious and nonconscious, the right brain is the one that seems to be acutely perceptive of emotional and viscerally felt experiences in others (Decety and Chaminade, 2003; Schore, 2005, 2007). These writers and others conclude that the analyst's sensitivity, or her right-brain readiness to be fully attuned to nonverbal communication, is a necessary therapeutic skill. Becoming entangled in an enactment, although at first out of awareness, is a surprising facet of such sensitivity.

Relevant to the clinical observation that many enactments give voice to painful emotions are the findings by Sato and Aoki (2006) and Kimora et al (2004), who emphasize the right hemisphere's role in receiving and processing negative emotional stimuli. Others conclude that the right hemisphere is the one involved in recognizing other people's emotional expressions and is connected to internally generated bodily sensations (see McGilchrist, 2009; Schore, 1994, 2003, 2005, 2009, 2012). Thus, the right brain, with its ability to perceive subtle cues and activate its own bodily and emotional sensations, allows the therapist immediate and direct modes of interaction. These unconscious exchanges are essential on two levels; on becoming conscious they open crucial windows into the patient's dynamics, but at the same time they reverberate empathically with the patient's internal states, acknowledging and regulating them (Schore, 2012).

The ongoing communication between interacting brains is particularly intense in close relationships where the participants are attuned to each other's messages (Bromberg, 2006; Maroda, 1991), especially during times of heightened and mutually dysregulated emotions (Schore, 2012). This finding may explain the prevalence of enactments and projections within couples and the difficulties they often encounter in trying to resolve them on their own. The activation of these implicit relational patterns within the therapeutic dyad, however, presents the only opportunity patients may have to become aware of their interpersonal difficulties. The therapeutic relationship, intermixed with the therapist's unique personality structure, can serve as retrieval cues (Carroll, 2003; Rustin and Sekael, 2004) for the early interactional schemes of the patients, in turn affecting those of the therapist. Both activate, according to Bucci (2007a, 2007b), past dissociated, maladaptive emotional schemas that are largely implicit and have affected the patient's life before therapy.

Within the therapeutic dyad, implicit and explicit information is mutually communicated on an ongoing basis (Bromberg, 2006, 2011; Ginot, 2007, 2009; Miller, 2008). The neural and emotional arousal that occurs in response to perceived interpersonal cues is physical and real, operating through the thalamic-amygdalar circuit, and is similar in nature to the response experienced in reaction to the original event itself (LeDoux, 2002, 2014; LeDoux and Doyere, 2011; Mancia, 2006, 2007). The fact that we can emotionally access very complex relational aspects through an intense involvement with our patients turns enactments into such valuable processes. In their largely unconscious modality they go beyond more readily recognized countertransferential feelings and connect with what is most hidden and implicit. In this way, the premise that the unconscious is more knowable through action finds a concrete illustration within the intersubjective field.

THE CASE OF TINA: PART 3

During one especially difficult session, when my behavior seemed to communicate to Tina that wherever she was, it was not where I wanted her to be, Tina burst into tears, her face and body displaying great agitation. Amid sobs, she described how pushed and prodded she felt, how very anxious and alone. She said that she really wanted to please me but did not know how, and now she felt deeply disappointed in both of us. Just as with her former analyst, she felt hopeless, lost, and misunderstood. I wanted something from her, and she did not know what it was. All she felt was pushed and coerced.

Tina felt deeply wounded and held me responsible for "totally missing the boat." "Why is it so important to you to control what I need to say, to push your agenda?" she asked angrily. Feeling defensive, I answered that I was not quite sure what had taken place during the past few sessions and for some time before, but I was certain that as difficult as the experiences between us were, we needed to understand what they meant. I apologized for being pushy and hurtful, and said that what had happened, our mutual emotional misses, had been building up for a while and could teach us a great deal about her internal world and mine. As the session ended, I did not have a chance to describe the feeling that was most disturbing to me—the sense of deadening suffocation.

Tina left that session agitated. At the next session, she reported the following dream: we are both sitting in my office and she is asking me, "Why are we here? There are no windows in this office." She feels a growing panic, and with dread realizes that I can't help her, that nobody can. She feels on the verge of suffocation and forces herself to wake up. While discussing the dream—noting that in reality the office has two windows—for the first time Tina experienced and expressed her thoughts and feelings in direct and immediate ways. She was clearly and openly angry, sad, and frightened. She became fully aware of an intolerable sensation of being enclosed, held down, and suffocated. Her heart was racing, and her head felt light with panic. She felt like her chest and her head "were going to explode."

While disclosing to Tina my own frequent sense of being controlled and suffocated by her and how closely these feelings echoed her own, her distress intensified. But she was not running away from her frightening feelings and experiences this time. On the contrary, she desperately wanted to understand our tumultuous interactions. As we talked, it became clear to both of us that something very important was embedded in our seemingly mismatched communications. It was not just her need to take care of her mother that colored Tina's interactions, nor was it her argumentative and evasive behavior. The painful, protracted enactment exposed core, unconscious relational patterns and affective memories that characterized almost all of Tina's interactions with others—an intense fear of being emotionally violated and forced to adapt to the other—and myriad automatic defenses designed to preserve her sense of autonomy. Unaware, I came to embody her parents' deadened affect and also their implicit demand for her to join them. At the same time, Tina's own unconscious self-systems—the one succumbing to her parents and the one that could find its voice only through stubbornly clinging to a sense of autonomy—were also part of our interaction.

Exchanging unconscious communications, we simultaneously reacted to and triggered implicit affective memories, fantasies, and defenses. In our subsymbolic (Bucci, 2007a, 2007b, 2011) interchange, I was the one "called on" to enact what was most frightening, almost annihilating—becoming through my behavior the emotionally oppressing parents. Like Tina, in the face of her emotional control I also experienced an increasing pressure to resist the feeling of suffocation, to withdraw and preserve my own subjectivity.

The defensive control Tina exerted on the sessions was something we had observed and discussed numerous times, but merely acknowledging and analyzing it did not create the interpersonal space in which to authentically experience and understand its multilayered meaning. On the contrary, talking only seemed to perpetuate and strengthen the oscillation between compliance and defiance. The enactment between us opened the therapeutic space to new experiences; by introjecting Tina's projected dread of being invaded, and by experiencing the fear of suffocation and defenses against it, her unconscious but enacted self-systems could be addressed.

In Tina's case, having an insight into her tendency to oppose and argue was not sufficient for integration and growth. Rather, an intersubjective stirring of her implicitly encoded early emotional and interpersonal attachment patterns gave voice to what was sensed but still not a part of a conscious sense of self. As Chapter 8 discusses further, insight is not enough: enduring change almost always demands a lived emotional experience. Such intense experiences are most often an inextricable aspect of therapeutic enactments. Being enacted by both of us, and in the context of the emotional aftermath, early implicitly encoded patterns had the opportunity to be recognized, analyzed, and integrated.

THE MIRROR NEURON SYSTEM
AND THERAPEUTIC ENACTMENTS

Another dramatic development in our effort to understand how people "get" the emotional states and behavioral intentions of others is the field identifying and studying the mirror neuron system. Although this field is still in its infancy, some neuroscientists have already advanced theories linking the mirror neuron system to our ability to inhabit the emotional states of others. In an interesting confluence of psychoanalytic thought and neuroscientific research, this developing field reflects the growing clinical recognition of intersubjectivity as an essential aspect of human interaction. At the very least, the consistent studies showing brain structures' activity in response to observing others have paved the way to a more comprehensive picture of what happens biologically when individuals, including strangers, are engaged with each other. Research has so far indicated that the mirroring system is connected to imitation, language development, shared emotions, empathy, the mediation of pain, and the development of the sense of self and others, among other things (Fadiga and Craighero, 2007; Gallese, 2008; Hari, 2007; Iacoboni, 2008; Rizzolati et al., 2002). These neural processes have been emphasized in other chapters discussing the significant influences intersubjective experiences have.

The mirror neuron system found in the premotor cortex and other areas is activated in monkeys and in people observing others engaged in purposeful behaviors (Iacoboni et al., 2005; Rizzolatti and Luppino, 2001). Further findings have shown that the mirror neuron system fires when we are watching or mimicking others' facial expressions or when anticipating others to be in pain, which has led some researchers to describe its functions as underpinning our ability to automatically and involuntarily simulate the emotional states of others (Gallese, 2006, 2008; Gallese et al., 2007; Goldman, 2006; Iacoboni, 2006, 2007, 2008; Ramachandran, 2011). This biological propensity—consistently shown through magnetic resonance imaging and other techniques—to replicate someone else's neural activity in one's own system or embedded simulation seems to be at the heart of our capacity to understand the feelings of others, according to these researchers.

Gallese and Iacoboni see this built-in mirroring ability as a neuropsychological expression of empathic responses, or in Gallese's words, "the empathic shared manifold of intersubjectivity" (2006, p. 271). Not surprisingly, perhaps, adults as well as children who scored higher on general empathy scales also showed stronger brain activity when they perceived their partners to be in pain or when observing others' emotional expressions (Dapretto et al., 2006; Pfeifer et al., 2008; Singer et

al., 2004, 2006). Studies indicating that mirror neuron structures "communicate" with the emotional brain have led Iacoboni to state that
"These results clearly supported the idea that mirror neurons areas help
us understand the emotions of other people by some form of inner
imitation" (2008, p. 119). Through embodied simulation, then, the mirror neuron system seems to automatically establish a direct experiential
link between subjects. In Iacoboni's words, "This simulation process is
an *effortless*, automatic, and unconscious inner mirroring" (2008, p. 120;
emphasis in original).

The various subtle characteristics of neural mirroring responses studied and described by neuroscientists are all the more interesting and
significant in light of our clinical experiences. Indeed, when we try to
deconstruct the nature of nonconscious communication of enacted systems, what gets to be highlighted through these studies is our ability to
connect with others' emotions and intentions often before we can articulate what we feel. Contrary to understanding others by intentionally
putting oneself in the other's situation or imagining how the other feels,
Gallese's and Iacoboni's conclusions present a very different way to view
empathy and enactments. The neural process of embodied simulation
creates automatic, unconscious, and prereflexive empathic responses,
ones that do not depend on deliberate efforts to understand the other or
cognitively trying to interpret their situation.

Adding to Schore's (2003, 2007, 2012) conclusions regarding the right
hemisphere's role in unconscious communication are findings regarding
the mirror neuron system. Some of Iacoboni's studies (2006, 2007, 2008)
highlight the right amygdala's part in perceiving and processing scary
emotional facial expressions. Similarly, other researchers have found
that the right hemisphere's mirror neuron system became more active
among children and adults when observing and imitating emotional facial
expressions in others. Dapretto et al. (2006) demonstrated that in comparison to normally developing children, a group of 12-year-old children
with autism displayed a lower mirror neuron system activity within the
right hemisphere. Furthermore, the more severe the autistic impairment,
the less activity was detected in mirror neuron areas. The researchers
concluded that social and emotional mirroring largely depends on the
right brain mirroring areas connected to the limbic system.

Another group working with Iacoboni (Uddin et al., 2004), exploring
the relationship of the mirror neuron system to self-other recognition,
found that in tasks requiring subjects to recognize their own morph-
ing face (as opposed to that of their best friend), two areas in the right
hemisphere became active: the parietal and frontal lobes, both mirror
neuron structures. Interestingly, these findings also fit with research
describing the right hemisphere as the "location" of one's sense of self
(Schore, 2012).

In a further refinement of what it means to resonate empathetically, and with great relevance to the psychoanalytic encounter, Gallese and Iacoboni assert that the shared neural processes do not imply a self-less merging phenomenon between participants, but an emotional and communicational permeability between them. In Gallese's words, "empathy entails the capacity to experience what others experience while still attributing these experiences to others and not to the self" (2006, p. 288). Similarly, while demonstrating the role of the mirror neuron system in self-other recognition, Iacoboni and his group (Iacoboni, 2008) confirmed subjects' ability to maintain their own sense of self when observing pictures of themselves and of others, a point emphasized by Gazzaniga (2008) as well.

Perhaps the most significant finding to the psychotherapeutic dyad is the one delineating the relationship between mirror neurons and the limbic system. Exploring this connection, Iacoboni (2007, 2008) and Carr et al. (2003) have demonstrated that mirror neurons send signals to the emotional centers located in the limbic system, enabling us to experience feelings associated with observed and imitated emotions. The anterior insula was found to be the anatomical pathway that connects mirror neuron structures to the limbic areas, and especially the amygdala. Some of the visceral sensations can then reach consciousness and become subjective feelings (Gazzaniga, 2008; Iacoboni, 2008; Ramachandran, 2011). Of particular interest are Iacoboni's (2008) assumptions that the mirror neuron system itself is greatly affected and sculpted by early care-taking experiences. This finding is a significant contribution to the growing body of evidence showing the effects of early attachment patterns on the brain/mind.

THE NEED FOR FUTURE RESEARCH

The implications of these studies to the understanding the communicated elements embedded in enactments are intriguing. But as some writers have rightfully pointed out, the mere activity of mirror neuron structures in response to others does not tell a full story yet (Gazzaniga, 2008; Goldman, 2006; Stueber, 2006; Watt, 2005). Some significant questions, not yet answered by research, have been asked as to the causal relationship between mirror neurons and the *felt* experience of empathy. By the same token, the differences between a more aware experience of empathy on the one hand and a direct experience of emotional contagion on the other need to be delineated as well (Watt, 2005; Zept and Hartmann, 2008). The phenomenon of emotional contagion, according to Watt (2005), is carried by neural pathways that act faster and are more primitive than the mirror neuron system.

As researchers, philosophers and clinicians struggle to explicate the connection between neural activation and the experience of getting the other's conscious and nonconscious patterns, much remains unknown. In this context, the current limitation of our understanding of how the mirror neuron system explicates the complex and often shifting phenomenon of empathy needs to be taken into account (Gazzaniga, 2008; Goldman, 2006; Watt, 2005; Zept and Hartmann, 2008). Nonetheless, the enthusiasm accompanying this research is also understandable. The opportunity to glimpse at a link between our biology and our human behavior has once again proven incredibly irresistible, engaging, and promising. Understanding how another's person's unconscious systems are not just enacted but also received and acknowledged by the other—a parent, a patient, a partner, or a therapist—takes the neuropsychological findings about enacted representations to a different level. The current state of research can still explain, for example, how and why patient and therapist react to each other's emotional and bodily cues, suffusing their perceptions with their own internal representations and defensive adaptations (Gallese et al., 2007; Iacoboni, 2008). As Gallese (2008, p. 774) maintains "mirroring is always a process in which others' behavior is metabolized by and filtered through the observer's idiosyncratic past experiences, capacities and mental attitudes."

At this point in time, we could say that although questions regarding the leap from neural firing to subjective feelings of unmediated understanding of an enacted neuropsychological map are not answered yet, mirror neuron system research still offers us some understanding. It explains what takes place within the intersubjective matrix, shedding light on familiar clinical experiences. One could also argue that when trying to understand what takes place in enactments within the psychotherapeutic dyad and outside of it, it is possible to see the role of the mirror neuron system not as structures that faithfully replicate observed emotional reactions but as neuropsychological processes that result in mutual, idiosyncratic attunement to each other's visceral/feelings states and intentions. At times, depending on the degree to which reflectiveness is lost, this mutual involuntary reactivity will culminate in enactments.

The mirror neuron system, then, may underpin the complex web of interpersonal communication in or out of awareness (Decety and Chaminade, 2003). This may be accomplished not by experiencing compassion for the other in a predictable, comforting way necessarily, but by being able to reverberate with a wide range of implicit encoded patterns that can only be enacted. Because these interactions might give expression to unconscious painful, angry, and defensive self-systems, the empathetic aspects in enactments do not depend on the analyst's ability to experience empathy for the patient's difficulties. The empathetic component is found in her readiness and ability to resonate with what is not verbalized but nonconsciously transmitted nonetheless. Here is where we return to the original premise: although enactments may seem at times to be misattuned events that threaten the therapeutic process, by inhabiting the other's nonconscious affects, defenses, and automatic interpretations, they also embody an interpersonal resonance and direct emotional knowledge.

ENACTMENTS AS INTERSUBJECTIVE WAYS OF KNOWING

The realization that the verbal content of an interaction constitutes only part of a much larger whole is highlighted by what has been discussed in other chapters: most of the information encoded and enacted in response to environmental demands operates out of awareness. Taking into account the limited verbal and cognitive access into our neural brain/mind maps or self-systems, it may be that enactments offer the only ways to emotionally know patients and really experience some of their earliest emotional memories and narratives. In this way, enactments may be the only authentic venue that can bring to life implicit affective and relational patterns, as we often witness in our intimate relationships.

Thus, enactments do not just indicate an unconscious transference–countertransference process run amuck, but may express moments of meetings (Stern et al. 1998), when two subjectivities are totally, albeit temporarily, immersed in each other's unknowable needs, expectations, and defenses.

The enacted self-systems activated in the therapeutic environment offer an authentic and direct way for both patient and therapist to negotiate unconscious patterns. What gets revealed through enactments, just as through any enacted patterns, are the underlying characteristics of a particular brain/mind map or pattern. Perceptual tendencies, emotional convictions, automatic interpretations of interpersonal cues, and defensive behaviors—all become part of the mutual interaction. Within the emotional environment of promise and disappointment, hope and potential terror, old relational and emotional patterns are unavoidably activated and enacted. By simultaneously providing a safe environment and the opportunity for reflective awareness, the psychotherapeutic relationship is the one relationship where unconscious self-systems can be experienced, identified, and understood.

We could rightly worry, as some have when discussing enactments, that mutual embodied simulation, where each participant automatically and nonconsciously activates the other's neural systems, would lead to a hopeless interpersonal mess. If enactments cannot be avoided because of the permeable boundaries between brains/minds of interacting sub-jectivities—think of the automatic firing of mirror neurons (Iacoboni, 2007, 2008) or the right brain's sensitivity (Schore, 2007, 2012)—how can we know what's going on? How can we extricate ourselves as analysts from an entanglement that may stand in the way of our work? We can see why clinical writings have portrayed enactments as impasses that can derail the analytic endeavor, particularly with patients experiencing rigid dissociative defenses (Chused, 1998; Ivey, 2008; Pizer, 2003).

In actuality, the mutual process of embodied simulation results in a direct, unmediated, and visceral knowing of the other, eventually affording both patient and analyst a way to further recognize and under-stand dissociated self-narratives and relational patterns and integrate them into a more reflective and cohesive self. Both are affected partic-ipants, and both may learn about themselves. The therapeutic way to achieve these important goals is bound with the process of mentaliza-tion (Fonagy and Target, 2006) or mindful awareness (Siegel, 2007; Wal-lin, 2007) that is essential for regaining the cooperative shared reflective space. When coming out of an enactment, as the analyst becomes aware of her own contribution, usually (but not always) both participants can start examining the meaning of the mutually determined interaction. A regained state of mindfulness will restore the therapist's ability to listen again with a "tension between empathic identification and observing distance" (Zwiebel, 2004, p. 259). The therapist's self-disclosure of her feelings, thoughts, and role in an enactment can further enhance the process of reflective awareness in both participants. It is particularly powerful in helping the patient better understand how an enacted self-state within the therapy debilitates his wellbeing, rather than promoting it. The therapist's disclosed experience, which in actuality is rooted in the intersubjective field, can help the patient directly and emotionally become aware of an important part of his internal life (Ginot, 1997). As modeled by the therapist, the patient can gain the sense that his behav-ior is not being judged or repudiated; rather, it is being examined as an unconscious emotional and interpersonal adaptation that, although successful in the past, no longer works.

CHAPTER 5

Aspects of Affective Dysregulation: Self-Narratives as Expression of Unconscious Self-Systems

THIS CHAPTER EXPLORES ONE OF the more salient aspects of dysregulated affective states: the automatic, repetitive beliefs and ruminations about the self that are often an inseparable part of unregulated emotions. Such self-narratives can acquire an intrusive, autonomous life; they surface unbidden and flare up as familiar thoughts, fantasies, or images and end up dominating our intrapsychic and interpersonal experience. In addition to the visceral sensations and disturbingly negative emotions that characterize a dysregulated state—the aspects that make a dysregulated state so unsettling and unpleasant—an unregulated state frequently includes a particular narrative. These narratives or ruminations take the form of recurrent negative thoughts about the self, irrational convictions, denigrating evaluations of one's efficacy or self-worth, and an exaggerated preoccupation with the projected negative judgment of others, to name a few examples.

In essence, a recurrent narrative gives a dysregulated state its familiar shape and feel and intensifies its harmful qualities. In the midst of a dysregulated state the visceral, emotional, and cognitive are totally intertwined; feelings are fueled by words, and the words we tell ourselves reinforce the negative state. Neurally and therefore experientially, they are one and the same (Sergerie and Armony, 2006). To quote Panksepp and Biven (2012, p. 451): "in humans these [affective states] are always accompanied by cognitive changes, such as emotionally entangled attributions, ruminations, all sort of plans and worries." These joined expressions of emotion and thought embody an important aspect of our unconscious. This chapter presents a psychodynamic model that integrates the interlocked processes of body, affect, cognition, and developmental forces. Together these brain/mind functions come to characterize the dysregulated aspects of an unconscious self-system and its consciously felt self-state.

Throughout my clinical work, repeated encounters with patients' negative narratives about themselves have raised persistent questions. For example, why do these narratives—easily activated during stressful situations—tend to be so harsh, so turned against one's self? Why are they distorted, at times clearly removed from one's experiences in the external world? How is it that a more balanced perspective is lost and what remains is the conviction that one's negative assessment of the present situation is the only correct one? Why are these narratives so stubborn and persistent, telling the same story that, in a reciprocal loop, ends up reinforcing dysregulation? Importantly, can recurrent narratives help us better understand patients' unconscious self-systems, their internal representations, and defensive systems? If so, what are the implications for treatment?

A BRIEF EXAMPLE: THE CASE OF ANDREW

Andrew, a professional man in his thirties, sought therapy on starting a new job, for which he had undergone weeks of stressful interviews. In spite of his wish for a smooth transition, he experienced strong feelings of discomfort and anxiety from the first day in his new position, as well as physical symptoms of light-headedness, palpitations, and shortness of breath. These feelings were followed by a state of inertia and fatigue.

He was terrified he might not be able to fulfill the demands of the new job. Thoughts of inevitable failure were constantly on his mind. He was certain he was already failing because he was not proving himself fast enough, and thereby disappointing those who had placed trust in him. Attempting to unsuccessfully fight his anxious feelings and the familiar sense of lethargy that followed only made him feel more defeated. At this point he came for treatment.

From the beginning of therapy, Andrew knew that in the past he had successfully held a great deal of responsibility in very visible positions. He was quite familiar with the new job's environment, if not its details. In spite of these realizations, his discomfort did not lessen; on the contrary, it grew to a painful and distracting level.

Glumly, he said that because he felt so exhausted, he had a difficult time actually achieving what he most wanted: to become engaged again and perform successfully. What quickly became apparent was Andrew's repeated pattern of "falling apart" each time he started a new project, always sinking for a while into what he experienced as a confusing disconnect from reality. He knew he was capable, and yet he had no access to his feelings of competency. In school each new grade and later each new work situation began with the same self-doubts and intense fears of being judged. The question that perplexed him most concerned his inability to learn from reality, since he had gone through these transitions in the past and had ended up performing well, ultimately enjoying both school and work.

Andrew's predicament is familiar, which underscores the debilitating effects of a compromised ability for affect regulation as an enacted expression of an unconscious self-system. His puzzlement about the repetitious nature of his dysregulated states captured, in effect, the tenacity of implicit cognitive/affective states associated with particular situations. It highlighted the difficult if not impossible task of differentiating between the dysregulated affect triggered by perceived threat and the automatic way of thinking that is part of it. Andrew's difficulties remind us that during dysregulation, the automatic and familiar narratives about the self are subjectively experienced as entirely couched in objective facts. In this case, an unconscious internal reality becomes the only dimension of one's experience.

THE NATURE OF NARRATIVES

As depicted in Andrew's case, these self-narratives or ruminations in effect give a more conscious articulation to unconscious self-other representations. By embodying early intersubjective and developmental processes, self-narratives represent an integrated portrait of the conscious and the implicit, the affective and the cognitive, collapsed into an unshakable story line that becomes an inseparable part of one's self-definition during a dysregulated self-state.

More specifically, self-narratives originate from the child's efforts to give meaning to his or her internal and interpersonal experiences. In attempting to make sense of and interpret physical and feeling sensations as they are occurring, the child's "conclusions" regarding the self largely echo the quality of the emotional experience generated within a particular condition. These interpretations and beliefs become part of the unconscious self-models, maps, or self-systems (Damasio, 2010; Wilson, 2002, 2003, 2011), and because of immature brain/mind processes, they will often be painfully distorted.

During heightened emotional arousal, or conversely, depressed detachment, this set of distorted ruminations can be experienced as an internal monologue or verbal expressions. (To narrow the scope, this chapter focuses on narratives that automatically express negative feelings and thoughts about the self.) Other narratives are also prevalent, such as those that externalize or blame others, and of course, a range of grandiose ideas about the self. As the expression of a largely implicit intersubjective past, self-narratives are often also triggered within the psychotherapeutic dyad. Like enactments, they can become an inescapable part of the therapeutic interaction and reveal a great deal about a particular unconscious self-system.

The expressed convictions, then, convey not just thoughts about the self, but represent an entire unconscious self-system, with its unique emotional tones, physical sensations, implicit and explicit attachment memories, and the cognitive interpretations given to them—conscious and unconscious alike (Bromberg, 2006). In this way, self-narratives can be seen as the consciously felt manifestation of an unconscious system (Bromberg, 2006; Bucci, 2007a, 2007b; Damasio, 2010; Ginot, 2007, 2009; Lewis and Todd, 2004, 2007; Panksepp, 2012). The development of language itself is a process that is largely embedded in the world of experience (McGilchrist, 2009), so understanding what verbal self-narratives convey will lead us back to the world of experience.

In a broader sense, self-narratives are a specific demonstration of how brain/mind processes are integrated: visceral physiology, affect, cognition, and action tendencies are intertwined within the brain, even if we don't consciously recognize it (Damasio, 1999, 2010; LeDoux, 2002; Lewis and Todd, 2007; Panksepp and Biven, 2012; Wilson, 2011). We are used to regarding these as separate entities, holding on to the somewhat intuitive notion that in our felt experience, as well as within the brain, affects and thoughts are different and distinct phenomena. This view is understandable in light of the occasional splits between these modes that we see in patients. At times, although verbally expressing intense negative evaluation about the self, narratives appear to be devoid of affect, strengthening their mechanical, automatic, and inevitable nature.

As we dig deeper clinically, we often see that even when experientially dissociated from the conscious sense of self, emotions can be conveyed through narratives or one's actions in the world. One may feel numbness, defeat, or emptiness, but the accompanying narratives still embody a feeling state, albeit a hypoaroused one. In extreme splits seen among highly dissociative patients, self-narratives may be the only manifestation of their hidden emotional and relational core.

In the course of development, raw feelings mix with higher mental abilities, resulting in complex self-systems whose core is made of more nuanced emotions, such as shame, self-denigration, or self-blame. As the next sections demonstrate, this wide range of combined affects and the meaning given to them shape our narratives (Wilkinson, 2010).

Within us all, different unconscious self-systems may give rise to different narratives, but they all are imbued with the original core affects typical to a particular brain/mind system. This integration occurs due to the many pathways of interaction between the lower regions of the brain and newer cortical areas. Even complex or abstract ideas are intertwined with affect and actually would not be there without it. Primary affective dynamics control secondary learning and memory reservoirs, as well as tertiary learning processes. These integrated functions become part of higher, more conscious mental mechanisms such as reflection (Damasio, 2010; Fonagy et al., 2002; Gazzaniga, 2008; Koziol and Budding, 2010; McGilchrist, 2009; Panksepp and Biven, 2012; Schore, 2012; Siegel, 1999, 2007).

Although I often mention affect, cognition, and visceral sensations as separate processes, this is only for convenience. The more detailed exploration of self-narratives, what they represent, and what they mean as well as their developmental roots clearly demonstrates how they embody a highly integrated interaction.

THE ROOTS OF NARRATIVES: ATTACHMENT AND INTERSUBJECTIVITY

Although narratives are expressed through words, their first emotional foundations can be found in the quality of early intersubjective experiences. Prolonged states of affective dysregulation brought on by misattunement will affect much of the child's rapidly evolving self/other representations. Due to the infant's limited resources, the acquisition of a robust, internal capacity for regulation is largely dependent on the caregiver's psychobiological sensitivity to the infant's shifting physiological and emotional arousal states (Beebe and Lachmann, 2002; Cozolino, 2006; Fonagy, 2008; Schore, 1994, 2003; Siegel, 1999, 2007; Stern 1985; Tronick, 2007; Wallin, 2007). Neglect, severe abuse, and abandonment have been shown to have lasting traumatic effects (Bowlby, 1973, 1982). Children's dependency on their caretakers also makes them vulnerable to a wide range of mismatched interactions where seemingly benign exchanges may cause substantial emotional injury and growing doubts as to one's self-worth.

While emphasizing the role of parental attunement in the child's emotional development—especially in regard to adaptive affect regulation capacities—we should also remember that the field of genetics is increasingly showing us that the picture is even more complicated. Innate temperament, inborn brain connectivity, the infant's degree of resilience, and embryonic developmental factors may affect the trajectory of our emotional growth as well (see, for example, Gardner, 2011). Recently, for example, specific proteins were found to transmit ways of coping with stress from mother rats to their pups (Zaidan et al., 2013). Significantly, such findings embody the old nature versus nurture debate, showing that not only are both involved but that some of our seemingly innate qualities are affected by parental traits. Finally, a parent's ability to be attuned to and validate a child's needs as well as his or her unique internal world is correlated with the parent's level of reflective awareness (see Fonagy et al., 2002; Gergely and Unoka, 2008a, 2008b; Slade, 2005). Developmental forces, then, are found in the interaction between genes and the environment, and more specifically in the process of gene expression in the context of environmental influences. These interpersonal effects are specifically rooted in the intersubjective bonds between infants, children, and their parents, although evidence also points to the importance of the child's and adolescent's peer groups on one's growing sense of self (Grawe, 2007).

As Schore (1994, 2003, 2005, 2012) emphasizes, since myelination of the central nervous system is already extensive during the first 18 months of life, the infant is particularly vulnerable to hyper- or hypoaroused physioaffective states. Most often (although again not always) an attuned parent can successfully modulate them. Repeated failures at attunement during infancy and childhood, for example, can result in heightened sense of danger and intense dread that may lead to chronic hyperarousal states. Even with the first rudimentary seeds of language, such words as *good, bad, yes, no*, primitive narratives become embedded in the felt affect of the unconscious core self (Damasio, 2010; Panksepp, 2012).

As we saw in Chapter 2, hyperaroused fear states may lead to progressing narratives of impending danger and insecurity, for example. Conversely, defensive dissociative detachment mobilized against arousal will lead to depressed or defeated states (Kagan, 1998; Schore, 1994, 2003, 2012), resulting in narratives of total helplessness; "what's the point of trying?" or justifications for avoidance are an example.

The Certainty of Negative Spin:
The Case of Claire, Part 1

The following vignette illustrates the intersection of the visceral, affective, and cognitive elements characterizing a particular unconscious self-state and the various stages of the therapeutic processes it has gone through. Claire, a single, attractive woman, started therapy in her late twenties due to persistent but vague feelings of anxiety and sadness that she said, "came and went, depending on what was going on." She had moved to New York to pursue a graduate degree, and she felt lonely and insecure. Describing a pattern of short-term relationships, with long periods of time in between, she expressed worries about her difficulties in dating men and wondered about her inability to stay engaged in a lasting, long-term relationship.

Claire is the youngest of three children, with two older brothers. Her Israeli-born mother was the only daughter of two Holocaust survivors, who had Claire later in life and seemed to have raised her with love, but also with many fears and an overprotectiveness that bordered on suffocation.

According to Claire, who visited her grandparents in Israel, "a sense of doom was hanging in their apartment, a depressed atmosphere that felt uncomfortable" to her as a child. Claire's mother had met her American husband when she went to college in the United States. When they got married she dropped out of college and moved to his home state, never resuming her studies. Ever since Claire could perceive and understand her parents' histories, her mother's inability to pursue her own career had caused Claire a great deal of anguish.

Claire's father became a successful businessman, but her mother became increasingly frustrated with her professional underachievement. According to Claire, she often appeared to be angry and impatient. As her memories centered more and more on her mother's volatile behavior, she remembered that as a child she was scared of her mother's intense reactions and angry outbursts, which seemed beyond comprehension to Claire. She recalled that she avoided bringing friends home, fearing her mother's unpredictable moods.

At the beginning of therapy Claire related that her empathy was always with her father, with whom she identified. She saw him as "the unjustifiably attacked victim in the marriage," as the peacemaker who had to put up with "a crazy wife." She initially described him as the stable parent; later on, as her recollections became richer and more nuanced, she realized that her father was also controlling and self-involved, needing a great deal of validation for his achievements. She also remembered fun times with her mother and her older brothers.

As to Claire's own difficulties, quite soon into the therapy her negative self-states appeared to be easily activated each time she felt anxious or stressed. At these times, her self-confidence sank and she repeatedly told herself she was less intelligent and less competent than others. Utterly believing that unless her presentations were perfect she would be found out and judged as not good enough, she spent a great deal of energy on redoing her work and second-guessing her assignments. She was also certain that she could never attract somebody she could love back, and in her recurrent narrative, "once somebody got to really know her he would be disappointed." In these moments she frequently used the word *doomed*.

Self-Narrative as a Marker of Intersubjectivity:
Shared Experiences

Intersubjectivity can be defined as the ongoing mutual experiences driven by conscious and unconscious communication and the need for emotional resonance. As a result, at all times, alongside the child's essential separateness and inherent temperament, there are always self-states that are utterly attuned to and entangled with the caregiver's physical presence, emotions, and vocal communications.

This lack of differentiation is a result not simply of the child's supposed nonexistent subjectivity but of an active, evolutionarily determined psychobiological need (Ainsworth, 1993; Beebe and Lachmann, 2002; Braten, 2007; Braten and Trevarthen, 2007; Bromberg, 2006; Cozolino, 2006; Lyons-Ruth, 2003; Schore, 2012; Siegel, 1999, 2007; Stern, 1985; Tronick, 2007).

In their model of intersubjectivity, for example, Braten and Trevarthen (2007; Braten, 2007) describe an interactional model that changes over time but still has one enduring feature: the child's other-centered focus. From primary intersubjective dialogue and mutual mirroring, the child and the caregiver progress to secondary intersubjective attunement, where the child seeks shared intentions and interests. During this period the toddler is animated by feelings of pride, autonomy, and shame. Similarly to Schore (2003), Braten and Trevarthen (2007) consider the age of about 18 months as central to these feelings. Developing verbal skills enable new forms of intersubjectivity, new modes of interaction, and ongoing involvement in the emotions, language, and behaviors of significant others. The example they give is the mutual mouth movement when feeding a toddler—mutual action and joint satisfaction.

Tertiary intersubjective participation occurs around three to six years and is defined by the even greater understanding of and absorption in the minds and emotions of others. Verbal exchanges, self-dialogues anchored in a rich narrative imagination, and repeated simulation of conversations (some predetermined by already encoded previous experiences) lead to the development of representations, cognitive styles, and narratives of the self and other (Braten, 2007; Bucci, 2007a, 2007b; Grawe, 2007; Lyons-Ruth, 2003; Olds, 2006; Wilkinson, 2010).

As higher-order developments continue, children increasingly see themselves as responsible coauthors of anything they feel or think, even though the experiences they are immersed in emanate from a parent (Braten, 2007; Hermans, 2004; Lewis and Todd, 2004, 2007). It is interesting to note that two interwoven developmental forces eventually determine our developing sense of self and personal identity: the inevitable intersubjective immersion in the parent's emotional world on the one hand, and the child's tendency to perceive events from a self-centered point of view. Eventually, entrenched narratives embody representational aspects of self-other experiences, as well as representations of one's own idiosyncratic interpretations of them.

LANGUAGE AS A BRIDGE BETWEEN AFFECT AND COGNITION

Self-narratives that automatically surface during dysregulation may also provide a bridge between the conscious and the unconscious, most likely linking unconscious images and representations to more subjectively conscious self-states. Although fully embedded in emotion—and in unconscious self-systems—the link that narratives provide is through language (Damasio, 2000, 2010; Daniel, 2009; Mancia, 2006; Panksepp, 2012; Pinker, 2007; Siegel, 2007). In this context, research has shown that positive and negative moods are associated with distinctly different cognitive processing of both intrapsychic and interpersonal events. Furthermore, these researchers have delineated the role of words in the experience of feelings. Language is the connotative carrier of inchoate emotions and bodily sensations, so words inevitably shape and form the meanings and perception of our internal and external worlds on all levels of consciousness (Clore and Ortony, 2000; Davidson, 2000; Pinker, 2007).

Language develops within "a (m)other-centered" dyadic participation as well (Braten, 2007, p. 123), whereby the child will nonconsciously but actively coarticulate the speaker's intensions and actual words as if he himself were a co-originator of what is being said. The implications of this model are clear. Negative criticism from a parent, hostile communications, neglect, and any other painful interactions will be co-opted by the child, in essence perceived as originating from within him. The parents' actions and communications become the child's own. This other-centered speech resonance is at play in all levels of conversation. Moreover, parental emotional states (irritation, depression, frustration, self-denigration) that have nothing to do with the child will also be co-opted by him as if they were his own. This process is part of the child's meaning making (Braten, 2007; Conboy and Kuhl, 2007; Hermans, 2004; Kuhl, 1998; Rall and Harris, 2000; Schore, 2005; Stern, 1985; Tomasello, 2001) and also constitutes a building block of the developing unconscious maps.

Through the course of development, a joint body of meaning is created and consolidated in the context of the intersubjective relationship. This happens "in the form of scripts, representations, or working models" (Papastathopoulos and Kugiumutzakis, 2007, p. 224), schemas (Bucci 2007a, 2007b), or implicit self-systems that underpin our more conscious self-states. As these co-created meanings become part of the child's representational world, the developing narratives about the self

are also immersed in shared experiences (Papastathopoulos and Kugiumutzakis, 2007).

As the term *intersubjectivity* implies, both parties consciously and
nonconsciously affect each other and operate from an other-centered
point of view. They are engaged in a process of mutual influence. Within
the parent–child dyad the latter is the one most vulnerable. Paradoxically, by being so essential for survival, the bonds of intersubjectivity
can also carry within them the seeds for dysregulated self-states that
are made up of painful, traumatizing, humiliating, and confusing interactions. Simultaneously, cognitive characteristics are added and become
part of that particular self-system and the more conscious self-state. As
Claire's case continues in the following sections, it is clear that many
emotional messages, verbal and nonverbal, shaped the nature of her
self-narratives. In particular, her mother's lingering unprocessed feelings alternating between fear and anger became part of Claire's own
self-system.

As we clearly have seen in Claire's recurrent narratives, language—in
the form of words, concepts, images, or metaphors—derived from intersubjective attachment situations will inevitably be suffused with a wide
range of sensory and affective experiences. Although the emotions or
the emotional memories themselves may never be accessible, their content is encoded prior to the maturity of explicit memory and they still
color the rapidly developing cognitive skills.

An important implication of these findings is the necessity to consider the developmental phases of middle and late childhood as well
as adolescence and view them as being powerfully influential as early
infancy. In actuality, the potential of painful and humiliating experiences to engender dysregulation and shape negative meaning needs to
be considered throughout development. This is especially true during
preadolescence and adolescence, when acceptance by one's cohort
group is most significant. During childhood, for example, parental conflict or a difficult divorce will contribute a developing negative narrative,
whereby the child may interpret feelings of loss or panic as indications
of his own self-worth or guilt.

THE ROOTS OF DISTORTION: CHILDHOOD
LIMITATIONS AND MEANING MAKING

We cannot forget the child's limited ability to make sense or give meaning to an emotional state, and as Braten and Trevarthen (2007) say, to
locate the source of the negativity in the parent, outside the self. The
other-centric focus ends up as a self-centric one in terms of how the
child understands an experience. Interpretations and meanings given to

painful experiences are inevitably rooted in the child's immature cognitive abilities, leading to the centric belief that a negative experience
emanates from him, that the pain he feels is his fault.

The distorted explanations given by the child are made even more
destructive by the slower-developing left hemisphere—the explainer
(Gazzaniga, 2008; Gazzaniga et al., 2014; McGilchrist, 2009)—and the
PFC as a whole. This immaturity adds to the process of the self-centric
meaning given to an emotional state. Consequently, while in the midst of
traumatic, painful, or shameful experiences, the child has no choice but
to arrive at distorted conclusions about his self-worth, competency, and
importance to the parent and to his age group. Because the child is not
yet able yet to attribute events and emotions to their appropriate sources
or place them in a larger, more reasoned context, even completely distorted and negative conclusions about the self are perceived as utterly
authentic. Such immature interpretations span the range from complete
self-blame for the negative feelings to extreme defensive attempts to
externalize them. As Chapter 7 explores, narcissistic defenses and the
narratives that accompany them may very well start with such defensive
attempts.

In addition, the early maturing right hemisphere, greatly involved
in unconscious communication, does not allow for a differentiation
between the mother's mood and intent from the child's own. Recalling
Braten and Trevarthen's model, we can see how damaging these immature process are. This is especially so because of the right brain's sensitivity to negative affect and the attentional system's propensity toward
negative emotions (Hanson and Mendius, 2009; Koziol and Budding,
2010).

The far-reaching effects of the amygdala further clarify our inclination for distorted associations and personal meanings unconsciously
originating in a state of emotional arousal. Because the amygdala projects to many cortical areas, including those it doesn't receive reciprocal
input from, it can determine levels of affective and cognitive dysregulation. It influences short- and long-term memories, as well as other cognitive functions (Damasio, 2010; LeDoux and Doyere, 2011; Wilson, 2011).
Rubino et al. (2007), for example, found that the amygdala was activated
by language regardless of personality styles. As has been demonstrated,
the amygdala has a pivotal role in linking external stimuli, somatic
responses, and automatic coping attempts (see Chapter 2). Throughout
life, sensory stimuli activate memory traces in the limbic system without passing through higher cortical areas. This out-of-awareness process
results in unconscious perceptions, feelings, cognitions, and behavioral
tendencies (Gainotti, 2006; Ginot, 2012; Huether, 1998; LeDoux, 2002;
Ohman, 2009, Ohman et al., 2007; Sergerie and Armony, 2006). Since
the narratives themselves are unconsciously embedded within a negative

map or self-system, they will be automatically reactivated and become an inseparable part of a dysregulated self-state.

Self-Narratives and the Developing Identity

What become conditioned and automated are the child's impressions of particular interpersonal situations, and the many-layered emotional meaning assigned to them. This meaning is tied to attachment dysregulation or repeated violations of the need for autonomy and self-esteem among older children and adolescents. Frequent parental criticism, disapproval, intrusiveness, and demeaning attitude will become the child's own implicit core self (Grawe, 2007). As is largely accepted (see Braten, 2007; Panksepp and Biven, 2012), the searing feeling of humiliation develops around 18 months, side by side with a much more limited capacity for reasoning or understanding. Negative self-narratives—centering on the child as the source of the bad feelings—become the integrative bridge between painful, traumatic, and humiliating emotions and the inevitable efforts to explain them (Gazzaniga, 2008; Lewis and Todd, 2004, 2007; Papastathopoulos and Kugiumutzakis, 2007). Although the actual memories and the amalgam of associations in their wake are not accessible, narratives give them conscious voice and representation.

Emphasizing the integration between working memory, cognition, and emotion, Grawe (2007) further contributes to the understanding of self-narratives as an essential part of dysregulation. An anxious dysregulated self-state will require four components: (1) working memory for conscious experience, (2) involvement of the amygdala, (3) activation of the arousal system, and (4) feedback of fear-specific somatic sensations. What becomes conditioned and automated is the emotional meaning and cognitive assessment of a particular situation. This meaning is tied to attachment dysregulation or repeated violations of the needs for autonomy and self-esteem among older children. Later on, automatic responses follow the meaning perceived in particular situations, triggering emotional and behavioral tendencies. These, coupled with old encoded representations, impede a more direct and accurate evaluation of one's competence, and strengths.

Self-Narratives and the Conscious– Unconscious Continuum

Viewing negative self-narratives as a bridge between painful emotional experiences and the inevitable efforts to explain them and give them meaning via fast-developing linguistic skills enables us to better understand the shades and contours that comprise the consciously felt experience of an unconscious self-system. Our narratives, indeed, can be seen as an emotionally "true" reflection of our negative self-systems. When they are activated, they are in essence an important manifestation of our identity. This explains why they seem so "real and convincing" when we are in the midst of a dysregualted state with its particular narratives. It also explains why, when such states are stronger than others, the individual senses that only the negative narrative is "authentic and true" to the conscious sense of self while a positive one is not, and is often considered fraudulent and ephemeral. In effect, elaborating on the link between attachment styles and the various mental narratives embedded within them, Siegel (2007) considers identity to be shaped by memory and narrative, forged through the unconscious adaptation to the caregiver's attunement.

As the bedrock of the coping styles that have been consistently observed in attachment studies, Siegel mentions four narrative structures. Secure, avoidant/dismissive, disorganized/dissociated, and ambivalent/anxious attachment and narrative patterns are seen as closely related to the level of empathetic attunement, as well as to the caregiver nonconscious intrusiveness. For instance, in disorganized attachment, a recurrent state of fear leads to neurally encoded experiences of moving away from the origin of terror while another set of circuits will encode a move toward the parent for comfort. As the source of terror, the parent cannot provide comfort or resolution, leading to a narrative characterized by fragmentation and eventually dissociative processes (Bromberg, 2006; Ginot, 2012; Grawe, 2007; Lyons-Ruth, 1999; Schore, 2012; Siegel, 2007).

Considering the developmental roots of the Adult Attachment Interview, Main et al. (1985) and Daniel (2009) examined the relationship between attachment and narrative structures in adulthood and determined the existence of different narrative characteristics in secure and insecure attachment patterns. Adults with dismissing narratives and few explicit childhood memories were found to actually suppress emotional reactions, measured by dermal activity (Dozier and Kobak, 1992; Roisman et al, 2004). Ambivalently attached children and adults, who are constantly in a vigilant state of alarm, display a narrative focused on the other, but at the same time lacking in reflection and contextual understanding (Daniel, 2009).

Although the narrative structures described by these researchers may highlight the more generalized aspects of meaning making inherent in attachment, rather than individual fantasies and narratives, they nevertheless describe a link between attachment experiences and developing internal working models (Bucci, 2007a, 2007b, 2011; Main et al., 1985). Reflecting again on Andrew's difficulties with new challenges, we can understand how his debilitating dysregulated state and the narrative that characterized it reflected his parents' difficulties with empathetic resonance and unrealistic expectations; emotional attitudes that were part of many conscious and nonconscious interactions from early on. These became automatically enacted components of any situation in which he expected to be judged. The shared emotional/cognitive space between himself and his parents, now internalized and felt to be entirely his own, was the only neuropsychological reality available to him during these stressful situations, expressed through intense fearful fantasies and verbal narratives.

Recent research into brain regions that constitute the default network further illustrates how the integration of memories, experience, and self-referential ideation might culminate in self-narratives (see Chapter 1). The posterior and anterior cingulate cortex, the medial PFC, and the temporoparietal junctions have all shown significantly greater metabolic activity when the brain is at rest (Raichle et al., 2001) and engaged in internally focused tasks such as rehearsing emotional experiences and memories, envisioning the future, and thinking about the self and others (Buckner and Carroll, 2007). These integrated and synchronized regions seem to be involved in selecting and storing memories according to their emotional meaning and context. Additionally, while at rest, the default network is in constant communication with the hippocampus, rehearsing and going over the selectively stored memories (Greicious et al., 2008).

The importance of the default system to self and other monitoring is also suggested by others (Northoff and Panksepp, 2008; Uddin et al., 2007) who suggest that self-referential and affective processing occur in cortical and subcortical midline regions when the brain is in a neural resting state. In spite of what might seem as a leap from neuroscientific findings to a hypothesis of how narratives take hold, one can still arrive at some intriguing assumptions about how certain brain/mind characteristics develop and endure. What is exciting in this attempt to integrate neuroscience with subjectively felt experiences is the specificity of the subject matter. One can imagine the child's immersion in the emotions and behaviors of the attachment figures; we can imagine her perceptions and affective responses and the subsequent self-referential rehearsed rumination (Ginot, 2012). All these processes occur on a continuum of awareness, and if reinforced over time, they become part of an unconscious map. Without becoming aware of such existing response tendencies—verbal, emotional, and behavioral—the adult woman will continue to experience them as inevitable and, during dysregulation, as a totally justified reaction. Reality-bound evidence to the contrary, such as a positive track record or the existence of a loving support disappears from consciousness.

THE CASE OF CLAIRE, PART 2

With time Claire became aware of how anxious her mother had been, how disappointed with her life, and how she blamed her husband for "not doing anything with her life." But some part of Claire's emotional world also resonated with her mother's helpless frustration and disappointment. For the first time, through her own feelings, Claire understood the extent of her mother's anxiety, her endless fears about the kids' daily activities and their need to be independent.

Her mother did not prevent them from doing things, but there was in the house, Claire realized, an atmosphere similar to the one she had experienced in her grandparents' home. Often, her mother would warn the kids, especially Claire, about potential dangers, things that could go wrong, making sure they remembered to be careful at all times. This combination of fear and frustration found its way into Claire's unconscious, shaping an entire implicit self-system.

Getting to know her mother anew, Claire began to understand why in the face of any task that demanded "self-exposure," such as a presentation or going on a date, her anxiety and automatic self-dismissive thinking would be reactivated. Although she had a circle of good and loyal friends and was quite successful at her internships, she still felt unworthy, as if these positive experiences were not to be trusted; disaster was waiting. What slowly became clear to us was how Claire's internalizing of her mother's fears and attitudes—both verbalized and unspoken—increasingly linked interpersonal encounters with the fear of failing and the belief that she will be found lacking. Her mother's fears about life's potential dangers and her obvious disappointments became part of Claire's unconscious self-system and were generalized to situations that carried the risks of being judged. In these situations her fearful self-narratives would repeatedly remind her of the need to stay safe by not taking risks, even in the face of objective evidence to the contrary.

AFFECTIVE SYSTEMS AND THE DEVELOPING NARRATIVES

As Panksepp and Biven (2012) have shown, some of our innate affective systems are capable of inducing negative raw emotions, which later interact with higher mental functions. The fear as well as the panic/grief systems are central to the generation of unpleasant arousal states. When devastatingly activated, they result in a range of anxious states and ruminations. Separation anxiety, embedded in the panic/grief system, leads to dysregulated social anxiety, for example.

The fear system, according to them, creates its own set of anxieties and ruminations about the insecure nature of one's existence and the prevalence of impending danger. Autonomic defenses are employed as a response to both emotional threats. In Chapter 2 we examined the amygdala's role in enhancing the brain's focus on danger and fear, thus contributing to and enhancing dysregulation. Panksepp suggested that the amygdala, which shows activation during emotional-cognitive tasks, is a hub that creates an interface between affective and cognitive functions. If we remember that emotions generated through the amygdala influence implicit and explicit memories we can further appreciate the ease with which the meaning given to difficult experiences tends to be negative. Combined with the child's other-centered immersion (Braten and Trevarthen, 2007), negative self-centric, left-brain interpretations are inevitable (Gazzaniga, 2008; Wilkinson, 2010).

As language develops and becomes the symbolic carrier of emotions, narratives provide a link through words that are fully embedded in this wide range of affect. An interesting finding for this discussion is a neuroimaging study demonstrating that the right hemisphere's counterpart areas for Brocca's and Wernicke's regions (the verbal skills regions) also provide support for language performance (van Ettinger-Veenstra et al., 2010). This interaction further strengthens the embodied and integrative nature of language and the complex processes that integrate emotion and cognition into a coherent, emotionally convincing narrative.

As clarified by Colombetti (2010), emotional arousal is experientially and automatically coupled with appraisal, a process that on all levels of the conscious to unconscious continuum gives meaning to an experience. As appraisal and arousal are structurally integrated within the whole embodied organism, the words that give shape to the negative experience are totally situated within the dysregulated emotion.

THE CASE OF CLAIRE, PART 3

Once again, Claire's therapeutic process is quite illustrative of what has been discussed here. In spite of her growing ability to modulate some of her narratives, their debilitating power resurfaced when a new stressful situation presented itself. After about two and a half years in therapy, Claire fell in love with a man who genuinely loved and respected her as much as she loved and respected him. They formed a stable loving relationship and planned to move in together. In spite of a significant improvement in her capacity for affect regulation, this stressor triggered Claire's tortured internal monologues.

The stuff of life—taking a risk on an apartment and a neighborhood—mushroomed into an emotionally fraught confusion suffused with anxiety and dread. Claire's verbalized need to make sure her boyfriend was totally happy with their choice overshadowed her own preferences. It sounded eerily familiar to both of us; echoes of her mother's act of giving up her own educational goals were unconsciously being enacted. As a result, the anticipated search for a place with a boyfriend—an event she had often fantasized about in the past but had been convinced was an impossibility—became a source of self-doubt, with constant questioning as to what was the perfect neighborhood and the perfect apartment. In a variation of past fears and old beliefs that life could never be worry-free, Claire also kept thinking that her current happiness with her boyfriend was destined to be short-lived: it was all a "mirage," and therefore very fragile.

At these dysregulated moments she entirely forgot how well she and her boyfriend got along and how calm and helpful he was, and instead saw him as also awash in anxiety and doubt, just as she mostly saw her mother. The intense affects and negative thinking triggered by this happy occasion allowed Claire to realize the depth of her unconscious immersion in her mother's unconscious self-system. She felt as if her mother came alive through her own feelings and thinking. The more she experienced her fearful emotions in therapy, the more she recognized how deeply embedded were her mother's fears and convictions. It was as if, she said, she "did not have a choice"; she was her mother, "afraid of everything, with a very negative outlook of life."

At the same time, Claire's memories and ideas of her mother became more emotionally mixed and nuanced. She could remember that she was indeed very attuned to her mother's moods, trying her best not to burden her. She realized that much of her energy went into protecting her mother from her demons, tiptoeing around her. She now thought that not bringing friends home was not just because of fearing her mother's outbursts, but was really a way to lessen her mother's burden and housework. This reason is also why she seldom turned to her mother for help. The thought of involving her mother with her problems made her feel inexplicably upset. Now she identified the feeling and the narrative that went with it as sadness and guilt.

FOCUSED ATTENTION AND THE DEVELOPING NARRATIVES

The level of attentional readiness within the perceptual system seems to drive the interchange between emotion and cognition and further determine the tone and quality of the developing narrative. Cortical attention regulates emotion through downstream paths, while emotional arousal generated by the limbic system and lower regions activates the attentional focus (Lewis, 2005; Lewis and Todd, 2004, 2007). In a reciprocal loop, attention amplifies the focus on negative emotions and their personal meaning. Adding to the child's vulnerability is the amygdala's innate tendency to focus the mind on what signifies danger, on what is intense and out of the ordinary. As we have seen, since Claire was deeply attuned to her mother's negative affective states, the effects of this focus and its arousing qualities were particularly devastating.

Indeed, consistent findings demonstrated that the level of attentional readiness within the perceptual system seems to drive the interchange between emotion and cognition and further determines the tone of the developing narrative. This process explains Claire's hyperfocus on her mother's emotional life, both its conscious and unconscious aspects.

Emotions such as sadness, anger, and anxiety are especially powerful in narrowing the focus of attention and anchoring it to specific aspects of the interaction or the situation. Within the self-states associated with heightened negative emotions, this will result in exaggerated negative appraisals and conclusions, all encoded in specific neural networks (Cozolino, 2002, 2006; Davidson, 2000; Lewis and Todd, 2004). The combination of the automaticity of the mirror neuron system, the efficacy of right-brain-to-left-brain communication, and the heightened attention they generate set the stage for dysregulated affective states, including their add-on fantasies and narratives (Clore and Ortony, 2000; Derryberry and Tucker, 1994; Kaplan et al., 1999; LeDoux, 2002; Lewis and Todd, 2004; Ohman, 2009, Ohman et al., 2007; Wilson, 2011).

Lewis and Todd (2004) locate the starting point of internal dialogue in the neural circuits between the frontocortical and limbic regions. These reciprocal connections generate global attention states and the emotions they focus on emerge, usually in conjunction with anticipated action from the other. The center of one attentional system is the orbitofrontal cortex, which has dense connections to the amygdala. It is also connected to the temporal lobes where perceptual information is processed, to regions attending to potential rewards, threats, and behavioral plans, and to Broca's area, which controls speech. A second attentional system involves the anterior cingulated cortex that integrates more diverse information into a larger whole, and seems to be less emotionally driven (Lewis and Todd, 2004).

These findings indicate that parental emotions, behaviors, and voices are especially powerful in focusing the child's attention on the negative aspects of the interaction, enhancing the development of harmful internal monologues. Lewis and Todd (2004) suggest that these monologues progress through and inhabit many shades of emotional content. This susceptibility to negative emotions, fantasies, and self-monologues driven by the attentional systems seem to be an inevitable part of the intersubjective aspects of development, especially when the child's temperament is taken into account (Braten 2007; Braten and Trevarthen, 2007; Davidson, 2000; Kagan, 1998; Lewis and Todd, 2004, 2007). Remember that the amygdalas of infants exposed to facial expressions were more active when viewing neutral expressions than scary or angry ones (see Chapter 2). The opposite is true for children and adolescents, whose amygdalas are more reactive to angry or scary faces (Hamann, 2009; Phelps, 2009). Infants, then, are more sensitive to expressionless faces and neglectful interactions often enacted by the caretaker via an emotionless expression. Tronick (2007), in his now much-cited experiment, found the same: in the face of maternal facial passivity and indifference, the infant collapses in despair.

Think about the depressed mother who cannot muster enough energy to interact with her baby, express genuine joy, or mirror his exuberance. Even subtle stimuli, such as different facial expressions, are mediated by the amygdala and its circuits. These become intertwined with other affective systems, such as panic/grief and rage. When activated by dysregulating situations, negative affective systems dominate and control the PFC and the hypothalamus with its neuroendocrine activity. As a result, painful feelings and the self-blaming ruminations that go with them take over conscious experience. While more positive or affirming aspects of a current situation are simply not there.

The Mirror Neuron System and Self-Narratives

As has already been mentioned, nonconscious self-systems can develop not only from what is directly done to and said to the child but by being absorbed in and imitating a parental self-state. We can see this very clearly in Claire's burden of anxious ruminations. Recent research on the mirror neuron system demonstrates a child's susceptibility to negative states and the development of negative narratives. The mirror neuron system has been shown to establish a neuropsychological link between interacting subjectivities that observe or relate to each other. Specifically, these specialized neurons found in the premotor cortex, seem to mediate action understanding, imitation, and empathy—interpersonal processes that also make up our intersubjective building blocks (Gallese, 2006; Iacoboni, 2008; Rizzolati et al., 2002).

This direct, nonverbal understanding is mediated by what Gallese (2006, 2008) calls a neuropsychological process of embodied simulation, creating in our own brains the affects and intentions of those we observe or interact with. This process, according to Gallese (2009) and Iacoboni (2008) constitutes the roots of empathy and intersubjectivity. Here we have the mechanism that underpins the child's absorption in a parent's emotional self-state, identifying with and internalizing parental emotions and traits. This of course enables a child to resonate with a parent's pain and anxiety or conversely, joy, happiness, and other positive affects. The child's brain/mind will simulate the parents' neuropsychological states and understand their intent and the emotions behind the spoken word. Chapter 9 further discusses the centrality of the mirror neuron system to intergenerational transmission of trauma. Here we need to consider innate brain connectivity. As Dapretto et al. (2006)

showed, children on the autistic spectrum showed a less active mirror neuron system than nonautistic ones. The more severe the syndrome, the less activity was noticed.

The Mirror Neuron System and Language Development

Recent research is starting to explore the role of the mirror neuron system in the development of cognitive skills that are an inextricable part of imitation and shared mental states (Fadiga and Craighero, 2007; Gallese, 2008; Iacoboni, 2008; Rizzolati et al., 2002). In researching the association between this system and social cognition, Gallese (2006, 2008) has proposed that the neurobiological functional mechanism that underpins the mirror neuron system—embodied simulation—is also responsible for the development of social meaning and symbolic language.

Via the neural exploitation hypothesis, Gallese and Lakoff (2005) suggest that key aspects of social cognition have become linked to brain mechanisms that originally evolved to enable sensory-motor imitation, namely, the mirror neuron system. Networks originally responsible for embodied simulation—automatically imitating action, intention, and emotion—later evolved to become new neural scaffolding for thought and language. These researchers, ever conscious of the intersubjective elements embedded in all interactions generated by the shared neural mapping, also emphasize the interpersonal elements of this newer neural adaptation (Gallese and Lakoff, 2005). Similarly, Knox (2009) implicates the mirror neuron system in the child's sense of self-agency, speculating that during the early stages of development, when the separation between primary and secondary sensory-motor areas is not yet complete, imagination and thoughts are inherently intertwined with physical action and emotional states. Thus, language, originating from mirror neuron–driven perceptions of action and intention, is intimately entrenched within the various sensory-motor experiences and the emotional meanings attached to them. In this way the mirror neuron system seems to affect many experiential aspects of self-organization such as emotional identification and language development (Gallese 2006, 2008; Iacoboni, 2008; Olds, 2006, 2012).

The emphasis on the mirror neuron system as linking cognition, fantasy, and affect highlights their inseparable existence within one's phenomenological experience and elucidates how self-narratives develop. Language derived from intersubjective attachment situations will inevitably be suffused with a wide range of automatic simulation of parental intentions and emotions. Although the emotions themselves may be dissociated, they underlie a recurrent self-narrative. As Iacoboni (2008) and Gallese (2006) have stressed, the mirror neuron system seems to automatically establish a direct experiential link between subjects, effort-lessly and unconsciously, and predominantly via the right hemisphere (Schore, 2012).

Again, one can appreciate the emerging realization that the intense intersubjective communication between parent and child primes the lat-ter to be particularly attuned and vulnerable to negative interpersonal experiences on explicit and implicit levels. Reinforced neural activa-tions eventually coalesce into a solid pattern of fantasies and linguis-tic "knowledge" about various aspects of the self. Claire's unconscious self-system and its recurrent narratives are a good example.

Gallese's (2006, 2008) hypothesis seems to correspond to Braten's (2007) emphasis on the intersubjective properties of language develop-ment. Bear in mind that they consider language development as firmly rooted in the context of a mother-centered context. Hence, language that originates from mirror neuron–driven perceptions of action, intent, and emotion is embedded within interpersonal perceptions and experi-ences, as well as the emotional meanings attached to them. Indeed, as Tomasello (2001) suggests, the shared perceptions of intentions, which emerges around nine months, is crucial for language acquisition and the development of a sense of self. As there are no explicit memories from this age, these processes become part of future enacted unconscious processes.

MEMORIES AND SELF-NARRATIVES

The important field of memory research further illuminates how distor-tions in narratives may occur. Our memory reservoirs constitute who we are in our conscious narratives. But as we now know, memories—emotional and implicit ones included—are not an accurate replica of an event or an experience. Emotional memories and the meaning given to them influence the tenacity of self-narratives in several ways. First and possibly most important, we need to consider the intertwined link between the emotional tone of the memories populating an unconscious system and their influence on self-narratives. As we have already seen, inaccessible or implicit memories of painful interpersonal experiences can still generate self-blaming or other narratives turned against the self.

Second, memories are entwined with one's current mood—negative moods will lead to negative memories and vice versa. Memories are also colored by the already established unconscious emotional/cognitive self-systems within which they are encoded and through which they are recalled (Churchland, 2013; Damasio, 2010; Fernyhough, 2013; Pank-sepp and Biven, 2012). What is relevant to us is that an unconscious self-system assembled of negatively slanted memories will tend to generate negative self-narratives that then become part of a more conscious self-state.

In addition to the influence of mood, memories are vulnerable to a wide range of distortions, which heavily influence narratives linked to unconscious emotional memories. Memory systems differ in their levels of rigidity and in what is consciously accessible. What is remembered, accurate or otherwise, has a great deal of significance if it is underpinned by the power of emotion (Damasio, 2010; Panksepp, 2008). When remembering events or emotional experiences, the gist of the experience or the processed and distilled mental narrative is usually more important than the accuracy of the details. Often, the emotional impact determines how influential a memory becomes in terms of its effects on narratives about the self. As Dudai says: "Narratives can assimilate and parsimoniously represent the value impact of experience. . . . In the process of forming mental narratives, engrams merge, losing much of their original individuality. They join the distributed, large and dynamic 'society of engrams' that comes to constitute our memory" (Dudai, 2011, p. 38).

Another potential distortion results from the memory system's tendency to level off memories and mingle them together (Fernyhough, 2013). Forgoing a great deal of detail could allow the brain to promote generalizations and facilitate appropriate responses to both expected and unexpected stimuli. Some part of the hippocampus may generate auto-associative memory capable of linking together quite arbitrary co-occurring inputs, including emotional inputs from the amygdala. The context that is stored with memory also influences recall, affective states, affect processes, and the storage and retrieval of memories. Such processes clearly illustrate the interactive nature of the conscious and unconscious realms.

DISTORTED MEMORIES AND DISTORTED SELF-NARRATIVES

When trying to understand the distortions that characterize negative self-narratives, we can clearly see how an amalgam of emotional memories affects implicit self-systems as well as more conscious narratives about ourselves. Often, especially within an unconscious, dysregulated self-system, these narratives are distorted as well; negative systems will result in negatively biased interpretations of experience. Again, in Dudai's words: "In the process of forming mental narratives, engrams merge, losing much of their original individuality. They join the distributed, large and dynamic 'society of engrams' that comes to constitute our memory. In real life, engrams are palimpsests, reflecting physical traces of many layers of past events" (Dudai, 2011, p. 38). Memories, then, can be accurate, but they are often prone to distortions and biases, colored by the already existing unconscious memories. This process can clearly lead to a biased emphasis on negative memories and to the negative meaning given to them. To emphasize the narrative component of memory, the "made-up" self-hating or removed-from-reality distortions, as it were, are not intended to simply undermine the accuracy of our memories. But the more we know about memory, and the more we realize how vulnerable to distortions memories and narratives are, the more we can help patients cope with them.

Significantly, neuroimaging studies as well as observations of brain-damaged individuals reveal that similar neural systems underpin memory and story telling. Rubin (2006) sees memory and narratives as totally intertwined. As a key organizer of experience, self-narratives incorporate autobiographical memories with all their biases and emotional stamp. If information does not fit into the developing system, it has less of a chance to make it into a conscious memory. As children we take on other people's emotional states and verbal behaviors—mediated by the mirror neuron system—and are immersed in the caregiver's emotional states. So are our memories, emotional and contextual.

In spite of this knowledge, when we experience the familiar convincing feeling of remembering, especially within an emotional state, memories still seem totally true (Fernyhough, 2013). This feeling of remembering seems to be important to our consistent sense of self. When we consider again the narratives that develop within an unconscious dysregulated affective state, one based on and reinforced by past emotional memories, we can see another aspect that underpins the development of narratives and why they are harsh but so convincing. When triggered within a dysregulated state, these narratives are the only memory/experience that "feel" true. Furthermore, the negative spin of these narratives will continue to create negative meanings that in essence do not match reality. Without mindfulness, positive or contradictory information will not be easily believed.

SELF-NARRATIVES AND THE FLEXIBILITY–RIGIDITY CONTINUUM

The tenacity of a negative self-state and the narratives or images attached to it can also be explained by the rigidity that memory structures acquire. Once a memory is consolidated, it is advantageous for the brain to exclude new information that it automatically deems to be of no value or only of temporary value. On the other hand, the "updating" process of memories—allowing new experiences to form old ones—is also highly beneficial for survival. Memories that are too robust can be maladaptive and prevent new responses to a changing environment. A memory system that is too rigid, will lead to poor imagination. In this case, we can see the future only in terms of the past. Thus the neural mechanisms that allow recurrent updating of items in long-term memory may also permit a more effective and free imagination.

If memory traces of intersubjective experiences become rigid and are entirely dependent on the unconscious system, the meaning and interpretations attached to them will be based on past experiences alone, and new experiences will be unconsciously seen through old emotions and old narratives. A more flexible memory system, both conscious and unconscious—or more accurately, on the continuum—will be more open to new, more reality-bound interpretations of one's competence or self-worth. During therapy, reflective awareness on the dysregulated state in real time may mitigate some of the effects of a rigid system.

THE CASE OF CLAIRE, PART 4

We can understand how Claire came to inhabit and enact so much of her mother's anxiety as well as her "forgotten" reactions to her father's controlling attitudes, and how it was so difficult for her to develop a sense of competency and approach life with more ease. The unconscious identification with her mother's suffering and perceived failure and her painful reactions to her father's know-it-all implied criticalness became the building blocks of Claire's ideas about herself. Her mother's anxious system became her own: the sense of failure and disappointment of her life fed into Claire's own dread about failure and making the wrong decisions. The mother's Holocaust legacy, and her passive role in her own life—both unreflected on and therefore readily enacted—became an active part of Claire, blending with the sense of insecurity reinforced by her father.

As therapy progressed, Claire decided that she was not going to be like her mother: angry, fearful, or critical of her husband. She wanted to be different and create a different kind of relationship altogether. Out of therapy, she purposefully tried to become aware and reflect on automatic affects and thoughts that essentially echoed her past.

As Claire and her boyfriend chose a neighborhood and apartment, she relaxed and negotiated the move with maturity and relative calm. A year later, they got married; Claire was working at the firm she truly liked, and she mostly experienced optimism and a positive view about life. Although her narratives still reemerged under pressure, the therapeutic process was powerful enough to shift something fundamental in how she related to her past and its aftermath. The more she understood her past and distorted conclusions about herself, the more tolerant of her affects she became. She began to reflect on disturbing feelings and narratives in real time, telling herself the story of their origin, soothing and reminding herself that she was not her mother and did not have to live her life.

Negative self-narratives can be seen as the point of contact between affect and cognition, forming a bridge to between these inseparable modes of neuropsychological functioning. Although a recurrent negative narrative is expressed through words, at times entirely removed from affect, its very essence is embedded in neurally encoded emotional memories of early attachment experiences (Gergely and Unoka, 2008a, 2008b; Grawe, 2007; Mancia, 2006). Thus, narratives become the cognitive expression of emotional dysregulation, containing within them past interactions, emotional memories, defenses, and distorted conclusions all triggered by emotional stresses similar to the original ones. Often, especially among more dissociative patients, narratives are the only manifestation of one's hidden emotional and relational core.

Although narratives are expressed through words, their very first emotional roots can be found in the quality of attunement characterizing the earliest intersubjective experiences.

SELF-NARRATIVES AND THERAPEUTIC ENACTMENTS

Because dysregulation-embedded internal monologues reflect and enact an unconscious self-system, their inevitable reactivation within the therapeutic dyad provides a valuable opportunity to experientially access unconscious connection between emotional memories and their representational narratives. In the entangled dyadic context of mutual expectations, need, and disappointments, the enactment of dysregulated self-states is bound to become part of the transference-countertransference relationship. This observation is particularly compelling in light of the ongoing unconscious and nonverbal affective communication that often results in enactments (Aron, 1996; Braten, 2007; Bromberg, 2006; Chefetz and Bromberg, 2004; Chused, 1998; Gallese, 2006; Ginot, 2007, 2009; Jacobs, 1991; Pizer, 2003; Schore, 2012; Stern, 2010). An internalized, fully articulated parental voice could be activated in the intersubjective matrix, triggering emotional and behavioral reactions, entirely out of awareness. Quickly, old patterns triggered by the therapeutic relationship can grow from a barely conscious emotional sense mediated by the orbitofrontal cortex into an aroused self-state. This dysregulated state will be composed of old certainties and vigilant emotional and cognitive appraisals that will guide the perception of external reality through old, familiar lenses. As often witnessed in clinical situations, a blurring of internal and external realities ensues. At these moments the more modulated attentional system controlled by the anterior cingulate cortex is not active. Indeed, synchrony of the two becomes important during therapy (Ecker and Toomie, 2008; Lewis and Todd, 2004), especially through the development of reflectiveness.

Because enactments are rooted in unconscious emotional communications, recognizing them can provide important information about unconscious self-systems (Bromberg, 2006; Ginot, 2007, 2009, 2012; Stern, 2004). Similarly, fantasies and self-narratives expressed during states of high or low arousal levels can convey a great deal of emotional knowledge as well. Like enactments, dysregulated narratives, when fully experienced and enacted within the session, can start an integrative process in the context of the reflective space provided by the analytic process. Words embedded in experiences not yet part of the conscious sense of self will help the patient reconnect with the implicit, this time questioning rigid and automatic beliefs. By their very enmeshment within a hyper- or hypoaroused state, dysregulated narratives, although at times affectively dissociated, can still lead to more integrative experiences.

THE CASE OF CLAIRE, PART 5

Such an enactment served to enhance Claire's understanding of the unconscious forces guiding her emotions, narratives, and behaviors. A few times during our therapeutic process, her negativity and insistent predictions of doom tried my patience and even my empathy. Similarly to other unconscious communication leading to enactment, her verbal communication was only part of the story. Only on understanding the immense and paralyzing power of her words—their at once numbing and infuriating effect on me—did we realize that she was in effect pleading with me to see beyond these words. Another self-system, one that secretly sought to feel free of the constriction of the past, could not directly express itself; its power was dwarfed in the face of a rigid system that could only repeat the internalized voices of her parents.

As played out between us, and as between Claire and her boyfriend, stress activated a particular affective state and familiar ruminations. During these times, her amalgam of implicit memories and the distorted self-concepts attached to them were the most prominent aspect of an unconscious-conscious self-system. As the repeated negative states and their familiar narratives persisted around the time of the search for the new apartment, any attempts to reflect on them, to understand their interpersonal and desperate messages—to her mother, to herself, to me—were met with hurt and a feeling of being unsupported and misunderstood. Claire insisted that when overwhelmed she could only experience what came naturally. When I eventually shared my genuine feelings of impatience, and later of defeat and hopelessness, surprisingly she jumped to my defense, offering apologies and expressing concern. Enacting a different self-state, Claire was trying to take care of me. But just as quickly, she tearfully asserted that she was not in therapy to "provide me" with what I "needed to hear," but only to express her own feelings. I was on the verge of tears as well, simultaneously feeling criticized but also elated at the manifestation of her need to express herself and assert her needs.

This emotional exchange and others similar to it further helped us grasp with our bodies and affects, and with Claire's warring self-states, a struggle that clearly affected her quest to forge an identity of her own. This process became possible through my emotional reactions; reactions that snuck up on me, making it almost impossible to contain the mixture of suffocation, anger, impatience, and defeat. As our interactions drifted between interlocking, difficult emotional states and the reflection on them, Claire came to fully appreciate the power her words had on others; they had the same devastating effects that her mother's negative words had had on her. The heated exchanges between us also rattled her and connected her to dissociated sets of feelings and thoughts: deep concern for me, guilt for causing me to be upset, and a great desire to assert herself and find her own way apart from me and on her own terms. As Claire saw it, that was something she couldn't do with her mother.

On a deep level, Claire's spontaneous assertion of her own needs was a real expression of her movement toward a stronger sense of self-determination. This strengthened self-state was increasingly present as the therapy continued, especially in the aftermath of the recurrent entanglements between us.

CHAPTER 6

Repetition and Resistance

THIS CHAPTER REEXAMINES THE IMPORTANT concepts of repetition compulsion and resistance as aspects of unconscious processes. These interrelated phenomena are inseparable parts of any therapeutic process and are often perceived as obstacles for growth. What validates this clinical position is the fact that resistance and unconscious repetitions are indeed entirely intertwined with the observable difficulties in changing emotional and behavioral patterns. The following sections demonstrate how the structure and function of the brain/mind in essence work against any attempts to acquire fresh ways of seeing and being with oneself and others. Such processes result in what we usually call resistance and repetition—the difficulties to implement new insights and replace old rigid patterns with more adaptable ones. What is so intriguing about the innate pull to enact nonconscious self-systems is the recurrent realization that in spite of wishes to alter how one feels, inherent neuropsychological processes ensure that change is truly difficult to execute. Conversely, repeating old patterns is natural, automatic, and bypasses consciousness. The resistance to change and the reliance on the familiar are the embodiment of the flexibility–rigidity continuum and express the balance between automaticity and change and between repetition and change.

THE POWER OF NEURAL LESSONS:
WE ONLY KNOW WHAT WE LEARN

A patient's resistance to change can take many forms: from missing sessions to the subtle but consistent inability to internalize and utilize the therapeutic interaction. It is not surprising that the notion of resistance has been central in psychoanalytic and psychotherapeutic literature, and that all therapeutic approaches have had to contend with what it means and how to overcome it. Although the phenomenon of resistance has been traditionally understood as a necessary defense, a mental bulwark against the unfamiliar, its embeddedness in brain/mind processes is increasingly changing its meaning and our understanding of how it functions. Deeply entrenched in mind/brain processes that rely on what worked in the past to alleviate physio/affective distress, there is indeed the reflexive and automatic move to repeat old patterns and consequently resist changes to emotional and relational patterns.

To start the discussion I raise a difficult question: why would we fear change if becoming more flexible and less reliant on entrenched patterns can make our lives less tumultuous? Why would we resist to know who we are, avoid confronting searing old pains and the elaborate defenses against them? Why do we become disconnected from childhood experiences, from learning about the many facets our parents had, if understanding ourselves can bring about a better sense of well-being or more satisfying relationships?

As part of the attempts to resolve the dilemma of why patients resist that which they often say has brought them to therapy—change—resistance has had many interpretations. In Freud's unconscious model, repetition is the inevitable and compulsive breakthrough of unconscious fantasy, which finds ways to affect behavior as part of the unconscious internal reality (see Freud, 1905, 1914, 1915). In later dynamic models, resistance and repetition have been seen as being motivated by an unconscious determination to hold on to old patterns, especially as a way to stay connected to attachment figures. Patients, it is assumed, are terrified of change, afraid to let go of old patterns without new ones to replace them. Alternatively, it is presumed that they are comfortable with the secondary gains that maladaptive patterns may have brought about. Resistance is also seen as an inevitable part of the transference–countertransference interaction, whereby patients may reject internalizing new relational patterns, again motivated by an unconscious need to maintain old ones. This motivation to resist the therapist's influence or continue to fight for a total sense of autonomy may also be seen as a defense against feeling taken over by another subjectivity

Above all, the sense that patients are afraid to confront their past-related painful states, that they would continue to employ their typical defenses against potential devastating memories for as long as they can, is prevalent in our therapeutic conceptualization. From a psychodynamic point of view, these interpretations are instructive and helpful; they describe a felt experience, a recognizable state of holding on to what is known, and an insistence on repeating old ways of relating to oneself and others. The neuropsychological model of the unconscious yields a more nuanced picture as to why we repeat dysfunctional patterns, why we are quick to rely on defenses that worked in the past, and why it is so hard to change.

On a subjective level, repetitions feel natural and necessary—they are all we know. The multilayered underpinnings of behavioral patterns and how we approach others and ourselves cannot be accessible, of course, but neither are some of the more salient features of our behaviors and how they affect others and ourselves. What we largely fail to appreciate is how the brain/mind's habitual ways of functioning "resist" new alternatives in real time, when old self-systems are activated. At the most fundamental but important level, this resistance is rooted in the biological reality that dictates that any felt and implemented changes need to first be registered and encoded on a neurological level. As brain/mind processes dictate, only neural shifts can lead to a psychological one, a fact that further explains the roadblocks to change. This process is especially significant in light of the countless networks and connections that constitute the brain/mind functioning. The motivational aspects of resistance are often less of a factor than this evolutionary determined propensity for the brain to conserve energy and automatically use established maps and networks (Damasio, 2010; Gazzaniga et al., 2014; Koziol, 2014; Lewis and Todd, 2005, 2007). But this brain/mind dynamic is not all biased toward enacting only the known. Recall the importance of the flexibility–rigidity continuum, the ability of the PFC to integrate new information, and, again for evolutionary purposes, try new behaviors when the old ones fail to help with survival. For this adaptive purpose, memory systems are dynamic, unstable, and changeable. When needed, processes of retrieval and updating offer a big advantage over memories that are too robust and stable (Dudai, 2011).

As we know, due to the ever-shifting relationship between the rigid and the flexible aspects of brain/mind processes such efforts are sometimes not easily accomplished, and some patients continue enacting their behavioral and defensive patterns for many years. In spite of what seems to be the tenacity of brain/mind functioning, a neuropsychological model does not present a hopeless position. On the contrary, by underscoring what brain/mind aspects stand in the way of change and how, we can try to tackle them more successfully. For example, in the context of an empathetic relationship, therapists may become more actively engaged with the patient's habitual but unsuccessful self-other emotional patterns. The therapist's "activity" and ability to communicate observations and her own emotional experiences are especially valuable in the wake of repeated enactments with the therapist and with others.

With its built-in goal of identifying and improving unconscious emotional self-systems and defensive patterns that prolong a painful existence rather than alleviate it, the therapeutic process offers a unique place in which such patterns can be fully seen and understood. This goal is entirely within reach, especially in the context of a trusting and accepting therapeutic relationship. Therapeutic interactions embedded in empathy and lack of judgment may enable patients to internalize and reflect on the therapist's attempts at helping them confront the unknowables. The patient's recognition of the stubbornness brain/mind processes can greatly contribute to a judgment-free understanding as to why feelings, thoughts, and behaviors persist. Only on recognizing and becoming aware of the nature of our emotional and behavioral neural patterns, the childhood necessity for an array of defenses, the emotional and interpersonal learning that took place unconsciously and without our conscious will or participation, our helplessness as children to affect the course of events, can we start and attempt to connect with painful self-systems.

Resistance and repetition affect both therapeutic participants. Therapists may get to feel frustrated and incompetent, while patients may become hopeless and discouraged at the pace of change. Digging deeper into the characteristics of nonconscious processes offers a clearer picture of what underlies the tenacity of resistance and the difficulties involved in psychic and behavioral change. In actuality, the insights gained from neuroscience research makes clear that any shift in our mental functioning is even more difficult to achieve than we would like to believe. The motivation to hold on is not directed by conscious or unconscious needs for stability, fears of the unknown, or fear of not feeling comfortable in a new skin. Rather, these tendencies are determined by the way that the brain/mind works and by the enacted tenaciousness of unconscious self-systems. As was already mentioned, the process of learning and change are totally intertwined with the creation as well as the process of extinction of neural pathways (Kandel, 1999, 2001; LeDoux and Doyere, 2011; LeDoux and Schiller, 2009; among many others). Accordingly, we cannot view the motivation to enact what is familiar as a choice; in actuality it is guided by nonconscious processes that control one's ability to shift between an automatic response system and a more flexible response structure that affords openness to new learning and reflectiveness. The following sections and therapeutic process explore in some detail the neuropsychological forces that underlie the propensity for enacted repetition.

THE INEVITABILITY OF REPETITION

One of the central brain/mind characteristics that can account for the power of resistance is its built-in preference for repeating what has already been learned and reinforced. As was previously illustrated,

• stimulus-control - based reflexes
• higher order (slower, more reflective) reactions

powerful and rigid self-systems are surprisingly successful at choreo-
graphing emotional environments and interpersonal dynamics that
closely resemble and enact the internal expectations and predictions
comprising one's unconscious self-system. Theoretically we seem to
acknowledge this tendency, but still do not fully appreciate its innate
nonconscious and ongoing control of all perceptions and behaviors. As
Koziol and Budding (2010) suggest, all behavioral processing can be
categorized as either stimulus control–based reflexes or a higher-order
responses that involve slower, more reflective reactions. It is important to remember that these brain/mind processes are not only simple
reflexes that only involve motor skills we perform without thinking—
the examples we usually think of are riding a bike, driving, or playing tennis. In effect, our stimulus-based reflexes include all forms of
reinforced learning, from reactions embodying unregulated raw affects
to sophisticated, subtle defenses. Such innate learning occurs automatically and out of awareness, and its function is to safeguard physical and
psychic survival.

Obviously, the concept of evolutionary survival needs to significantly
expand to include the need for emotional survival and the sense of
personal comfort and well-being. Such needs are especially invoked
within the intersubjective sphere, where attunement and empathy (or
lack thereof) give rise to many learned reactions and defenses. As the
internal thermostat of adaptation is always at work, seeking to restore
homeostasis and a sense of control, the responses that best achieve the
goal of restoring the sense of well-being (even if illusory) will be maintained. Styles of affect regulation, for example, relational and attachment styles as well as cognitive defenses marshaled to defend one's
self-worth, are the result of what seemed to work for adaptation. In a
predictable environment, such emotional and behavioral styles acquire
fast and automatic qualities, especially in their unreflected response to
familiar environments.

As a quick resolution to emotional distress, a child's stimulus-based
control of behavior has clear advantages for adapting to a predictable
environment by affording reactions that are already tested and known
to work (Toates, 2006). But it also has obvious disadvantages, ingrain-
ing whole patterns of behaviors with little opportunity for reexamina-
tion or spontaneity: a stimulus will evoke the same reaction each time.
Even in ambiguous or new conditions, if there is any remnant of the
familiar stimulus, the same responses will ensue. Furthermore, the
entrenched connections will seek the stimulus even when it is not fully
there (Toates, 2006). When confronting new situations that may require
different behavioral patterns, if the entrenched unconscious system is
inflexible, it will seek to fold new situations and stimuli into the old.

NOTHING TO SAY: THE CASE OF AMY

A case example here can provide a good illustration of what we might call a stubborn resistance to continue old patterns. Amy, a professional woman in her early forties, came to therapy to "save" her year-old relationship. In effect, she came at the request of her boyfriend, a therapist, who had insisted on her starting therapy. As their relationship grew, she said, her boyfriend became increasingly upset every time Amy caved in to him during a disagreement or a discussion that might lead to an argument. At those moments she quickly withdrew both physically and mentally, became very quiet, and seemed to be entirely engrossed in her internal world. When challenged by her boyfriend as to what she was feeling or thinking, she insisted that she "had nothing to say." What particularly upset the boyfriend was the fact that in spite of all his assurances that it was okay to argue, that he would never hold it against her, she was still withdrawing and shutting him out. Being in the therapeutic world, he understood that her behavior was not simply directed at him, but he said he felt cheated out of a more equal partner.

Amy's tendency to retreat into an uncomfortable silence was also enacted in our interactions. As we both learned, she withdrew when she felt the pressure to actively contribute to a conversation. For a while, I could not relinquish my expectations for her participation, but the more I nonverbally demanded that of her, the more she retreated. At the slightest discomfort, for example, when the conversation focused on her mother, she would say that she had "nothing interesting to say." Frequently, sessions felt awkward and disjointed, and the silence was sad and helpless.

Although at times I felt impatient with Amy's silences and her retreat into her inner world, I could also feel her acute and all-consuming discomfort when trying to put things into words. But when entirely "forgetting" her history or her unconsciously guided withdrawal, I experienced her as being willfully resistant and oppositional, not making an effort to transcend her difficulties. At times I thought that her silence was calculated to punish those who wanted something from her, thereby getting back at her mother, who needed Amy to be an adult before she was ready to be. Occasionally I took her silence personally, feeling helpless to affect any change in her behavior. During particularly difficult patches in our interaction, I tried to explicate some of these thoughts, and Amy usually agreed with me. Inquiring about what she had thought between sessions, she said that nothing from the sessions stayed with her. These thoughts about Amy's willful resistance surfaced in me especially when she would report lively conversations at work, but persistent difficulties with her boyfriend and with me. At the same time, I had to remind myself that Amy's unconscious self-system had to be enacted in her close relationships, where the most significant triggers reside.

As therapy progressed, however, and she was increasingly able to express herself, Amy's withdrawing reactions became understood as a repetitive lifelong pattern that developed in response to her emotionally difficult childhood. In her descriptions, her mother was "a real powerhouse." Both at her job and in the home she was the moving force "responsible for everything." She felt a mixture of love, pity, and empathy for her mother; not only did her mother take care of Amy and her brother, she had to take care of their father. After some years of emotional and behavioral problems, inexplicable outbursts, and wasteful spending, he was diagnosed as bipolar. Tearfully Amy remembered her mother's exasperation at her husband's erratic behavior: his lack of control over money and his emotions, his inability to keep to a schedule, and his inattentive behavior toward their children.

For as long as Amy could remember, she had tried to be the good girl and not burden her already overworked and visibly unhappy mother. When the mother would become enraged at the father, at times taking it out on the children as well, Amy understood her misery and "forgave her." When an inevitable conflict came up pitting her wishes against the mother's hurried needs, she quickly gave up and each time consciously resolved to avoid getting into any conflict with her mother. When it happened again, invariably when she needed something and her mother was busy or inattentive, she felt it as her own failure for not dealing with things herself. She became very adept at reading her mother's affective states, knowing when to offer help and when to be quiet so as not to upset her any further. In her experience, her mother truly "could not handle any more bad stuff, any more trouble. Her constantly cleaning up after my father was more than enough. What bad luck she had with him . . . he made her so miserable, he did not mean to, but he did."

From early on, within a self-system trained on her mother's emotions and actions, the boundaries between her own actions and those of her mother became totally blurred, leaving Amy to experience herself as the injuring party in any conflict even when her mother's emotional outbursts had nothing to do with her. She was not aware of the sad fact that as much as she tried to take the burden from her mother, her frazzled mother did not have much time or patience for her. She made sure Amy and her brother were well-fed and did well in school, but she paid little attention to who they really were. In effect, at times she sensed that her mother's unhappiness also extended to having the burden of her and her brother, and though nothing was ever verbalized, Amy still wondered about it.

Amy's room became her refuge from her parents' frequent fights; read-

ing and a strong fantasy life—imagining different scenarios of happier
family life—provided some comfort. Above all, hiding her own needs,
keeping to herself, and avoiding conflict so as not to injure the other
became second nature to her. As a teenager, the tendency to withdraw
into her own world became intertwined with a growing conviction that
she "had nothing interesting to say," and that others were more interesting than she. Amy did have a few good friends, but she felt safest in the
comfort of her room, especially in the context of a looming conflict with
any of them. If she felt flashes of anger, she kept it to herself.

What developed was an unconscious impulse to avoid conflict, remain
invisible, and hide her internal life when an interaction became stressful
and demanded her full participation. Unconsciously, her own subjectivity and her point of view, her needs, or disagreements seldom became
part of her conscious sense of self and the intersubjective field. She was
aware of her discomfort and fears, she was aware of how hard it was
for her to express her own side in a disagreement or a fight. Amy was
entirely unconscious, however, of the enacted surrender to the other's
subjectivity. She was equally unaware of her automatic retreat from the
interaction deep into her own fantasies. These enacted reactions were
accompanied by the more conscious narrative saying that what she had
to offer was not important, that she had nothing to say.

Prior to her current relationship, Amy was married for 10 years to a
man as quiet and withdrawn as she is. After the birth of their only son,
they settled into an amicable relationship that did not require much in
the way of interaction, and the growing distance between them finally
ended the marriage. Amy realized that the marriage essentially accom-
modated that part of her that wished to stay away from conflict and
strife. Her current boyfriend, however, did not accommodate that system; he valued her company and wanted her full participation as an
equal partner. Finally, she had to come face to face with her unconscious system and the painful limitation it imposed on her emotional
and interpersonal life. Until her painful memories of having to—or in
her words, "choosing to"—give herself up to her mother's well-being
were reflected on and understood, her unconscious way of being could
only be enacted. Indeed, the more aware she became of her internal
state of discomfort, and the more she expressed herself with her boyfriend and me, the more she felt alive within both relationships.

LEARNED BEHAVIORS, RESISTANCE, AND
THE FLEXIBILITY RIGIDITY CONTINUUM

From the very beginning, all movement and sensory-motor developments are learned and organized within the brain in patterns that

allow easy interaction with the environment. The same is true for complex self-systems that internalize and integrate affective, cognitive, and
behavioral patterns. These more complicated systems are understood by
Koziol and Budding (2010) as extensions of the motor control system.
Consequently, complex brain processes unconsciously support thinking,
feelings, and reacting to stimuli, internal and interpersonal (Churchland,
2013). These well-known processes emphasize some of the points made
throughout the book; it's not that as clinicians we are not aware of
procedural learning or implicit memory systems. But when it comes to
understanding patients' difficulties and struggle with change, we tend
not take these brain/mind nonconscious processes into account.

The core of an automatic response system is made of procedural
learning and consolidated memories that involve connections between
subcortical and higher cortical regions. Theoretically and clinically, however, we do not usually consider the inevitability of learning systems and
procedural habits, which are essential for adaptation, and their effects
on automatic repetition. Procedural learning is so important, according
to Koziol and Budding (2010) that the brain/mind has two systems dedicated to it: the corticostriatal, which mediates the acquisition of habits,
and the corticocerebellar, which mediates responses to a changing environment. All self-systems require the combination of these two systems.

Because these processes involve not just simple adaptation routines,
the implications are significant. Consider, for example, defensive reactions
mobilized in response to predictable and repeated hurtful interactions. To
sustain a minimal level of emotional well-being or regain some internal
order in an emotionally chaotic turbulence, a child will employ bodily,
emotional, and cognitive defensive maneuvers to fend off such external
or internal stressors. In the realm of social procedural learning, Lieberman (2003) proposes two brain systems linked to automatic behavior: the
reflexive and the reflective ones. The reflexive system is activated under
conditions that generate nonconscious, implicit, or automatic processing
of social information. Framing social adaptation within this context is
offered by diverse neuropsychological approaches. Automatic social skills
include noticing or intuitively "reading" the emotions of others, responding with unconscious empathy, nonconsciously communicating with
others, and fully engaging with them in a personally meaningful way,
both negative and positive. These social procedures are executed nonconsciously, without higher-order mediation (Gallese, 2007; Iacoboni, 2008;
Koziol and Budding, 2010; Lieberman, 2003; Schore, 2012).

As has been emphasized when discussing development, the amalgam
of learned behaviors include the parental internalized patterns as well
as parental coping strategies. Whether learned patterns are subtle and
imperceptible, such as avoidant reactions that are embedded in one's
emotional and behavioral system, or more bold and noticeable, such as

reflexive and reflective ✓

self-protective aggrandizing narratives, the child and then the adult has no choice but to repeat what works best. Internalized parental traits also become a part of any unconscious system, and as such are also enacted without awareness. What makes this automatic response tendency so effective is that the behaviors involved are reinforced by their very action (Koziol and Budding, 2010).

The wider implications of these conclusions add to our understanding of why we repeat behaviors even when they are not even effective at reducing stress or anxiety and even when they cause more upheaval in our emotional and relational lives. If what reinforces behavior is just its repeated implementation in response to situations, to real and perceived threats, whether or not a particular behavior achieves the desired effects may be secondary. It is interesting to speculate on the consequences resulting from the desperation to regain an internal sense of well-being. Under certain situations, in the face of emotional injury, even reactions that provide only a momentary illusion of relief are learned and reinforced. Behaviors may resist tinkering or new direction even if they are not actually helpful in their current form. Such links between stimulus and behaviors, self-tripping as they may be, are remembered and reinforced by their activation each time. Such recurrent activation may not allow for new ways of adaptation.

This out-of-awareness learning process seems to be a major source of the difficulties patients experience in spite of repeated insights. As long as the higher-order adaptive system does not kick into gear to derail the automatic response tendency, new perceptions, feelings, and behaviors cannot be established. Since the stimulus-behavior system is literally out of our conscious control, and automatically reacts to familiar stimuli (real or imagined) in the same known way, it is important to place it in a more adaptable and aware realm. Some of the following chapters discuss some therapeutic modalities that can help introduce reflectiveness and therefore flexibility into one's stimulus-behavior system.

Procedural and automatic behaviors include whole patterns of organized emotional and cognitive reactions that become encoded, thereby accomplishing the important evolutionary task of psychological survival efficiently and without thinking (Koziol and Budding, 2010). With each repetition emotional, cognitive, and behavioral patterns become more automatic and therefore efficient. Similarly, as a result of being immersed in one's parents' emotional world and unconsciously imitating their typical ways of being emotionally and interpersonally, learned behaviors and emotional styles also become part of an unconscious amalgam (Braten, 2007; Olds, 2006, 2012; Seligman, 2009).

When both the reflexive and reflective systems operate in tandem, alternating adaptively, they will lead to greater flexibility and the ability to change perceptions, interpretations, and behaviors. The rigidity–

flexibility continuum seems to be an important aspect contributing to one's readiness to undergo neuropsychological change. One must still ask why some patients, for example, are more flexible than others. Why is it that much harder for some patients to adopt more adaptive modes of behaviors, enhance their ability to regulate difficult affects, and be more open to mutuality in relationship? Finally, why is it so difficult for some self-systems, especially the negative ones, to learn from "reality," to change one's assessment of oneself according to a positive track record, for example?

An important aspect of one's level of flexibility is the ease of the oscillation between the two response systems: the one based entirely on a subcortical stimulus-response mode and the higher-order response system, which promotes fresh assessments and reactions to new situations. Successful behaviors and adaptations are based on efficiently alternating between the two modes of response processing (Ito, 2008; Koziol and Budding, 2010). To function well, we need to combine both tendencies at any given moment. Less adaptive behaviors are the ones that don't change at all, that only rely on the model that rigidly predicts and enacts behaviors without being corrected by the cerebellum. Such behavioral patterns—from the simplest to the most complex and nuanced—become automatic and do not require conscious control or thoughtful "supervision" any longer (Ito, 2008). In this case we rely on the cerebellum and the basal ganglia's experience with that particular behavioral pattern, leading to a process that is independent of conscious mediation. The unconscious reciprocal loop between the stimulus and the reaction feels as intuitive as the act of walking. We simply do not give it any thought.

BALANCE AND IMBALANCE: THE SHIFTING RELATIONSHIP BETWEEN CORTICAL AND SUBCORTICAL AREAS

To better understand the cause of rigid behaviors that repeat themselves without reflective awareness, we need to recall the important integration between cortical and subcortical areas. As was already mentioned, Koziol and Budding (2010) conclude that as in the case of the enactment of movement, affect and cognition are also affected by the coordination between three systems that need to operate in tandem: the cerebellum, the basal ganglia, and the prefrontal cortex. Higher functions in the cortical areas actually find expressions through the subcortical regions and are dependent on them for efficient functioning (Ito, 2008).

With an imbalance in the process of cooperation, behaviors can become rigidified, entirely under the control of the automatic system, without the modulating effects of either the correcting cerebellum or the conscious PFC. In this case, even reflective awareness is not enough to modulate

the automaticity of an emotional or behavioral pattern, or offer the comfort of affect regulation (Koziol and Budding, 2010). Within a very rigid
system, reflection may be easily recruited by existing affects, narratives,
and behavioral patterns, thus failing to provide fresh or reality-bound
emotional and cognitive perspective. As we often see in the therapeutic
process, such difficulties in developing an observing self-state are quite
common among patients with rigid systems. Although we may conclude
that these patients are resistant to change or to the therapist's interpretations, we need to be reminded that such "holding on" to habitual ways
of being is really the result of the unique balance each person possesses
between subcortical maps and more conscious functioning. The nature of
this balance will be further determined by the pace of actual neural shifts
and changes to existing pathways and networks (Koziol, 2014; Koziol and
Budding, 2010; LeDoux and Schiller, 2009; Siegel, 1999, 2007).

What is significant about this complex balance between the rigid and
the flexible (and everything in between) is that we are entirely unaware
of the extent of its influence on our response tendencies, on our ways
of treating ourselves and others, on how an entrenched narrative or
interpersonal expectation creeps up into our consciousness, unbidden.
In this context, an unconscious system is enacted out of awareness,
responding fast to an activating emotion or an intersubjective communication. Whereas we may be aware of the discomfort they create, we are
not aware of what generated our response, what nonconscious communication made us feel unconsciously vulnerable or injured.

To start with, unconscious systems, as we have seen, tend to be
enacted, thus revealing some of their hidden dynamics. But the fact that
a self-system is unconscious does not mean that it will necessarily be
repeated mindlessly. When a nonconscious pattern is activated, reflective
awareness—either directed by the correcting power of the cerebellum
or earned through practice—curbs repetition and resistance. This process can become greatly compromised when a behavior is emotionally
driven to rigid defensive responses, as we just saw in the case of Amy.
In rigid configuration where perception and response are determined by
past experiences alone, an encounter with a fear-arousing situation, for
example, will be tightly linked to a distorted but involuntary evaluation
of the potential danger. In response, a rigid self-system would reenact
behaviors that in the past provided relief from intense negative feelings.
Without being "corrected" or refined by the loop between the cortical
and subcortical regions these defensive behaviors may lead to maladaptive repetitions. Here again, it is important to remember that such rigid
patterns run the gamut from reflexive responses to very specific objects
or situations, such as phobias, to very complex interpersonal patterns
that repeat themselves without awareness.

It is important to reiterate that optimally, the higher-function responses, the ones that can "learn from reality," are also under the sway of unconscious processes. Good, intuitive judgment and adaptation often occur without any deliberate thinking. To guarantee a strengthened ability to process emotions and provide one with an adaptive perspective, however, the therapist can help the patient to recruit reflective awareness of one's dyregulating emotions, fantasies, and narratives. As often witnessed during the therapeutic process, although effortful to start with, such reflective processing can become automatic and second nature as well.

Significantly, the balance that determines how rigid and how resistant to change our unconscious maps are should be considered an important aspect of the nonconscious realm. Often, becoming aware of how the various parts of our mind work together—how we automatically resort to defensive and self-protective behaviors, how we do not learn from our current situation and still cling to old patterns, how susceptible we are to negative affective states and their attack on our sense of self—is the most important part of making the unconscious conscious. As patients learn in the course of therapy, in the face of a distressing hyperaroused emotional state, some of the defensive behaviors they automatically employ in response are the ones that have become hijacked by a rigid system. Since higher-level functions of the cortex are also linked to deeper regions, these cortical-subcortical interactions are critical to our ability to modulate the levels of automaticity according to a particular situation. When these structures are well coordinated, they guide behaviors that are adaptive in the service of reducing stress and psychological pain and in promoting emotional and behavioral patterns that are in the best interest of the individual and his goals (Panksepp and Biven, 2012). If the influence of executive functions is greatly compromised, automatic behaviors that no longer work for the overall well-being of the individual take the lead and underpin repetitive self-states that feel entirely justified and natural even though they might be highly unadaptive. In other words, no new learning can take place.

Avoidance, for example, seems to be an innate part of functioning. We may even think about it as a symptom. In actuality, however, avoidance expresses an entirely nonconscious and instinctive behavioral pattern that in its tenacity as a very early defense seems to have a life of its own. What makes this particular pattern so resistant to change is the lack of awareness that usually accompanies it. Avoidance is just enacted, not questioned or challenged. Often, even when it is suggested to patients that they reflect on the session or on their avoidant reactions in between sessions, they later report a total lack of recall of the assignment. Their behavior and mental preoccupation portray a seamless maintenance of old ways of being that at the moment of execution (passivity, avoidance) seem the only possible option. This is not a volitional process, as no thought goes into it in real time.

THE TIP OF THE CONSCIOUS-UNCONSCIOUS CONTINUUM: DISSOCIATION

At times, patients who have difficulties implementing change are viewed as being under the influence of dissociative defenses that prevent them from being connected to that part of themselves that wishes to change. Dissociative processes are assumed to be used in the service of protecting one's sense of psychic integrity, especially in the case severe trauma. This is thought to be carried out by pushing painful or intolerable experiences out of awareness, placing (or more accurately, locking) them within an unconscious self-state (Bromberg, 2006; D. B. Stern, 2010). Noticeably, the notion of defensive dissociation has replaced the more traditional concept of repression. Although taking for granted that such a process essentially gets rid of unwanted memories or experiences, the notion of dissociation is still far from clearly understood.

As we recall, neuroscientists have maintained that as far as protective measures are concerned, there is no one single agency or function that unconsciously guides what is to be put out of awareness (Churchland, 2013; Damasio, 2010; Hassin et al., 2007; Koziol and Budding, 2010; Ramachandran, 2011). The question, then, is how is such a decision made? Why do some experiences remain conscious and others do not? Lastly, is the process in any way volitional, unconscious, or some combination of both? These questions are especially intriguing in light of studies showing that it possible for subjects to consciously suppress information, resulting in a compromised recall of it (Andersen et al., 2007). It is possible, as Fernyhough (2013) suggests, that dissociation is a more volitional process, and that what we consider to have been dissociated or unconscious in essence has been there in consciousness, but not really thought about.

However, if we consider dissociative processes as part of the balancing act among the interacting cortical and subcortical regions, we can look at it as another manifestation of a rigid way of being. While out of awareness, the automaticity of self-systems renders enacted behavioral patterns mindless and repetitive, coloring the conscious self-states they underlie with a similar sense of automaticity and lack of awareness. From a functional point of view, dissociative states can be considered more procedural and repetitious than protective. The lack of awareness embodied by a dissociated state makes it more resistant to conscious examination and naturally to change (Dell, 2009; Steele et al.,

2009). When the imbalance among the various brain/mind processes precludes awareness or flexibility of perception and behavior or an adaptive coordination between conscious and unconscious a state of dissociation exists. Similarly, in the presence of a flexible correction to how we perceive a situation, how we feel and act in response to it, and most important how connected we are to our internal state at the time, there is a good coordination between the different realms. What gets dissociated these times is the chance for the coexistence of multiple self-systems, the possibility of different self-states, and therefore the potential for an open and fresh approach to new situations (Bromberg, 1998, 2006, 2011; Bucci, 2007a, 2007b). A dissociative state is in essence too successful at separating a particular self-state from more adaptable ones. Drowning in an emotional state and in the narratives that accompany it, for example, experiencing no other reminders or possibilities, can be considered a dissociative state. The dissociation is not of content put away necessarily, but is more about a lack of awareness about other states and external information (Bromberg, 1998, 2006).

In another aspect of dissociation, when the natural ability to experience oneself—one's emotions, needs, and thoughts within a current moment and owning them as emanating from one's own subjectivity—is compromised, dissociation is also at work (Bromberg, 2006). What is dissociated in this case is the opportunity for open and nondefensive emotional and cognitive approach to our internal life, free of parental voices or old recriminations.

Ideally this flexibility and the ability to experience the moment in an adaptive way and not only according to rigid patterns is helped by a healthy coordination between cortical and subcortical regions, with the latter providing the appropriate regulation and guidance. In the absence of such facility between these systems, enhancing the reflective ability can be helpful in reestablishing adaptive responses. Starting with effortful attempts, mindfulness and emotional awareness can modulate rigid response patterns and help regulate emotions that feel too overwhelming. One of the goals in psychotherapy will be to establish such mindful abilities to regulate one's emotions and behaviors.

We can view dissociation, then, not necessarily in term of content but as a dynamic continuum relegating specific self-systems to rigid and automatic repetitions that do not take into account the characteristics of a wide range of intra- as well as interpersonal conditions. A dissociated capacity for reflectiveness at such repetitions magnifies the potential damage that they incur. Without the participation of the PFC and its ability to reflect and plan, subcortical maps take over, executing their behavioral patterns automatically and routinely, without coordinating them with the cortex. In other words, the interplay between automaticity and openness, between routine and novelty, between safe and familiar and risk-taking behavior is broken. As rigid states gain supremacy in one's functioning, other systems that could infuse one's more conscious self-states with emotional knowledge of other possibilities, and thus promote overall integration and well-being, do not have access to expressing themselves.

As we have seen, embedded in the cortical-subcortical loop are the processes that determine how flexible and how relatively free of automaticity we are. This interconnected unified system also fashions the level of dissociation, as well as the compulsion to repeat old patterns and resist changing them. The next section discusses one of the important determinants behind the repetition of rigid old patterns.

THE ROLE OF DOPAMINE

The answer to the question of why people persist in doing things that bring negative outcomes seems to be intertwined with the dopamine reward system that governs the corticostriatal learning loop. Together with the PFC, the basal ganglia function as a reinforcement of learning systems, contain the highest dopamine concentration, and construes critical reward circuitries (Koziol and Budding, 2010). Dips in dopaminergic activity result in negative reinforcement and avoidance; a surge, of dopamine in reinforced behaviors. External positive feedback or positive interactions with the environment result in spikes of activity above baseline level and positive learning. Conversely, negative feedback or negative experiences are associated with a decrease below baseline levels and cause a decline in dopamine (Niv, 2007). Dips in dopamine encourage the avoidance of painful choices or behaviors that are perceived as leading to increased anxiety and discomfort. This occurrence explains much of Ron's unconscious repetitions of passive behaviors in the context of an authority figure (see Chapter 2).

It seems then that what we often deem as resistance to therapeutic change are neurally based difficulties that patients display in "taking in" and implementing new ways of being. Patients' initial tendency to dissociate from the therapeutic process itself is in actuality a function of brain/mind processes. In particular, avoidant behavior is hard to change. We might say that the behavior has become such a part of an instinctive, automatic response system that it just "occurs." We just find ourselves not doing something, postponing activities without even realizing it.

Often, when patients demonstrate "resistance" to change, they really give expression to the level of coordination between conscious and nonconscious processes. It's not that they are somehow motivated to resist change; they are not aware of their rigid pull toward the enactment of primarily established unconscious systems. This continuum of rigidity phenomenon finds manifestation in our enacted communications and behaviors, internal as well as interpersonal. This fact leads us to consider the unconscious as a global influence on all behaviors. Enactments so prevalent in psychotherapy are actually only a more dramatic illustration of this fact.

THE POWER OF UNCONSCIOUS CONVICTIONS AND RESISTANCE TO CHANGE: THE CASE OF JULIE

Julie's case illustrates a struggle through an unconscious persistence to repeat a self-system enacting intersubjective experiences suffused with painful affects and self-denigrating narratives. The seemingly stubborn and prolonged repetition of her internal convictions is not seen as an unconscious need to preserve early attachments, but as resulting from a complex self-system that developed in response to particular emotional stressors. In understanding such a system, internalized representations, learning experiences, and coalesced memories naturally maintain a connection to the past, but this connection is not volitional and does not continue out of need. With time, such a system is enacted as part of the brain/mind organization (Lewis and Todd, 2007).

Julie, a 36-year-old woman, sought therapy due to recurrent feelings of insecurity and confusion accompanying her relationship. She desperately wished to get married and start a family, while her boyfriend of two years, Jon, kept avoiding any decision about a long-term commitment. His reluctance to commit seemed to be a part of a larger pattern of confusing messages—promises and declarations of love interspersed with dismissing criticism and doubts about the relationship. Julie repeatedly said she loved Jon, and when describing their fights, she glossed over and even justified his behavior.

At this point, Julie's sense of herself was almost entirely tied to the ebb and flow of her relationship with Jon. She had a successful career, but felt content and secure only when her relationship went well. When they were fighting, or when she felt criticized, she would drown in a miserable self-state, with self-narratives constantly "reminding" her how worthless she was, not worthy of being loved or taken care of. She did not question his vicious attacks on many aspects of her personality, nor did she wonder how it was that at times of dysregulation all good feelings and reality-bound achievements disappeared.

The picture that emerged of Julie's mother was one of a career woman, who sometimes appeared to be cold, uncaring, critical, and belittling. She would often discourage her daughter from feeling good about herself, directly saying things like "don't hope for too much. You know that things won't turn up well for you." "Don't think you are that smart . . . don't think too much of yourself." When Julie expressed some need or asked for something that might be out of the way, her mother often saw her as selfish and demanding. As a matter of fact, *selfish* and *inconsiderate* were the most often expressed words about her daughters (Julie had a sister three years younger).

Throughout childhood and beyond, Julie couldn't talk to her mother about any of her experiences in school or with friends, dreading her mother's critical assessment of her, belittling her feelings. Her father was often away for business, for days at a time, and although he was warmer and more affectionate than her mother, each time he returned she felt she "did not get enough of him." She longed to be closer to her father— when he was home she would feel more secure and content—but came to accept his absences as another inevitable painful event in her life.

In a recurrent childhood dream, Julie's parents would tell her that they could no longer support her and keep her at home (her younger sibling was exempt), and as a result she had to find another place to live. She would wake up feeling great panic and unspeakable despair. During the day she would "forget" the dream, but began dreading falling asleep.

As therapy began, Julie's growing emotional connections with her painful memories intensified her sense of helplessness and despair. During difficult sessions, when the meaning of her difficulties was discussed, the intensity of her negative feelings about herself and her persistent dismissal of Jon's hurtful provocations was palpable. Listening to her, I often experienced her as resistant, as someone totally "committed" to her past experiences. Although intellectually I knew that Julie had no choice but to enact rigid self-systems until something in them shifted, I still wished for her to feel better, to move forward. "Why can't she realize that she is an attractive, smart woman who can find a man who truly loves her?" I sometimes asked myself silently. Julie's repeated need to defend Jon at her own expense lasted for months, as did her shifting moods. If he was happy, so was she, and vice versa. Later we understood this automatic defense of Jon and her dependence on his emotional tenor as a repetition of her adaptation at home to her parents' behaviors and moods. Only later did she realize that in actuality she had no choice but to adopt her parents' behaviors and moods, and especially her mother's "opinion" of her, and see them entirely as her own, as emanating from her rather than from them.

My physical and emotional exhaustion resulting from Julie's negativity was interrupted by her following dream, in which the family visits a vacation resort, and she and her mother go to the playground there. But as they get ready to use the swings in the empty space, she realizes that her mother starts walking away, leaving the playground. Julie runs after her, calling her to come back, but her mother seems determined to get away from her and does not turn back.

While describing the dream and connecting to its emotional meaning, Julie expressed visible emotions and tears. The depth of her internalized view of herself as one destined to be abandoned came to the forefront and collided with her relationship reality. Indeed, just a few weeks prior, Jon ended the relationship. Although devastated, at this time Julie was more ready to confront her unconscious fantasies as the one destined to be unloved. She began to understand that her severe grief was not just about Jon's betrayal—part of her was not surprised—but mainly about her emotionally bereft childhood.

She realized that her love for Jon was complicated. Waiting for him to change, to love her as much as she loved him, enacted childhood daydreaming focusing on profound sadness, feeling rejected by her mother, and missing her busy father. These inward preoccupations and ruminations became part of the process of unconsciously constructing her self-systems, the many associations attached to them, and the repeated enactments that gave them voice. Real experiences grew and intensified, becoming encoded and reinforced. Remember here the role of the default network, which while the brain is at rest, mediates imagination, ruminations, cognitive interpretations, and thoughts about the future (Raichle et al., 2001). This process further encodes the painful experiences and weaves them into a developing self-system.

Julie's road was still characterized by the stubborn rigidity of her unconscious system, which occasionally overtook her whole experiential space. Nearly two years into the therapy, she seemed to oscillate between some hope that things could be different and her old negative expectations. She even decided to try online dating. This decision triggered a new bout of self-doubts and shameful feelings. If she "winked" at somebody and he didn't respond, she felt rejected. After a few attempts to connect with people, she practically gave up. She was still a member but her lack of actions betrayed a great deal of anxious passivity.

The most recurrent sentence during this phase was "what is the point?," followed by an elaborate justification to why nothing will change and how helpless she actually was to make something different happen. This consuming sense that nothing can change, that what the self feels is the only experience available, explains why such systems are rarely challenged, why they are so convincing to the patient, and why a patient often seems resistant to change, even in the midst of the working through phase of therapy. For Julie, the feelings of not deserving love, of being so wronged, and the belief that nothing could change seemed to be who she truly was. In spite of her conscious decision to take care of herself, especially in regard to dating, as soon as she had left the office, as she later reported, she "just forgot" what we had talked about and totally avoided the dating site.

As therapy continued, we understood Julie's complaints and her convictions about being doomed as enacted expressions of much deeper painful experiences—the early emotional deprivation that could not find a voice. They were created too early to remember and later were deliberately defended against and pushed away from consciousness because of her need to defend her parents.

At this point in time, Julie described another dream: "In the dream," she said, "there is a little girl, may be six years old. I realize that she is tired and groggy, that she doesn't know what's going on. For some reason she has to climb up a hill in the distance. She's walking with difficulty, but she knows that she has to do it, that she has no choice. She is dressed in old and tattered clothes; her shoes are torn with holes, like a homeless child. She is alone, exhausted and walking, too tired to call out for help. When she tries to yell for help, no voice comes out. But she has to keep walking, with nobody helping her." Julie woke up crying, her heart broken with sadness for the little girl.

After a few minutes she continued: "This is what I have been carrying with me, that feeling of being alone, not understanding what they wanted from me, why was nobody helping me . . . taking care of me . . . I bring this struggle with me everywhere."

It took about three years to get to this point in the treatment, and increasingly, Julie came to recognize, identify, and examine much of what plagued her during her adult life, especially in her relationships. What was so resistant to change was in effect an unconscious system that automatically guided complex patterns of emotions, thoughts, and behaviors.

How can we understand Julie's insistent choice of her very compromised life with Jon? How to explain her tolerance of enormous ambivalence, criticalness, and belittling behaviors? How could an intelligent woman who was simultaneously aware of Jon's reluctance to marry her and her own desire to get married not fully get what was going on? As the preceding discussion indicates, her cumulative traumatic experiences with her parents, especially her mother, coalesced into enduring implicit systems that although unconscious in terms of what they contained, nonetheless continually found an enacted voice in her life.

It's not that Julie was completely unaware of how problematic her relationship with Jon was and how unhappy she was in reaction to his behaviors. She knew she was mistreated; she was unaware of the amalgam of implicit memories, emotional lessons, underlying expectations and beliefs, as well as and behavioral tendencies that underpinned her complex love life. She realized that something was preventing her from meeting new men who might be better for her. Self-reflection was limited to ruminations about her conscious needs, disappointments, and her "lack of luck in life." During dysregulated affective states, she obviously would be aware of her very negative and denigrating self-narratives, but being entirely unaware as to their meaning, the negative self-state would take over and become the one possible experience.

As with all our stubbornly rigid self-systems, it was her entrenched pattern that was greatly resistant to change, and not the conscious or unconscious wishes to reenact her suffering or a simple "attachment" to misery. Like many patients, she had to struggle with a system that, because of its rigid subcortical networks and a compromised activity in the PFC, could not easily integrate novel experiences into existing maps. Furthermore, as we saw, when a rigid system evaluates and predicts reality according to what is internally but unconsciously anticipated, such powerful expectations are sought after and recreated. Julie was attracted to difficult relationships in which she lived out that old relational map of yearning and disappointment. Such a map made it difficult for her to seek new experiences; the self-system that yearned for love and acceptance was not developed or strong enough to get its wishes.

At this point, Julie was ready to carry her increasing reflective awareness and growing affect regulation outside of treatment and use them in real time. She did this when she felt despair at not being loved, self-denigrating about the hopelessness of it all, enraged at her fate. She was encouraged to engage her reflective abilities while experiencing dysregulation and become aware of and tolerate her emotions for what they were, echoes of the past. Her developed sense of herself as an agency, as an individual no longer living under her mother's emotional rules, freed her to gain an authentic connection to her own needs and goals. With time, her mother's voice became weaker and weaker, whereas Julie's empathy toward her own subjectivity grew. She could now embrace the suffering girl and treat her well.

loving kindness to self.

just "thoughts"
just "emotion".

CHAPTER 7

Injury, Defense, and Narcissistic Personality Structure

O F THE RANGE OF EMOTIONAL and personal difficulties we typically see in the therapy office, narcissistic personality disorders
seem to embody much of what this book describes. In a clear way,
narcissistic patients often exemplify the intricate behavioral patterns
we all develop in our attempts to cope with psychic pain. When crush-
ing and intolerable feelings of shame, humiliation, and self-blame over-
whelm a toddler, a young child (Braten, 2007; Braten and Trevarthen,
2007; Schore, 2012), or an adolescent (Grawe, 2007), innate defensive
processes automatically and unconsciously struggle to compensate and
restore a sense of well-being. The emotional injury, on the one hand,
and the various defenses employed against it, on the other, result in
unconscious self-systems that embody both experiences, often through
self-states entirely disconnected from each other. These maps (Damasio, 2010), including their accumulated implicit learning and associations, are activated in different contexts, giving rise to the complex
narcissistic symptomatology.

Most often, the emotions that make up the painful tangle of injury
are implicit, and only when enacted do they reveal some of the intensity embedded in them. What is communicated is a self-state that is
not fully aware of the underlying hurt but is nonetheless activated to
repeat its painful manifestations and/or the enacted defenses automatically employed to self-regulate. Drawing from his immense clinical
experience, Bach (2006) describes narcissistic personality disorders
as made up of two emotional pathologies: feeling victimized and
deflated, with considerable low self-esteem, and conversely tending
to display grandiose, hypomanic, or sadistic patterns. By experiencing

and articulating a depth of negative feelings and thoughts regarding one's self-worth, the deflated narcissist often appears to be depressed and clingy. The ones who repeatedly come across as self-inflating tirelessly seek the approval of others, compete with them, and need to feel superior.

More specifically, in the midst of affective dysregulation, the self-narrative of deflated narcissists focuses on their insignificance in relation to others and their perceived inferiority. In therapy and in their relationship, they often look to the other to validate their inferior, hurt, or victimized position, experiencing anger when these unconscious expectations are frustrated. The overinflated narcissist, who often comes across as arrogant and all knowing (Kerenberg, 2007) automatically emphasizes their superiority, often at the expanse of the other. They consciously experience themselves as the center of the universe and expect others, including their therapists, to mirror their subjectivity without any doubt or skepticism (Bach, 2006). As Kernberg (2007) observes, the core issue of some narcissistic patients is their inability to depend on the therapist because any dependency is unconsciously experienced as humiliating. As a defense, these patients try to control the therapist and the therapeutic process.

Often, while engaged in the therapeutic process with narcissistic patients—witnessing their wide mood swings, becoming embroiled in very negative or, conversely, grandiose self-states, being indirectly asked to confirm either or both—I also realize that directly or indirectly all narcissistic self-states convey a great deal of misery (Kohut, 1971). At times, when being attacked for failing to "see" a patient's point of view, or when being subtly and competitively put down, I momentarily lose my own regulatory capacities and sink into a victimized mood or into a sullen, somewhat hostile withdrawal. Usually, however, holding on to my reflective awareness, I maintain the fragile thread of connection to the injured part. As the patient and I get to know and immerse ourselves in that vulnerable self-system, I find myself more empathetic with the patient's desperate but unconscious attempts to save face.

What has always been so compelling to me about the therapeutic engagement with patients suffering from an array of narcissistic characteristics—the injury hidden or acutely lived and the unproductive but resolute defenses—is the hope that the patient can find new ways to cope with feelings and convictions that seem so dreadful that they threaten to destabilize his trust in his very survival. The challenge of helping a patient reach his core of pain—experiencing it together and helping him let go of coping mechanisms that really do not work for his well-being—keeps the treatment alive even in the face of rigid patterns that seem to create transferential-countertransferential obstacles throughout the treatment (Kernberg, 2007).

A NONNEGOTIABLE NEED FOR PERFECTIONISM:
THE CASE OF MELODY

Melody was a physician in training when she sought therapy because of severe and persistent anxiety. She could not explain what made her so stressed and anxious, except for the competitive atmosphere, frequent evaluations, and the high stakes attached to her performance. Pretty soon it became clear that her professional and interpersonal life embodied a constant struggle with self-doubts and nagging thoughts of imminent failure. She was utterly convinced that she would be found out as a fraud, and then all would be lost. In one of the first dreams she brought to treatment, she could not diagnose a patient, and both the head of the ward and her direct supervisor were becoming increasingly short and angry with her. She woke up in total panic, with inchoate and inarticulate feelings of dreadful shame.

From the very beginning of the therapy, it was evident that Melody was actually living this nightmare in her daily internal life, in her constant doubts and fears of being found out as not as smart as the others around her. She became aware of how afraid she was to be seen as incompetent. If she were judged as such, she felt she would be rejected and unloved; unless she was perfect, she would not be good enough. Her unshakable and unexamined conviction that unless she were perfect she was an utter failure personifies the torture chamber that characterizes some of the deflated (Bach, 2006) narcissistic internal structure. It is a no-win situation, where perfection is not possible and a sense of self dependent on perfection as a lifeline is not connected to real strength and continually feels crushed.

How is it that an unconscious injured self-system and its accompanying conscious dysregulated self-state often compels intelligent—and often highly functional—people like Melody to lose sight of the irrational aspects of their experience? As is often witnessed, dysregulated states display such intense negative convictions that they end up underpinning faulty thought processes (Bach, 2006), which are representative of narcissistic dysregulation or collapse. The following sections will further examine how the narcissistic unconscious systems—although factually removed from the here and now—still exert an enormous power on perception, emotions, and cognition.

VULNERABILITY AND DEFENSIVE SELF-REGULATION

Melody's emotional and cognitive patterns demonstrated complex aspects of a deflated structure, accompanied by a great deal of anxiety and depressed affect. Her automatic attempts at securing a sense of well-being reflected an ineffective and unrealistic conviction that perfection was proof of self-worth. She did not actually experience herself as perfect—only the desire to be seen as a perfect and flawless professional. At the risk of presenting this case too superficially, I will only mention here that growing up with a bitter, critical mother, she often witnessed her mother being belittled and put down by her maternal grandmother, who lived with them.

We need to remember, however, that although the pervasiveness of dysregulation and self-regulatory defenses in narcissistic disorders may be more obvious than usual, we all embody the dual systems of hurt and protection—both occupying spaces on the continuums of consciousness and flexibility. In effect, our sophisticated self-regulating maneuvers are surely among the most essential and intriguing aspects of the human brain/mind. Subjected to her mother's criticalness and sarcasm—a mother who herself had had a garrulous and demanding mother— Melody had no choice but to develop an unconscious self-system that oscillated between two self-states; the first embodied her shameful, self-doubting, and critical self-other representation. The protective state, on the other hand, constantly arrived at unrealistic pacts and imposed childlike conditions to achieve the sense of well-being; only perfection would do. We can also imagine the role of the default network (Gusnard et al., 2001; Raichle et al., 2001)—the brain's activity at rest—being preoccupied with the inward processing of feelings, memories, and ruminations about what it felt like to be criticized and humiliated and what "life-saving" defenses worked best.

It is interesting to start the inquiry into the duality of psychic pain and self-protection by recalling that throughout evolution, the instinctive avoidance of light witnessed among one-cell organisms developed into a wide range of physiological and mental processes dedicated to restore homeostasis within us. The fact that our neuropsychological defenses do not operate under one central and conscious self-agency that decides what should be defended against and how but are determined by the simultaneous activity of many brain areas (Cappelli, 2006; Churchland, 2012; Damasio, 2010; Koziol, 2014; LeDoux, 2014; Lewis and Todd, 2007; Mesulam, 2000)—only adds to the complicated nature of defenses. Defenses are innately and unconsciously derived as responses to any threat. They are also underpinned by the amygdala's quick detection of real or perceived danger (LeDoux, 2002), and continue to operate even when the original emotional threats no longer exist.

Defenses can be seen as global and synchronized brain/mind processes used in the service of well-being, homeostasis, and survival (Damasio, 2010; A. Freud, 1968; LeDoux, 2002, 2014; Panksepp and Biven, 2012). They arise instinctively as innate responses to negative

shame

self-states that the brain/mind and body cannot tolerate for long. Intense shame, experienced as complete loss of self-worth and thereby endangering psychic integrity, seems to be at the core of many narcissistic dysregulated states (Kohut, 1971; Schore, 2012). As development continues, defenses gain complexity and intellectual sophistication. Together, incoming cognitive abilities and the growing rationalizing capacities of the left brain (Gazzaniga, 2008; Gazzaniga et al., 2014) provide a network of justifications and compensations designed to ameliorate intolerable affects. The defenses that work to achieve the goal of homeostasis will be reinforced and become a part of the self-system.

The deflated narcissist, for example, embodies such emotional collapse and loss of self-esteem, experiencing exaggerated flaws as if they were completely real and without any realistic perspective. Melody's extreme doubts about her self-competency developed as a response to a critical mother, who was often humiliated by her own mother. As she came to understand, watching her mother constantly put down by an angry and rigid grandmother caused Melody a great deal of pain. By identifying with her mother's shame, it became hers as well. Being criticized by her own mother seemed natural and justified—the negative self-system was never questioned.

In reaction, a defensive need to avoid failure at all costs may lead to a faulty system that demands nothing short of perfection; anything else is proof of the dreaded sense of unworthiness. In other cases, an unconscious capitulation to parental voices and the involuntary internalization of a parental attitude that views the child as an extension, for example, stand in the way of the child developing a separate subjectivity. Such patients will look to others for external validation for much of their internal experiences and decisions. Deflated narcissists, who during dysregulation display self-critical states and intense fears of being found out, may not have had the capacity or innate inclination to develop either the protective illusion of perfection or a grandiose defense.

Among overinflated narcissists, automatic expressions of arrogance, aggression, self-enhancement, convictions about one's constant righteousness, and biases about one's self-worth in relation to others (Bach, 2006; Kernberg, 2007) are also called into action to defend against self-crushing experiences. In opposition to the deflated patient, the overinflated narcissist does not consciously experience the shame and fear of being psychically annihilated, but has learned to fight them with all he has (Kohut, 1971).

As we see in clinical practice, deflated patients are often preoccupied with comparing themselves to others, constantly trying to assess their perceived value, usually judging themselves as lacking or inferior. They feel diminished when others succeed, as if such successes are a statement on their own self-worth. In extreme cases, patients are loath to read, learn new material, or seek help, unconsciously convinced that such acts are proof of not being good enough. Overinflated patients, on the other hand, are extremely sensitive to any intimation that they harbor within them human weakness or flaws. It is as if the very admission to a human need, vulnerability, or flaw will throw them right back into the unconscious web of intense and intolerable shame. As was mentioned, even dependency on a therapist is such an indication (Kernberg, 2007). For them, having a human flaw is totally humiliating. For that reason, they have a difficult time seeing their role in interpersonal disagreements or conflict; to avoid the dreaded experience of the "bad self," they have to be right. As part of the constant and unconscious campaign to promote the self, some unconsciously seize any opportunity to assert their superiority, and remind others preemptively that they hold the power. Being unaware of themselves, they are often unaware of others existing as separate subjectivities, with needs, perceptions, and opinions different than their own (Kerenberg, 1997, 2002).

VICTIM AND VICTIMIZER: THE CASE OF ROGER

When he was about three years old and growing up in an upper-middle-class family, Roger's older brother started abusing him verbally and physically. His parents denied the severity of their son's aggressive bullying and refused to acknowledge it even when they were alerted to it. As he remembered, throughout his childhood, when Roger complained about being bullied by his brother, his parents did not take him seriously, told him to "be a man," and insisted that both assume equal responsibility. He felt helpless and without any resources to fight back; even when he tried, his brother accused him of instigating the fights, and at times indeed convinced Roger that he was to blame. After many such fights, Roger felt that his parents also blamed him for them, but he concealed his felt helplessness and rage.

Roger started therapy in his forties due to serious problems in his marriage: repeated fights and disagreements that caused a great deal of stress for the whole family. Paradoxically, he appeared at once brittle and arrogant. He was convinced that he was the victim in the marriage and that the main problems in the relationship were his wife's unfulfilling career and her frustrations at having to sacrifice her professional life to take care of their two sons (she worked part-time). His frequent expressions of righteous indignation, self-confidence in his own assessments, total lack of self-doubt, and a withering attitude toward his wife were delivered without any reflective awareness. The greatest difficulty in our initial therapeutic encounter was Roger's sensitivity to any exploration that required some sort of self-examination or a more nuanced understanding of his marriage and other relationships. He would bristle when asked to reflect on the connection between his difficult past and his present relationships.

It's not that Roger did not recognize that his past affected his present problems, but that understanding was only couched in the context of being a victim. In his narrative he was a victim of his brother's bullying, his parents' unempathetic neglect, and his wife's dissatisfaction. The possible links between painful emotions and the enacted need to be on top, control others, and at the same time see himself as the only victim were rejected. Similarly, his automatic expressions of self-aggrandizing and the importance of being vindicated at all costs remained unconscious as well. For more than a year into the therapy, Roger would get angry with me when he perceived—sometimes rightly, other times with a great deal of projected certainty—the intrusion of my own subjectivity in the interaction. I could not freely express my own ideas about what was going on; it was most often perceived as a disagreement and an insult. I was to totally accept only his version of who he was and the nature of our interaction.

The level of sensitivity to disagreement and perceived slights permeated his relationship with his wife. If she disagreed with him or insisted that he examine his behavior, he felt attacked and devalued. Only when Roger viscerally realized that some of his intense and recurrent problems with his two boys might be related to his past experiences, that his frequent complaints about his wife are an expression of the deep wounds within him, did he slowly begin to take our interactions in with less defensive argumentative. "Fear for my marriage and my sons made me brave," he later said. As his therapy continued for the next few years, it still encountered the automatic enactment of his entrenched defensive modes and the inevitable entanglements that our interactions created.

The lengthy therapy was an important aspect of Roger's progress toward an enhanced ability to look inwardly with less panic and defensiveness. During that time, again and again, his life experiences, his many interactional difficulties, and the many distortions embedded in the ways he saw himself and others were felt, identified, and analyzed. Whereas Melody's internal shifts occurred relatively rapidly—within a year both her internal states and her encounters with her external environment changed considerably—Roger's path was more difficult. It is entirely possible that from the onset Melody possessed more flexible and thus open connections between cortical and subcortical systems, allowing for a quicker attunement to and integration of novel ways of feeling and thinking about herself and others. Roger's learning curve, on the other hand, was impeded by the enactment of the more entrenched narcissistic self-system. With time, his complicated and rigid web of hurts, resentments, and defenses softened as well. A growing reflective ability as well as an increased affect tolerance enabled him to eventually construct entirely new ways of understanding himself and others. The realization that he embodied and enacted both victim and victimizer, helplessness, hurt, and rage as well as the defenses against them enabled Roger to modify his internal reactions and interpersonal behaviors. His capacity to tolerate and sit with difficult feelings—feelings that in the past would quickly be responded to with familiar patterns—grew as well. With his growing awareness, the automaticity of his emotional, cognitive and behavioral reactions greatly diminished. As will be discussed in the following chapters, time may indeed be an important aspect of the therapeutic process; changing entrenched neural pathways takes time.

LEARNING AND AUTOMATICITY OF DEFENSES

The process of developing unconscious and automatic defensive systems is closely intertwined with implicit and explicit learning processes. Learning occurs when specific behaviors, emotional reactions, comforting thoughts, or soothing internal monologues lead to the favorable outcome of restored well-being. We can fully understand how such internal or external responses, from simple avoidance to complex cognitive machinations such as the tendency toward grandiose self-soothing, take hold in the face of an immense blow to the self. Learning is also crucial when a very negative and faulty self-evaluation develops; a child has no choice but to internalize as his own his parents' impatience, criticism, neglect, or lack of acceptance. These communications become the dominant measure of his self-worth. We saw this clearly in Melody's case.

Whether defenses are automatically recruited to reestablish a more positive emotional state or whether the child succumbs to the parent's definition of himself—in itself a possible reaction against defying them to secure their love—learning determines the strength of the response. In the case of a positive outcome, the corticostriatal synapses are strengthened with each successful result. That set of neurons is likely to be activated in similar situations, and the same affect, conviction, behavior, or defensive mechanism is likely to be executed.

As discussed in previous chapters, the basal ganglia and the cerebellum are sensitive to the context that generates the behavior, and they bias the PFC with information about the most appropriate reactions. This is always done within the context of the present emotional, cognitive, and perceptual patterns it detects (Damasio, 2010; Gollwitzer et al., 2007; Koziol and Budding, 2010; McClelland, 2011). Based on prior experiences with similar conditions, a defense mechanism that successfully regulates affect, for example, will also include learning to anticipate or expect this rewarding result. Consequently, a self- protective behavior or thought is automatically triggered out of awareness even before the activating situation fully unfolds. Within intimate relationships, for example, unconsciously expected threats will be triggered and simultaneously activate those defenses that proved affective (Andersen et al., 2007).

The tenacity and automaticity of compromising and often debilitating coping strategies is explained by the various brain/mind processes that were described in previous chapters. I mention here the role of the cerebellum and the neocerebellum (Koziol and Budding, 2010; Thach, 1996) in linking the representations of specific behavioral contexts with the relevant movement/response generator. Consequently, complex behaviors and patterns are mapped onto specific environmental features and context. Eventually these patterns are being triggered and guided automatically by informational input from the internal or external environment, bypassing conscious control.

Furthermore, cerebellar output extends to the main planning areas of the brain, the PFC, thereby underpinning the unconscious enaction of very intricate and sophisticated response patterns. The tendency to shore up the self in the face of a perceived threat to one's well-being, in the case of a narcissist, will occur out of awareness. Melody was not aware of the frequent fluctuations she underwent while comparing herself to others, nor was she cognizant of how unrealistic and impossible her demands from herself were. This reinforced unconscious tendency to react a certain way will automatically guide internal or interpersonal defensive responses. Preemptively, grandiose ideation, for instance, may be embedded in a profound contempt toward others, or sadistic attitudes of dismissal (Bach, 2006; Kernberg, 1997, 2007; Kohut, 1971). Similarly, internalizing the aggressor's insults and drowning in negative self-states that repeat the sense of failure and unworthiness will also repeat itself as a complex pattern, automatically and without conscious participation.

The inherent variety seen in the emotional and/or cognitive maneuvers mobilized to protect the child's sense of self becomes clear when we remember the important function of meaning making (Colombetti, 2010; Sheets-Johnson, 2010, 2012). In this context, the very individual paths to restore well-being use ways of giving new meaning to devastating encounters and internal experiences; the left brain with its explanatory powers will create the only meaning that makes sense for that moment. A forced belief in a parent's world is protected at one's own expense; similarly, convictions of the devastation of failure and the redemption of perfection make sense at moments of dysregulation and a grandiose and self-inflating stance may become as natural and undetectable as the act of breathing.

UNCONSCIOUS SYSTEMS AND THE EITHER-OR RESPONSES

Often narcissistic patients who have just entered therapy seem to enact unconscious self-systems with a remarkable degree of obliviousness as to the opposing emotional and behavioral poles that characterize them. An either-or way of relating to oneself, others, and the world at large is common. For example, Melody frequently shifted between a self-state that felt like an utter failure and a self-state that was convinced that only perfection confirmed her self-worth. In Roger's system, people were always correct or mistaken, inferior or superior, victims or victimizers. For both of them, "gray" perceptions or interpretations were nonexistent. Bach (2006) describes such thinking as polarized; one is either good or bad, guilty or totally absolved of guilt, experiencing pleasure or pain, attached to others or utterly alone. Bach sees this polarization as a failure to develop a "useable transitional area in which dichotomy, ambiguity, and paradox can be acknowledged and contained" (Bach, 2006, p. 76).

The disconnect between self-systems containing enactive representations of injury and defense develops when parallel—but unconsciously interacting—self-systems of pain and defense become exceedingly robust. Although the nature of the relationship between these two emotionally significant maps is not conscious, it nonetheless fosters separate ways of self-experience. The more pronounced and rigid the dissociation between the unconsciously held injury and defense, the more vacillation between them is experienced and enacted. As a result, an either-or pattern of experience dominates each self-state. Good and bad intersubjective encounters come to inhabit different self-systems and self-states, resulting in an unlinked split between them (Bromberg, 2006, 2011; Kerenberg, 1975, 1997, 2007). For some patients, the more devastating the emotional quality of the injury, the more it may become split from the defenses used against it. What may remain unconscious is not so much the actual memories of injury to the self; many patients can recount such traumatic experiences. Instead, what facilitates the persistence of the split between the two self-systems is the enormous emotional significance that shaming, criticizing, and diminishing experiences carry for the state of well-being and the survival of one's self-integrity.

Zachar and Ellis (2012) suggest the existence of a bidimensional affective systems that innately reacts to and emphasizes the positive or negative valence and the perceived values embedded in every situation. This perceived—and often projected—value inherent in any internal or external context in actuality reflects high and low arousal states. Evolutionarily determined, this innate dual approach helps explain the binary way of thinking often noticed among narcissistic patients. From early on, driven by an actual or perceived blow to the sense of self, good or bad valence is automatically generated by what Zachar and Ellis call the core affect, a concept paralleling that of Panksepp and Biven (2012) as well as Damasio (1999, 2000, 2010), Schore (2012), and Tsuchiya and Adolphs (2007), all underscoring the centrality of innate affects.

The core affect, whether positive or negative, is the basis for our emotional life, and our cognitive and behavioral choices. Within its innate and automatic nature, it will certainly influence the all-or-nothing binary perceptions of oneself and of others and will shape the binary nature of narcissistic approaches to oneself—all good or all bad. The developing defenses will be shaped by a similar binary assessment; grandiosity or unconscious humiliation and narcissistic collapse.

Similarly, emphasizing homeostatic goals as the guiding principle of our response tendencies, Damasio (2010) adds reward and punishment as the all-important incentives for exploration, action, or withdrawal. Paradoxically, there is no one designated agency acting as a "rewarder" or a "punisher" (Damasio, 2010, p. 55). "Yet, 'rewards' and 'punishments' are administered based on the design of response policy systems" (Damasio, 2010, p. 55). The emotional value of an experience is what ultimately determines how we react to it, internally and interpersonally.

From a neuropsychological point of view, hormones and neuromodulators orchestrate internal states of value, reward, and punishment, which are central to survival. These chemical patterns allow unconscious processes to detect and measure departures from the homeostatic range and thus act as sensors for various internal needs. This action leads to corrective processes designed to ensure survival and well-being (Damasio, 2010). Further underpinning the oscillating enactment of injury or the defenses against it is the fact that within working memory, the representations of one's intentions—accessible to conscious awareness—are stored in different structures from the unconscious representations that are used to guide action.

What is so compelling about this neuropsychological model is the basis it provides for the duality of the intense sense of injury and potential annihilation and the automatic necessity to restore integrity and well-being. On various levels of awareness, the physiological and the psychological are entirely intertwined and meet to produce a system so exquisitely sensitive to slights that it sees them where they do not really exist. The slights signal to the system that the intolerable emotional disintegration experienced in the past is possible again in the here and now. Recalling the enduring emotional and interpersonal lessons that each unconscious self-system contains and then uses as a filter for all other interactions with the environment, it is easy to see how a devastating sense of annihilation, for example, would sensitize a system to automatically respond to both real and perceived threats.

This process is the basis for neural/psychological systems that reinforce the narcissists' unconscious and acute sensitivity to perceived threats to the self-worth, as well as their emotional reactivity and defensive patterns. The lack of linkage between conscious awareness and intention on the one hand and the operation of complex motor and goal representations on the other (Prinz, 2003) further explains how whole patterns of behavior are enacted and repeated without one's awareness. In the case of narcissistic patterns, unconscious learned behaviors, for example, result in a deflated pattern that in spite of the best intentions to feel good still repeats a victimized, depressed stance. An overinflated, grandiose self-system will express and enact the unconscious innate need to restore well-being and homeostasis, in spite of a conscious wish to be accepted by the other. As we have seen throughout this book, the connection between perception and action is inseparable, and unless attended to with reflective awareness, it bypasses any conscious input from the PFC.

THE UNCONSCIOUS DEFENSIVE SYSTEMS AND PERSONALITY TRAITS

Given that the restoration of homeostasis and emotional well-being, even if temporary, is the cornerstone of life management (Damasio, 2010; Panksepp and Biven, 2012; Schore, 2012), we can see how central defenses are and how they come to constitute some of our major personality traits. In an interaction with one's temperament (Kagan, 1998), a wide range of coping measures will develop. A total identification with parental self-states at the expense of one's own sense of autonomous subjectivity, rebelliousness designed to achieve autonomy at all costs, a need to be perfect, a wide range of avoiding thoughts and behaviors, and grandiose thoughts intended to enhance good feelings about the self are only some of the manifestations of such defenses.

Based on these processes, we should view defenses as inevitable and widespread processes, procedures automatically embedded in our neurochemical responses to the emotional attributes of internal and external stimuli. In the context of injurious interactions, when the child's still fragile sense of self is inundated by hurtful experiences, successful defenses can bring an internal respite. Of course, although they restore well-being, many emotional and cognitive maneuvers compromise the adult's ability to adapt to new situations unencumbered by unconscious expectations and response tendencies. In the case of the narcissistic structure of immense injury and defense, where the threat to survival feels entirely real, both the underlying emotion and the attempts to regulate it are more pronounced and therefore more damaging.

Experience and reaction, injury and defense, and what is learned, discarded, or retained are all part of the conscious–unconscious continuum and develop along the rigidity–flexibility continuum. Although defenses may be quite effective as strategies to cope with internal turmoil, they are also quite maladaptive when throughout adulthood they continue to operate automatically and out of awareness in response to any perceived threats to the integrity of the self. This is especially the case when the child's needs for healthy expressions of autonomy, achievement, separateness, and a sense of being important to the parent are severely undermined (Grawe, 2007). It does not simply feel bad to be treated a certain way; it literally threatens one's psychic survival and endangers one's emotional integrity.

THE COST OF NARCISSISTIC STRUCTURE: A CONTINUUM OF CONSCIOUS–UNCONSCIOUS AFFECT DYSREGULATION AND COGNITIVE DISTORTIONS

In a confluence of emotional dysregulation and rigid coping mechanisms a narcissistic self-structure is characterized by an unconscious and unyielding conviction that the sense of self is fragile and very vulnerable, needing to be defended at all costs. How else can we understand a patient's repeated oscillation between a bottomless pool of negative assessments of one self-state and the need to be the best at all things and never fail, or a patient's unconsciously enacted overinflated and careless attitude? Some defensive systems enact a voracious need—at times an insistent demand—to be adored, recognized, and appreciated. Others frequently look for validation and agreement and, as in the case of the garrulous, grandiose patients, do not understand the reason for their interpersonal difficulties.

At its core, a narcissistic structure of injury and coping may not be very different than any other conscious/unconscious self-organizations. As we saw in previous chapters, we all embody variations on the human vulnerability to hurt and trauma and the innate need to psychologically survive. It seems, however, that the narcissistic internal organizations and the splits between self-systems are particularly attuned to and sensitive to vulnerability, its rigid defenses fueled by the passionate need to protect an inordinate sense that the self is so fragile it cannot survive any more attacks on its integrity.

In the midst of dysregulation, when one's sense of self is threatened, an amalgam of conscious and unconscious emotions and cognitive convictions get triggered, swinging between the unconscious sense of being obliterated and the enacted defense. Whether coping was achieved through complete identification with the injuring voice or through automatic expressions of self-importance and self-aggrandizement, a narcissistic patient often demonstrates what Bach so apply terms "thought disorder" (Bach, 2006, p. 21). The intense emotional experience, at times experienced as overly dramatic, and the cognitive distortions involved in the faulty assessment of the situation are the intertwined embodiments of poor affect regulation. In the narcissistic structure, such compromised regulation is expressed in very specific and predictable ways, both in the depth of the injury and the exaggerated efforts to thwart it.

At first glance this assessment may seem excessive, but on close examination we can recognize that what characterizes a narcissistic coping mechanism is indeed the tendency during dysregulation to be fully attuned to one's feelings and thoughts alone. The internal reality becomes the only reality, even when it does not comply with or does not take into account current conditions. A deflated mode of dealing with threat by inhabiting and enacting a felt self-state of complete shame and failure is just as removed from reality as the knee-jerk inclination to aggrandize oneself and look for constant validation. These modes of functioning affect all levels of the narcissist's relationship to himself and to others: his cognitive ability to assess reality in reflective and fresh ways, his ability to self-regulate adaptively, the language he uses and his expectations from others—especially within an intimate relationship. Narcissistic pathology in particular presents an extreme example of failing to take reality into account, tolerate ambiguity, or accept multiple points of view (Bach, 2006; Kohut, 1971).

The unconscious excessive preoccupation with protecting the sense of self may lead to a lack of awareness about the consequences of one's behavior with others. Such patients may come across as insensitive and selfish. As Baumeister and Vohs (2001) suggest, narcissists are addicted to receiving and experiencing positive self-esteem. Conversely, others may be incredibly sensitive to strangers' looks or reaction to them, to casual remarks and innuendo not really directed at them. At either extreme, the main preoccupation and approach to the external world is embedded in and filtered through one's unconscious systems.

As a patient's typical ways of responding to dysregulation become a way of feeling, thinking, and acting, they actually come to represent a major personality trait. Consequently, it seems that the biggest cost to a narcissistic personality structure are the many potential interpersonal entanglements created by their honed sensitivity and unconscious defense. A tendency to disregard the other, or in more extreme cases, disallow them to have subjectivities of their own, or the tendency to idealize others and diminish one self are often part of the transference (Kernberg, 1997, 2007).

This difficulty is especially noticeable when others do not confirm to the narcissist's position or express disagreement. It is not just that such patients do not consider others' needs or even think about them, but that the other's subjectivity is often perceived as threatening by its very existence. For this reason therapeutic interaction often get bogged down by projective identifications, empathetic failures, and therapeutic enactments. As Bach observes, narcissists have difficulty in establishing a sense of self as an agent in the context of other selves (2006, p. 23), while Kernberg stresses their rejection of dependency and their repeated attempts to control the therapy. This was my experience with Roger, especially at the start of our relationship. The noticeable drive to show his superior knowledge and have the last word was expressed through frequent attempts to challenge my observations and put his stamp on what was said and understood.

The interpersonal limitations demonstrated by the narcissistic personality disorder are linked to the failure to develop a theory of mind in relation to significant others (Bateman and Fonagy, 2012; Fonagy et al., 2002). Described by these researchers as linked to early intersubjective difficulties, the failure to develop a theory of mind dovetails with the excessive feelings of panic in regard to the survival of the integrity of the self. An unconscious system easily threatened with disintegration and always on guard cannot easily develop adequate pathways dedicated to the consideration of the other as an equal subjectivity; it may prove too much of a risk. Together, the difficulties in taking the other's subjectivity into account and the general tendency toward unconsciousness as to one's feelings and actions present particular therapeutic challenges.

IMPLICATIONS FOR TRANSFERENCE–COUNTERTRANSFERENCE ENTANGLEMENTS

The enacted duality of both dysregulation and self-regulatory responses often occur within the transference–countertransference interactions and, as a matter of fact, in all of the patient's intersubjective experiences. The ensuing entanglements present a particular therapeutic challenge. Frequently, the therapist will be perceived as failing the patient with a misfiring interpretation or an unempathetic intervention that does not really "get" the patient, or, in more intense engagements, as an attacking figure. The patient is not aware that his unconscious self-system fears being annihilated and discarded, but he will perceive, feel, and act according to those unconscious expectations. What is dissociated from consciousness is not simply the content of a self-system— as we understand now, most of its neuropsychological foundations can never become accessible—but the ability to reflect on what is going on.

This inability to naturally mentalize and reflect on the meaning of one's experiences and actions, as well as of those of others, characterizes the narcissistic structure.

It is not only the patient's system that activates the therapist's. The opposite may be true as well, or more accurately, they affect each other in a way that makes it difficult sometimes to identify who does what to whom (Benjamin, 1995, 2004; Bromberg, 2011). Within the many unconscious mutual cues embedded within the intersubjective space, patients and therapists simultaneously respond with their injured system and their typical defenses. Any sign that the self is threatened with criticism, lack of empathy, and objectification may unconsciously activate unconscious systems in both participants.

In addition, while interacting with a very depressed patient or a patient with grandiose defenses, the therapist's own past injuries and defensive systems may be activated and enacted out of awareness. These potential impasses are almost inevitable because for patient and therapist, the original unconscious loop of injury and defense begins within the realm of intersubjective interactions. The compromised implicit relational knowing, the disturbances in reality testing, and its accompanying faulty thinking (Bach, 2006) create many pitfalls for both participants. A patient's insistent repetitions of the victimized and helpless self-system—with all its emotional intensity, possible frequent projections of being insulted or misunderstood, and the subtle or overt sense of superiority, to mention just a few examples—will threaten the therapist's own homeostasis.

When attempting to resolve an enactment, the purpose is not necessarily to unearth some buried experiences, as we know most of our underlying memories and associations cannot become accessible, particularly those acquired during relational patterns established early in life. Recalling the chapter on therapeutic enactments, what seems to be important in their resolution is the conscious attention and focus that is directed toward the unconscious system as a whole: its unacknowledged pain, its complex defensive attempts at regulation, and its relational style.

Alternatively, some patients will react to a threat to the sense of self with idealizing the therapist and protecting the relationship above all (Bach, 2006; Kernberg, 1998, 2007; Kohut, 1971), repeating a relational dynamic that needs to be recognized as well. This mode of relating serves as a self-regulatory defense (Andersen and Chen, 2002), and is often enacted with a great emotional investment is "erasing" the self and elevating the other. Researching the tendency to self-regulate within negatively or positively perceived relationships, Andersen et al. (2007) found that the "dreaded self," out of our multiplicity of selves, gets activated in the transference. A therapist may react with a range of conscious and unconscious perceptions, feelings, and thoughts, all couched in her particular maps. She may feel reluctance to be idealized to such a degree, fearing the consequences or the responsibility; she may feel needed and useful, and much in between. Without awareness as to her feelings, she may contribute to an unfolding enactment.

The therapist may be reluctant to upset the patient with direct reflections and interpretations, afraid of hurting his feelings, inviting his wrath; she may avoid taking a more active therapeutic role for fear of losing the patient altogether. Such cautiousness, whether conscious or unconscious, can lead to a prolonged and stagnant therapeutic process with no discernible progress. Similarly, a patient's enacted deflated system can interact with the therapist's own anxieties regarding narcissistic injuries, thus engendering and mutually amplifying a sense of hopelessness, defeat, and doubt about the value of the therapeutic process. When mixed with the fear of pushing the patient too much, such an enactment can indeed bring the treatment to a halt. It can be concluded, then, that much of the clinical difficulties encountered when treating the narcissistic patient stem from an encounter with unconscious self-systems that are at far extremes of the conscious and the rigid continuums.

This situation may create an especially difficult intersubjective field, fraught with underlying fears and anxieties. The intense fear seems to center on the patient's desperate and continued defense against the unconsciously held injury, as well as any reflective awareness of the defenses used. The therapist, consciously and unconsciously, may mirror and identify with that fear, entirely submerging her own subjectivity. She may consciously feel that she is being empathetic to the patient's needs, and that by letting herself be used as a self-object, she is promoting the patient's growth.

THE DIFFICULT PATIENT

When narcissistic relational patterns are without any reflection, understanding, or deliberation, many interpersonal difficulties may ensue. In extreme cases of narcissistic disorder, patients are so sensitive and defended that they are all but unreachable. They will always see their position as right and justified: to him, the others are the ones who are wrong, hurtful, or destructive (Berenson and Andersen, 2004; Reznik and Andersen, 2007). Consciously a therapist may become angry and defeated, unconsciously acting out and losing all threads of empathy. Indeed, with such patients, it is sometimes difficult to maintain empathy for the patient's hidden pain when all that is expressed is the ferociousness of the defensive system.

In light of such rigid systems, however, the therapeutic questions are complex, and the answers are not so clear-cut. A main therapeutic issue, it seems, questions whether a therapeutic emphasis on the patient's seeming needs to remain unconscious (rather than on interpretive work) constitutes an enactment; it may be an unconscious mutual admission that the system must go on as is, without any disruptions caused by the therapist's reflections, interpretations, and possible dissensions from the patient's version of things.

Consider a therapeutic process reported by a supervisee over a period of a few months into the second year of treatment. Repeatedly the therapist related that whenever she tried to probe into the patient's memories and feelings about his childhood, he would balk and become evasive. Without realizing it, the therapist retreated from further inquiries, reasoning first to herself and then to me that "obviously he is not ready to deal with his painful childhood. Maybe he needs some time before he can talk about his past." What did become clear was the therapist's cautiousness. She was hesitant in her reflections, questions, and interpretations, aligning herself closely with the patient's verbalizations. But she also felt that the treatment was stuck. Both felt therapy was "boring and not going anywhere."

Similar therapeutic enactments with narcissistic patients can amplify the dilemma we often have with our patients. Who determines the emotional atmosphere and the verbal exchanges—us or them? Obviously the answer is that we are both contributors. What does such an interaction really mean? What if the supervisee's anxieties added to the patient's difficulties in accessing his past? Conversely, were her unconscious reactions a complementary empathetic response that facilitated trust and the feeling of being understood? Should we have seen the process as an enactment or as an empathetic environment? There are many ways to understand this process, of course, but for this therapist the answer came when she became aware of her cautiousness and passivity. Feeling increasingly uncomfortable with her careful behavior during their sessions, she understood her reactions as the complex mix that they were: empathetic resonance mingled with her own anxieties about confronting painful experiences.

Only on becoming aware could she free herself from her fixed emotional position and explore other possible interventions that could move the treatment forward. In spite of her trepidations, she disclosed some of her ongoing feelings of hesitancy to the patient and invited him to consider what they might mean. Over a period of time, while they openly dealt with their possible effects on each other; the patient, now emotionally engaged, started to slowly become curious about his dissociated pain, his past traumas, and the inevitable defenses against them. For her part, the therapist learned a great deal about herself.

An additional interesting question about treating a narcissistic patient but which can be easily generalized is whether empathy and what we consider to be holding a therapeutic environment are expressed through empathetic agreement alone or whether more active and interactive forms of empathy are more effective in moving therapeutic process forward (Ginot, 1997, 2005, 2007, 2009, 2012). The therapist's fears of upsetting the patient and the therapeutic process—conscious or unconscious and anywhere on the continuum—can easily become a pact of avoidance. Such collusion can consciously be explained by the often repeated assertion that patients in general and narcissists in particular are too vulnerable to encounter their hurt and defenses; we convince ourselves that they are not ready, that they are too vulnerable. In every therapeutic process we need to ask ourselves whom we are protecting: the patient or ourselves. It is much easier, after all, not to rock the boat.

IMPLICATIONS FOR TREATMENT

Throughout the past few decades, major advances in the treatment of narcissistic disorders have been discussed. Kohut's seminal work focused on the therapist's role as a self-object to the patient, designed to help the injured, stunted self grow (see Kohut, 1971). But Kohut also emphasized rupture and repair as inevitable and necessary interactional processes that on resolution strengthen the patient's ability to tolerate emotional turmoil, internally and interpersonally. Clearly, treatments can never avoid such ruptures or enactments. Kohut, and others established therapeutic approaches that focused on empathetic reflection and on various forms of holding (for example, Ferenczi, 1932; Lessem, 2005; Rogers, 1951; Slochower, 1996; Stolorow et al., 1995; Winnicott, 1969). In some ways, Schore's emphasis of the importance of mutual regulation within the therapeutic dyad—especially the therapist's ability to use her emotional right brain to modify the patient's dysregulated state—parallels Kohut's ideas regarding the therapist's role as a regulating force.

Obviously, much empathy is needed when offering any intervention addressing emotional pain or defense. With the changing view of intersubjectivity, however, the view of empathy has changed as well. It is not seen simply as the feelings of sympathy or understanding, but as being part of an honest, freeing exchange between patient and therapist (Aron, 1989; Ginot, 2001). This more interactive and authentic understanding of empathy implies a flow of communication, especially when attempting to resolve an enactment, including the therapist's disclosure of her own experiences within an enactment (Bromberg, 2006; Chused, 1998; Ginot, 1997). Any disclosure of the therapist's experience within the interaction, however, should be sensitive to the patient's emotional states as well and to the interactional history between them. For this reason, it is not out of the question even with narcissistic patients to establish mutual interactions that explore the intersubjective entanglements from early on.

What points us toward a more engaging and confronting interactions with the narcissistic patient (Kernberg, 2007), to my mind, is the knowledge that once choosing to seek therapy, a patient likely knows that something in his way of being does not work. Often, these patients live their lives with emotional, professional, and interpersonal difficulties. As defended and sensitive as they are, a part of them still wants to get a handle on their lives, to feel more balanced and less destructive. A sensitive and unafraid therapist can create a place for honest examination, even if it involves hard questions long avoided. The defenses themselves should be seen empathetically and analyzed in the context of one's past. Transference–countertransference, inevitable in all treatments and potentially more intense here, provide more "grist for the mill" as the phrase goes. What I stress here is the ability to analyze much of the patient's difficult implicit, automatic systems earlier rather than later in therapy.

This was the case with Roger's and Melody's therapeutic processes. In spite of Roger's need to always be right, to fight for and establish his autonomy at any cost to the other, part of him was also engaged, surreptitiously taking me and our interactions in. This was especially noticeable when his defenses were lived and experienced in the session and understood in terms of his past. As treatment continued, he became increasingly curious as to how his behavior affected the therapy and me.

Melody's therapeutic process also addressed the emotional and the interpersonal costs of her unconscious self-systems and self-states from the very beginning of therapy. In her eagerness to reduce her intolerable distress and suffering, she was open to a different kind of dysregulation: the one she experienced with me during sessions. But this time, she was simultaneously accessing her most painful past experiences and memories while reflecting on them in real time. Each time she could regulate her affect and negative thinking within the session, she took that ability with her to the hospital and to her social life. The growing elucidation of her dual volatile system of pain and defense greatly contributed to Melody's ability to become more aware and integrated. This very brief description of her treatment leads us to the next chapter. Continuing with the theme of reflective awareness and mentalization, it will discuss their centrality to the therapeutic process.

CHAPTER 8

Implicit and Explicit Therapeutic Processes: The Elements of Enduring and Sustained Change

A S OFTEN MENTIONED IN THESE chapters, the significance of a neuropsychological model of the unconscious is found in the potential therapeutic implications that can be drawn from it. Echoing the continuum of unconscious–conscious processes, therapeutic endeavors reflect the explicit and the implicit aspects embedded in human interaction. In addition to each therapist's preferred therapeutic models, verbal and nonverbal exchanges, mutual perceptions and communications, projected expectations, and enacted emotions and behaviors are at work as well. From these elements, each therapeutic modality and each individual therapist seeks to reexamine, question, and ultimately modify self-systems and behaviors that are no longer adaptive. Although specific therapeutic approaches may greatly differ, all therapists try to help patients achieve greater affect regulation, a sense of personal fulfillment and well-being. Undoubtedly, a neuropsychological understanding of the unconscious can provide us with more nuanced approaches to the nature of change and to its underlying factors, the potential impediments to enduring internal shifts, and conversely the therapeutic processes that may contribute to positive changes.

THE (IM)POSSIBILITY OF CHANGE

The question of what facilitates enduring change is especially urgent in light of what has been discussed so far—the fast and automatic action of emotional, cognitive, and behavioral habits, our unconscious self-systems, and their expression as self-states and personality traits. Significantly, even higher mental functions that take part in goal pursuit do not have to operate consciously (Bargh, 2007, 2014; Papie and Aarts, 2013). Out-of-awareness enaction of emotional and behavioral patterns tend to overshadow conscious intentions. The implementation process of conscious intention itself can become automated and enacted without deliberation (Gollwitzer and Oettinger, 2013). Consequently, even the execution of consciously articulated drives, goals, and desires are often derailed by unconscious self-systems.

Such unconscious processes explain the question asked each time we engage in an act that clearly and predictably goes against our own self-interest: "What was I thinking?" Sadly, the answer is: not too much thinking was taking place. When a series of unconsciously executed behaviors, simple or complex, is invoked, the reflective capacity that can imagine and deliberate the wisdom and potential consequences of an enaction does not seem to operate. Mesulam (2000) introduced the concept of the default mode of brain function—different from the more recently described default network (Raichle et al., 2001). The default mode describes a more automatic way of functioning, driven by subcortical automatic regions rather than by more cortical areas. States of emotional dysregulation and need may increase the grip unconscious systems have (Panksepp and Biven, 2012; Schore, 2012), especially when, under the sway of an emotion system, we react to contextual stimuli without any awareness of doing so.

In light of such entrenched processes, one can feel quite discouraged about the possibility of altering ingrained personality patterns that once learned and reinforced acquire a life of their own. Although it has been demonstrated that the brain's plasticity is retained throughout our lives (e.g., Ecker et al., 2012; Gazzaniga et al., 2014), we can all acknowledge how hard it is to change the way we feel, think, and behave; regulate distressing feelings and thoughts in real time; or retain a reality-bound perspective during dysregulation. At the same time, repeated attempts to find ways to ameliorate suffering and improve functioning have been at the heart of all therapeutic modalities, from Freud's analysis of impulse derivatives to current emphasis on a wide range of focused technics such as CBT and eye movement desensitization and reprocessing (EMDR).

Therapeutic modalities try to address these basic but entirely interconnected questions: why are we so vulnerable to negative affects, such as anxiety and depression? Why do we tend to engage in self-defeating emotional, relational, and behavioral patterns, often against our better judgment? What do we need to do to feel better and change undesired patterns?

As discussed in previous chapters, an expanded picture of the inter-active processes between conscious and unconscious states not only addresses the why but can provide clues as to what therapeutic elements may work best. Within this expanded understanding of the unconscious, we can reexamine concepts such as psychodynamic insight on the one hand and techniques that stress symptom-focused, short-term therapy on the other. In addition, findings from studies that have compared different approaches can also illuminate the therapeutic dynamics that can lead to and sustain improved mood functioning.

One of the more interesting issues today—an issue attached to political and economical realities—is the one doubting the length of time required for therapeutic efficacy. Can 12 or 20 sessions offered by a CBT clinician, for example, be enough to induce change beyond temporary symptom relief? In the context of such developments in the field, and using the accumulating neuropsychological knowledge, we need to better understand the elements that may impede structural change as well as the ones that enhance and sustain it. It is not that neuropsychology can provide us with the only answers we need to gain a better understanding of how to promote health. There is little doubt that an enhanced appreciation for the origins, tenacity, and all-encompassing brain/mind processes can only help us understand what we are dealing with when we try to help people overcome compromised affect regulation and old thinking patterns.

I am using the term *structural change* because it actually conveys the essence of unconscious neural maps and self-systems that dictate enacted patterns. A structural change may mean a change in the way one feels about oneself in general and even in the midst of distress, including the regulation of negative self-narratives; it may indicate a significant change in one's relational patterns and the ability to see the other not just through one's needs; it may involve actual changes in how one approaches conscious life goals and pursuits, changes stemming from an increased sense of agency, a clearer sense of identity, and enhanced self-esteem; and importantly, it may entail the development of sufficient reflective awareness. Obviously, such fundamental changes in one's self-systems, and consequently consciously felt self-states, are the ultimate therapeutic goal, a goal that subsumes within it the amelioration of symptomatic suffering.

All therapeutic changes are really changes in neural networks and the connections among them, and change may be more difficult for some patients compared with others. The potential effects of the flexible–rigid continuum are always at work, and they need to be recognized and addressed. Beyond this, enduring therapeutic change exceedingly seems to be based on many disparate elements; from the quality of the therapeutic relationship to the direct ways a therapist can help a patient develop reflective awareness to regulate thoughts and affects. Therapeutic change also seems to mean not the total erasure of anxiety, disvaluing self-states, dysregulation, and even recurrent symptoms, but how we process them in real time. In spite of recent finding showing the power of reconsolidation of old memories to alter their affective bite (LeDoux and Schiller, 2009; Ecker et al., 2012; Toomey and Ecker, 2009), it is also suggested that early emotional memories are indelible (Fernyhough, 2013). The power of preverbal emotional experiences and early arousal levels in shaping unconscious maps was already discussed, but their lasting consequences need to be acknowledged by therapists as well. Such a wider understanding can guide the essential therapeutic goal of structural transformation while at the same time realizing that a deep change also entails the development of the ability to live with and automatically regulate recurrent patterns until they no longer have an effect.

Therapists often encounter the puzzling and frustrating experience of realizing that despite the obvious importance of therapy, some patients still forget the content of sessions and report not thinking of therapy outside the office. The triggers for such shifts most likely remain totally out of awareness, hiding the meaning behind the forgetful enaction. Again, taking the vast unconscious into account, it is not simply resistance or intentional avoidance but an automatic change of self-states and the reestablishment of old, rehearsed ones. In addition, when we consider, the weekly therapeutic hour (which in effect is only 45 minutes in most cases), we cannot help but ask ourselves: how can it have any enduring effect at all? As we have seen until now, entrenched neural patterns easily and automatically revert to what they learned, to what they do best and with minimal expenditure of energy (Mesulam, 2000).

Taking the neuropsychological model of the unconscious into account, we can better appreciate the forces that cause repetition rather than reflection, and the possible methods that can help slow down an automatic system. What the unconscious model also teaches us is that a great deal of learning takes place out of awareness, subject to intra- and interpersonal unconscious processes. The fuller picture of how conscious and unconscious processes mutually affect each other; of the ongoing loops between subcortical, limbic, and cortical regions; of the inextricable links among body, affect, cognition, and enaction can also educate us as to what may induce enduring change. In light of such intertwined brain/mind structures and processes, it seems that therapeutic change can be accomplished through many paths, all inevitably intersecting and affecting each other.

For example, considering the inextricable link and crucial interaction between affect and reflective awareness or mindfulness, we can devise better paths to enhanced emotion regulation (Cozolino, 2002; Ginot,

2001; Jurist, 2008; Lane et al., 2014; McRae et al., 2013; Ochsner and Gross, 2005; Schore, 2012; Siegel, 2007; Wallin, 2007), especially in the midst of experiencing and reflecting on an emotional state in real time (Bateman and Fonagy, 2012; Jurist, 2008, Falkenstrom et al., 2014; Lane, 2008, Lane et al., 2014). Similarly, an emotionally suffused therapeutic process, especially as enacted between therapist and patient, will add the needed dimension of affectivity, helping the patient (and therapist) integrate affect, behavior, and cognition (Bromberg, 2006, 2011; Ginot, 2009, 2012; Schore, 2012). Using bodily sensations in therapy will also enhance the ability to tolerate affective states and achieve an integrative regulation (P. Ogden et al., 2006); approaches employing bodily sensations, EMDR, affectivity, and reflective awareness have proven successful as well (Beck, 1979; Beck et al., 1990; Ecker et al., 2012; Shapiro, 2002). Finally, remembering the action ready propensity of brain/mind processes, and the links between bodily activity and learning, there may not be a substitute for actual implementations of newly acquired insights and their behavioral practice (Grawe, 2007) in therapy.

Subsequently, the questions of what enhances and sustains enduring change in one's internal structure—in essence our unconscious-conscious self-systems—may be resolved when we recognize that all facets of our mental functioning should be equally recruited in therapy: affect, thoughts, the quality of the therapeutic relationship, and the implementation of new behaviors. In light of the unconscious model, therapy can be seen as the indispensable intersubjective space where a wide range of explicit and implicit (Fosshage, 2005, 2011) interpersonal experiences attempt to internally shift entrenched patterns and substitute them with new ways of being. In other words, explicit and implicit, interpersonal and intrapersonal learning processes need to take place for such changes to happen. The following sections discuss some of the factors that may be most responsible for sustained change and examine the unconscious model in the context of therapeutic processes.

THE COMPLEXITIES OF THERAPEUTIC INSIGHT

Increasingly, it seems that the nature of insight is more complex than simply gaining an understanding about one's past, psychodynamic make-up, and maladaptive repeated patterns. In the face of such powerful unconscious self-systems, can a conscious understanding—even one that arises spontaneously in the midst of an emotional experience—maintain a sustained change? Moreover, is a conscious insight always the desired antidote that can bring about better regulation and adaptive change? Schore and Schore's (2008) work, for example, emphasizes mutual regulation as the condition capable of fostering the necessary neuropsychological changes in the cortical and subcortical regions of the right hemisphere. Other therapeutic approaches stress the emotional qualities of the therapeutic relationship, the indispensable importance of empathy, and the therapist's ability to serve as a self-object for any therapeutic gains (e.g., Ferenczi, 1932; Kohut, 1971; Lessem, 2005; Rogers 1951; Slochower, 1996).

Within the dynamically oriented therapeutic approaches, however, the concept of insight and the expectations that it can lead to changed affect and behavior maintains its primacy. Since Freud (1914, 1915) the quest for conscious awareness and integration has been bound up with the concept of insight. Gaining awareness into one's internal conflicts, unconscious motivation, and fantasies has always been an important therapeutic goal. Insight has been especially important, for example, in the analysis of transference, the unconscious influence of childhood events and experiences, and the resolution of an enactment.

As we often witness, although many patients arrive at insightful realizations, they still cannot change the way they feel or do things. It is not uncommon that after experiencing intense emotional insight into a particular dynamic, patients report that the session, its content, and intensity "disappeared" shortly after leaving the office. As discussed in the following sections, such forgetfulness (often described as dissociation) is guided by unconscious processes that may seem defensive but in essence reflect the brain/mind's tendency to revert to more powerful and automatically engendered states.

Additionally, as has been noted by numerous studies, efforts to maintain reflectiveness about one's moods, emotions, actions, and thoughts tend to quickly deplete one's consciously experienced resources, such as attention, persistence, and focus. One's automatic, habitual ways of experiencing and doing things quickly resume, demanding much less brain/mind exertion (Mischel and Ayduk, 2013; Rothman et al., 2013). The slower, more deliberate efforts of being aware at times may need to fight for survival, remain at the foreground, and thus exercise more conscious influence on unconscious habits.

The importance of emotional insight should be front-and-center as well. On the way to the successful enacted affect regulation in real time, when a negative self-system is activated, many affective "know-hows" need to shift. Within the mutual self-regulation afforded by the therapist's ability to regulate herself, a patient may internalize and assimilate new ways of dealing with arousal states (Schore, 2012; Schore and Schore, 2008). Recalling the role of the mirror neuron system in mediating empathy and the emotionally resonant understanding of the other in the dyad (Gallese, 2006; Iacoboni, 2008), Schore's therapeutic model is incredibly prescient. This internalized capacity for regulation is translated to more integrative ways of being.

We can ask, however, if it is necessary to put into words—a verbal insight—whatever emotional gains have been achieved, whether any additional reflective awareness can strengthen the states of well-being and emotional and integrative progress. The understanding that affect and cognition are intertwined throughout the brain/mind (Koziol and Budding, 2010; Lewis and Todd, 2007; Panksepp and Biven, 2012) points toward an answer. Based on neuropsychological evidence and, more important, clinical experiences, we can assume that both aspects of mental functioning are needed for new internal and external patterns take hold. Reflective awareness focusing on many therapeutic interactions, especially as they are happening, can greatly consolidate affective states. Just as an emotional experience affects cognitive aspects, the reverse is true as well, expanding the nature of insight.

INSIGHT IS NOT ENOUGH

Insight by itself—by definition an act of reflection bringing together affect and cognition—is necessary but not sufficient for change. If a therapeutic realization is not followed by repeated efforts to hold on to it and further experience and reflect on it in real time, its effectiveness is lost. The occasional understanding, even if accompanied by intense emotions during therapy, is no match for the automatic and habitual forces of nonconscious processes. On the other hand, identifying brain/mind characteristics that either fight or promote enduring insight will enable us to better understand what can help patients hold on to a realization and implement desired changes.

As we often see in our work, insight without continued awareness and attempts at regulation through self-talk or gained perspective, for example, are not enough for sustained change. We have repeatedly seen that our brain/mind operates under the control of both conscious and unconscious forces, the latter having a distinct advantage. Studies have shown that it is difficult for the more deliberate faculties to hold on and slow down the automaticity of brain/mind processes (Bargh, 2007, 2014; Damasio, 2010; Gollwitzer and Oettinger, 2013; Gollwitzer et al., 2007). Indeed, when it comes to maladaptive automatic enaction of unconscious systems, we often witness the difficulties in holding on to reflectiveness in the face of overwhelming emotions or the distorted convictions of negative self-narratives. In effect, insight cannot be separate from the process of working through, where repeated efforts are made to reinforce new understanding and new coping skills.

Newly experienced insights in a particular psychotherapy session are often not strong enough to endure, especially at the beginning of the therapeutic process, before the capacity for affect regulation and a lasting reflective ability take hold. One's habitual and automatic way of being feels more real and authentic than the newly acquired insight and thus quickly and automatically resumes. The dissociated self-systems can be negative or positive, but possibly because of their weaker neural connections, they are experienced as alien and not belonging to the "real" self. They often feel fraudulent. As old affects and behaviors take over, there is no new insight or state to mull over in between sessions; it fades as only the old one asserts itself. Without reflective awareness and no explicit reactivation, the long-term memories of the session are inhibited (Dudai, 2011).

AN EXPANDED DEFINITION OF INSIGHT

We need to expand our definition of what *insight* means. Insight does not end with the acquired new understanding of the roots of a difficulty or an unworkable pattern; a more active definition should take into account the efforts to maintain such new and meaningful understandings. This can be achieved through mindful reflection. As effortful as mindful reflections are at the beginning, with time—when sufficiently learned and fully encoded—they become automatically employed when needed. The transformative power of mindful awareness or reflective awareness lies in the process of becoming coupled with a dysregulated narrative or affect in real time (Bateman and Fonagy, 2004, 2012; Jurist, 2008; Lane, 2008; Lane et al., 2014; Lewis and Todd, 2007; Siegel, 1999, 2007; Wilson, 2011). This process actively recruits the power inherent in the integrated processes of affect and cognition (Lane et al., 2014; Lewis and Todd, 2007; Watt, 2012). The development of reflective awareness can ensure that reactions to internal cues or external circumstances are relatively free from the pull of the narrow personal meaning of triggering stimuli. An interpersonal difficulty may no longer automatically indicate a personal failure but will be understood in the context of wider, more reality-bound circumstances, for example.

We may hear from patients that they authentically wish to change the way they relate to themselves and others, that they want to become better at managing their dysregulated emotions, that they would like to separate from internal parental voices and establish their own sense of identity and agency. We often also hear a genuine wish for avoiding addictions, for engaging in less destructive interpersonal patterns, for less avoidant behaviors that protect against failure at all costs. Patients often know that to do anything else surely compromises one's quality of life. Yet it is difficult to translate such wishes and necessary choices into behavioral and psychological action. During dysregulation, the executed self-system seems not to be easily amenable to the corrections that are guided by the cortico–cerebellum connection.

Damasio (2010) sees this skewed balance between conscious and unconscious processes as stemming from neural competition for brain space and functions. Unconscious processes (evolutionarily ancient and individually linked to earlier developmental phases) control a wide range of learned patterns and behaviors. With repeated reinforcement, these become habitually tenacious. The unconscious realm, essentially the function of subcortical and emotional regions that guide meaningful behavioral patterns, easily "wins" out. The more under the influence of the lower brain regions, the more automated these emotional, behavioral, and defensive patterns are.

What makes reflectiveness absent in some patients is the fact that the prefrontal cortex does not function in isolation but interacts with the cerebellum and the basal ganglia. As we recall, both play a central role in deciding what incoming information reaches the cortex and is used by it (Koziol, 2014; Koziol and Budding, 2010). We see then, that our emotional, cognitive, and behavioral unconscious maps or self-systems occupy different spaces along a flexible/rigid gradient (Gazzaniga et al., 2014; Koziol and Budding, 2010). The greater the interaction between the interlocking systems that guide behaviors, the greater one's instinctive capacity to adapt to changing situations and disconnect from old learning and memory structures. This integration is at the heart of what we consider executive function, and by extrapolation, it is also the central determinant of the flexibility–rigidity continuum. An increased reflective awareness is closely linked to strengthening the functions of PFC regions that in turn inform subcortical areas about the necessary course of action (Lane, 2008; Lane et al., 2014; McRae et al., 2013; Ochsner and Barrett, 2001). Sustained reflective awareness slows down one's responses, allowing for more flexible reactions to novel situations over time and with greater consistency.

THE ACTION OF THERAPEUTIC CHANGE: THE EXPLICIT REALM OF THE THERAPEUTIC PROCESS

The tension between conscious and unconscious processes renders these two modes of functioning more open to improved integrative communication. In effect this potential is precisely what enables psychotherapy to work. The mutual effects between conscious and unconscious processes mean that many potential influences reside in both realms; once implemented and incorporated, such neuropsychological changes affect both. Hence, together, explicit and implicit processes are responsible for therapeutic change, some easily identifiable, others not at all. It is also important to realize that even when we think that a particular technique or reflective exercise have helped in the explicit realm, this realm of functioning is entwined with the implicit one. As a result, it is impossible to truly ascertain what is explicit as opposed to implicit, because we cannot know how the verbal interacts with the nonverbal. For this discussion and for convenience sake, explicit and implicit therapeutic actions are discussed separately.

In the explicit realm, the ability of the prefrontal regions to modulate behavior has been greatly studied. For example, due to the participation of PFC executive functions, themselves influenced by subcortical areas (Koziol, 2014), transforming maps give rise to more conscious images and as a result to more adaptive behaviors (Damasio, 2010; Panksepp and Biven, 2012; Wilson, 2011). Having direct connection to subcortical regions, circuits in the PFC can modulate complex patterns of behavior (Viamontes, 2011). As a result they can mediate adaptable, flexible, and goal-directed behaviors that consider short- and long-term internal and interpersonal consequences. In tandem, the conscious recruitment of working memory may help in self-awareness and regulation (McRae et al., 2012; Viamontes, 2011).

As both the conscious and unconscious realms are intertwined, the persistent push of unconscious systems may be slowed, derailed, and modulated, trying, learning, and encoding more efficient connections between the fast and the slow functions (LeDoux, 2002). Interestingly, the effect of more conscious processes is seen by Damasio (2010) as the ability to deliberate, reflect, and plan rather than exert rigid control. Reflective awareness and the enhanced emotion regulation it can promote seem to present some counterbalance to automatic repetitions of maladaptive patterns, internal and interpersonal, the value of reflectiveness in therapy has begun to soar (Bateman and Fonagy 2004, 2012; Beck, 1979; Cozolino, 2002, 2006; Fonagy, 2008; Jurist, 2008; Kanter et al., 2009; Lane, 2008, Lane et al., 2014; Wallin, 2007).

Underpinning the shifts between conscious and unconscious control is the changing relationship between subcortical and cortical areas. Although the basal ganglia and the cerebellum are involved in unconsciously selecting the appropriate response, habit, or procedure, it does not necessarily mean a behavioral output. This is because the frontal cortex is receiving information from other cortical regions as well. The additional input of the current situation may lead to more deliberate and analyzed response, more adaptive to the new situation. It bears repeating again that optimally higher-level processes resulting in slower, more deliberative reactions to internal and external events are mediated automatically as well. It is only in the face of a "disappeaing" reflective ability, especially during stress or dysregulation, that we need to encourage patients to recruit deliberate and effortful attempts at awareness and cognitive processing.

THE ROLE OF THE FLEXIBLE–RIGID CONTINUUM

A shifting change in the flexible–rigid tension is clearly behind the important adaptational ability to learn from reality, to let new information inform old lessons and reinforced convictions. When a self-system is rigid, operating mostly from old maps, it does not take a new reality into account. A therapeutic focus on enhancing a patient's reflecting abilities will reduce his tendency to incorporate new situations into old ones, blur the distinctions between them, and interpret them in the only one familiar way.

In the context of social behavior, Lieberman (2003) proposes two brain systems: the reflexive and the reflective. The reflexive system is activated under conditions that generate unconscious, implicit, or automatic processing of social and intersubjective information. Subcortical pathways and the limbic system mediate the implicit integration of affects, drives, and object associations, and as such they underpin the implicit processing of emotional/social information. Data from mirror neuron system studies confirm the role of the limbic system in intersubjective unconscious emotional processing; neural activation in response to others reaches the amygdala via the insula (Carr et al., 2003; Gallese, 2008). We make quick intuitive social judgments and acquire behavioral sequences and procedures that are necessary for interaction and adaptation in much the same way we acquire motor skills (Bargh, 2014). Like any acquired pattern, unconscious interpersonal ones can harden into rigid, maladaptive response tendencies, especially if rooted in painful childhood experiences. Here, the slower, more deliberate reflective awareness in real time can provide effective brakes on hyperaroused reactivity.

The centrality of reflection to regulation and well-being echoes in the importance of theory of mind in both children and adults (Fonagy, 2000, 2008). Both functions are linked to self-understanding and the grasping of other people's minds, to the ability to become aware of emotional and behavioral patterns and regulate them in real time (Bateman and Fonagy, 2008; Ginot, 2012; Iacoboni, 2008; Jurist, 2008; Lane et al., 2014). In other words, reflective awareness can greatly contribute to one's adaptive move from unwanted unconscious reactions to an aware mindfulness that gives us choices. The capacity to understand other people's minds has been also recently linked to the medial prefrontal regions, emphasizing their importance to interpersonal reflective awareness (Ghaznavi et al., 2011).

Calkins and Leekers for example, describe emotional self-regulation as "those behaviors, skills, and strategies, whether conscious or unconscious, automatic or effortful, that serve to modulate, inhibit, and enhance emotional experiences and expression" (2013, p. 355). As part of the therapeutic process, reflective awareness is most likely the first step toward regulation. This step starts with the capacity to experience strong affect, the building block of a core self-state, while simultaneously reflecting on it and its behavioral and verbal expressions (Ecker et al., 2012; Jurist, 2008; Siegel, 1999). Even more important, repeated reflective efforts will lead to the integration of regulation skills, rendering them more automatic rather than only effortful and therefore less fragile (Blair and Ursache, 2013; Calkins and Leekers, 2013; Kanter et al., 2009).

In an important reminder of the potential countervalence to automaticity, reflection enables a more adaptive conscious control, especially to new situations—an advantage over merely automatic actions that enact the past in the present. This balance (or tug-of-war, as it were) between conscious control and unconscious lack of awareness is always at play. As we already saw, this balance largely shapes the specific features of the conscious–unconscious continuum in each of us. It determines the level of flexibility and openness to change—attributes that may determine therapeutic progress.

MENTALIZED AFFECTIVITY: A THERAPEUTIC ACTION INTEGRATING AFFECT AND COGNITION

What we know so far from neuroscience research is that the substrate of dysregulated as well as regulated states is found in the image and map-making regions in the cerebellum and the basal ganglia. Once any of these trigger regions is activated, a chain of events occurs—chemical molecules are secreted by the endocrine glands and by subcortical nuclei and delivered to both the body and the brain. These influence the more conscious mediating areas in the cerebral cortex; cognitive and emotional functions, including defenses that were successful in the past, are automatically employed (Damasio, 2010; Koziol and Budding, 2010; Panksepp and Biven, 2012). (See Damasio, 2010, for a discussion on how consciousness comes to be.)

As we try to understand the implications of such brain/mind systems, the importance of including affect and cognition in our therapeutic interventions naturally comes to mind. Hence, the act of reflective awareness itself is never far away from the emotions or negative narratives it sets to modulate. The idea that an emotional experience is essential for enduring changes of behavioral and interpersonal patterns is not new, of course, and many have stressed that change without it is merely short-lived (Bromberg, 2006; Cozolino, 2002; Fosha, 2000; Schore, 2011, 2012). The inclusion of the body as a carrier of experience has been showing significant therapeutic benefits as well (P. Ogden, 2009, P. Ogden et al., 2006; Schore, 2012). What is added here is the inclusion of reflectiveness while in the midst of emotional dysregulation (mentalized affectivity), thus integrating affect and cognition in our therapeutic efforts.

Further strengthening the links between affect and cognition Blair and Ursache (2013, p. 304) demonstrated that executive functions are intertwined with and dependent on emotional, attentional, and stress-related systems. Although executive functions are primarily involved in top-down regulation, they are still linked to attention and emotion mediated by bottom-up, nonexecutive regulation. When subcortical and limbic emotional systems register internal or external stimuli, they activate stress and attention physiology. Recall here the role of the amygdala in directing attention toward any new or emotion-inducing stimuli. With overwhelming physio/emotional responses, PFC activity is reduced, and the anterior cingulate cortex and limbic systems induce stress responses and increased neuroendocrine hormone activity (Critchley, 2005).

In line with Schore's model, Blair and Ursache (2013) maintain that because executive functions are affected by levels of stress hormones, compromised early experiences can result in the development of an overwhelming stress physiology. In chaotic, unpredictable environments, infants and children's attention, emotion, and stress physiology are more reactive. These children are less likely to develop efficient cognitive and executive functions. As adults, the compromised reflective awareness makes it difficult for them to be able to hold the other—the therapist—in mind, reflect on their own internal experiences, and importantly develop adaptive regulation (Fonagy, 2001). Consequently, often therapeutic processes that engage such patients benefit from helping them develop reflective ability and mentalization.

Leaving content aside, the therapist can, for example, engage a patient who frequently misses sessions in trying to become aware of her frequent absences. Because we know that the patient's automatic behavior tends toward lack of reflection, a series of questions and tasks designed to encourage her to actively reflect on her behavior can be developed together. Following a "forgetful" absence, the patient can be asked if she thought of the therapist waiting for her, or if she thought about the therapy at all on the day of the appointment. The patient can be instructed to think of the therapist waiting for her and about their relationship and what it means to her. Indeed, more structured manuals for treating dysregulated reflective abilities have been developed and used, especially with borderline patients (Fonagy, 2001, 2008; Kerenberg, 1975, 1997; Levy et al., 2011).

What is new in this discussion is the realization that because all mental processes are structurally and functionally entwined, we can use any aspect of a maladaptive state as a venue to induce mindfulness and change the course of enaction. Negative self-narratives, for example, can become the focus of reflectiveness with the goal of reframing debilitating emotional ideas about the self. Similarly, enhanced regulation can be achieved through simultaneously linking emotional experience and reflectiveness. Jurist's (2008) notion of mentalized affectivity, engaging the patient's reflectiveness while still maintaining the affective qualities of the experience, seems to indicate a movement toward a fruitful integration of the affective and the cognitive elements of dysregulated states. Reflecting on one's emotions, narratives, or behaviors while in the midst of them can potentially enhance regulation (Bateman and Fonagy, 2012; Lane, 2008 Pally, 2007; 2012; Siegel, 2007; Wilson, 2011).

Uncoupling present emotions and thoughts from their past origin and understanding their old purpose, differentiating between internal states and present circumstances that in reality do not correspond to them, and gaining the ability to gain a flexible frame of reference contribute to affect regulation. But as has been mentioned a few times, for some patients, in order for such a capacity to develop, active efforts need to be learned, implemented, and rehearsed. If patients are able to do it in real time, while in the midst of a dysregulated state both in the session and out of it, the chance of enduring change is tangible.

The development of mindful awareness through becoming aware of one's internal states and not being afraid of them, but rather reframing them through self-talk and a more reality-bound perspective, are some of the more common reflective techniques utilized today (Ecker et al., 2012; Gollwitzer and Oettinger, 2013; Jurist, 2008). These approaches, however, are entirely couched in the emotional glue that holds a maladaptive self-state together. As emotion and cognition are so closely intertwined, the act of reflectiveness, while in the midst of an emotional state that distorts one's capacity for wellbeing, serves to reshape and restore the balance between the two (Lewis, 2005; Lewis and Todd, 2007). As emotions and automatic behaviors become more modulated they do not take over one's entire conscious experience. Perspective gains a foothold and can calm one down. In turn, more regulated states also affect the quality of attention and cognition, specifically the level of one's negative thinking.

By widening the concept of reflectiveness to include both the cognitive and the affective aspects of the therapeutic experiences, Jurist and Lane have recognized the inextricable connection between the verbal and the emotional, emphasizing their inherent link and its importance to the process of affect regulation (Damasio, 2000; LeDoux, 2002; Lewis and Todd, 2007; Panksepp, 2012; Toomey and Ecker, 2009).

*cf. mindfulness class
homework focuses on noticing
emotions and "turning towards"
(ie. regulating)*

Implicit and Explicit Therapeutic Processes   177

REFLECTIVE AWARENESS IN ACTION

In an interesting development, the conclusions coming out of neuro-psychological studies echo some basic concepts of psychodynamic therapies. For example, perceived self-efficacy was found as an important characteristic underpinning the ability to maintain awareness and reframe overwhelming emotional situations (Gollwitzer and Oettinger, 2013). Such feelings of self-efficacy are clearly the goal of most therapeutic approaches and are greatly affected by many aspects of the therapeutic process, both explicit and implicit. Papie and Aarts (2013) also stress the importance of self-agency for maintaining awareness and regulation. Successful attempts at regulation have also been linked to action performance—in other words, the practice of newly learned regulation approaches (Prinz, 2003; Wegner, 2002). According to these clinicians, a sense of agency is the result of comparing an action—mental or behavioral—to a preconceived intended goal. Gollwitzer and Oettinger (2013) maintain that self-agency only emerges from conscious intention to pursue a specific goal.

These conclusions emphasize the relationship between intentional actions and a growing sense of agency. Whether taking place in session or outside of it, an active persistent intention to reflect on one's dysregulated emotion clearly contributes to effective regulation. As I stress again later, such attempts at reflection in real time are not intended to erase an emotion or a disturbing thought. Rather, an emotional/cognitive state is experienced to its fullness and total intensity, but the patient is not entirely drowning in it (Jurist, 2008; Lane et al., 2014). When the act of forming an intentional goal is consciously pursued, when a plan is actively held in one's mind, regulation has a chance to increasingly take hold (Bayer et al., 2010; McRae et al., 2013).

In the context of the brain/mind's propensity to enact existing patterns, such conclusions are at once practical and interesting; they emphasize action control rather than changing the self to enhance regulation. It is not that the centrality of more fundamental shifts in unconscious systems themselves are disregarded. By remembering the entwined links among mental functions, what psychodynamic clinicians gain are additional therapeutic tools for fostering regulation and change. Regulation abilities fostered by reflection in turn affect whole internal systems.

The implication of these studies is that a patient is capable of committing himself to hold on to mentalized affectivity and regulation in the session and outside of it. Moods, feelings of anxiety and agitation, and a sense of safety or calmness can all benefit from an active and intentional reframing and recontextualizing. The implementation of intention is an efficient way to overcome the automatic habitual responses guided by implicit systems (Gollwitzer and Oettinger, 2013; Ochsner and Gross, 2005). This process may start through an imagined conscious intent to regulate developed in the session, but then can be implemented in real time in the context of the patient's life.

WHAT NEUROSCIENCE HAS TO OFFER CLINICIANS

In the clinical realm, Toomey and Ecker (2009) and more recently Ecker et al. (2012) propose that therapeutic change can be achieved through a process of "disconfirmation" or recontexualization of an unconscious disturbing emotional state. Underlying their clinical approach is the recent discovery that on resurrection implicit memories reconsolidate again, giving us the opportunity to erase the emotional learning embedded within them (LeDoux, 2014; LeDoux and Schiller, 2009; Milner et al., 1998). During erasure of maladaptive emotional learning, old constructs receive a direct disconfirmation via new and vivid emotional experiences. At those intense therapeutic moments, "what had seemed real is finally recognized as being only one's own fallible construct" (Ecker et al., 2012, p. 55). In a larger sense, as we saw in previous sections of this chapter, such a process of recontextualization couples the direct experience of disturbing affects, memories, or automatic defenses with reflective awareness that questions their validity in relation to the present. These clinicians suggest that within a safe, empathetic environment allowing a disturbing memory to "slide" from the (unconscious and affective) right hemisphere into the left (more conscious and deliberate) will generate change through the enhancement of reappraisal or reframing processes. This approach is supported by studies exploring the benefits of various self-distancing, distracting, and "cooling" techniques used in the midst of overwhelming "hot" affects (Mischel and Ayduk, 2013).

The therapeutic action of mentalized affectivity is further illustrated through a growing number of studies exploring the effects of cognitive reappraisal on emotional reactions. Subjects who were instructed to reappraise their reactions (reactions to films, startle eye blink) reported feeling less negative in response to films, anticipation of painful shock, negative autobiographical memories, and stressful speech tasks. Reappraisal was also shown to reduce cortisol response to stressors (Lane, 2008; Lane et al., 2014) and reduce negative association with emotional arousal (Deveney and Pizzagalli, 2008). Interestingly, such coupling of affect and awareness also lies at the base of mindful awareness promoted and enhanced by various meditation practices. The positive effects of continuous mediation practice on affect regulation have been repeatedly confirmed in studies using imaging of brain structures before and after meditative sessions (for example, Davidson, 2000; Davidson and Begley, 2012; Goleman, 2003; Hanson and Mendius, 2009).

In other neuroimaging studies, subjects were able to increase or decrease amygdala response according to their regulatory goals. Instructed to evaluate fear-inducing film clips as more intense (up-regulation), or conversely less so (down-regulation), subjects actively influenced the intensity of their of amygdalar activation (Bauer and Baumeister, 2013; Gollwitzer and Oettinger, 2013; McRae et al., 2013; Rothman et al., 2013). Those who reframed the emotional value of the clips to down-regulate reduced the levels of amygdala activation. The authors conclude that individuals can either amplify or diminish their amygdalar responses in accordance with their affect regulation goals. These writers and others contribute to the growing understanding that as affect and cognition inform each other, thought processes clearly shape the emotional hub.

Other instructions called for distracting oneself from overwhelming negative emotions and deliberate suppression of feelings, mainly through not showing any affect to others. Not surprisingly, suppression of negative affects was much less effective than reframing. In an interesting implication for therapeutic techniques, a decrease in amygdala activation due to reappraisal was greater than the one due to distraction. Both reduced amygdala activity, but the reappraisal more so. Reappraisal was more effective at reducing the subjective experience of emotion through the cognitive process of manipulating the affective *meaning* of negative stimuli. Not surprisingly, and in line with clinical experiences, distraction and deliberate suppression of affect were the least effective at regulation.

These conclusions are significant in light of findings that depressed patients have exhibited an increased activation of the amygdala in response to masked negative stimuli (Sharpley, 2010). Conversely, they have showed reduced responsiveness to positive stimuli (see Whalen et al., 2009). In concert with clinicians who have found awareness of emotional states essential for regulation, integrating these findings further opens the possibility that helping depressed patients become aware of their internal states while reflecting on them might affect amygdala activation. When we remember the multifaceted role of the amygdala in our emotional life and in the building of unconscious self-systems, any change its activation should be noted. Indeed, if mentalized affectivity—the attempts to reevaluate the meaning of a stimulus, its context, and relevance to current time—can induce neuropsychological changes, it should become part of any therapeutic process. When sustained and repeated reflectiveness can modulate the intensity of the amygdala's response, the effect of emotional memories, the attention given to negative stimuli, and the physiological reactions that accompany these, affect regulation can be achieved (Phelps and LeDoux, 2005; Wager et al., 2008).

Interestingly, subjects suffering from post-traumatic stress disorder (PTSD) were less successful when using reappraisal to reduce self-reported negative affects; they also failed to recruit prefrontal regions that healthier subjects could (McRae et al., 2013). It is possible that effortful reflection—reappraisal—is much more taxing within this population, indicating the need for repeated attempts within a safe therapeutic environment. The notion of mentalized affectivity—or in the language of the studies, reported reappraisal of emotions in real time—seems to be particularly relevant when working with survivors of trauma.

Although neuropsychological research following psychotherapy is scant so far, a vast body of accumulated clinical experience has demonstrated that repeated awareness of one's feelings and reflecting on the meaning embedded in one's actions, narratives, or fantasies often leads to emotion regulation and enhanced integration in one's conscious sense of self (Cozolino, 2002, 2006; Damasio, 2010; Panksepp and Biven, 2012; Wallin, 2007; Wilkinson, 2010). Unless we consider both affect and the cognitions embedded within it, something important in our therapeutic efforts is lost.

According to Lewis and Todd (2007) as well as Siegel (2007), the real-time linking of emotion, awareness, and reflection will alter the interactive loop between the anterior cingulate cortex, the PFC, the amygdala, and other subcortical areas. Consequently, new integrative links will be created. This approach, as demonstrated by Toomey and Eckers (2009) and Ecker et al. (2012) can be practiced in session and also used in therapeutic homework. A process of reevaluation of meaning and relevance can change the trajectory of a maladaptive emotional reaction (McRae, Ochsner, and Gross, 2013). This process of coupling affect and reflection in dream work and analysis of transference–countertransference entanglements can also enhance the patient's neuropsychological ability to search for new and creative ways of feeling and understanding oneself (Domash, 2010).

Often, however, reflecting on one's dysregulated state is not an easy process, and without the safe space provided by psychotherapy, it is not generally an option that can take place. Entrenched unconscious coping strategies or defenses ensure that no new learning occurs, allowing overwhelming emotions to take over. Efforts to develop an emotional awareness of one's narratives during dysregulation are difficult. They are met with the difficulties inherent in the brain/mind's tendency to repeat and enact what it knows, in this case, dysregulated states.

Without efficient ways to provide a new context, a new way of under-standing and acting, the resultant state with its embedded predictable narrative signals that nothing has changed. This is where therapy's enor-mous contributions come in: when narratives and the emotions they embody are reflected on within the empathetic conditions of treatment, the emotion will become regulated as well.

In Jurist's words: "Mentalized affectivity entails revaluing, not just modulating, affect. Mentalized affectivity captures what is most chal-lenging in adult affect regulation: that new meaning can be created and specified by reflecting upon affective experiences" (2008, p. 105). Such reflectiveness further integrates affect and cognition and will enhance one's familiarity with a particular self-state, including some of its uncon-scious underpinnings.

NEW DIRECTIONS IN THERAPEUTIC EFFICACY

These are some of the ideas behind CBT (Beck, 1979; Beck et al., 1990) and they also seem to explain the reported efficacy of EMDR (see Ecker et al., 2012; Panksepp and Biven, 2012). The act of reflecting on an experience in real time is also an important part of understanding and using therapeutic enactments (see Chapter 4). What this chapter has sought to add is the idea that although insight is irreplaceable, if it only happens within the therapeutic encounter and sporadically at best, its efficacy will be limited. Without the efforts of mentalized affectivity, the insightful self-state will be replaced, sometimes immediately after a session, by the more habitual state. Even though we sometimes refer to these shifts as dissociative, the process is inherent in the brain/mind's habitual nonconscious activity, which automatically favors already exist-ing networks to the creation of new ones.

Reflectiveness, as understood and discussed here, is not to be con-fused with cognitive approaches such as trying to talk one out of dysreg-ulation. As mentioned before, subjects instructed to suppress negative affects were not successful at regulating their reactions to a negative situation (Mischel and Ayduk, 2013). The potential effectiveness of men-talized affectivity during therapy and outside it seems to be rooted in the patient's ability to experience a dysregulated state underpinned by a unconscious system and attempt to reframe it at the same time. Similar to Lane (2008) and Lane et al.'s (2014) findings showing the importance of emotional awareness to affect regulation, Suvic-Wrana et al. (2011) showed that rather than increase dysregulation, emotional awareness aids it. Suppression of negative feelings among people suffering from anxiety and depression led to ineffective regulation strategies. Conversely, conscious awareness of one's internal states and the ability to articulate them, according to these researchers, is a precondition for the use of reappraisal as an adaptive affect regulation strategy.

IMPLICIT THERAPEUTIC ACTION

Obviously, we can't directly reflect on the state of our amygdalas or other neural structures; nor can we become more aware of the incremental neurochemical changes resulting from the therapeutic work. Although the role of reflective awareness is considerable, other therapeutic actions affect both internal and external structures. Dimensions of the therapeutic relationship and its mutual regulation, the level of empathetic acceptance on the therapist's part, and many unconscious identification processes are as important as reflection. In particular, Bion (1984, 1990), Kohut (1971), and Schore's (2012) work—among others—illuminate the implicit and nonverbal mutual influences that the therapeutic encounter offers. Other clinicians such as Fosshage (2005, 2011) and Bromberg (1998, 2006) clearly integrate both explicit and implicit elements in their therapeutic models.

Following the importance of learning processes in the formation of conscious and unconscious systems, we also need to consider such processes as an important part of successful therapy. In some essential way, the therapeutic relationship is a learning ground for new ways of being, for fresh ways to relate to oneself and others. Such learning may be slow, but it is also inevitable, especially when repeated lessons and practice are part of the process inside the therapy and outside of it. This inevitability is one of the most hopeful aspects of therapy. Even when patients display a great deal of rigid systems that make them seem resistant and in some cases immovable, if they remain in therapy, chances are good that they will internalize many new understandings and behaviors that culminate in structural changes.

The processes of learning and internalization that continually occur within the intersubjective realm of therapy are also tied up with the important function of unconscious identification with the therapist. What underpins interpersonal imitation, identification, and modeling is the automatic activation of the mirror neuron system (Olds, 2012). Returning to Schore's model, the therapist's capacity to stay regulated in the face of a stormy arousal state, the patient's and possibly her own, will directly affect the patient's ability to regulate. There is little doubt that in addition to the mutual activation of right-brain regions, unconscious learning is also taking place. In other learning processes, the mutual resolution of enactments and therapeutic impasses "teaches" patients how to overcome interpersonal hurdles and how to integrate the old with the new.

IS IT THE THERAPEUTIC APPROACH OR
TIME SPENT IN THERAPY?

Although we mostly cannot see or measure the implicit elements promoting and sustaining therapeutic change, they are part of any therapeutic encounter. At the same time, considering the repetitive and rigid tendencies of unconscious systems, one has to question whether therapeutic approaches that offer a limited number of sessions can be effective in promoting substantial and lasting change. Quite a few studies have compared short-term therapeutic approaches such as CBT and dialectical behavior therapy (DBT) with psychodynamically oriented long-term therapies. In spite of the accepted wisdom, backed by some evidence (Beck et al., 1979), that symptom-focused approaches are as effective, the results of recent studies are much more interesting. In light of the unconscious model, they also are not surprising.

In a large meta-analysis study Shedler (2011) presents compelling evidence that psychodynamic therapy is as effective in ameliorating symptoms as other, more "evidence-based" approaches, such as CBT. Moreover, patients who received psychodynamic psychotherapy maintained their gains. These therapeutic gains continued to strengthen with time. Similarly, Rabung and Leichsenring (2011), as well as Huber et al. (2011) report on the therapeutic efficacy of long-term psychotherapy and psychoanalysis. Both were found to be more effective than short-term therapy, at termination and afterward. Luyten et al. (2011) found that even after termination patients demonstrated a "sleeper" effect, reporting that their therapeutic gains held up and even strengthened with time.

In an interesting study, Knekt et al. (2011) examined three therapeutic modalities: (1) solution-focused therapy that lasted 12 session; (2) short-term psychodynamic therapy that lasted for 20 sessions; and (3) long-term dynamic psychotherapy that lasted for three years. In addition, a group of patients underwent psychoanalysis with four weekly sessions. At the five-year follow-up, the long-term psychotherapy and psychoanalysis were the most effective at reducing symptoms and maintaining change. Last, Taylor (2011) and Slavin-Mulford and Hilsenroth (2011) also maintain that on termination, patients of long-term dynamic psychotherapy achieve structural change, maintain their gains, and continue to build on them after therapy is over.

When trying to decipher the meaning of these studies, we are still faced with not knowing exactly the determining factors that have contributed to change (Safran and Shaker, 2011). One of the common conclusions is that intense, emotionally focused dynamic therapy is more conducive to structural change—certainly a conclusion that strengthens the importance of coupling emotion with reflectiveness. Long-term psychotherapies most likely also emphasize the therapeutic relationship, the power of empathy, the therapist's self-disclosure of her own experiences during an enactment (Ginot, 1997), and the process of reflective awareness on transference–countertransference impasses (Ginot, 2001, 2007, 2009).

What is so interesting about these and other studies is the fact that with a CBT approach the reduction of symptoms occurs quicker in comparison with psychodynamic approaches. At the same time, with the completion of therapy the therapeutic effects fade (Slavin-Mulford and Hilsenroth, 2011). In the same vain, Levy et al. (2011) compared different modalities of treating patients with diagnosed with borderline disorder. One group received transference-focused therapy (Kerenberg, 2007), together with mentalization-focused therapy (Bateman and Fonagy, 2004), while another group received DBT. They found that while patients who received DBT treatment showed similar benefits to those receiving transference-focused and mentalization therapy, only patients in the latter group retained improvements in reflective awareness and attachment patterns as measured by the Adult Attachment Interview. The authors interpret these indexes to reflect structural change.

Can we state for a fact that the important therapeutic action reside in the dynamic orientation alone, or is the factor of time just as important? Certainly the results can strongly hint that with a lengthy therapy, the opportunities for internalized learning make the process very effective at inducing structural changes or changes in entrenched self-systems. The possibility that new, healthier behaviors have a chance to be reflected on, encouraged, executed, and reinforced increases the chance that they will stick. As implementation occurs, reported and repeated, new pathways continue to develop, strengthening new networks.

As a whole, this accumulating body of data is obviously very significant to contemporary therapeutic approaches. As much as one would wish for easy solutions for very complicated human conditions, as much as we would like to quickly fix a wide range of symptoms and emotional difficulties, what is emerging is entirely in concert with what we know about unconscious brain/mind processes. Approaches that emphasize short-term symptom relief will possibly succeed in promoting lasting change if more time is allotted to the difficult job of tackling unconscious processes that in effect underlie all emotional difficulties.

THE CASE OF LEAH: BETWEEN YEARNING AND FLIGHT

The following case, describing a long-tern therapy process, further illustrates the intersection of affective, bodily, and cognitive elements that together brought a significant transformation in the patient's internal world. Changes in her work life and relationships ensued.

Leah was a 31-year-old married woman when she started therapy (about 7 years ago). She described ambivalence about her marriage but could not specify what made her dissatisfied. She expressed an acute confusion about her new career choice. She had just finished law school and passed the bar exam. On completing this long and arduous journey, she became extremely anxious and distressed, so much so that she could barely eat or sleep. Thinking about her lined up job only made her more dysregulated.

Leah could not understand what was "driving her crazy," why she was so anxious and dispirited, so unable to be happy in her marriage with a man who loved her and with her career. She wanted to enjoy her success more, but she couldn't. As therapy continued, she described ambivalent feelings about most things in her life. As far as she could remember, she was seldom satisfied with where she was, with her group of friends, or where she lived. Her feelings about her mother and her two sisters were especially fraught, and often Leah would express a great deal of guilt for not feeling closer to them and not loving them more. Her father was the only figure in her life that seemed to elicit more stable, loving feelings.

Leah, however, was far from her family. She immigrated to this country in her early twenties, following her then-boyfriend to his new job. Until she joined the army, Leah grew up in a kibbutz, where from about two months of age she spent most of the time in the group home. Parents would visit the infants, but most of the time, certainly at night, the infants were watched over by designated caretakers and later on by teachers. Like all other children, she visited home every afternoon for a few hours and was always happy to play and spend time with her older sisters. Her parents, however, were very active members of the community and were often busy.

With time Leah's bodily sense of her experiences as a child intensified; she remembered other children crying in response to each other's distress; the continuous noise in the children's room, especially at night; the way different caretakers would handle the kids under their charge. Most of all, she became aware of her yearning to see her parents as much as possible and her frequent disappointment when even during family time they were elsewhere. Her consciously felt resentment toward her parents grew alongside unconscious bereft feelings of abandonment and helplessness.

Leah's worst memories described a frightened girl who felt alone, with nobody to turn to. Her feelings were always kept away from her parents, sisters, and friends. As much as she tried to adopt her friends' carefree existence, she still remained mostly unsettled, unsure about herself and unhappy. She could not wait to flee the kibbutz, but when she did, and made a new life for herself, she still felt just the way she did "when she was 5 and 15." One of Leah's dreams brought her back to the communal dinning room table, where in the midst of the noisy din that she was familiar with, she was forced to finish a big plate of food. She was hungry before, and was happy with the food, but then, plate after plate full of food continued to arrive, and she was expected to finish them all. If she didn't, something bad was going to happen to her. She woke up feeling helpless and in a great panic. The dream reminded her of how she felt while growing up. The kibbutz and her parents, she said, knew nothing about what she needed or craved. They raised her, but not in the way that was good for her. Things were done for her, food was given, but her need for a comforting presence was more unreachable. Leah looked for it among friends, but she always wondered how it must feel to be really important to a loving parent who could focus on her.

As time went on, Leah realized that her tremendous anxiety about her career and marriage was a manifestation of a deeper, almost all-consuming inability to surrender to a situation, experience herself in the moment, and enjoy where she was. In her unconscious self-system, a surrender without being on guard, without bracing her self in tense anticipation, meant experiencing an overwhelming fear. Her amygdala, from the very beginning attuned to noises and unpredictable events, and her mirror neuron systems attuned to the crying of other kids, coalesced into a self-system that became sensitized to interpersonal danger while craving it immensely. The amalgam of thwarted needs and disappointments, of repeated fears that only reinforced fleeing, resulted in an enacted emotional ambivalence; close relationships were the source of both potential comfort and hurtful disappointments. In Leah's case, the part that craved a supportive and loving person in her life was strong enough to actively "participate" in the choice of a mate. A system that unconsciously sought love "recognized" this possibility in her husband. There was enough internalized relational health in Leah's unconscious to bring this about. The injured and disappointed system, however, was not far behind and thus was easily triggered when expectations that precluded love and attunement were easily activated within the interactions with her husband. This system constantly "told" her that whatever she had with him and how much he said he loved her, it was bound to disappoint her. It was better to be alone rather than rely on others.

As Leah's understanding of her past and its continuous enactment in the present grew, so did her ability to reflect on her difficulties within her marriage. She chafed at her husband's attention, but simultaneously craved it and was upset when he became distant in response to her rejection. She was attracted to him, to his body and sense of humor, yet she often wanted to be left alone, rejecting his offers for help and his attempts to cheer her up. She loved him and wanted to stay with him, but she also wanted to leave and be on her own for the first time in her life. She could also better understand her ambivalent feelings about her career and the city she moved to; she had decided to leave Israel for good, and yet, upon becoming an attorney, she could not tolerate the thought of never going back.

Leah's high levels of anxiety and sense of paralysis about all areas of her life subsided early on, but the tormenting ambivalence between the need for others and the need to be away from them, between the yearning for security and a sense of agency and the pull of her old panic at being trapped, continued to occupy much of the therapy. It took a few years of intense analytic work for her to develop affect tolerance for very painful memories while being able to reflect on them and put them in the specific context of her childhood. It was not others she was running away from but the frightening and incomprehensible associations attached to being with them. Many experiences of being with adults were not comforting; on the contrary, they led to meager measures of warmth and certainty. Turning to other kids, naturally, did not provide the yearned-for stable warmth as well, and Leah was left with some sense that something big was missing from her life. On meeting her husband, she hoped that he could provide that "missing something," but he "disappointed her as well."

Only with continued therapeutic work and practiced reflective awareness at home—for example, paying attention to her feelings when her husband approached her with warmth—was Leah able to tolerate, identify, and regulate her feelings of automatic anxiety and the impulse to flee. The ability to regulate her feelings generalized to her work as well. It was not the law that paralyzed her and made her feel as if her life was over, but the commitment she made to something secure: the unfamiliar stability of staying in one place. Out of habit she always needed to be somewhere else, another place that potentially had more to offer.

Although Leah's case is firmly anchored in a particular past and emotional history, her internal and interpersonal patterns reflect common brain/mind processes. A grossly compromised need for empathetic attunement and manifestations of love and an overwhelmed fear system associated with early interactional experiences are quite common. Obviously, like Leah, the particular conditioned fears, the defenses against them, the numerous interpersonal experiences, and the endless associations to them are always unique, resulting in different self-systems and self-states in each one of us. The presenting symptoms of anxiety, depression, confusion, and ambivalence were their enacted manifestations. Whereas it is possible that Leah could have been helped by short-term therapy such as CBT, which would encourage her to think differently about her anxiety so as to regulate it, it is highly unlikely that such an approach would have been sufficient to derail entrenched patterns that started preverbally and affected many experiences since then. Without recurrent working through (which may take years for some people), older brain/mind patterns overtake one's functioning, canceling out the new efforts at regulation.

Most significant, the therapeutic efficacy of recontexualizing anxiety or other disturbing feelings without touching the unconscious self-system feeding it—especially if carried out in a period of a limited number of sessions—may be quite limited. As Safran and Shaker (2011) observed, in the context of short-term therapy (especially CBT), the rapid symptom relief does not have the staying power of changes occurring in the course of an experientially informed, intense long-term therapy. As mentioned, only in the setting of the intersubjective therapeutic interaction can the many nonverbal implicit learning and identificatory processes take place.

Fittingly, to close this discussion about the explicit and the implicit elements of therapeutic change, we need to remember that effective therapy is a process that can happen in the framework of two subjectivities where feelings of trust and mistrust, fear and safety, openness and closeness can all be experienced, explored, and reflected on, thus embodying all aspects underlying enduring therapeutic change. In Leah's case, there is little doubt that we needed several years to repeatedly deepen, expand, and experience together the many aspects of her unconscious-conscious states. Her developing reflective awareness was an important part of her therapeutic progress, but so were her identification with our work, the way we resolved our impasses, and her growing ability (which can only stay inarticulate) to surrender into the relationship with me. As the previously mentioned studies showed (Huber et al., 2011; Knekt et al., 2011; Rabung and Leichsenring, 2011; Safran and Shaker, 2001; Shedler, 2011), even after termination patients undergoing long-term therapy showed a growing increase in therapeutic gains.

As Leah increasingly practiced reflective awareness in real time while she was in the midst of a difficult dysregulating affect, her ability to regulate such states transformed from effortful to more natural and automatic. Similarly to the complex learning processes that took place throughout her childhood, the emotionally suffused and intersubjective environment of the therapeutic environment encouraged new learning, conditioned responses, and many new associations to them. As new responses and experiences—conscious and unconscious—are practiced, implicitly or explicitly, they encourage stronger connections among the new networks that are eventually capable of competing for neural space with old ones (Damasio, 2010). With time, they become powerful and automatic in their own right.

CHAPTER 9

Intergenerational Enactment of Trauma: The Role of Unconscious Self-Systems

THE PHENOMENON OF INTERGENERATIONAL TRANSMISSION of trauma is one of the most pronounced manifestations of unconscious processes and the ongoing pervasive effects they have on children of trauma survivors. The damaging consequences of trauma for victims and the next generation shape the nature of unconscious self-systems as well as their emotional, cognitive, and behavioral manifestations. The physio/affective reactions embedded in traumatic events, then, do not only touch survivors. Their enacted expressions—conscious and unconscious alike—deeply mark the children of survivors as well. This seems to be the case regardless of the time of the trauma in the parent's life or its scope—whether it occurred in childhood or adulthood, a result of one devastating event or recurring and cumulative developmental trauma.

In addition to decades of studying the effects of the Holocaust trauma on the survivors' children (Danieli, 1998, Felsen, 1998; Laub and Auerhahn, 1993; Yehuda et al., 2008; among many others), a wide range of parents who were exposed to severe traumas have been studied. In a meta-analysis study of research pertaining to paternal and maternal trauma, parents' PTSD symptoms were significantly associated with child distress and behavioral problems (Lambert et al., 2014). Parents with PTSD demonstrated compromised parental functioning (Solomon et al., 2011), higher parental stress (Renner, 2009), severe conflicts with their children (Ruscio et al., 2002), and tended to impose strict discipline (Cohen et al., 2008).

The range of trauma studies has widened considerably and currently includes parental traumatization by war combat, terrorist attacks, inter-personal violence, sexual violence, victimization by torture, and natural disaster. For example, women who experienced childhood abuse (sex-ual and physical) have been diagnosed as having PTSD at a rate rang-ing from 26 percent to 52 percent (Cloitre et al., 2010). In studying the effects of intergenerational transmission of sexual abuse, McClosky and Bailey (2000) and Testa et al. (2009) for example, found that daughters of sexually abused mothers have a higher risk at being sexually victim-ized themselves.

Researching the relationship between early physical violence early in life and subsequent attachment styles, Lyons-Ruth and Block (1996) and Lyons-Ruth et al. (2005) found that women who were physically abused as children tended to engage in either hostile or withdrawn emotional patterns with their children. The mothers who were abused as chil-dren established disorganized attachment styles with their infants, a result confirmed by other studies (e.g., Lieberman and Knorr, 2007). Significantly, what children of traumatized parents also carry are the physiological markers for PTSD symptoms, chronic hyperarousal, and stress—abnormally high cortisol levels (van der Kolk, 1994; Yehuda, et al., 1996, 2005, 2008).

The findings showing a relationship between parental trauma and its physio/affective marks on the next generations are important. Most studies, however, focus on general patterns of emotional and behavioral difficulties as seen in the family system (Harkness, 1991; Lambert et al., 2014). As some researchers note (Deckel et al., 2013; Kaitz et al., 2009; Seng et al., 2013; Yehuda et al., 2008), more understanding is needed in regard to the possible psychological and physiological processes under-lying intergenerational transmission of parental trauma. Furthermore, psychotherapeutic work with children and adults will benefit greatly from getting a fuller picture of what specific patterns, difficulties, or even resilience tendencies become part of the second generation's brain/mind structure.

In the context of the expanded understanding of unconscious pro-cesses presented in this book, the examination of what takes place within the phenomenon of intergenerational transmission of trauma relies on what we already know about the prevalence of unconscious communication (McGilchrist, 2009; Schore, 2012), the automatic enac-tion of encoded, widespread brain/mind patterns (Damasio, 2010; Sheets-Johnstone, 2010; Stewart, 2010), the centrality of the affective sys-tem to well-being (LeDoux, 2002, 2014; Panksepp and Biven, 2012), and the child's innate susceptibility to the parent's emotional states (Braten, 2007; Bromberg, 2006, 2011; Schore, 2012; Tronick, 2007). By becoming part of the ongoing and co-constructed intersubjective world between survivors of trauma and their children, the trauma—its memories and affects and defenses against them—inevitably influence the second generation's course of development. The overarching purpose is not just to identify what processes take place and how, but to convey the resulting experiences of children exposed to parents who were traumatized from the "inside out," to use Bromberg's (1998, 2006) profound term.

Exploring the unique parameters of intergenerational transmission of trauma, this chapter explores some of the unconscious-conscious processes that underpin it. These processes result in a particular emotional patterns—from the vaguely felt sense of a split consciousness typical to the victims of trauma and to their children (Boulanger, 2007; Danieli, 1998; Wardi, 1992) to an automatic and unconscious tendency to repeat and enact aspects of the parent's trauma (Kestenberg, 1982; Rashkin, 1999). As in all cases where unconscious self-systems are enacted without reflection, the level of dissociation between the trauma and its emotional and behavioral residues—between the wish to forget and the involuntary enactments (Bromberg, 2006; Stern, 2010; Waelde et al., 2009)—determines the effects of parental trauma on the child's adaptive capacity.

THE NATURE OF TRAUMA: DIVIDED CONSCIOUSNESS

Unsurprisingly, the well-documented phenomenon of intergenerational spread of trauma (Danieli, 1998; Felsen, 1998; Kaplan, 1995; Kestenberg, 1982; Moses, 1993; Rashkin, 1999; Wardi, 1992, among others) takes place whether the parent speaks of the past or is utterly silent about it, whether the past has been made coherent (Fonagy, 2008) or is still raw and undigested; it happens without volition or intent. Often, the child is exposed to repeated acting-out behaviors that have been shown to accompany the presence of PTSD symptoms (Kaitz et al., 2009; Lambert et al., 2014; Seng et al., 2013). The child of traumatized parents will internalize essential aspects of the traumatic past, absorbing the destabilizing affect and the maladaptive defenses against it. As a result, a child who herself did not suffer sexual abuse, for example, but is nonetheless subjected to her mother's overly promiscuous attitudes (or conversely, a strict approach to dating) will inhabit many shades of her mother's fears, emotional reactions to men, and defensive adaptations.

Daughters of mothers with sexual abuse in their past may even enact their mother's past. In a study conducted using therapy sessions (Lev-Wiesel, 2007), mothers who were victims of incest and whose daughters became victims of sexual abuse were grouped into four types: the Unaware mothers, who showed complete lack of knowledge of the sexual abuse occurring at home; the Unwitting Accomplice, characterized by latent cooperation with the abuser; the Enabler, who overtly or covertly encouraged her spouse to abuse their daughter; and the Common Fate mothers, who saw their fate intertwined with that of their daughters. In other cases, children of abused fathers will suffer the consequences of the fathers' automatically enacted violent reactions. In turn, the child will internalize and learn to employ reactive violence as a way of responding to frustrations, never achieving an adaptive style of affect regulation (Siegel, 2013). Similarly, the effects of war trauma on the consequential quality mother–child interaction were examined as well. Mothers exposed to war displayed a higher level of unstructured and/or hostile style of interaction, while their infants showed lower levels of responsiveness to and involvement with their traumatized mothers (Van Ee et al., 2012).

As we see, the process of intergenerational transmission of parental trauma does not differ essentially from the inevitable developmental processes that underpin the child's immersion in and identification with parental emotional states and behavioral enaction (Braten, 2007; Braten and Trevarthen, 2007; Schore, 2012). But they differ in their excessive emotional intensity among survivors and their children—expressed in hyper- or hypoarousal affective states, such as fear, mistrust, and helplessness Consequently, the child's trauma-suffused unconscious map (unique to each individual, of course) is made up of many shades of emotions and meanings echoing a parental emotional and cognitive self-state. It is a self-system spanning the unconscious–conscious continuum, and giving center stage to specific images, emotions, meanings, and even imagined memories—all related to the parent's silent or enacted trauma. Meanwhile, other states, fully rooted in the present, may attempt to thrive with the business of life. The experientially divided existence common in survivors of trauma and their children (Bergman and Jucovy, 1982; Epstein, 1979) illuminates the complex workings of brain/mind processes, in particular the cleaving effects of intense emotions such as grief/panic and intense fear on the developing self-states of the growing child (Boulanger, 2007; Panksepp and Biven, 2012).

The experiential quality of divided consciousness has been widely studied in Holocaust survivors and their grown children (Bergman and Jucovy, 1982; Kaplan, 1995; Kestenberg, 1982; Moses, 1993; Rashkin, 1999; Wardi, 1992). In their discussion of knowing and not knowing the experience of trauma, Laub and Auerhahn (1993) describe what can be called degrees of consciousness, paralleling this book's theme of the conscious–unconscious continuum. A state of not knowing occupies one end of a continuum, followed by what they define as screen memories, fugue states, split-off fragmented memories and narratives, transference phenomena, the enactment of the trauma as a way of knowing, witnessed narratives, and finally the ability to use metaphor for trauma at the other end. All these describe ways of knowing and not knowing embodied within the survivors' efforts to live with intolerable memories and at the same time go on with their present lives. This form of loose and dynamic dissociative processes are then unconsciously picked up and adopted by the children they raise (Felsen, 1998; Wardi, 1992).

The experience of divided consciousness is characterized by a wide span ranging from obliviousness to awareness as to its features. At an extreme pole, full dissociation may block any awareness of past events (van der Kolk, 1994). Mostly, however, aware and unaware states shift and intermingle, creating the simultaneous experience of both knowing and not knowing the full details and significance of horrific events. At the other extreme, a child may become fully immersed in the parent's experience so as not to allow himself a sense of self separate from the trauma (Lyons-Ruth et al., 2005; Renn, 2012).

In the realm of the emotional field between parent and child, conscious and unconscious fragmented affects, images, and behaviors representing the parent's past trauma are often embedded in his or her experiences as a parent. From overprotectiveness and enmeshment (Rowland-Klein and Dunlop, 1998) to fears of handling the baby among abused mothers (Grosskopf, 1999), parenting role reversal (Macfie et al., 2005), identification with an abused father's past violent abuse (Kwong et al., 2003), or combat experience (Harkness, 1991; Lambert et al., 2012), the child's developing unconscious self-system internalizes the parent's unconscious communications. These communications, some expressing different self-systems while others enact angry or violent patterns as a result of dysregulation, confuse the growing child, resulting in dissociated self-states that are not aware of their roots or meaning (Bromberg, 2006, 2011; Stern, 2010).

THE NATURE OF MEMORY AND ENACTED TRAUMA

An important window into the self-states of trauma survivors, especially in regard to the nature of traumatic memories, is provided by Langer (1991) who studied the memories of Holocaust survivors. His depiction of survivors' fragmented memories further illuminates what gets communicated to their children and the children's reactions to these communications. After witnessing hundreds of recorded testimonies of survivors struggling to recall what they went through during the war, Langer describe the many layers and interplay between declarative and nondeclarative memories and the various mental defenses used against them. In the interviews, according to Langer, survivors strained to put into narrative form events, perceptions, feelings, and memories that in actuality confounded a linear account. The testimonies seemed to embody a battleground between what Langer calls "the disruptive" memory and the efforts to maintain a semblance of normal life. In his words: "Contemporality becomes the controlling principle of these testimonies, as witnesses struggle with the impossible task of making their recollections of the camp experience coalesce with the rest of their lives. If one theme links their narratives more than any other, it is the unintended, unexpected, but invariably unavoidable failure of such efforts" (1991, p. 3).

What is so compelling about Langer's descriptions is their relevance to what is known about the effects of trauma on dysregulation, dissociative processes, and fractured physio/affective memories (Boulanger, 2007; Bromberg, 2006; Fernyhough, 2013; van der Kolk, 1994). The memories that are known and not known by survivors—the physicality of abuse, for example, or the helpless and incomprehensible sense of violation—become part of the interaction. Images, involuntary flashbacks, and the raw affects that accompany them throw the parent back into a past that in essence is lived in the present.

Indeed, Kaplan (1995), Kestenberg (1982), Laub and Auerhahn (1993), Macfie et al. (2005), and Wardi (1992) describe trauma survivors' inability to fully integrate traumatic memories so they can mourn their past. As a result, they experience suppressed rage and a shattered sense of strength and competence. It is not difficult to generalize these findings to children of parents who endured a wide range of traumatic experiences. War veterans who suffer from flashbacks, who carry fractured and unintegrated memories or images of death and destruction, for example, will struggle with the power of such memories to engender an almost constant state of hyperarousal with no relief (Dekel and Goldblatt, 2008; Grosskopf, 1999; Harkness, 1991; van der Kolk, 1987, 1996).

Although not cognitively understanding the nature of the fractured memory or the flashbacks that has overtaken a parent, the infant and child is still exposed to their emotional intensity and the behavioral manifestations that they unconsciously and automatically engender. This will affect the child's ability to negotiate internal working models as well as external emotional challenges. Some grown children will live out and enact their fathers' or mothers' unreflected-on trauma (van Ee et al., 2012), giving voice to the pain, the defense against it, and the resultant maladaptive—or resilient—self-narratives.

INTERGENERATIONAL TRANSMISSION OF TRAUMA

One cannot start to approach the subject of intergenerational transmission of trauma without considering the ever-present and lasting effects of intersubjectivity. As discussed in previous chapters, the child's immersion in his parent's emotional, cognitive, and behavioral states will lead to an identification process that internalizes them, and he will learn to incorporate them as his own. Furthermore, emotional states such as sadness, rage, helplessness, fear, and pessimism emanating from the parent will be experienced as arising from the child himself (Braten, 2007; Braten and Trevarthen, 2007; Schore, 2012; Tronick, 2007; Wallin, 2007). This process may be particularly damaging for optimal development in light of the fragmented nature of traumatic experiences and memories and their tendency to be enacted (Bromberg, 2006). In a process of what could be called an identificatory traumatization (Braten, 2007; Olds, 2006), children internalize their parents' trauma and its enacted manifestations. Children will also unconsciously learn and adopt their parents' typical coping styles.

As I have witnesses in some patients—second- and third-generation children of Holocaust survivors—once becoming conscious of a parent's pain and the defense against it, some children will actively attempt to reject the parent's internal turmoil, almost desperately running toward a pain-free way of being. Such attempts, however, are seldom entirely successful. The unconscious learning and immersion processes that have taken place inevitably become part of an unconscious self-system, and thereby are bound to be enacted as well. Similarly, among my patients, children born just after their fathers had died in war had a lifelong struggle not only with coming to terms with losing a father but with finding adaptive ways to cope with their mothers' grief. In many cases, from the very first day, their mothers' sadness and sense of helplessness became their own, alongside unconscious and ongoing attempts to ease the mother's emotional burden.

Kogan (1995) reports a tendency among survivors and their children toward numbness on one hand and a preoccupation with death on the other, and describes four dimensions of intergenerational trauma: traumatization through loss of the child's separate sense of self: traumatization through parental exploitation of the child as a life-saving substitute; traumatization through lack of empathy and abandonment of the child; and traumatization through intense focus on helplessness, lack of hope, and a frightened approach to life's challenges. In Kaplan's words: "The children of survivors were living out and dreaming out their parents' nightmares. The children were enacting experiences and relating fantasies that could only come from a person who had actually been in a ghetto or extermination camp and actually observed the slaughter of her loved ones. The child of survivor had been sheltered from the truth. But the child was living the nightmare" (1995, pp. 222–23).

As documented by many clinical writings, the therapeutic experience of working with adult children of trauma survivors has shed a great deal of light on the process of intergenerational transmission of traumas. According to Kestenberg (1982), for example, through a process of transposition, the inner lives of children of survivors become crowded and preoccupied with traumatic content not belonging to them. Consequently, they experience and enact nightmarish fantasies directly related to the nature of their parent's trauma. The mechanism of transposition goes beyond identification—the child identifies with her parent as an individual and with a real historical past filled with suffering, submission, and helplessness. Recalling Braten and Trevarthen's model (2007), it is easy to understand how the normal states of immersion with a parent's emotional states, the verbal and conscious as well as the nonverbal, become disproportionately large, crowding out those parts of the child that should be dedicated to the development of an individual and differentiated sense of self.

Intersubjectivity, however, implies that at any given time the mutual needs for attachment, connection, and validation generate a co-constructed emotional reality where it is impossible to entirely differentiate the parent from the child (Aron, 1996; Benjamin, 2004). A parent's needs to find an emotional echo in the child will surely intensify the child's absorption in that state. This is true for the unconscious mutual exchange between Mary and her daughter, highlighted in the case study a bit later. An unconscious tendency to rely on the emotional resources of the child—or conversely, casting her as the bad, persecuting object during dysregulation—will also disrupt a normal course of closeness and separation, resulting in difficulties in the establishment of a coherent sense of self.

Kaplan (1995) sees transposition as a distorted enactment by which parents unconsciously transmit their wishes, fears, and rage unto the child. What is so destructive to the child in the cases of parental traumas is the amount of brain/mind space claimed by the traumatic past. The transposition of trauma, according to Kaplan, originates in the parent's unconscious need to use the child's vulnerability and susceptibility— that very building block of immersion and identification (Braten, 2007; Olds, 2006)—to rework or compensate for unmourned losses. Moreover, with tragic results for the child, the process of transposition entails repeated failures of empathy on the part of a very depressed, angry, or otherwise emotionally preoccupied parent.

Tronick (2007) sees the dyadic expansion of consciousness as an intersubjective frame in which each self-organizing entity of the dyad is responding to and collaborating with the other self-organizing system—a significant other. Such a collaboration results in an expansion in which each individual incorporates elements of the other's consciousness into his own. This process elucidates how interacting subjectivities know each other's mind, and such exchanges are essential for both the infant and the adult. What the child internalizes is not just another subjectivity but a self in relation to another subjectivity, an amalgam of representations that cannot be understood on the basis of one participant alone. Seligman (2009) notes that within their continuously interactive exchanges, monitoring, and imitation, infants and then children internalize the parent's inner working models or unconscious self-systems. These identifications are not with just a single affect or behavior but with a relational system that includes the parent's coping mechanisms and self-states; like the parent, the child oscillates between them, unconsciously reacting to contextual triggers.

MOTHER AND DAUGHTER IN THE WEB
OF SEXUAL ABUSE: THE CASE OF MARY

At the age of 39, Mary sought therapy because of growing anxiety about her status as a single woman. Although she wanted to get married and have a family, she could not find the right man to fall in love with. She was very critical of her past boyfriends, and as she described past relationships, her derision came through. She blamed their shortcomings for her inability to "really get attracted to them." In effect, her sexual desire was very uneven; once a relationship developed, she completely lost any sexual interest. When the relationship did not recover from her lack of sexual interest and outright rejection of her partner's sexual desire, she told herself that she obviously was not "sexually interested in them." Mary came to treatment when she realized that she would miss the boat and not have a family unless she understood her problematic interactions with men.

Mary grew up with a single mother, Susan, who lost her mother when she was nine. Susan, an only child, was left with her father, a much older man, who after his wife's death became very preoccupied with his career as an academic. Very soon after the funeral, her mother's brother moved into the household to help his brother-in-law cope with the many new responsibilities, especially those pertaining to Mary's daily care. As the father saw it, a family member was preferable to outside help.

Susan's sexual abuse by her uncle started then and lasted until she was 14 and was no longer afraid of him. Although Mary claimed she only knows fragments of information told to her by her mother, a picture emerged of an emotionally devastated little girl—Susan—who was left alone to deal with her grief and an emotionally distant father. Her uncle, on the other hand, "paid her all the attention in the world," and convinced her that only he loved her the right way, and that his love would make up for the loss of her mother.

As an adult, Susan became a hard-working businesswoman. She was married for a short time and ended the marriage when Mary was about four years old. Following the divorce she only dated sporadically, and these relationships "slowly disappeared, for one reason or another," as Mary put it. There might had been a serious guy or two, she remembered, but no enduring relationship developed. Mary's knowledge into her mother's past was short on details; until her early twenties she did not know about the abuse, but she had the vague sense that something terrible had happened to her mother when she was young.

What Mary could recall was her frequent exposure to her mother's critical assessment of all the men she knew through work and her sarcastic contempt for the men she had dated. Her anger at one of her first superiors drove her to start her own business. Mary also remembered Susan's unconcealed rage against her father—Mary's grandfather—and the abusing uncle. As Mary grew up, she became aware of the numerous messages to be careful around boys; the topic of date rape came up throughout high school and college. Not understanding her mother's obvious anxiety when she had a party to go to, Mary was consciously torn between trying to placate Susan by curtailing her social activities and the wish to have a worry-free dating life and follow her newly experienced crushes on boys. She knew Susan expected her to adopt her fearful aptitudes, but she was very confused as to why. What she did not know was the extent to which she already had unwittingly internalized them.

Only as therapy progressed did Mary realize how ensnared she was in her mother's emotional life, long before she ever knew of the actual sexual abuse. Being attuned to her mother's shifting affective states, she became identified with her rage and mistrust of men, unconsciously enacted and verbalized from Mary's early life. As a child, when she asked Susan about the lack of photos of her grandfather and uncle, for example, her mother slipped into an angry silence and then quickly changed the subject. Much of Susan's communications regarding men remained unconscious, and in her adult life Mary enacted her mother's experiences. Reaching a defensive compromise, she still wished to date and experience relationships but invariably found ways to end them.

Many memories, experiences, and learned patterns of behavior went into Mary's unconscious self-system. Out of awareness her mother's verbal and nonverbal messages regarding men greatly shaped Mary's internal feelings, attitudes, and enacted behaviors that stemmed from them. She could not, of course, eradicate her sexuality, but as a little girl and especially during her adolescence, affects of anger and fear and cognitive notions about the untrustworthiness or the "necessity" of men became embedded within her own desires for an emotional and sexual attachment. Her mother's notions became part of her developing unconscious self-system, with all its associative connections.

Like Claire (see Chapter 4), the first few years of the therapeutic process focused on Mary's journey toward an emotional and identificational separation from her mother's internal world. This process was difficult; being an only child with a great deal of empathy for a single mother who worked hard to raise her increased Mary's immersion in her mother's emotional states (Braten and Trevarthen, 2007, Tronick, 2007). Whereas Claire was attuned to her mother's Holocaust legacy, transmitted to her through her own parent, Mary was attuned to her mother's abuse-related dysregulation and the numerous behavioral, emotional, and nonverbal ways in which they enacted.

Realizing that she had a right to forge her own separate way, a right to express her need for attachment and sexuality according to her own needs, Mary was determined to pursue her own desires and worry less about her mother's confused and unprocessed ones. For Claire and Mary, therapy seemed to grant permission to become viscerally connected with their own desires for life and happiness. Once experiencing a right to her separate subjectivity, Mary used her growing reflective abilities in times of dysregulation. She tried to stay aware of her feelings and thoughts, to ask herself why she was anxious and whether she really needs to run away from an intimate encounter. As she continued to allow herself new feelings and behaviors, her nascent emotional and sexual sense of self grew. As a new relationship became more stable and less anxiety-inducing, a more reality-bound relational pattern developed and was reinforced. The old system, much of which was bound with her mother's emotional past, receded. When it did surface—inevitably so—Mary, like Claire, was able to reflect on it. As time went by, this reflection became more second nature to Mary; it was there because it was there. From an effortful, forced exercise, it became an automatic habit, only this time, one that was on her side.

NEUROPSYCHOLOGICAL ASPECTS OF INTERGENERATIONAL TRANSMISSION OF TRAUMA

The challenge to better comprehend—from the inside out—how children experience their intersubjective and co-constructed encounters with traumatized parents (Benjamin, 2004; Bromberg, 2006; Cozolino, 2002; Wallin, 2007) can be best facilitated by a further discussion of the brain/mind processes. As we have seen throughout this book, the neuropsychological underpinnings of such processes as intersubjectivity, the centrality of emotional memories, unconscious learning, and identification can help us grasp how parental self-states become the child's and why they acquire such power. Only a few relevant systems will be mentioned here—enough to highlight those brain/mind dynamics essential for intersubjective transmission of trauma and its enactment by the child throughout his adult life. This section will recap the integrated activities of the right brain, the affective systems, the amygdala, and the mirror neuron system.

Schore's (1994, 2003, 2005, 2009, 2012) conclusions regarding the development of the social brain greatly explain the process of unconscious transmission of parental self-states. Initially regulated by the physio/affective attunement between the right hemispheres of mother and infant, the mother's self-states are transmitted to the child's through myriad nonverbal and verbal communications. Extensively connected to the limbic system and thus sensitive to interpersonal appraisal and emotional processing, the right hemispheres of mother and child are especially active in the infant's first two years. During this time, according to Schore, the mother's right hemisphere is the child's first reality. Her emotional preoccupations with the child and her efforts at attunement are the bedrock for implicit memories and relational modes, projected to the child's receptive right hemisphere (Cozolino, 2002, 2006; Schore, 2012; Wallin, 2007). Conversely, an unattuned mother who is preoccupied much of the time with fighting off disturbing memories, who is drowning in recurrent resentment, rage, or a depressive, helpless feeling state, will not assist the child when he most needs her, during dysregulation. In effect, in spite of her best intentions, her distractibility will increase the child's arousal, at times leading to a depressive, dissociative state (Schore, 2012).

Further supporting the role of the right brain in processing nonverbal communication are Schore's observations that the infant's ability to efficiently process visual cues from the caregiver resides in the right hemisphere and not the left. A positron emission tomography study of two-month-old infants looking at images of a woman's face detected activation in the infants' right visual area and the right fusiform gyrus (Tzourio-Mazoyer et al., 2002). Stressing the power of the intersubjective transmission of affect, a functional MRI study examined brain activity of healthy mothers watching videos of their own infants and looking at videos of unfamiliar infants (Ranote et al., 2004). The findings showed that watching one's babies resulted in greater activation of the mothers' bilateral visual areas and their amygdalas. Watching the unfamiliar infants resulted in greater activation of their bilateral orbitofrontal cortex. The authors suggest that the amygdala and the temporal pole are important to the mother's response to her infant, and thereby reaffirms their importance to face emotion processing and social behavior. Similarly, LeDoux (2002) maintains that facial misattunements register in the infant's right hemisphere and are perceived as danger in the amygdala region.

Ongoing, intersubjective communications—widely found on the unconscious–conscious continuum—occur on all levels, from emotional facial expressions, gestures, and tone of voice. These mutual communications can span the range from the very subtle to the loud and unmistakable emotional, cognitive, and behavioral enacted expressions. All these co-constructed expressions—with their endless levels of intensity or subtlety—are mediated by the right hemisphere from early on (McGilchrist, 2009; Schore, 2012).

Mary's mother, Susan, oscillated between barely simmering rage at men and an unacknowledged fear of them on the one hand, and a perpetual attitude of ambivalence about her tortured desire for a relationship on the other. Out of awareness, Susan's interactions with Mary were suffused with implicit emotional memories, cognitive beliefs, and shameful and self-loathing self-narratives—none of which were fully acknowledge, reflected on, or understood. This enacted internal turmoil was, of course, related to her violation at the hands of her uncle, but with her natural need to willfully suppress the prolonged traumatic nightmare (Anderson and Green, 2001; Anderson and Levy, 2009), Susan could not make these connections.

Susan's half-articulated but still negative communications regarding men, in particular her gaze and facial expressions when she and her daughter engaged in conversations about Mary's social life, conveyed immense fears, dismissal, and a sense that little about men was safe. Her own sporadic and unfulfilling dating life only reinforced her implicit and explicit messages. The half-concealed messages were that she and her daughter did not really need a man in their lives, and that they both needed to protect themselves from their inevitable aggression.

Schore's contributions delineating the enduring effects of arousal levels are supported by a large body of data illustrating the centrality of the amygdala's role in chronic self-states of anxiety, prolonged stress, and dread. When these arousal states unconsciously become a part of the interactional field, they engender arousal states in the child as well. Here the affective system and the role of the amygdala as the vigilance center for fear and other emotions are central (see Chapter 2). With reciprocal connections to subcortical arousal centers as well as to higher cortical areas, the amygdala contributes to arousal states and a state of hypervigilance, often leading to nonspecific arousal states even when they are not warranted. As often seen while treating adult children of trauma survivors (and even third-generation adults), survivors' ability to provide consistent and sustained regulation and calm, to reduce rather than increase states of arousal, can be compromised (Badenoch, 2008; Cozolino, 2002, 2006; Lambert et al., 2014; Siegel, 2013). When immersed in a self-state in which they relive the past, parents often cannot see their children's need for empathy or for assistance in achieving regulation and facing up to life's challenges. On a behavioral level, if the unconscious trauma-related self-system is fully activated in the presence of the child's needs, the parent may turn to the child for comfort, or conversely, ignore his needs all together (Grosskopf, 1999; Kestenberg, 1982).

Consequently, the innate affective system of fear (see Panksepp and Biven, 2012) and the function of the amygdala interact to greatly affect both the victims of trauma and their children. In the context of parental inexplicable anxiety and intense fear reactions, or when faced with a parent's inability to stay calm in the face of any minor upset—physical or emotional—the child's amygdala becomes sensitized to automatically and indiscriminately perceive danger and fear, which are then activated in a wide range of challenges and interpersonal situations (Hamann, 2009; LeDoux and Doyere, 2011). By affecting cortical and attentional/perceptual processes, as well as the memory center in the hippocampus, the amygdala and the affective arousal it generates influences the child's own encoded memories and their contextual emotions and meanings (Cozolino, 2006; Damasio, 2010; LeDoux, 2002; Mancia, 2006; Seligman, 2009).

This process is especially significant in light of the relatively late development of the PFC. Without much capacity to provide contextual understanding of internal states, and with a limited ability—greatly driven by temperament—to self-regulate, the child is highly affected by interactions leading to overwhelming affects (Gainotti, 2006; Grawe, 2007; Kagan, 1998; LeDoux, 2002; Mancia, 2006; Schore, 2005; Siegel, 2007). Indeed, wide-ranging studies have demonstrated that children of trauma survivors suffer from generally higher levels of cortisol (the stress hormone) in some cases and low levels in others. In either case, these levels indicate a constant state of arousal and numbing defense (Grosskopf, 1999; Renn, 2012; Yehuda et al., 1996, 2005, 2008). These findings are far from surprising; following a massive trauma, the adult amygdala's perpetual state of vigilance and the hormonal changes they generate become part of the child's physio/emotional system and an anchor to a hyperaroused brain/mind self-state.

Mary was both hyperaroused in terms of her anxiety about men and hypoaroused when it came to a continued expression of her own healthy sexuality. At the start of a relationship, she could still give voice to her libido, but as the relationship continued and became more serious, her sexuality waned and she physically lost interest. Mary's relational patterns as an adult woman seemed to unconsciously represent her mother's ambivalent relational patterns. At the same time they gave voice to her own needs for intimacy: that need gave voice to her healthy sexuality at the beginning of a relationship and her identification with her mother to increased anxiety and a waning libido. There was nothing volitional about Mary's shifting self-states, her reduced sexuality was enacted by an unconscious self-system comprised of self-other representations, needs defenses mingling many emotion systems.

The innate systems of fear and grief/panic and the amygdala's sensitivity to all of their internal and external expressions make it clear that a parent who is carrying physical and emotional memories of terror and abuse cannot avoid experiencing some of them while with his or her child. Memories and experiences may not be wholly accessible, and their narrative, as Langer (1991) observed, may be fragmented and incoherent; yet their emotional weight and meaning cannot be fully obliterated. In the face of event-based and dysregulating raw fears, mistrust of others, or rage, the child's amygdala becomes sensitized to all potential fears, and just like the parent's, maintains a state of hypervigilance in all interpersonal relationships. Not experiencing or witnessing the terror themselves, children of trauma survivors feel as if they did; their fear system, in tandem with the striatal-cortico and cerebellar-cortico loops, has learned to anticipate danger where it does not exist and treat it as real (Chapters 1 and 2).

THE ROLE OF THE MIRROR NEURON SYSTEM AND EMPATHY IN INTERGENERATIONAL TRANSMISSION OF TRAUMA

The adoption of another person's fear system and the appropriation of it as one's own is a testament to the power of subcortical affect regions working together with the mirror neuron system that mediates an indirect and unmediated emotional knowing of the other (Gallese, 2008; Iacoboni, 2008). The mirror neuron system operating early and in tandem with the right brain further mediates processes of empathy, imitation, and internalization of the parent's states. The process is mutual, but the still-developing child is very vulnerable to the parent's emotional states. The mirror neuron system most likely underpins that self-state in child that is always attuned to the parent's unconsciously and consciously communicated emotions, beliefs, and behaviors (Beebe and Lachmann, 2002; Braten, 2007; Braten and Trevarthen, 2007; Gallese, 2007, 2009; Iacoboni, 2008; Stern, 1985; Tronick, 2007). It further guides the child's innate propensity to identify with a parental state, to internalize it as his own, all entirely out of awareness.

As Carr et al. (2003) have shown, the neural information carried by the mirror neuron system travels to the limbic system and the amygdala through the insula. It is no surprise, then, that the child's innate affect systems, such as grief/panic, fear, and attachment, become intertwined with those of the parent's. These processes clarify Langer's (1991) observations that the experience of being a witness to another person's trauma is by definition an interpersonal act, far from being fixed in a passive role. In the most primal of relationships, composed of infinite, ongoing reciprocal communications, the parent–child intertwined emotional lives cannot help but result in mutual influence (Beebe and Lachmann, 2002; Schore, 2012; Siegel, 1999, 2007; Stern, 1985; Tronick, 2007).

The mirror neuron system doesn't just enable automatic emotional learning and identification (Olds, 2006; Seligman, 2009) on the part of the child, it also underpins the child's empathetic connections to the parent's internal life. Here again, the process is unconscious (Hasson et al., 2011). For reasons he could not quite understand as a child, Rob, for example, grew up feeling sorry for his often anxious and fretful mother. He felt he had to protect her, to make sure he did not upset her. Indeed, he was "a model boy," as he said. In his early twenties he found out that his mother was severely neglected by her parents, and in effect was raised by her maternal grandparents. Taking over for their daughter, they made sure that their granddaughter was physically taken care of but could not provide the emotional support she was craving. In spite of not knowing the facts about his mother's difficult and neglectful upbringing, Rob had intersubjective knowledge of his mother's sad past. Sensing her sadness and anxiety about raising him and his sister, he set up to protect her from any further distress.

Another example can be seen in Josh, whose tormented but disso- ciated self-systems were greatly shaped by a father who, following the Vietnam War, could not control his temper. Such emotional and behav- ioral states created an atmosphere of dysregulation and fearful unpre- dictability around him, sensitizing Josh's amygdala to be ever vigilant for his father's frightening outbursts. Defending against his father's rage and trying to avoid his outbursts, Josh developed an all-or-nothing pat- tern in relation to others. On the one hand he needed to be in full control of the interaction and relationship—reacting with anger when things did not go his way—while on the other he avoided all manners of confrontation, especially angry ones.

Some of Josh's early internal responses were also shaped by his empathetic connections to his father's nonverbal suffering, a sad and brooding emotional state that "really talked" to Josh, according to him. Mediated by his mirror neuron system (Carr et al., 2003; Gallese, 2007, 2008; Iacoboni, 2008), Josh also internalized his father's terror and sad- ness about his war experiences. Although he learned to respond with anger to even minor frustrations, like his father, he was also capable of a great deal of empathy. More than anything, Josh was utterly con- fused and distressed about the very mixed and seemingly contradictory feelings he brought to every relationship—the need for control and low tolerance for frustrating interactions, mixed with the opposite fear of disagreement from the other. The therapy quickly progressed after an incident in which Josh felt intense remorse and panic, fearing again that he hurt his own child beyond repair. He recognized this pattern, but this time in therapy, he was able to start reflect on its roots, and ways to avoid the very repetition of what he dreaded most.

There is an inevitability for some children to emotionally reverberate with their parents' pain, but perhaps the process of intergenerational transmission of trauma is more complex, reflecting the nature of the co-constructed intersubjectivity between parents and children (Benjamin, 1995; Braten, 2007). In light of the exchanged emotional communications and the child's active mirror neuron system–guided empathy, perhaps what is being projected into the child's unconscious system is not simply "content" of the parent's fractured emotional memories or even acting-out behaviors per se. Rather, what seems to be transmitted in many cases is a certain atmosphere, vague and specific at the same time: an atmosphere also steeped in hidden pain and hinting of events from which one can never escape or forget (Grosskopf, 1999; Lieberman, 2003; Renn, 2012). As Langer (1991) saw in the survivors' narratives, the memories were there, but because of the emotional weight, they had a fragmented narrative structure and lacked coherence.

ENACTED TRAUMA AND THE CHILD'S FIGHT FOR INDIVIDUATION

A parallel process to the divided consciousness characterizing trauma victims occurs among their children as well. A state suffused with memories that will not go away and the negative convictions and narratives bound up with them comprise a self-state that is closely intertwined with that of the parent's trauma. At the same time, a defensive system that automatically needs to preserve the sense of well-being (Damasio, 2010; LeDoux, 2014) also springs into action. A self-system expressing the child's innate motivation to thrive apart from the trauma develops and, depending on the strength of the enmeshment with the parent will gain various levels of unconscious "permission" to separate. All these processes underpin the frequent shifts between self-states experienced by children of trauma survivors: reliving the trauma through a child's eyes and imagination, attempting to defend against the feelings of horror and helplessness, and a self-state that is fully ensconced in current life with all its joys and challenges (Bromberg, 1998, 2006).

As Aron has suggested (1996), the child possesses a curiosity and need to get to know the parent. Similarly, Benjamin (2004) emphasizes the mother–child mutuality, highlighting the intersubjective tension between recognizing the other and oneself as separate subjectivities and the need for full identification and love. This tension is particularly central among children of trauma survivors who are unconsciously caught between an intense empathy with—and immersion in—the parent's suffering. The child's innate need to be nurtured as the child rather than parenting the parent and the wish to see one's parents as strong and protective and not as helpless victims may conflict with the trauma related self-state. Among some of these children, these warring unconscious self-systems and their enacted tendencies impede development as a separate and confident subjectivity, possessing a sense of agency and individuation.

But it is not only affects writ large that are intersubjectively enmeshed, learned, and internalized between trauma survivors and their children. As discussed in Chapter 5, exploring the centrality of self-narratives to our mental functioning, a wide range of cognitive meanings and narratives is embedded within and intertwined with the devastating affects. The repeated attempts to give meaning to the perceived parental affect, results in a host of fantasies and narratives focusing on the specifics of the parent's trauma (Danieli, 1998; Epstein, 1979; Kaplan, 1995; Kestenberg, 1982; Wardi, 1992). The dissonance between the enmeshed self-other emotional existence and the meaning given to them and the child's own experiences in the world is one of the challenges faced by children of traumatized adults.

The therapeutic process seems to be an irreplaceable tool in helping children who grew up with traumatized parents to achieve their own sense of individuated subjectivity. The internal separation from the parent's emotional patterns of perceiving and reacting to the world, and from the various self-narratives foisted on the child, is an important therapeutic goal as we saw in Claire's case (see Chapter 5). Such a dissonance between what was learned and what needs to be developed may be further determined by the content and rigidity of the child's unconscious self-systems, the level of enmeshment with the parent's suffering, and the self-given permission to separate and experience life on one's own terms.

As therapy progressed, Mary realized that she was not as helpless as her mother was, and she could protect herself from "bad guys" in her own way and according to her own judgment. Her oscillation between unconsciously reliving her mother's past and her externally defiant behavior and fights with her mother utterly preoccupied her, not leaving much psychological brain/mind space to achieve her own emotional development. With time, however, she was increasingly able to differentiate herself from those feelings, thoughts, and behaviors that in essence belonged to her mother and not to her.

Among children of trauma survivors, then, what seem to pay the highest price are those self-states that innately strive for individuation. Not only is the seeking system the most likely to become curtailed (Panksepp and Biven, 2012), but the affects that become prominent, as we saw, are fear and anxiety. In agreement with Fonagy and Target (1998),

Stern (2010) maintains that the child's alien identifications are embedded in the interactional field, and as they become the child's foundation of a self-state, they crowd out needs, affects, and strivings. As a result a wide swath of the child's personality becomes dissociated. Among others, positive self-regard, the need to be different from the parent, and innate pride in oneself as a separate subjectivity are largely lost as a vital, significant part of the sense of self.

ENACTED TRAUMA AND THE POWER OF REFLECTION REVISITED

In the context of what we know about how self-systems maps are created within the brain/mind, the plight of children of trauma survivors presents a particular manifestation of the intrinsic relationship between unconscious systems and their inevitable enacted tendencies. Recall that unconscious–conscious systems are entirely tied up with the automatic tendency to enact and express internal representations (Bargh, 2014; Koziol, 2014; Stewart, 2010). When we think of the experiential straddling of two realities characterizing children of trauma survivors—the child's own and that of the parent—we can appreciate the powerful effects of parental trauma on the conscious and unconscious brain/mind functioning. The divided consciousness is not passive and dormant, but like all self-systems is automatically enacted out of awareness. Even when the "content" of a particular self-system is rarely contemplated, only vaguely sensed (Laub and Auerhahn, 1993), or fully acknowledged, the triggers giving rise to an enaction of this state are most often unconscious, the neuropsychological process automatic. The result is a state of enacted knowing, characterizing children of trauma survivors. It is not a rational, cognition-based knowledge of trauma, but an enacted knowledge expressed through the unconscious expression of implicit maps and their myriad patterns.

The importance of reflection is unsurprisingly central to the issue of intergenerational transmission. As Fonagy and his colleagues (Busch, 2008; Fonagy, 2008; Fonagy et al., 2002; Jurist, 2008; Lyons-Ruth et al., 2005; Main and Hesse, 1990; Slade, 2005) show, the presence of a reflective functioning in parents acts as a protective mechanism against disorganized attachment. Using the Adult Attachment Interview, they found that the mother's sense of personal security is greatly related to her ability to coherently reflect on past experiences, including traumatic ones. What is being implied is that it is not necessarily the severity of the trauma that determines one's level of felt security and ability to engage in secure attachment, but the extent to which a victim of trauma has allowed himself or herself to think about it and attempted to integrate it into a coherent meaning and sense of self.

Main's (1991) concept of metacognitive monitoring supports the idea that reflective processing allows a better adaptation to one's traumatic past. In studies, the presence of mentalization among mothers with a traumatic past resulted in secure attachment relational styles, greatly benefiting their children. They were able to hold their children's subjectivities in mind, allowing them to focus on their needs and view them as separate from them. In this way they avoided enmeshing the children in their anxieties and fears. As an expression of an intergenerational dimension, attachment styles mirror the nature of the interaction. In Coats's words: "the child's sense of security is in fact, a function of measureable psychological characteristics in the parent" (1998, p. 139).

The repeated finding regarding the positive effect of reflective abilities among mothers who endured trauma in their past greatly underscores the centrality of such abilities for healthy child-raising and child development. Subsequently, the implications for the intersubjective exchanges between trauma survivors and their children are obvious. Mentalization, the ability to put the trauma in a more tolerable and coherent context and remember it without the raw dysregulating affect (LeDoux, 2014; LeDoux and Schiller, 2009), is especially crucial in light of data showing that trauma affects brain/mind organization (Bromberg, 1998; Dell, 2009; van der Kolk, 1987, 1996). More specifically, Beebe (2010) and Beebe and Lachmann (2002) assert that trauma significantly alters the brain's ability to flexibly update perceptions and representations, creating a fertile field for unconscious repetitions. Significantly, this conclusion totally dovetails with the balancing act between cortical and subcortical regions, a balance that determines one's level of rigid repetitions, which then deprive one of new input from cortical areas (Koziol and Budding, 2010).

When considering the power of traumas such as wars, terrorism, sexual and physical abuse, and the cumulative devastation of developmental traumas endured by so many children generation after generation, the importance of ameliorating or altogether preventing the generational chain of trauma and abuse is more important than ever. If, as has been repeatedly shown, a parent's reflective ability and the ability to recontextualize a traumatic experience (Ecker et al., 2012; Toomey and Ecker, 2009) and give it a coherent meaning (Fonagy, 2008) protects the child from internalizing dysregulating affects and cognitions, the implications for clinical work are clear.

At the same time, however, it seems very likely that in spite of a parent's ability to integrate past traumas in a lucid and relatively integrated fashion, the child's attachment needs will nonetheless assert themselves. It is reasonable to assume that even in such circumstances, with a reflective and attentive parent, the child who knows the parent's past will still connect with its painful and frightening aspects. A wide range of interactions—from sensed emotional states to hearing stories of the trauma to historical knowledge of what happened—will ignite many emotions in the child. We can easily imagine that this is the case for the children of the many soldiers who came back from war. Projecting him- or herself into the parent's military past and feeling the fear, guilt, and horror at what the soldier did and saw (Harkness, 1991), the child will inevitably develop a self-system dedicated to the parent's actual and imagined experiences. Accordingly, even when the power of intolerable and painful memories may be modulated by the integrative force of reflective awareness, the bare facts of the parent's suffering will endure. It is possible that the mere existence and knowledge of the parent's personal history is sufficient to trigger a child's empathy, imagination, and enmeshment in the parent's past.

We see, then, that the child susceptibility to the parent's traumatic past can include many paths. Unconscious identification with the traumatic self-state and an acute empathy toward lingering affective states of suffering constitute one path. Developing dysregulated hyper- or hypoaroused states due to the parent's emotional preoccupation with the trauma's aftermath is another. It needs to be mentioned that this chapter's focus on intergenerational transmission of trauma excluded studies attempting to explore the resiliency of children and the possible factors in the home that may shield them from the more harmful effects of trauma transmission.

THE LEGACY OF TRAUMA IN THERAPEUTIC ENACTMENTS

While treating adult children of trauma survivors and the second or third generation, an especially important goal is combining the raw emotional experience enacted by the trauma-related self-state with reflective awareness. This process is also central to resolving the inevitable transference–countertransference entanglements and enactments typical when treating adults growing in the shadow of their parents' trauma (Davies and Frawley, 1994). The opportunities for therapeutic collusions are many; the therapist herself may unconsciously need to avoid the intense pain embodied in the patient's communications or minimize its wide-ranging effects. As Danieli (1998) and others stress, the difficulty of treating these patients are sometimes due to the ever-present internalized aspects of the parental trauma and the strong emotions and countertransference they evoke (Prince, 1999).

The therapeutic process can become the safe place where the divided self-states can be fully experienced, explored, and integrated (Bromberg, 1998, 2006). But because of the emotional weight embedded in the grown child's traumatic self-state, and the loyalty to the parent he tried to save and sometimes actually had to parent, the activated self-state possesses a particular power. Before awareness informs the automatically enacted implicit relational patterns, the therapeutic process may be the sole venue for the enacted knowledge the child possesses. As the therapist is there to fully (albeit also unconsciously) respond to these enacted expression of the patient's unconscious systems, the ensuing enactments can be the only way to reconnect with the adult child's traumatized self-state (Bromberg, 2006; Ginot, 1997, 2007, 2009; Stern, 2010).

During Mary's treatment, I often felt as helpless and hopeless as she did, convinced that indeed, due to her negative expectations and convictions, she would never achieve happiness. At these times, her relationship with men seemed doomed and incorrigible, just like her mother's. Other times, "forgetting" her difficult past, I caught myself inordinately focusing on the possibility of meeting a man and creating a family with a "good father." These conversations enraged and upset Mary, who insisted that nothing could happen before she was "totally ready," and of course, she was right. But these mismatched interactional processes—revealing much about each of us and about the meaning of our mutual enactments—were very helpful once we analyzed and reflected on them. We understood that many of these enactments gave expression to Mary's experiences, her own as well as her mother's. Her mother's alternating states of anxiety, despair, and rage found their way into our interactions, as did my unconscious filtering of the intense emotions that were present in the space between us.

CHAPTER 10

Intersubjectivity and Unconscious Self-Systems: The Coexistence of Conflicting Processes

T HE THERAPEUTIC GOAL OF TRYING to objectively identify unconscious patterns and their enacted self-states inevitably faces various clinical and theoretical challenges. A renewed recognition of the
ongoing expressions of our unconscious maps also necessitates a thor-
ough understanding of attachment and emotional patterns; the particular self-states unique to each patient need to become deeply known
experientially and reflectively. This therapeutic aim, however, may be
in conflict with the multilayered facets of intersubjectivity: the continuing conscious and unconscious mutual influences and the resulting out
of awareness processes such as projective identification. In effect, the
interpersonal entanglements and enactments that inevitably take place
between the two participants of the therapeutic dyad present the following dilemma: can therapists steer patients toward an "objective"
acceptance of a self-system in a way that is relatively untainted by the
therapists' own unconscious?

This question is especially relevant in light of the expanded neuropsychological model of the unconscious, addressed in Chapter 1. In particular, the neuropsychological characteristics of unconscious processes
and maps—their early affective origin, stable but widely interconnected
structures, and their automatically enacted features—raise interesting
questions concerning some of our assumptions about the therapeutic
process. Specifically, it is important to reexamine how the pervasive
nature of unconscious processes belonging to both patient and therapist
interact with innate and unavoidable intersubjective forces. The ques-

tion of whether therapists can properly identify and analyze a patient's maladaptive patterns independently and without the context of the intersubjective interaction is central. To paraphrase Winnicott's (1967, 1969) assertion about infants and mothers, is there a patient without a therapist? Can a true understanding of the patient's dynamics exist outside the interpersonal context of the therapeutic dyad?

A related issue raises more questions involving the validity of the therapist's knowing authority. While observing and experiencing a patient's repeated patterns inside therapy and hearing how they are enacted outside of it, can the therapist gain a better grasp on the patient's dynamics than the patient himself does? We could wonder whether therapists can arrive at an accurate assessment of patient's internal lives, how they should communicate their conclusions, and with what level of confidence. Finally, how do we square off the fluid and interpenetrable nature of the intersubjective encounter between two participants who react to and affect each other with the more stable, habitual, and projective nature of their unconscious systems? Taking into account the automatic, defensive, and repetitive nature of unconscious processes—the tendency to expect, predict, perceive, and act according to subcortical maps—it is important to further examine how two separate subjectivities meet in psychotherapy.

These questions highlight the need to revisit some of our conceptual and clinical understanding of the therapeutic endeavor, especially in the context of intersubjectivity. One of the more intriguing issues addresses the previously mentioned and seemingly contradictory processes of helping patients recognize their implicit patterns while still staying cognizant of the unconscious aspects potentially involved in any interpretive interaction. As we have seen so far, the enactive properties of unconscious self-systems give habitual expression to each person's implicit and procedural memories, unconscious associations, and the distorted affective and cognitive meaning given to all experiences. Consequently, each sphere of social relatedness contains within it a mix of the individuals' unique implicit selves and the selves in interaction with each other (Bromberg, 2006; Stern, 1985, 2004; Stern et al., 1998). In essence, the interplay between the individual and the intersubjective parallels the interchange between explicit and implicit domains (Renn, 2012) or the continuum of conscious and unconscious processes.

SEPARATENESS AND INTERCONNECTION: THE PARADOX OF BEING APART AND A PART OF THE THERAPEUTIC DYAD

As has been illustrated in this book, the neural machinery of unconscious processes is entirely out of awareness and can never be accessible (Churchland, 2013; Damasio, 2010; Koziol, 2014; Panksepp and Biven, 2012). Consequently, its influence on every aspect of our functioning is involuntary, automatic, and repetitive—continually expressing entrenched ways of perceiving and interpreting the world. Bearing in mind the repetitive and often rigid quality of unconscious maps, we can ask how much are we actually "open" to the neuropsychological influences of another? In other words, we need to ask ourselves how effectively we can step out of the continual influence that our unconscious exerts on us to really listen to, see, and understand the other. If patients and therapists are the products of separate unconscious systems, their unique internal neuropsychological webs may render them unreceptive to and defensive about other interpretations of who they are. Rigid emotional and relational habits also may assimilate the other's intentions into existing relational memories. Obviously, the resulting biases may occur for both patients and therapists.

The questions raised by the stable and entrenched nature of unconscious systems are especially pertinent in the context of the continued expansion of the concept of intersubjectivity. As clinicians seek to further explicate the complex aspects of mutual and unconscious interchanges and the emotional sphere they engender, some proposed models negate the importance of separate subjectivities altogether. In such theoretical and clinical models, the major therapeutic action is found in the attention to and analysis of the co-created interactional processes of the here and now (Bohleber, 2013). For example, a focus on transference–countertransference interactions and how they reveal the unconscious and enacted dynamics of both participants may take center stage during the therapeutic process.

As the examination of the meaning of intersubjectivity has evolved, its nature has continued to expand beyond the inevitability of mutual and reciprocal effects. The additional conceptualizations have begun to emphasize the co-created facets of the interaction and the intersubjective third (Aron, 1996; Benjamin, 1995, 2004; Bohleber, 2013; Mitchell, 1993, 2000; T. Ogden, 1986, 2004). In these models the co-constructed third is the main subject of investigation; neither the patient's nor the therapist's internal realities alone can be examined separately (Bohleber, 2013). With Mitchell (1988, 1993, 2000) and Aron's (1996) suggestion that the patient's emerging dynamics, history, and internal experiences are co-created with the therapist, a significant conceptual shift has occurred.

It is not just that the historical veracity has stopped being the most important representation of the patient's life's experiences; more significantly, the patient's emerging self-knowledge cannot be disconnected from the intersubjective process. There is no single, distinct version of the dynamic past, only one that is continually co-constructed by both

participants. Therefore, the value of an objective, observable, reality
has become less important to Mitchell (1988, 1993, 1997, 2000) and
other relational theorists such as Aron (1996). In Mitchell's model of
mind, reality itself is experienced through imagination and fantasy, and
these seemingly different domains interpenetrate and enrich each other
(2000, p. 84). Consequently, the patient's past is co-constructed with the
therapist. Moreover, the many aspects constituting the patient's internal
world—conscious and unconscious—can be understood and interpreted
in multiple ways, each corresponding to the unique qualities of the dyad
(Renn, 2012). The patient's surfacing material is also shaped by the therapist's internal life, and the whole process expresses inevitable intersubjective mutual influences (Aron, 1996; Mitchell, 1993, 2000).

Among other clinicians who have continued to develop the concept
of intersubjectivity, T. Ogden (1986, 1994, 2004) sees patient and therapist as completely interdependent; their internal worlds react to each
other and change as a result. In this conceptualization, all therapeutic
experiences are mutually determined and unconsciously create a newly
constructed experience—the analytic third, an intersubjective psychological space co-constructed by both participants in the dyad. This
encounter unconsciously generates an interpersonal phenomenon "that
has not previously existed in the form it was now taking" (T. Ogden,
2004, p. 184). In this way, intersubjectivity engenders intimacy and an
authentic experience of relatedness. According to Ogden, intersubjectivity also facilitates an important venue for therapeutic progress. Out of
this jointly created third, a new sense of separateness and individuality
emerges, enhancing the patient's sense of self.

This therapeutic outcome happens through an unconscious process
of projective identification, in which both participants subjugate themselves to the mutually generated intersubjective third (T. Ogden, 2004).
As part of this therapeutic development, both patient and therapist free
themselves from their individual limitations, arriving at a state where
they are simultaneously intertwined with and independent of each
other. Of particular importance is Ogden's assertion that the experience
of unconsciously recognizing and being recognized by the other ensures
a strengthened individual subjectivity.

Similarly, Benjamin's conceptualization of intersubjectivity views
the process as grounded in mutual recognition. She also discusses the
notion of a third. The necessity to surrender, to perceive and feel things
from the other's point of view, is important in her model as a process
that is rooted in the mutually created third between mother and infant
(1995, 2004). Within the therapeutic relationship, both participants allow
enactments to occur by creating an intersubjective third, thereby affording reflection on the nature of the interaction and each participant's role
in it. The resulting mutual recognition reflects a more egalitarian view

all thought is construction

of the therapeutic process, an important outcome that depends on the therapist's acceptance of his own unconscious contribution.

Bion's (1984, 1990) notions of the container/contained and "dreaming for two" are relevant here as well. Similarly, Brown (2011) defines intersubjectivity as an unconscious process of communication and meaning making between two intrapsychic worlds. This intertwined exchange results in changes between and within each member of the analytical dyad. The mutual unconscious communication and the co-constructed intersubjectivity process occur through projective identification (Bion, 1984, 1990; Brown, 2011). More radical yet, Baranger and Baranger (in Bohleber. 2013) maintain that within the therapeutic process, the sole subject of investigation is the combined unconscious fantasy emanating from the intersubjective field. All these approaches emphasize a shared psychological amalgam co-created by the unconscious minds of both patient and therapist. Felt experiences of unconscious communication, projections or repeated enactments within couples and within the therapeutic relationship clearly exemplify the entangled nature of relationships.

But without acknowledging the power of unconscious self-systems— which until becoming known operate the only way they know how— these models for understanding the clinical encounter may be inherently limited. Such potential limitations may result from the possible overestimation of the power of intersubjectivity to override unconsciously guided, ingrained patterns. In therapeutic models that view the patient's history, dynamics, and even perceptions of his internal life as mostly co-constructed rather than internally fixed and driven, individual subjectivities do not really exist as such (Bohleber, 2013; Ogden 1998, 2004; Renn, 2012). Given the pervasiveness and automaticity of unconscious processes dedicated to maintain implicit emotional learning, memories, and defenses, therapists are faced with the quandary of whether it is wise or even possible to abandon the notion of the patient's separate and actively enacted distinct subjectivity.

ENACTMENTS AS THE EMBODIMENT
OF THE CO-CONSTRUCTED THIRD

As has been indicated, stable and inflexible adult subjectivities span the important continuums of unconsciousness–consciousness and rigidity–flexibility. Enduring perceptions, emotions, interpretations, and behaviors inhabiting different levels of unconsciousness and rigidity may make it difficult for both patient and therapist to unconsciously subjugate their perceptions to the other or abandon their typical ways of experiencing themselves and others, including their unconscious defensive operations. Patients as well as therapists with rigid unconscious systems and automatically enacted self-states will involuntarily revert to their deep-rooted and typical ways of perceiving and behaving. Both patient and therapist might filter interactions through their unconscious maps, giving them an unexamined, familiar meaning. This inevitable neuropsychologically determined tendency to enact internal complex maps may end up in entangled interaction and repeated enactments (see Chapters 3 and 4).

Reexamining the inevitability of enactments in the therapeutic relationship offers us an opportunity to understand intersubjectivity in a more nuanced way. It is likely that the more meaningful and noticeable manifestations of the third are processes that most of the time are emblematic of enactments. Ongoing mutual effects occur under the conscious radar of both patient and therapist at any given moment; such processes characterize all meaningful human interactions. These unconscious influences support unconscious attunement, interpersonal imitation, and the acquisition of new models for affect regulation (Ginot, 2001, 2009; Fosshage, 2005, 2011; Schore, 2012). But what we consciously experience as the third in fact may be the culmination of an enactment, the moment when the effects of unconscious processes and the failure of mutual attunement and recognition cross the line from the unconscious to conscious experiences (Aron, 1996; Benjamin, 2004; Bromberg, 1998, 2006, 2011; Chused, 1998; Maroda, 1991; Schore, 2012; Stern, 2010). Consequently, the infinite mutual influences and their repercussions can also be perceived as occupying different spaces on the unconscious–conscious continuum, operating quietly and unobserved until states of hyper- or hypoarousal trigger emotional and behavioral entanglement (Schore, 2012).

In this way, enactments themselves represent a co-constructed third. Rather than giving an expression to a mutual surrender within the dyad, enactments mostly embody the unconscious–conscious intermingling of two entrenched systems, activated by unconscious–conscious cues within hyper- or hypoaroused physio/affective states. The therapeutic importance of enactments is rooted in their inevitable shifting between different, often conflicting self-states. As clinical experiences indicate, during an enactment, both patient and therapist may oscillate between emotional assault and victimization. It is as if at any time during such interpersonal and often hurtful impasses, one participant is either the aggressor or the misunderstood victim (Benjamin, 1998, 2004; Maroda, 1991).

Most often, however, both participants of a dyad—whether therapeutic, romantic, or just business partners—will feel and enact both self-states of rage and victimization at different times and in response to an escalating emotional state of hyperarousal. Within such an enactment, for example, anger will be justified and the sense of being misunderstood and victim-ized totally embraced without reflection. These shifting positions signify early internalizations of all aspects of the intersubjective sphere: the parent's behavior and emotional messages, the child's felt humiliation and/or trauma, and the myriad self-focused and negative meanings attached to such painful interactions (Braten, 2007; Braten and Trevarthen, 2007; Diamond, 2004; Hermans, 2004; Lewis and Todd, 2007).

The understanding of enactments as the expression of activated two rigid unconscious systems opens a window into unconscious patterns and their enacted manifestations (Bromberg, 2006; Ginot, 2001, 2007, 2009; Stern, 2010). At the same time, enactments remind us that even in the midst of an entangled intersubjectivity, participants hold on to their sense of separateness. In effect, the transference–countertransference dynamics that lead to enactments most often involve rigid and entrenched perceptions, expectations, and emotional beliefs that fix both participants in familiar, unyielding reactions to each other (see Chapters 3 and 4). Both members of the dyad are convinced that their perceptions are the true ones and are unaware of the triggers that activated them or of the automatic nature of their reactions (Bromberg, 2006; Maroda, 1991).

The reality of enacted individual unconscious systems in a dyad is not just a matter of philosophical or theoretical conceptualization; it is closely related to how much focus is given by the therapist to the patient's own enacted patterns. Furthermore, the question of how much the patient's patterns can be seen as separate from those of the therapist's—or for that matter, to what degree we can examine each system for its individual characteristics—is still important. If a therapist believes that a focused attempt to identify and work through patterns that have outlived their defensive usefulness is central, for example, she will look for effective therapeutic modalities to achieve this goal. When we acknowledge the power of a patient's unconscious self-system and its felt self-state to induce strong reactions in the therapist—distinct reactions to the patient's emotions, thoughts, and behaviors—we can also look for more efficient ways to ameliorate them (see Chapter 8).

THE THERAPIST'S SUBJECTIVITY: DOES IT PROVIDE THERAPEUTIC AUTHORITY?

As we try to further deconstruct the opposing pulls of separateness and intersubjectivity we must consider the issue of the therapist's objective "expertise"—the therapist as the participant observer who "knows" what ails the patient and what needs to be done. This issue is connected, of course, to old debates regarding the therapist's actual and perceived authority in the therapeutic interchange (Aron, 1996; Benjamin, 2004; Cozolino, 2002; Wallin, 2007). Furthermore, as some intersubjective models suggest, the therapist's assumed knowledge itself can be a hindrance to the therapeutic knowledge (Bion, 1990), and interfere with the patient's self-search (T. Ogden, 2004). After all, the therapist is under the influence of his own unconscious perceptions, expectations, fears, and defenses, all guiding his feelings, and interpretations of the patient and informing his ways of being a therapist (Cozolino, 2002; Wallin, 2007).

What do engrained, stable, and often rigid unconscious systems mean to the therapist's efforts? We have already seen that intersubjective pulls span the range from unconscious communication and imitational processes to the prevalence of therapeutic enactments: enacted feelings, expectations, assigned meanings and behaviors, and their resultant misunderstandings and emotional upheavals. Such unconscious pulls may characterize the therapist's approaches as well as that of the patient. As mentioned before, not dealing directly with patients' unconscious systems as separate entities exerting their unique influence may not help them become aware of what unconscious processes are guiding them, summon up the motivation to confront patterns, or take on the difficult task of "going against the grain." At the same time, not sufficiently recognizing inevitable unconscious influences on the therapist's reactions, interpretations and behaviors can also be greatly detrimental to the therapeutic engagement (Aron, 1996; Bromberg, 2011; Cozolino, 2002; Wallin, 2007).

This aspect of the therapeutic work—the therapist's job of being aware (as much as she can) of her own familiar emotional and relational patterns—does not mean, of course, that the therapist cannot approach the patient's dynamics as separate from her own. By doing so, she is still not the sole or authoritarian holder of the correct interpretation regarding the patient's internal and enacted life. What differentiates this kind of therapeutic assessment from the older, one-dynamic-fits-all understanding of human nature is the greater information provided by neuropsychology. Paralleling the need to attend to distinct internal patterns of both patient and therapist and the interpenetrations of them are brain/mind processes that support both. The reinforced properties of unconscious maps truly interact through unconscious communication, underpinned by the right hemisphere and the mirror neuron system. If we acknowledge, then, that unconscious and intersubjective forces possess the power to deeply shape the therapeutic process, perhaps we should not give primacy to either the individual or the intersubjective realms—both are needed.

SHARED EMOTIONS: EMPATHY AND SEPARATENESS

The mirror neuron system and the right brain mediate our capacity for an unmediated neuropsychological understanding of another's person emotional states. The mirror neuron system in particular creates imitational and emotional bridges between interacting subjectivities that observe and react to each other. Through neurological simulation observers of an action, intent, or an emotion neurally reproduce them in their own brains (Carr et al., 2003; Gallese, 2009; Iacoboni, 2008; McGilchrist, 2009; Ramachandran, 2011; Rizzolati et al., 2002). This built-in mirroring ability also underlies the neuropsychological expression of empathetic responses, or in Gallese's words: "the empathic shared manifold of intersubjectivity" (2006, p. 271). Through embodied simulation, the mirror neuron system seems to automatically establish a direct experiential link between subjects. The unmediated naturalness of this process is demonstrated when Iacoboni describes it as follows: "This simulation process is an *effortless*, automatic, and unconscious inner mirroring" (2008, p. 120, emphasis in original).

In a further refinement of what it means to resonate with the other, and with great relevance to the tension between intersubjectivity and separateness, Gallese, Iacoboni, and Ramachandran assert that the shared neural processes do not result in a self-less merging phenomenon. The mirror neuron system only underpins an emotional and communicational permeability between participants, a potential porousness that is a building block of intersubjectivity. It does not define one's sense of self entirely, even while this permeability is taking place. In Gallese's words: "empathy entails the capacity to experience what others experience while still attributing these experiences to others and not to the self" (2006, p. 288). While demonstrating the role of the mirror neuron system in the neuropsychological processes of self-other recognition, Iacoboni and his group (Iacoboni, 2008; Uddin et al., 2004) confirmed subjects' ability to maintain their own sense of self when viewing pictures of themselves and of others, a point also emphasized by Gazzaniga (2008; Gazzaniga et al., 2014).

To summarize this complex issue of connectedness and distinctiveness in the therapeutic process, we can conclude that the shifting balance between the pull of intersubjective resonance and each participant's enduring set of typical unconscious enactive self-systems is an ever-present phenomenon. The therapist's effectiveness is most likely dependent on her ability to shift between surrender to the third and a more aware, observant state that can help a patient explore his internal life as an independent entity.

These intertwined processes of more detached therapeutic understanding in the midst of unconscious mutual influences seem to make
the therapist's work more difficult if not potentially precarious. As
therapists need to concurrently straddle reflective therapeutic understanding—anchored in both observation and the transference–countertransference interactions—and the unconscious realm of intersubjective
exchanges, it may be harder to navigate them both with equal success.
Clinically, the continual shifts between the two realms is most likely
practiced by most therapists; even those adhering to behavioral or cognitive-behavioral models have come to recognize the power and the pull
of unconscious influences (Lane et al., 2014). It seems apparent that in
order to swim rather than sink in the choppy waters that form the psychotherapeutic endeavor, a modicum of balance between intersubjectivity and more objective assessment needs to be achieved.

Indeed, as most writers conclude, what is important is the tension
between the therapist' surrender and her individuality, between her
unconscious influences and the patient's unique history and reality. As
Aron (1996) states so succinctly, the therapeutic relationship is equal
but asymmetrical. Based on a model of the unconscious as an enduring, enactive system, this apt conclusion describes the two intertwined
realms: the intersubjective one created by two unconscious self-systems,
and the more therapeutic one which is anchored in the therapist's ability
to successfully use her aware understanding of the patient's difficulties.

A similar tension between the individual and the intersubjective dyad
is suggested by other clinicians, including those who see intersubjectivity as an important, if not the most important, aspect of psychodynamic
psychotherapy and psychoanalysis (Aron, 1996; Benjamin, 2004; Bromberg, 2006, 2011; Brown, 2011; T. Ogden, 2004). While Baranger and
Baranger (in Bohleber, 2013) argue that the most important subject of
analysis is the shared unconscious emanating from both participants,
their position maintains that while the patient is immersed in the field
the therapist is only partially so. In actuality, the therapist is a participant observer. Recognizing the centrality the patient's unconsciously
enacted and recurrent patterns as well as the shared unconscious, the
authors maintain that to help patients, a therapist needs to leave the
intersubjective field and examine the patient's internal world.

Consider a therapeutic process reported by a supervisee over a period
of a few months into the second year of treatment. Repeatedly the therapist related that whenever she tried to probe into the patient's memories
and feelings about his childhood, he would balk and become evasive.
Without realizing it, the therapist retreated from further inquiries, reasoning first to herself and then to me that "obviously he is not ready to
deal with his painful childhood. Maybe he needs some time before he
can talk about his past." What became clear was the therapist's cautious-

ness. She would be hesitant in her reflections, questions, and interpretations, aligning herself closely with the patient's verbalizations. But she also felt that the treatment was stuck. Both felt therapy was "boring and not going anywhere."

This is a dilemma we often have with our patients. Who determines the emotional atmosphere and the verbal exchanges—us or them? The answer within the intersubjective model is that we are both contributors. What does that really mean? What if the supervisee's own anxieties added to the patient's difficulties in accessing his past? It is possible, after all, that guided by his unconscious self-system, the patient's already sensitized amygdala was acutely attuned to the therapist's own felt but inchoate anxiety. In turn, this visceral perception, an emotional resonance aided by the patient's mirror neuron system, intensified whatever fears about the interpersonal he already had.

We can further speculate that as a result, in an ongoing bidirectional influence, the therapist also became more anxious; her mirror neuron system and amygdala were active parts of the unconscious–conscious interchange. Aware of the feeling but not of its source, she "decided" that it was best not to push the patient beyond what he could tolerate. Can we say in this case that the anxiety actually belonged to the therapist and made it harder for the patient to open up? Conversely, it is also possible that the therapist's reactions constituted a complementary empathetic response that showed the patient she understood and accepted his pace of self-exploration. In this scenario the therapist's reticence to pursue difficult interchanges resonated with what the patient needed from the her: time and empathy.

In our supervision dyad, while trying together to understand her feelings, confusion, and this particular therapeutic process as a whole, the therapist appeared concerned by the possibility of such an intersubjective resonance of affects and intentions. At times, while not knowing who affected whom, she felt as if she was on shaky ground. More than anything, she was deeply worried that she was in the midst of an enactment with this patient, not trusting her conscious choices and therapeutic interventions. She needed to know how to gain her footing: was the process she was in an enactment or in effect the embodiment of a supportive environment?

The intricacies of this particular therapeutic situation are specific to this pair, but in essence are reminiscent of many such processes during ongoing therapy. What we needed to explore was the important realm where both the patient's specific dynamic and her internal tendencies interacted, affected each other, and still retained some individual ownership. At the same time we needed to accept that a complete separation between their two subjectivities was not possible and that the enactment itself may be an empathetic echo of the patient's difficulties.

Due to unconscious on-communication and our capacity to perceive and react to it, the therapist's and the patient's individual dynamics shift and change places with their interaction. At times the patient's (and therapist's) individual subjectivity is at the foreground, at others times, the interactional resonance takes center stage. How do we know what's going on?

There are many ways to understand any particular process, of course, but the most authentic means to find our way out of a confusing situation (or an incipient one) may be rooted in our own experiences. If we are mindful of our internal system and its usual biases, our feelings and reactions to a patient can clarify a great deal. Indeed, for this supervisee the answer came when she became aware of her cautiousness and passivity. Feeling increasingly uncomfortable with her careful behavior during sessions, she understood her reactions as the complex mix that they were: empathetic resonance mingled with her own anxieties about confronting painful experiences.

Only after becoming aware could she free herself from her fixed emotional position and explore other possible interventions that could move the treatment forward. In spite of her trepidations, she disclosed some of her ongoing feelings of hesitancy to the patient and invited him to consider what they might mean. Over a period of time, while they both openly dealt with their possible effects on each other, the patient, now emotionally engaged, started to become curious about his dissociated pain, his past traumas, and the defenses against them. For her part, the therapist learned a great deal about herself.

MOTHERS AND INFANTS, THERAPISTS AND PATIENTS: SIMILAR DYADS?

The focus on intersubjectivity as an inseparable element of the therapeutic process is not only the result of the discovered functions of neuropsychological processes underpinned by the mirror neuron system and the right brain. This increased attention to intersubjective influences in psychoanalysis and psychotherapy has also gained strength as it has become deeply rooted first in the mother–infant relational model and then, more specifically, in infant and attachment research. Winnicott (1967, 1969) and later Beebe and Lachmann (2002), Diamond (2004), Schore (2012), and Tronick (2007), among others, have viewed the relational bond between mothers and infants as the prototype for the therapeutic relationship. Comparable to the mother's role in shaping and organizing her infant's emotional life, the intersubjective process gives shape and meaning to the patient's internal world and history (Mitchell, 2000; Renn, 2012; Schore, 2012).

A robust body of research has shown the effects of early parental attunement, attachment styles, and reflective awareness on infants and toddlers and, in a longitudinal study, also among young adults (Lyons-Roth, 2003). The repeated results seem to back up these current views of therapy as a parallel process to the first relationships. The obvious assumptions are that the many opportunities for mutual attunement embedded in the therapeutic relationship are capable of enhancing emotional growth and affect regulation, just as they can in our early relationships. Intense, nonverbal moments of meeting between mother and child, experiences that help integrate the child's emotional world (Beebe, 2010; Kohut, 1971; Stern, 1985, 2004; Tronick, 2007), and strengthen affect regulation (Schore, 1994; 2012) are also thought to be essential to therapeutic process. There is little debate regarding environmental and experiential effects on the growing brain, especially in the context of close relationships in which the baby and then the child is highly attuned to his parents' emotional and behavioral states (Beebe and Lachmann, 2002; Braten, 2007; Braten and Trevarthen, 2007; Diamond, 2004; Fonagy and Target, 1998; Lyons-Ruth, 2003; Mancia, 2006; Schore, 1994, 2012; Stern, 1985, 2004; Trevarthen, 1979; Tronick, 2007, to name just a few).

As a result, it is increasingly taken for granted that the enduring influences that parents' attunement and their empathetic sensitivity have on a growing child actually parallels the therapeutic situation. Taking into account what we know about formed, strengthened, and well-rehearsed unconscious maps and their automatically enacted manifestations, this assumption may not entirely reflect such a reality. Are patients ever as immersed in the therapist's self-states as a child is in his mother's and father's emotional states (Braten and Trevarthen, 2007)? Similarly, can the therapist be as immersed in the patient's self-state as a mother is in her newborn, with the same intense emotional preoccupation? Most significantly, what is being questioned here is whether the processes of intersubjective influence are as powerful between two adults with already formed and well-defined self-systems and self-states as between a developing child and his parents.

In spite of the ongoing subtle and unconscious mutual influences triggered by intersubjectivity, the stable nature of an unconscious system may not easily let itself become affected by others. Although we assume that the therapist's emotional attunement and empathy and her ability to tolerate intense feelings will generate a healing process, the patient's openness to the emotional benefits of such an environment may be hindered by existing self-systems that automatically enact only what worked in the past. It seems more likely that a patient whose central self-systems and self-states are organized around affects and narratives of thwarted interpersonal closeness will not be able to truly recognize or experience such a supportive environment. The self-state that might greatly benefit from attunement, and care may take quite some time to develop. Unlike a growing child whose developing brain is entirely affected by those around him, an adult patient enters therapy possessing a defined personality, well armed with a defensive system that has proved its usefulness over many years. It is not that an adult brain/mind ceases to be plastic and changeable, but that within an adult with well-formed self-systems, plasticity is not always immediately available. Here again, both the rigidity–flexibility and the time available for therapeutic change are highlighted.

In this case, questions regarding the openness of adult patients to therapeutic influence and change are very relevant as we seek effective curative modalities. What is so clear in almost every therapeutic process is the way very early experiences are enacted, giving an undeniable voice to the child self-state. As poignant and real as old experiences feel, as painful as past memories are, and as destructive as some relational patterns are, these self-states reside within the complex context of an adult personality. As Mitchell (1997, 2000) also observed, despite the power of early representations, the patient is not simply an infant; present in therapy are adult self-states he has developed as well.

There are some very unique qualities, then, to the complex interchanges—both conscious and unconscious—between adults. These properties differentiate the therapeutic connection with adult patients from the more fluid intersubjective relationship between parents and children. Although unconscious learning processes are an important part of psychotherapy, it is still not clear how easy it is for old patterns to yield to learning new ways of perceiving and acting. It is important to recall that one of the defining characteristics of unconscious maps is their stability and reinforced strength. Old patterns are invariable triggered, but the question is still whether they can be influenced by nonverbal communication to the degree that a child's growing sense of self is affected.

THE DEFENSIVE NEED TO BE INVULNERABLE WHILE YEARNING FOR CONNECTION: THE CASE OF LISA

Lisa, a divorced woman in her fifties, started therapy after an intense fight with one of her daughters, a fight that seemed to be the end result of many years of rancor and bitter clashes. In therapy, as in her other relationships, Lisa had great difficulty listening to the other and being empathetic to another's point of view. Although she genuinely felt and verbally stated that she recognized her "flawed tendencies," when she perceived she was slighted or when someone disagreed with her, she defensively rejected the other's point of view.

With me, despite her obvious suffering and her wish to get along with those close to her, Lisa repeatedly dismissed my contributions, often arguing and insisting on her perceptions. Although she created a combative interaction at times, I felt a great deal of empathy for her struggle. I realized that in her unconscious fantasy, any crack in her system, any letting in of the other led to intolerable vulnerability. For a long time, Lisa, an adult with a fully formed rigid system simply could not afford to let me in. Her case is not that different from therapeutic encounters where therapists—facing resistant, entrenched patterns of perception, affect, and behavior—may end up feeling hopeless and defeated.

ATTUNEMENT IN DEVELOPMENT AND IN THERAPY

Addressing the important issue of nonverbal influence of attunement, is Schore's (1994, 2003, 2012) model, which views the indispensable function of affect regulation as entirely dependent on the mother's ability to modulate arousal states, especially early in the child's life. This necessary level of attunement to the infant and the toddler is mediated by the right brain of mother and child. Through a good enough mutual regulation of hyper- or hypoaroused psychobiological states, the baby develops his own capacity for affect regulation. In parallel to these nonverbal processes, the therapist uses her own internal regulation to nonverbally help a patient achieve regulation, a process that is fundamental to internal and lasting change. What is modified through nonverbally attuned regulation, according to Schore, are the integrative functions between subcortical regions and the PFC within the right hemisphere specifically.

What was damaged or not achieved during the early years can be emotionally corrected with the therapist's reparative emotional communication and her ability, akin to an attuned mother, to use her own self-regulation to help the patient achieve his. Schore's interpersonal-biological model offers a basis for further conceptual understanding of the invaluable nonverbal aspects of the therapeutic relationship, especially its intersubjective mutual effects. Although the therapeutic relationship does not replicate the original childhood one, it still offers many chances for corrective experiences.

The length of time therapy requires—in Lisa's case a few years for her to feel more vulnerable and trusting—attests to the strength and hold of self-systems, and the slow learning process that is involved in changing them, especially if self-systems are a part of a rigid neuropsychological structure. Schore's model affords a second chance for patients to strengthen their affect regulation abilities. But it seems important to realize that the enormous opportunities offered by psychotherapy are specific to this relationship. As cognition and affect are entirely inter-

twined within the brain/mind, and since old self-states coexist with
adult ones, therapeutic approaches that combine emotional experiences
with reflective awareness in real time seem to be the most helpful (Fonagy, 2008; Jurist, 2008; Lane, 2008, Lane et al., 2014).

The power of the interactional field is always at work between patient
and therapist, or in fact within any other dyad. Out of awareness, whole
patterns of affect cognition and behavior are mutually and automatically
being triggered and enacted, creating an enmeshed and complementary
dynamics (Racker, 1991). At the same time, we cannot lose sight of the
fact that the interaction is guided by two independent systems that inevitably react to each other. In some ways, the intersubjective encounter
can also be seen as an arena where two separate subjectivities are both
inside and outside the enmeshment. The more rigid and unconscious a
system is, however, the more opportunities for a power struggle and the
ownership of truth, as often happens in enactment.

THE THERAPEUTIC CHALLENGE AND A DELICATE BALANCE

In light of the friction and continual tug between intersubjectivity and
separateness, between mutual influence and defensive repetitions, we
need to examine intersubjective influences with the understanding that
among adults the process is much more complicated. Unlike the emotional needs and urgency between children and parents, the shades
of intersubjectivity may be more nuanced among adults. As suggested
earlier, the heart of therapeutic intersubjectivity is not simply found in
the co-construction process; with a relatively self-aware therapist, the
patient's enacted unconscious patterns can be identified as his. The true
expressions of intersubjectivity, however, may mainly be in the form of
the myriad enactments themselves, small and large, intense or mild, that
characterize the therapeutic relationship.

This seeming equivocation does not take away from the power
of intersubjective influences as unavoidable aspects of therapy, but
by giving credence to the patient's enacted unconscious as a distinct
and recognizable pattern, it does shift the all-encompassing centrality
that intersubjectivity has recently received. There is no doubt that in
an ongoing way, mutual responses occur in a repeated feedback loop,
subtly affecting the way each participant perceives and experiences the
other. But because these mutual influences are also determined by each
participant's unconscious biases, it is hard to see how a co-constructed
experience is not also fully informed by separate self-systems.

In this way, intersubjectivity cannot be differentiated from the distinct unconscious influences that determine what shape it takes. These
two elements of human interaction—one's stable patterns and the pull

of the other—are completely intertwined, and both are entirely rooted in unconscious processes. The third or the co-constructed therapeutic experience is a new interpersonal entity that is created by the triggered, enacted manifestations of two distinct self-states and supported by unconscious communication. At the same time, the individual self-system does not lose its unique qualities. As a matter of fact, throughout the therapeutic process, each participant's internal structure, unconscious hurts, and defenses may find their most urgent voice in the transference–countertransference interchanges.

Operating out of awareness, the nonverbal dimension also creates a continuous space for moment-to-moment mutual influence (Beebe and Lachmann, 2002; Renn, 2012; Stern, 2004, Stern et al., 1998). Patient and therapist constantly adjust to each other's physical movements, gestures, and emotional states. This is fundamental to all social behaviors, underpinned by the mirror neuron system and the sensitivity of the right hemisphere. It is largely assumed that unconscious resonance and the therapist's ability to nonverbally regulate the patient's emotional state actually provide a corrective experience. It is possible, however, that to achieve therapeutic change, what is needed even more than acknowledged intersubjectivity is the direct experience of and a repeated process of working through the patient's destructive patterns (see Chapter 8). Encountering a patient's unconscious in action and identifying it as a system that no longer works may demand the therapist's confidence and conviction that by dealing directly with and focusing on the patient's subjectivity, such patterns can change.

Revisiting the debate about the therapist authority also brings to light that therapists need to simultaneously reside within the unconscious mutuality and outside of it, listening to the unique qualities of the patient's enaction while trying to be aware of the habitual biasing power of their own unconscious maps. Importantly, fully accepting the ever-present influence of unconscious processes opens up the therapeutic process to also accepting the importance of the therapist's role as the one who can help patients confront patterns that do not work and often hinder them from achieving their goals. With enough or good enough awareness of the double pull of enmeshed intersubjectivity and the patient's distinct internal world, therapists come to embody Aron's (1996) conceptualization of psychodynamic psychotherapy as equal but asymmetrical. Inevitable neuropsychological processes common to both participants render them susceptible to entrenched patterns. Once these nonverbal communications and the enacted unconscious characteristics they represent intermingle, a new and inclusive entity comes into play—the third (Benjamin, 2004; T. Ogden, 1986, 1994, 2004).

It seems that the therapist's position as the expert who can help patients decipher their behaviors is irreplaceable. Without the therapist's knowledge and consciousness, both participants run the risk of being forever locked in ongoing enactments. The therapeutic relationship, especially the therapist's ability to largely remain simultaneously inside and outside the sphere of unconscious influences, offers patients unique opportunities. As we contemplate people's emotional connections in general and the difficulties that are often embedded within them, we see that the therapeutic relationship is entirely unique. There seems to be no other relationship that offers a relational depth that is not merely lived out automatically but can also be understood and reflected on. In such an interpersonal context, with the therapist's guidance, all maladaptive manifestations of unconscious systems can be experienced, identified, and become subject for change. To achieve this therapeutic goal, the therapist needs to be able to maintain her observer function while always staying mindful of her own subjective involvement.

Last Thoughts on the Relationship Between Conscious and Unconscious Processes and Its Relevance to Psychotherapy

"BEFORE CONSCIOUSNESS LIFE REGULATION WAS entirely automated; after consciousness begins, life regulation retains its automation but gradually comes under the influence of self-oriented deliberation" (Damasio, 2010, p. 187). Consequently, "the entire fabric of a conscious mind is created from the same cloth-images generated by the brain's map-making abilities" (Damasio, 2010, p. 199).

It may seem curious to begin the conclusion of a book dedicated to unconscious processes with quotes explicating the nature of consciousness. But as has been shown in the previous chapters, unconscious processes and the largely inaccessible maps they generate affect and guide all aspects of our conscious mental life. In fact, Damasio's (1999, 2000, 2010) neuropsychological model describing the relationship between unconscious processes and their conscious expressions offers the most enlightening and apt lens for exploring the unconscious. Unconscious processes are vast and ever-present, and they are characterized by learned and reinforced neuropsychological patterns that essentially form the foundation for our conscious existence. In Damasio's (2010) model, neural dispositions—subcortically activation neurochemical patterns—located in the brain stem and hypothalamus regulate biological functions. In this way, they mediate all processes necessary for survival: reward and punishment, drives, needs, motivation, and emotions (see also Koziol, 2014; Koziol and Budding, 2010; Panksepp and Biven, 2012; Schore, 2012).

These essential but inaccessible neural dispositions humming in the background also provide the underlying mechanisms for mapping images in the realm of perception, recognition, and recall, and most important, for selecting and editing which images will gain access to consciousness. Sharing this view are Koziol and Budding (2009) and Koziol (2014) who describe the editing functions of subcortical regions and the resulting effects on how stimuli in the environments are perceived, processed, and interpreted. As many of the current researchers and thinkers mentioned in this book see it, consciousness is a latecomer to the life management processes necessary for survival. The emerging consciousness has provided humans with a conscious grasp of some of the automated efforts and lessons involved in survival and well-being.

This conscious learning capacity and the accessible memories of the most effective physical and emotional survival mechanisms enable us to participate in life with the unique power of awareness and deliberation. Despite an ever-present presence of a conscious, continuous sense of self in our wakeful life, deliberate consciousness often takes second stage to the ongoing automated processes of the unconscious. Indeed, we are cognizant of how our body feels, our continuous feeling states and ruminations, and are especially attuned to others around us. What we are not aware of are the ways we process stimuli—how we categorize, interpret, and arrive at predictable and preordained convictions about who we are and others' intentions toward us.

One of the important conclusions following from this understanding of how the unconscious guides our conscious beings is that viewing conscious and unconscious processes as a dichotomy is arbitrary and inaccurate. The two realms continually inform each other (Damasio, 2010, p. 189), and with significant implications for psychotherapy, they affect and transform each other. Essentially, according to many neuroscientists, the difference between a totally unconscious life regulation–based existence and a more conscious mentality is determined by gradations of automaticity versus reflectiveness—in other words, the conscious–unconscious continuum. If reflective awareness—one of the human embodiments of consciousness—can affect the unconscious realm, then therapy has the power to shift unconscious neuropsychological patterns. Whether through reinforced learning processes, identification with the therapist, an empathetic and nurturing emotional connection with the therapist, or reflective awareness of repeated transference–countertransference entanglements (among many possible interactional determinants), patients' unconscious processes are affected by the therapeutic process. In effect, such changes as a result of learning have been seen in all creatures, even sea snails (Kandel, 1999, 2001). Learning changes our brain.

Yet despite this fluid relationship and the bidirectional effects between the two realms, the mutual influence is not exactly even. As remarked on by Damasio and as demonstrated in the previous chapters, automated and well-rehearsed maps are readily enacted without awareness, and they often have the upper hand when guiding our behaviors and conscious experiences. As a result, the process of change is not simple or easy. As each chapter has laid out, although emotional and behavioral changes are the stated goals of most therapeutic processes, change is difficult to realize and implement for many patients. What seems to underlie this struggle is each person's unique interplay between conscious and unconscious processes, between flexible and rigid self-systems. More specifically, what stands in the way of quick and enduring therapeutic change is one's unconscious processes and their respective automatically enacted features.

The neuropsychological evidence for the notion of unconscious guidance of higher mental processes, such as interpersonal perceptions and behaviors as well as sophisticated goal pursuit, is compelling (Bargh, 2007, 2014; Hassin et al., 2007; Hutto, 2012; Pally, 2007). It helps us understand, for example, the often seen repeated choices of partners who "don't work out" as a very sophisticated system that pursues the goal of love but is guided by another self-system that repeats the only emotional and relational patterns it knows. The stable nature of unconscious processes, especially in patients with rigid emotional and cognitive patterns, raises the question of whether it is possible to access and work through destructive patterns without full appreciation of their enduring qualities. Such a nonjudgmental understanding, shared with patients, can greatly enhance the therapeutic process; guilt over "choosing" to be miserable is replaced by deep commitment to experience and work through those maladaptive and largely fixed patterns.

Habits are another manifestation of the seamless integration of conscious and unconscious brain activity. Much of our daily existence is made up of habits, from simple ones to very complex social interactions and pursuits, as we have seen in many of the case studies discussed in the book. The brain/mind's ability to form habits has been an enormously important characteristic in the evolution of our species. Realizing that social, emotional, and behavioral patterns acquired in childhood last for a lifetime, and that our unconscious habits essentially make us who we are, further underscores why it so difficult to change and why it takes time to do so. Such habits, which can be called implicit working models or unconscious systems, will always seek the quickest and most tried ways to understand the world, not because there's a central agency that commands them to do so but because this is what the brain/mind does (see Chapters 1 and 2).

DIFFERENT PATHS TO THERAPEUTIC CHANGE

At the same time, the still emerging picture of the neuropsychological nature of our pervasive unconscious systems—especially their evolutionarily determined tendency to repeat complex learned patterns out of awareness—should further inform us as to what needs to be therapeutically addressed and how (Divino and Moore, 2010). In effect, since Freud, all therapeutic modalities have had to confront affectively driven and maladaptive patterns of behavior, even if they are patterns that repeat the very same interpersonal difficulties or negative emotions, self-negating narratives, and distorted beliefs about one's self-value. As much as we wish to escape such moods, thoughts, and behaviors, the automatic enaction of unconscious systems or maps is at the crux of this difficulty. The tendency to enact unconscious processes—an innate predisposition that embodies the entwined relationship between unconscious systems and movement—often hijacks reflectiveness, making sure old patterns prevail (see Chapters 3, 4, and 6). The plethora of therapeutic approaches—there are about 450 forms of therapy (in Lane et al., 2014)—may attest to the fact that there is truly no one way to induce enduring change. But it is also possible that what this number signifies is the inherent complexity underlying emotional and behavioral modification, resulting in numerous efforts thought to bring about personal transformation.

An enhanced understanding of the brain/mind's tendency to interpret internal and external experiences according to an unconscious entrenched map and automatically enact and repeat complex established patterns can guide therapists toward more efficacious approaches. Such therapeutic models may call for a more actively involved therapist who, as part of the process, addresses the underlying unconscious systems and their enacted manifestations both in therapy and outside of it. For example, more active approaches that directly engage old, maladaptive patterns have been suggested. In such therapeutic models, including EMDR (Parnell, 2006; Shapiro, 2002), emotional memory recontextualization (Ecker et al., 2012; Toomey and Ecker, 2009), and emotion-focused therapy (Fosha, 2000; Greenberg, 2011), what seems to facilitate internal as well as external shifts in old patterns is the concurrent focus on the here-and-now emotional immersion in old affective memories while reexamining and reflecting on them in real time.

It is important to clarify that these suggested approaches are not simply intended as a prescription for various techniques. Rather, what is compelling in these techniques is that they represent genuine efforts to maximize the integration of the unconscious and the conscious, the affective and the cognitive. Moreover, by emphasizing the importance of reexperiencing the affect embedded in memories while reflecting on their meaning, these clinicians use the brain/mind's inherent processes of imbuing affect with a wide range of distorted unconscious meanings.

The ever-present influence of the affective, physiological, interpersonal, cognitive, behavioral, and neuropsychological building blocks of the unconscious—which in the brain/mind are utterly entwined—inevitably stresses to us the need to focus on therapeutic efforts to identify, experience, and reflect on the enacted patterns. The fact that unconscious systems and the enactments they generate are the accessible expression of widely distributed encoded contents only strengthens the need to help patients understand and modify defensive patterns and distorted expectations that no longer work. Certainly the therapeutic process is able to provide one of the few opportunities for such unconscious–conscious states to unfold. As enacted layers and shades of unconscious–conscious maps or systems inevitably find expression within the therapeutic relationship, the therapist becomes an immersed witness who also models new interactions and new perspectives (see Chapters 8, 9, and 10).

THE PLACE OF NEUROSCIENCE IN THE ART OF HEALING

As we have seen throughout the various chapters of this book, there exists a very delicate and shifting balance between the power of repetition and the genuine wish to change. We have also come to realize that in many ways this balance is most often tipped in favor of the tried and reinforced (see Chapters 1, 2, 4, 5, and 6). It is one thing for a therapist to understand that the unconscious continually operates under the radar, and yet another to be able to surrender to its emotional force while also stepping out of it to understand and analyze what is going on. While attending to the patient's self-systems and their enacted manifestations is an important therapeutic goal, the therapist also needs to be able to check her own possible unconscious contributions to that assessment (see Chapter 10).

This very brief summary of the complexities involved in the therapeutic process highlights the need for an explanatory frame that can help therapists appreciate the difficulties but at the same time not be deterred by them. In fact, such complexities—the therapist's intuitive skills, her unconscious as well as conscious choices of interventions, her attentiveness to emotional vibes, and her willingness to use her feelings and discuss them—have all been considered to be the embodiment of the artistic and creative aspects of the therapeutic endeavor. Because conscious processes are not always involved in social interactions or the execution of goals but can be triggered by the environment without conscious choice or intention (Bargh, 2007, 2014; Damasio, 2010; Koziol and Budding, 2010; Ramachandran, 2011), the therapist's intuitive artistry is critical. But can therapy's fluid, at times nonverbal, and often indescribable qualities still benefit from neuropsychology? With the growing influence of neuroscience, the question of its place and integration within existing models of healing has been hotly debated before (e.g., Modell, 2008; Solms and Zellner, 2012a, 2012b).

More specifically, the paradigm shift in our understanding of how unconscious processes lie at the core of all conscious activity also calls for the examination of doubts regarding the potential contributions of neuropsychological research. Although a number of clinicians have emphasized the importance of neuroscience for a better understanding of psychological processes such as emotions, memory, transference, identification, projection, projection identification, and empathy, such efforts are still in the minority (see Divino and Moore, 2010). Furthermore, some clinicians have completely negated the need to integrate neuroscience into psychoanalytical theory and practice, claiming that such efforts are essentially reductionist and a simplification of the enormously complex human mind. Furthermore they claim that psychoanalysis does not need the purported "legitimacy" conferred on it by neuroscience (e.g., Blass and Carmeli, 2007; Hoffman, 2009; T. Ogden, 1994).

As an added equivocation, Modell (2008) as well as Westen and Gabbard (2002) suggest that simply integrating neurocognitive concepts such as procedural and implicit memory systems into psychoanalysis does not serve analysts well; it may even interfere with what is unique to the psychoanalytic model of the human mind. Another arguments doubts the relevance of neuroscience to an enterprise wholly based on the "unscientific" nature of patients' verbal narratives (Mechelli, 2010; Pulver, 2003). Similarly, T. Ogden (2004) and Renn (2012) maintain that there is no necessity for an overarching integrative model combining psychotherapy and neuroscience, but think that it is for each clinician to arrive at such an integration. Renn (2012), for example, employs knowledge regarding the gut's sensitivity to emotions to explain bodily transference–countertransference feelings.

In light of the unified important purpose of all forms of psychotherapy—helping patients with their internal and external struggles—such opposition mostly misses the mark. In effect, the inevitable integration of neuroscience into our clinical understanding of the human mind should not be about turf wars but about maximizing our role as clinicians and the potential benefits for patients. In actuality, the quickly accumulating body of neuropsychological knowledge has much more to offer to clinicians; neuroscience offers brain/mind–based understanding of emotional and interpersonal phenomena. Although we frequently experience the many manifestations of unconscious processes with patients and ourselves, we can greatly gain from a better and clearer understanding of them—an understanding that is not based on assumptions but on brain/mind characteristics.

In all aspects of therapeutic theory and practice, the capacity of neuroscience to further clinical thinking and practice goes far beyond the implementations of isolated findings and bodily focused techniques (Fotopoulou, 2012; P. Ogden, 2009; Solms and Zellner, 2012a, 2012b). Skeptics might still ask whether it is important for clinicians to know the mechanisms underlying projective identification, for example. The affirmative answer does not only stem from the truism that knowledge is power. Rather, such information is designed to achieve the most important goal—that of helping patients confront their unworkable patterns with the best chance for change. Understanding the mechanisms of projection identification and how they are tied to the brain/mind's inherent tendencies can motivate patients to examine the uniqueness of their emotional and interpersonal patterns. Experiencing and analyzing early memories, relationships, and how they have affected the brain/ mind's interaction with others can take center stage for the patient with less guilt and self-recrimination.

Clinicians of all approaches have to consider the implications that stem from one certain fact: it is no longer possible to consider unconscious brain processes as separate from our conscious mental life. We do not just encounter minds in abstraction; our embodied minds interact with other embodied minds, all communicating and enacting unconscious activity patterns. The proposed unconscious model and its implications for psychotherapeutic work is an example of efforts to gain a better understanding of the mind through knowing the body and the brain.

The fact that the various chapters of this book refer to unconscious patterns as widespread activity patterns does not in any way reduce their human qualities. Studies in the fields of cognitive and social neuroscience, memory, emotion, and other areas explore what is human about the way our brains/minds function. The particular focus on unconscious processes can further expand our understanding of human behavior and its endless complexity.

Invariably, any discussion about the stability and fixedness of unconscious patterns raises the question of free will. In many ways the emphasis on predetermined actions stemming from the pervasive influence of the unconscious may be the wrong issue to focus on. In light of the evolutionary powers of automated unconscious maps, the issues that need to be examined are ones that explore reflective awareness and not just free will per se. As has been repeatedly seen in studies as well as in the clinical material, the continuum of unconscious to conscious mental processes is parallel to that of unconscious to reflective processes. Reflective awareness leads to free will; otherwise, we are all prisoners of old entrenched patterns, beliefs, and narratives.

One of the most commonly voiced doubts regarding the incorporation of neuroscience into psychological theories questions the leap from neuroscience to mental activity—from the body to the mind. Because so much about the nature of brain activity and especially the way the brain becomes our mind is not known yet, such doubts are not entirely unjustified. With the growing and consistent findings linking particular regions and neural activities to mental experiences, it is becoming exceedingly difficult to dismiss the conclusions generated by neuropsychological research. At this point of neuropsychological research we can no longer describe some of the conclusions derived from it as unreasonable leaps. As we have seen, convincing models of how unconscious neurochemical processes become consciousness have already been elucidated by neuroscientists such as Bargh (2014), Churchland (2013), Damasio (2010), Hassin et al. (2010), Koziol (2014), Mesulam (2000), Ramachandran (2011), and Stewart (2010), among many others.

The success of neuroscience at influencing our therapeutic understanding can be found, for example, in the neuropsychological areas of memory, fear systems, and research studying the effect of experience on the developing brain. These areas of study have unlocked much of the mystery underlying our neuropsychological experiences. Memory, for example, is not a photograph-like representation but in essence the culmination of electrical and biochemical activities spread across different regions (Dudai, 2011). As the protein components responsible for the transference of short-term to long-term memory are becoming understood (see Fernyhough, 2013), it is also becoming apparent that on retrieval, emotional memories become reconsolidated, giving the therapist the opportunity to alter their traumatic meaning (Dudai, 2011; Ecker et al., 2012; Lane et al., 2014; LeDoux and Doyere, 2011).

Similarly, the extensive research on emotions in general (e.g., Panksepp and Biven, 2012; Schore, 2012) and on the fear system in particular (LeDoux, 2002, 2014; LeDoux and Schiller, 2009) has also immeasurably enhanced our understanding of how maladaptive emotions and defenses develop. The indisputable and enduring effects of early experiences on brain/mind structures and processes (e.g., Fonagy, 2008; Schore, 2012) provide another example of how neuroscience has already influenced our thinking and our work. Again, such knowledge can only help patients and therapists as they embark on the difficult task of personal growth.

When considering the neuropsychological underpinnings of the unconscious, the prospect of integrating them into our work is challenging. What is especially daunting are the potential implications of such integration. Understanding the stable, pervasive, and automatically enacted properties of unconscious systems clearly forces us to rethink long-accepted concepts such as resistance, anxiety narcissism, and transference–countertransference entanglements, as well as concepts of intersubjectivity (see Chapters 2, 4, 7, and 10). Revisiting such therapeutic concepts is important and necessary and can only open the way to new therapeutic modalities using the new information. For example, based on growing information regarding emotional memories and the power of reconsolidation, new efficacious therapeutic methods such as emotion-focused therapy (Greenberg, 2011), EMDR (Parnell, 2006; Shapiro, 2002) and the emphasis on reflective awareness in real time, are being pursued (Bateman and Fonagy, 2012; Ecker et al., 2012; Jurist, 2008; Lane et al., 2014; Siegel, 2007).

The exceedingly accurate identification of various regions and the processes connected with them, the growing picture of global brain activity, and most of all the wealth of information from brain-damaged patients clearly underlie a wide range of brain/mind functions (Churchland, 2013; LeDoux, 2014; Panksepp and Biven, 2012; Ramachandran, 2011; Schore, 2012; Solms and Zelner, 2012a, 2012b; to name a few). As the sheer amount of accumulated knowledge regarding the intertwined functions of our brains/minds keeps growing and becomes more available to us, it will offer exciting opportunities for the therapeutic communities. It is no longer the question of whether we as therapists should benefit from integrating the knowledge offered by neuroscience into our understanding; not using existing information that explains human suffering goes against the goal of offering patients the best possible chance.

Looking at the opportunities afforded by an expanded model of the unconscious, for example, does not diminish the irreplaceable need for therapeutic intuition, emotional involvement, and the ineffable benefits of experience. Rather, as we understand more of the brain/mind processes underlying the unconscious and other human experiences, we can offer patients the best of both worlds.

REFERENCES

Ainsworth, M. D. S. (1993). Attachment as related to mother-infant interaction. *Advanced Infant Research*, 8, 1–50.

Andersen, S. M., and Chen, S. (2002). The relational self: An interpersonal social-cognitive theory. *Psychological Review*, 109, 619–45.

Andersen, S. M., Reznik, I., and Glassman, N. S. (2007). The unconscious
relational self. In R. R. Hassin, J. S. Uleman, and J. A. Bargh (eds.), *The
new unconscious* (pp. 421–85). New York: Oxford University Press.

Anderson, M. C., and Green, C. (2001). Suppressing unwanted memories
by executive control. *Nature*, 410, 366–69.

Anderson, M. C. and Levy, B. J. (2009). Suppressing unwanted memories. *Current Directions in Psychological Science*, 18, 189–94.

Andreasen, N. C., and Pierson, R. (2008). The role of the cerebellum in
schizophrenia. *Biological Psychiatry*, 64, 81–88.

Ansermet, F., and Magistrett I, P. (2004). *Biology of freedom:Neural
plasticity, experience, and the unconscious* (S. Fairfield, trans.). New
York: Other Press.

Aron, L. (1996). *A meeting of minds: Mutuality in psychoanalysis*. Hillsdale, NJ: Analytic Press.

Arsalidou, M., Duerden, E. G., and Taylor, M. J. (2013). The center of
the brain: Topographical model of cognitive, affective and, somatosensory functions of the basal ganglia. *Human Brain Mapping*, 34,
3031–54.

Awh, E., and Vogel, E. K. (2008). The bouncer in the brain. *Nature Neuroscience*, 11, 5–6.

Baars, B. (1989). *A cognitive theory of consciousness*. Cambridge, UK:
Cambridge University Press.

Bach, S. (2006). *Getting from here to there: Analytic love, analytic process*. Hillsdale, NJ: Analytic Press.

Badenoch, B. (2008). *Being a brain-wise therapist: A practical guide to
interpersonal neurobiology*. New York: Norton.

Bargh, J. A. (2007). Bypassing the will: Toward demystifying the nonconscious control of social behavior. In R. R. Hassin, J. S. Uleman, and J. A. Bargh (eds.), *The new unconscious* (pp. 37–61). New York: Oxford University Press.

Bargh, J. A. (2014). Our unconscious mind. *Scientific American*, 310, 30–38.

Bargh, J. A., Gollwitzer, P. M., Lee-Chai, A. Y., Barndollar, K., and Troetschel, R. (2001). The automated will: Nonconscious activation and pursuit of behavioral goals. *Journal of Personality and Social Psychology*, 81, 1014–1027.

Bargh, J. A. , and Morsella, E. (2008). The unconscious mind. *Perspectives in Psychological Science*, 3, 73–79.

Bateman, A., W., and Fonagy, P. (2004). *Psychotherapy for borderline personality disorder: Mentalization-based treatment.* Oxford: Oxford University Press.

Bateman, A. W. , and Fonagy, P. (2012). *Handbook of mentalizing in mental health practice.* Arlington, VA: American Psychiatric Publishing.

Bauer, I. M., and Baumeister, R. F. (2013). Self-regulatory strength. In K. D. Vohs, and R. F. Baumeister (eds.), *Handbook of self-regulation: Research, theory, and applications* (pp. 64–82). New York: Guilford Press.

Baumeister, R. F., and Vohs, K. D. (2001). Narcissism as addiction to esteem. *Psychological Inquiry*, 12, 206–10.

Bayer, U. C., Gollwitzer, P. M., and Achtziger, A. (2010). Staying on track: Planned goal striving is protected from disruptive internal states. *Journal of Experimental Social Psychology*, 146, 505–14.

Beck, A. T. (1979). *Cognitive therapy and the emotional disorders.* New York: Plume.

Beck, A. T., Freeman, A., Davis, D. D., and Associates (1990). *Cognitive therapy of personality disorders.* New York: Guilford Press.

Beebe, B. (2010). Mother-infant research informs mother-infant treatment. *Clinical Social Work Journal*, 38, 17–36.

Beebe, B., and Lachmann, F. (2002). *Infant research and adult treatment: Co-constructing interactions.* Hillsdale, NJ: Analytic Press.

Benjamin, J. (1995). *Recognition and destruction: An outline of intersubjectivity.* New Haven, CT: Yale University Press.

Benjamin, J. (2004). Beyond doer and done to: An intersubjective view of thirdness. *Psychoanalytic Quarterly*, 73, 5–46.

Berenson, K. and Andersen, S. M. (2004). *Emotional numbing in transference: Triggering a parental representation linked with childhood physical abuse.* Unpublished manuscript, New York University.

Bergman, M., and Jucovy, M. (1982). *Generations of the Holocaust.* New York: Basic Books.

Bion, W. R. (1984). *Elements of psychoanalysis.* London: Routledge.

Bion, W. R. (1990). *Second thoughts.* London: Routledge.

Blair, C., and Ursache, A. (2013). A bidirectional model of executive functions and self-regulation. In K. D. Vohs and R. F. Baumeister (eds.), *Handbook of self-regulation: Research, theory and applications* (pp. 300–320). New York: Guilford Press.

Blass, R.. B., and Carmeli, Z. (2007). The case against neuropsychoanalysis: On fallacies underlying psychoanalysis' latest scientific trend and its negative impact on psychoanalytic discourse. *International Journal of Psychoanalysis*, 88, 19–40.

Bohleber, W. (2013). The concept of intersubjectivity in psychoanalysis: Taking critical stock. *International Journal of Psychoanalysis*, 94, 799–823.

Bollas, C. (1987). *The shadow of the object: Psychoanalysis of the unthought known.* New York: Columbia University Press.

Borghi, A. M., and Cimatti, F. (2010). Embodied cognition and beyond: Acting and sensing the body. *Neuropsychologia*, 48, 763–73.

Boulanger, G. (2007). *Wounded by reality: Understanding and treating adult onset trauma.* New York: Analytic Press.

Bounomano, D. (2011). *Brain bugs: How the brain's flows shape Our lives.* New York: Norton.

Bowlby, J. (1973). *Attachment and loss: Vol. II. Separation.* NewYork: Basic Books.

Bowlby, J. (1982). *Attachment and loss: Vol. I. Attachment* (2nd ed.). New York: Basic Books.

Braten, S. (2007). Altercentric infants and adults: On the origin and manifestation of participant perception of others' acts and utterances. In S. Braten (ed.), *On being moved: From mirror neurons to empathy* (pp. 111–36). Amsterdam: Benjamins.

Braten, S., and Trevarthen, C. (2007). Prologue: From infant intersubjectivity and participant movements to simulation and conversation in cultural common sense. In S. Braten (ed.), *On being moved: From mirror neurons to empathy* (pp. 21–34). Amsterdam: Benjamins.

Bromberg, P. M. (1998). *Standing in the spaces: Essays on clinical process, trauma and dissociation.* Hillsdale, NJ: Analytic Press.

Bromberg, P. M. (2006). *Awakening the dreamer: Clinical journeys.* Mahwah, NJ: Analytic Press.

Bromberg, P. M. (2011). *The shadow of the tsunami and the growth of the relational mind.* London: Routledge.

Brown, L. J. (2011). *Intersubjective processes and the unconscious: An integration of Freudian, Kleinian and Bionian perspectives.* New York: Routledge.

Bucci, W. (2007a). Dissociation from the perspective of multiple code theory, part I: Psychological roots and implications for psychoanalytic treatment. *Contemporary Psychoanalysis*, 43, 165–84.

Bucci, W. (2007b). Dissociation from the perspective of multiple code theory, part II: The spectrum of dissociative processes in the psycho-analytic relationship. *Conremporary Psychoanalysis*, 43, 305–26.

Bucci, W. (2011). The interplay of subsymbolic and symbolic processesin psychoanalytic treatment: It takes two to tango—but who knows the steps, who's the leader? The choreography of psychoanalytic inter-change. *Psychoanalytic Dialogues*, 21, 45–54.

Buchanan, T. W., Tranel, D., and Adolphs, R. (2009). The human amyg-dala in social function. In P. J. Whalen, and E. A. Phelps (eds.), *The human amygdala* (pp. 289–320). New York: Guilford Press.

Buckner, R. L., and Carroll, D. C. (2007). Self-projection and the brain. *Trends in Cognitive Science*, 11, 49–57.

Busch, F. N. (2008). *Mentalization: Theoretical consideration, research findings, and clinical implications*. New York: Analytic Press.

Calkins, S. D., and Leekers, E. S. (2013). Early attachment processes and the development of emotional self-regulation. In K. D. Vohs and R. F. Baumeister (eds.), *Handbook of self-regulation: Research, theory and applications* (pp. 355–74). New York: Guilford Press.

Canli, T. (2009). Individual differences in human amygdala function. In P. J. Whalen, and E. A. Phelps (eds.), *The human amygdala* (pp. 250–64). New York: Guilford Press.

Cappelli, L. (2006). Psychoanalysis and neuroscience: Anxiety in per-spective. In M. Mancia (ed.), *Psychoanalysis and neuroscience* (pp. 175–92). Milan: Springer.

Cappuccio, M., and Wheeler, M. (2012) Ground-level intelligence: Action-oriented representation and the dynamic of the background. In Z. Radman (ed.), *Knowing without thinking: Mind, action, cogni-tion, and the phenomenon of the background* (pp. 13–36). New York: Palgrave Macmillan.

Carr, L., Iacoboni, M., Dubeau, M., Mazziotta, J. C., and Lenzi, G. L. (2003). Neural mechanisms of empathy in humans: A relay from neu-ral systems for imitation to limbic area. *Lexique*, 100, 5497–502.

Carrol, R. (2003). "At the border between chaos and order": What psy-chotherapy and neuroscience have in common. In J. Corrican and H. Wilkinson (eds.), *Revolutionary connections: Psychotherapy and neuroscience* (pp. 191–211) London: Karnac Books.

Changeux, J.-P. 2011. The epigenetic variability of memory: Brain plas-ticity and artistic creation. In S. Nalbantian, P. M. Matthews, and J. A. McClelland (eds.), *The memory process: Neuroscientific and humanis-tic perspectives* (pp. 55–72). Cambridge, MA: MIT Press.

Chartrand, T. L., Maddux, W. W., and Lakin, J. L. (2007). Beyond the perception-behavior link: The ubiquitous utility of motivational mod-erators of nonconscious mimicry. In R. R. Hassin, J. S. Uleman, and J. A. Bargh (eds.), *The new unconscious*. New York: Oxford University Press.

Chefetz, R. A., and Bromberg, P. M. (2004). Talking with "me" and not "me": A dialogue. *Contemporary Psychoanalysis*, 40, 409–64.

Churchland, P. S. (2013). *Touching a nerve: The self as brain.* New York: Norton.

Chused, J. F. (1998). The evocative power of enactment. In S. J. Ellman and M. Moskowitz (eds.), *Enactment: Toward a new approach to the therapeutic relationship* (pp. 93–109). Northvale, NJ: Aronson.

Cloitre, M., Stovall-McClough, K. C., Nooner, K., et al. (2010). Treatment for PTSD related to child abuse: A randomized controlled trial. *American Journal of Psychiatry*, 167: 915–24.

Clore, G. L., and Ortony, A. (2000). Cognition in emotion: Always, sometimes, or never? In R. D. Lane and L. Nadel (eds.), *Cognitive neuroscience of emotion* (pp. 24–61). New York: Oxford University Press.

Coats, S. W. (1998). Having a mind of one's own and holding the other in mind: Discussion of "Mentalization and the changing aims of child psychoanalysis" by Peter Fonagy and Mary Target. *Psychoanalytic Dialogues*, 8, 115–48.

Cockburn, J., and Frank, M. J. (2011). Reinforcement learning, conflict monitoring, and cognitive control: An integrative model of cingulate-striatal interactions and the ERN. In R. B. Mars et al. (eds.), *Neural basis of motivational and cognitive control.* Cambridge, MA: MIT Press.

Cohen, L. R., Hien, D. A., and Batchelder, S. (2008). The impact of cumulative maternal trauma and diagnosis on parental behavior. *Child Maltreatment*, 13, 27–38.

Colombetti, G. (2010). Enaction, sense-making, and emotion. In J. Stewart, O. Gapenne, and E. A. DiPaolo (eds.), *Enaction: Toward a new paradigm for cognitive science* (pp. 145–64). Cambridge, MA: MIT Press.

Conboy, B. T. and Kuhl, P. K. (2007). Early speech perception: Developing a culturally specific way of listening through social interactions. In S. Braten (ed.), *On being moved: From mirror neurons to empathy* (pp. 175–200). Amsterdam: Benjamins.

Cortina, M., and Liotti, G. (2007). New approaches to understanding unconscious processes: Implicit and explicit memory systems. *International Forum of Psychoanalysis*, 16, 204–12.

Cozolino, L. (2002). *The neuroscience of psychotherapy: Building and rebuilding the human brain.* New York: Norton.

Cozolino, L. (2006). *The neuroscience of human relationships: Attachment and the developing brain.* New York: Norton.

Craig, A. D. (2002). How do you feel? Interoception: The sense of the physiological condition of the body. *Nature Review Neuroscience*, 3, 655–66.

Critchley, H. D. (2005). Neural mechanism of autonomic, affective, and integration. *Journal of Comparative Neurology*, 493, 154–66.

Curtis, R. (2009). *Desire, self, mind and the psychotherapies: Underlying psychological science and psychoanalysis.* Northvale, NJ: Aronson.

Dalenberg, C. J., and Paulson, K. The case for the study of "normal" dissociative processes. In P. F. Dell and J. A. O'Neil (eds.), *Dissociation and the dissociative disorders: DSM-V and beyond* (pp. 145–54). New York: Routledge.

Damasio, A. R. (1999). *The feeling of what happens: Body and emotion in the making of consciousness.* New York: Harcourt Brace.

Damasio, A. R. (2000). A second chance for emotion. In R. D. Lane and L. Nadel (eds.), *Cognitive neuroscience of emotion* (pp. 12–23). New York: Oxford University Press.

Damasio, A. R. (2010). *Self comes to mind: Constructing the conscious brain.* New York: Vintage Press.

Daniel, I. F. (2009). The developmental roots of narrative expression in therapy: Contributions from attachment theory and research. *Psychotherapy: Theory, Research, Practice, Training,* 46, 301–16.

Danieli, Y. E. (1998). *International handbook of multigenerational legacies of trauma.* New York: Plenum Press.

Dapretto, M., Davis, M. S., Pfeifer, J. H., Scott, A. A., Sigman, M., Bookheimer, S. Y., and Iacoboni, M. (2006). Understanding emotions in others: Mirror neuron dysfunction in children with autism spectrum disorders. *Nature Neuroscience,* 9, 28–31.

Davidson, R. J. (2000). The functional neuroanatomy of affective style. In R. D. Lane and L. Nadel (eds.), *Cognitive neuroscience of emotion* (pp. 371–89). New York: Oxford University Press.

Davidson, R. J., and Begley, S. (2012). *The emotional life of your brain.* New York: Hudson Street Press.

Davies, L. M., and Frawley, M. G. (1994). *Treating the adult survivor of childhood sexual abuse.* New York: Basic Books.

Dawson, G., Frey, K., Panagiotides, H., Yamada, E., Hessl, D., and Osterling, J. 1999). Infants of depressed mothers exhibit atypical frontal electrical brain activity during interactions with mothers and with a familiar nondepressed adult. *Child Development,* 70, 1058–66.

Decety, J., and Chaminade, T. (2003). When the self represents the other: A new cognitive neuroscience view on psychological identification. *Consciousness and Cognition,* 12, 577–96.

Dekel, S., Mandle, C., and Solomon, Z. (2013). Is the Holocaust implicated in posttraumaic growth in second-generation Holocaust survivors? A proposed study. *Journal of Traumatic Stress,* 26, 530–33.

Dehaene, S., Changeux, J., Naccache, L., Sackur, J., and Sergent, C. (2006). Conscious, preconscious, and subliminal processing: A testable taxonomy. *Trends in Cognitive Science, 10,* 204–211.

Dehaene, S., and Changeux, J.-P. (2011). Experimental and theoretical approaches to conscious processing. *Neuron,* 70, 200–227.

Dell, P. F. (2009). The phenomenon of pathological dissociation. In P. F. Dell and J. A. O'Neil (eds.), *Dissociation and the dissociative disorders: DSM-V and beyond* (pp. 225–39). New York: Routledge.

Derryberry, D., and Tucker, D. M. (1994). Motivating the focus of attention. In p. M. Niedenthal and S. Kitayama (eds.), *The heart's eye: Emotional influences in perception and attention* (pp. 167–96). San Diego, CA: Academic Press.

Deveney, C. M., and Pizzagalli, D. A. (2008). The cognitive consequences of emotion regulation: An ERP investigation. *Psychophysiology*, 45, 435–44.

Diamond, D. (2004). Attachment disorganization: The reunion of attachment theory and psychoanalysis. *Psychoanalytic Psychology*, 21, 276–99.

Dekel, R., and Goldblatt, H. (2008). Is there intergenerational transmission of trauma? The case of combat veterans' children. *American Journal of Orthopsyciatry*, 78, 281–89.

Dijksterhuis, A., Aaarts, H., and Smith, P. K. (2007). The power of the subliminal: On subliminal persuasion and other potential applications. In R. R. Hassin, J. S. Uleman, and J. A. Bargh (eds.), *The new unconscious* (pp. 107–37). New York: Oxford University Press.

Di Paolo, E., Rohde, M., and D. Jaegher. (2010). Horizons for the enactive mind: Values, social interaction, and play. In J. Stewart, O. Gapenne, and E. A. DiPaolo (eds.), *Enaction: Toward a new paradigm for cognitive science* (pp. 33–87). Cambridge, MA: MIT Press.

Divino, C. L., and Moore, M. S. (2010). Integrating neurobiological findings into psychodynamic psychotherapy training and practice. *Psychoanalytic Dialogues*, 20, 337–55.

Doll, B., and Frank, M. J. (2009). The basal ganglia in reward and decision making: computational models and empirical studies. In J. C. Dreher and L. Tremblay (eds.), *Handbook of reward and decision making* (pp. 399–425). Oxford: Academic Press.

Domash, L. (2010). Unconscious freedom and the insight of the analyst: Exploring neuropsychological processes underlying "aha" moments. *Journal of the American Academy of Psychoanalysis*, 38, 315–39.

Donald, M. (2001). *A mind so rare*. New York: Norton.

Doyon, J., and Ungerleider, L. G. (2002). Functional anatomy of motor skill learning. In L. R. Squire and D. L. Schacter (eds.), The neuropsychology of memory (3rd ed., pp. 225–38). New York: Guilford Press.

Dozier, M., and Kobak, R. R. (1992). Psychophysiology in attachment interviews: Converging evidence for deactivating strategies. *Child Development*, 63, 1473–80.

Dudai, Y. (2011). The engram revisited: On the elusive permanence of memory. In S. Nalbantian, P. M. Matthews, and J. L. McClelland (eds.), *The memory process: Neuroscientific and humanistic perspectives* (pp. 29–40). Cambridge, MA: MIT Press.

Duhigg, C. (2012). *The power of habit: Why we do what we do in life and business*. New York: Random House.

Ecker, B., Ticic, R., and Hulley, L. (2012). *Unlocking the emotional brain: Eliminating symptoms at their roots using memory reconsolidation*. New York: Routledge.

Ecker, B., and Toomey, B. (2008). Depotentiation of symptom-producing implicit memory in coherence therapy. *Journal of Constructivist Psychology*, 21, 87–150.

Edelman, G. M., and Tononi, G. (2002). *A universe of consciousness*. New York: Basic Books.

Eitam, B., Hassin, R. R., and Schul, Y. (2008). Nonconscious goal pursuit in novel environments: The case of implicit learning. *Psychological Science*, 19, 261–67.

Engel, A. K. (2010). Directive minds: How dynamics shape cognition. In J. Stewart, O. Gapenne, and E. A. DiPaolo (eds.), *Enaction: Toward a new paradigm for cognitive science* (pp. 219–44). Cambridge, MA: MIT Press.

Epstein, H. (1979). *Children of the Holocaust: Conversations with sons and daughters of survivors*. New York: Putnam.

Fadiga, L. and Craighero, L. (2007). Cues on the origin of language: From electrophysiological data on mirror neurons and motor representation. In S. Braten (ed.), *On being moved: From mirror neurons to empathy* (pp. 101–10). Amsterdam: Benjamins.

Fairbairn, W. R. D. (1952). *Psychoanalytic studies of the personality*. London: Tavistock.

Falkenstrom F., Solbakken, O. A., Moller, C., Lech, B., Sandell, R., and Holmqvist, R. (2014). Reflective functioning, affect consciousness, and mindfulness: Are these different functions? *Psychoanalytic Psychology*, 31, 26–40.

Felsen, I. (1998). Transgenerational transmission of effects of the Holocaust: The North American research perspective. In Y. Danieli (ed.), *International handbook of multigenerational legacies of trauma*. New York: Plenum Press.

Ferenczi, S. (1932). *The clinical diaries of Sandor Ferenczi* (J. Dupont, ed.). Cambridge, MA: Harvard University Press (1988).

Fernyhough, C. (2013). *Pieces of light: How the new science of memory illuminates the stories we tell about our pasts*. New York: Harper Collins.

Fonagy, P. (2001). *Attachment theory and psychoanalysis*. New York: Other Press.

Fonagy, P. (2008). The mentalization-focused approach to social development. In F. N. Busch (ed.), *Mentalization: Theoretical considerations, research findings, and clinical implications* (pp. 3–56). New York: Analytic Press.

Fonagy, P., Gergely, G., Jurist, E. L., and Target, M. (2002). *Affect regulation, mentalization and the development of the self.* New York: Other Press.

Fonagy, P. and Target, M. (1998). An interpersonal view of the infant. In A. Hurry (ed.), Psychoanalysis and developmental therapy (pp. 3–31). London: Karnac Books.

Fosha, D. (2000). *The transforming power of affect: A model for accelerated change.* New York: Basic Books.

Fosshage, J. L. (2005). The explicit and implicit domains in psychoanalytic change. *Psychoanalytic Inquiry*, 25, 516–39.

Fosshage, J. L. (2011). How do we "know" what we "know" and change what we "know?" *Psychoanalytic Dialogues*, 21, 55–74.

Fotopoulou, A. (2012). Toward a psychodynamic neuroscience. In A. Fotopoulo, D. Plaff, and M. A. Conway (eds.), *From the couch to the lab: Trends in psychodynamic neuroscience* (pp. 25–49). New York: Oxford University Press.

Frank, M. J., and Claus, E. D. (2006). Anatomy of a decision: Striato-orbitofrontal interactions in reinforcement learning, decision making, and reversal. *Psychological Review*, 113, 300–326.

Freud, A. (1968). *The ego and the mechanisms of defenses.* London: Karnac Books.

Freud, S. (1900). *The interpretation of dreams.* J. Strachey (ed. and trans.). New York: Basic Books.

Freud, S. (1905). Three essays on the theory of sexuality. In J. Strachey (ed. and trans.), *The standard edition of the complete psychological works of Sigmund Freud* (vol. 7, pp. 125–245). London: Hogarth Press.

Freud, S. (1914). Remembering, repeating and working-through. In J. Strachey (ed. and trans.), *The standard edition of the complete psychological works of Sigmund Freud* (vol. 12). London: Hogarth Press.

Freud, S. (1915). Instincts and their vicissitudes. In J. Strachey (ed. and trans.), *The standard edition of the complete psychological works of Sigmund Freud* (vol. 14, pp. 111–40). London: Hogarth Press.

Freud, S. (1926). Inhibitions, symptoms and anxiety. In J. Strachey (ed. and trans.), *The standard edition of the complete psychological; works of Sigmund Freud* (vol. 20, pp. 77–174). London: Hogarth Press.

Freud, S., and Breuer, J. (1895). *Studies in hysteria* (N. Luckhurst, trans.). London: Penguin Books, 2004.

Frijda, N. H. (1986). *The emotions.* Cambridge, UK: Cambridge University Press.

Gainotti, G. (2006). Unconscious emotional memories and the right hemisphere. In M. Mancia (ed.), *Psychoanalysis and neuroscience* (pp. 151–73). Milan: Springer.

Gallagher, S. (2012). Social cognition, the Chinese room, and the robot relies. In Z. Radman (ed.), *Knowing without thinking: Mind, action, cognition, and the phenomenon of the background* (pp. 83–97). New York: Palgrave Macmillan.

Gallese, V. (2006). Intentional attunement: Embodied simulation and its role in social cognition. In M. Mancia (ed.), *Psychoanalysis and neuroscience* (pp. 269–301). Milan: Springer.

Gallese, V. (2008). Mirror neurons and the social nature of language: The neural exploitation hypothesis. *Social Neuroscience*, 3, 317–33.

Gallese, V. (2009). Mirror neurons, embodied simulation, and the neural basis of social identification. *Psychoanalytic Dialogues*, 19, 519–36.

Gallese, V., Eagle, M. N. and Migone, P. (2007). Intentional attunement: Mirror neurons and the neural underpinnings of interpersonal relations. *Journal of the American Psychoanalytic Association*, 55, 131–76.

Gallese, V., and Lakoff, G. (2005). The brain's concepts: The role of the sensory-motor system in conceptual knowledge. *Cognitive Neuropsychology*, 21, 1–25.

Gardner, H. (2011). *The unschooled mind: How children think and how schools should teach*. New York: Basic Books.

Gazzaniga, M. S. (2008). *Human: The science behind what makes us unique*. New York: Harper Collins.

Gazzaniga, M. S., Ivry, R. B., and Mangum, G. R. (2014). *Cognitive neuroscience: The biology of the mind* (4th ed.). New York: Norton.

Gendlin, E. T. (2012). Implicit precision. In Z. Radman (ed.), *Knowing without thinking: Mind, action, cognition, and the phenomenon of the background* (pp. 141–66). New York: Palgrave Macmillan.

Gergely, G., and Unoka, Z. (2008a). The development of the unreflective self. In F. N. Busch (ed.), *Mentalization: Theoretical consideration, research findings, and clinical implications* (pp. 57–102). Hillsdale, NJ: Analytic Press.

Gergely, G., and Unoka, Z. (2008b). Attachment and mentalization in humans. In E. L. Jurist, A. Slade, and S. Bergner (eds.), *Mind to mind: infant research, neuroscience, and psychoanalysis* (pp. 50–87). New York: Other Press.

Ghaznavi, S., Witte, J. M., Levy, R. A., and Roffman, J. L. (2011). Bridging technology and psychotherapy: Toward investigating psychological and neural correlates of psychodynamic psychotherapy. In R. A. Levy, J. C. Ablon, and H. K. Kachele (eds.), *Psychodynamic psychotherapy research: Evidence-based practice and practice-based evidence* (pp. 301–13). New York: Springer.

Gilhooley, D. (2008). Psychoanalysis and the cognitive unconscious: Implications for clinical techniques. *Modern Psychoanalysis*, 33, 91–127.

Ginot, E. (1997). The analyst use of self, self-disclosure, and enhanced integration. *Psychoanalytic Psychology*, 14, 365–81.

Ginot, E. (2001). The holding environment and intersubjectivity. *Psychoanalytic Quarterly*, 70, 417–46.

Ginot, E. (2007). Intersubjectivity and neuroscience: Understanding enactments and their therapeutic significance within emerging paradigms. *Psychoanalytic Psychology*, 24, 317–32.

Ginot, E. (2009). The empathic power of enactments: The link between neuropsychological processes and an expanded definition of empathy. *Psychoanalytic Psychology*, 26, 290–309.

Ginot, E. (2012). Self-narratives and dysregulated affective states: The neuropsychological links between self-narratives, attachment, affect, and cognition. Psychoanalytic Psychology, 29, 59–80.

Glaser, L., and Kihlstrom, J. F. (2007). Compensatory automaticity: Unconscious volition is not an oxymoron. In R. R. Hassin, L. S. Uleman, and J. A. Bargh (eds.), *The new unconscious* (pp. 171–96). New York: Oxford University Press.

Goldman, A. I. (2006). *Simulating minds: The philosophy, psychology, and neuroscience of mind reading.* New York: Oxford University Press.

Goleman, D. (2003). *Destructive emotions: A scientific dialogue with the Dalai Lama.* New York: Random House.

Gollwitzer, P. M., Bayer, U. C., and McCulloch, K. C. (2007). The control of the unwanted. In R. R. Hassin, J. S. Uleman, and J. L. A. Bargh (eds.), *The new unconscious* (pp. 485–516). New York: Springer.

Gollwitzer, P. M., and Oettinger, G. (2013). Planning promotes goal striving. In K. D. Vohs and R. F. Baumeister (eds.), *Handbook of self-regulation: Research, theory, and applications* (pp. 162–85). New York: Guilford Press.

Grawe, K. (2007). *Neuropsychotherapy: How the neurosciences inform effective psychotherapy.* Mahwah, NJ: Analytic Press.

Greenberg, L. S. (2011). *Emotion-focused therapy.* Washington, DC: American Psychological Association.

Greicious, M. D., Superkar, K., Menon, V., and Dougherty, R. F. (2008). Resting-state functional connectivity reflects structural connectivity in the default-mode network. *Cerebral Cortex*, 19, 72–78.

Grosskopf, B. (1999). *Forgive your parents, heal yourself.* New York: Free Press.

Gusnard, D. A., Akbrudak, R., Shulman, G. L., and Raichle, M. E. (2001). Medial prefrontal cortex and self-referential mental activity: Relation to default mode of brain function. *Proceedings of the National Academy of Science, USA*, 98, 4259–64.

Hamann, S. (2009). The human amygdala and memory. In Whalen, P. J. and Phelps, E. A. (eds.), *The human amygdala* (pp. 177–203). New York: Guilford Press.

Hanson, R., and Mendius, R. (2009). *Buddah's brain: The practical neuroscience of happiness, love and wisdom.* Oakland, CA: New Harbinger.

Happaney, K., Zelazo, P. D. and Stuss, D. T. (2004). Development and orbitofrontal function: Current themes and future directions. *Brain and Cognition*, 55, 1–10.

Hari, R. (2007). Human mirroring systems: On assessing mind by reading brain and body during social interaction. In S. Braten (ed.), *On being moved: From mirror neurons to empathy* (pp. 89–99). Philadelphia: Benjamins.

Harkness, L. (1991). The effect of combat-related PTSD on children. *National Center for PTSD Clinical Quarterly*, 2, 1–3.

Hassin, R. R. (2007). Nonconscious control and implicit working memory. In R. R. Hassin, J. A. Uleman, and J. A. Bargh (eds.), *The new unconscious* (pp. 196–225). New York: Oxford University Press.

Hassin, R. R., J. A. Uleman, and J. A. Bargh (eds.), 2007. *The new unconscious*. New York: Oxford University Press

Hasson, U., Ghazanfar, A. A., Galantucci, B., Garrod, S., and Keysers, C. (2011). Brain-to-brain coupling: A mechanism for creating and sharing a social world. *Trends in Cognitive Science*, 16, 114–21.

Heekeren, H. R., Wartenburger, I., Marschner, A., Mell, T., Villringer, A., and Reischies, F. M. (2007). Role of ventral striatum in reward-based decision making. *Neuroreport*, 18, 951–55.

Hermans, H. J. M. (2004). The dialogical self: Between exchange and power. In H. J. M. Hermans and G. Dimaggio (eds.), *The dialogical self in psychotherapy* (pp. 13–28). New York: Brunner-Routlege.

Hesse, E., and Main, M. (2000). Disorganized infant, child, and adult attachment: Collapse in behavioral and attentional strategies. *Journal of the American Psychoanalytic Association*, 48, 1097–148.

Hesse E., and Main, M. (2006). Frightened, threatening, and dissociative parental behavior: Description, discussion, and interpretation. *Development and Psychopathology*, 18, 309–43.

Hobson, J. A. (1988). *The dreaming brain: How the brain creates both the sense and the nonsense of dreams*. Washington, DC: American Psychiatric Association.

Hobson, J. A., and Stickgold, R. (1995). The conscious state paradigm: A neurocognitive approach to waking, sleeping and dreaming. In M. S. Gazzaniga et al. (eds.), *The cognitive neuroscience* (pp. 1373–89). Cambridge, MA: MIT Press.

Hoffman, I. Z. (2009). Doublethinking our way to "scientific" legitimacy: The desiccation of human experience. *Journal of the American Psychoanalytic Association*, 57, 1043–69.

Horga, G., and Maia, T. V. (2012). Conscious and unconscious processes in cognitive control: A theoretical perspective and a novel empirical approach. *Frontiers in Human Neuroscience*, 6, 199.

Huber, D., Henrich, G., Gastner, J., and Glug, G. (2011). Must all have prizes? The Munich psychotherapy study. In R. A. Levy, J. C. Ablon, and H. K. Kachele (eds.), *Psychodynamic psychotherapy research: Evidence-based practice and practice-based evidence* (pp. 51–70). New York: Springer.

Huether, G. (1998). Stress and the adaptive self-organization of neural connectivity during early childhood. *International Journal of Developmental Neuroscience*, 16, 297–306.

Hutto, D. D. (2012). Exposing the background: Deep and local. In Z. Radman (ed.), *Knowing without thinking: Mind, action, cognition, and the phenomenon of the background* (pp. 37–56). New York: Palgrave Macmillan.

Iacoboni, M. (2006). Existential empathy: The intimacy of self and other. In T. F. D. Farrow and W. R. Woodruff (eds.), *Empathy and mental illness* (pp. 310–21). Cambridge UK: Cambridge University Press.

Iacoboni, M. (2007). Face to face: The neural basis of social mirroring and empathy. *Psychiatric Annals*, 37, 1–6.

Iacoboni, M. (2008). *Mirroring people: The new science of how we connect with others*. New York: Farrar, Straus and Giroux.

Iacoboni, M., Molnar-Szakacs, I., Gallese, V., Buccino, G., Mazziotta, J. C., and Rizzolatti, G. (2005). Grasping the intentions of others with one's own mirror neurons. *PLoS Biology*, 3, 1–7.

Ito, M. (2005). Bases and implications of learning in the cerebellum: Adaptive control and internal model mechanism. *Progress in Brain Research*, 148, 95–109.

Ito, M. (2008). Control of mental activities by internal models of the cerebellum. *Nature Review Neuroscience*, 9, 304–13.

Ito, M. (2011). *The cerebellum: Brain for an implicit self.* Upper Saddle River, NJ: FT Press.

Jacobs, T. J. (1991). *The use of self: Countertransference and communication in the analytic situation*. Madison, CT: International universities Press.

Jacobs, T. J. (2005). Discussion of forms of intersubjectivity in infant research and adult treatment. In B. Beebe, S. Knoblauch, J. Rustin, and D. Sorter (eds.), *Forms of intersubjectivity in infant research and adult treatment: A system view* (pp. 165–89). New York: Other Press.

Janet, P. (1913) Psycho-analysis. *Report to the Section of Psychiatry*, XV11th International Congress of Medicine, London, 1913. London: Oxford University Press/Hodder and Stoughton.

Jung, C. G. (1957). The undiscovered self. (R. F. C. Hull trans.). New York: Signet Books.

Jurist, E. L. (2008). Minds and yours: New directions for mentalization theory. In E. Jurist, A. Slade, and S. Bergner (eds.), *Mind to mind: Infant research, neuroscience and psychoanalysis* (pp. 88–114). New York: Other Press.

Kagan, J. (1998). *Three seductive ideas*. Cambridge, MA: Harvard University Press.

Kahneman, D. (2011). *Thinking, fast and slow.* New York: Farrar, Straus and Giroux.

Kaitz, M., Levy, M., Ebstein, R., Faraone, S., and Maukuta, D. (2009). The intergenerational effects of trauma from terror: A real possibility. *Infant Mental Health Journal*, 30, 158–79.

Kandel, E. R. (1999). Biology and the future of psychoanalysis: A new intellectual framework for psychiatry revisited. *American Journal of Psychiatry*, 156, 505–24.

Kandel, E.. R. (2001). The molecular biology of memory storage: A dialogue between genes and synapses. *Bioscience Reports*, 21, 565–611.

Kanter, J. W., Rusch, L. C., Landes, S. J., Holman, G. I., Whiteside, U., and Sedivy, S. (2009). The use and nature of present-focused interventions in cognitive and behavioral therapies for depression. *Psychotherapy: Theory, Research, Practice, Training*, 46, 220–32.

Kaplan, L. (1995). *No voice is ever wholly lost.* New York: Simon and Schuster.

Kaplan, P. S., Bachorowski, J., and Zarllengo-Strouse, P. (1999). Child-directed speech produced by mothers with symptoms of depression fails to promote associative learning in 4-months-old infants. *Child Development*, 70, 560–70.

Kerenberg, O. F. (1975). *Borderline conditions and pathological narcissism.* New York: Aronson.

Kerenberg, O. F. (1997). Pathological narcissism and narssisitic personality disorder: Theoretical background and diagnostic classification. In E. F. Ronningstam (ed.), *Disorders of narcissism: Diagnostic, clinical, and empirical implications* (pp. 29–51). Washington, DC: American Psychiatric Press.

Kerenberg, O. F. (2007). The almost untreatable narcissistic patient. *Journal of the American Psychoanalytic Association*, 55, 503–40.

Kestenberg, J. (1982). Survivor-parents and their children. In M. Bergman and M. Jucovy (eds.), *Generations of the Holocaust.* New York: Basic Books.

Kimora, Y., Yohino, A., Takahashi, Y., and Nomura, S. (2004). Interhemispheric difference in emotional response witout awareness. *Physiology and Behavior*, 82, 727–31.

Knekt, P., Laaksonen, M. A., Harkanen, T., Maljanen, E. H., Virtala, E., and Lindfors, O. (2011). The Helsinki psychotherapy study: Effectiveness, sufficiency, and suitability of short-term and long-term psychotherapy. In R. A. Levy, J. C. Ablon, and H. K. Kachele (eds.), *Psychodynamic psychotherapy research: Evidence-based practice and practice-based evidence* (pp. 71–94). New York: Springer.

Knox, J. (2009). Mirror neurons and embodied simulation in the development of archetypes and self-agency. *Journal of Annals of Psychology*, 54, 307–23.

Kogan, I. (1995). *The cry of muted children: A psychoanalytic perspective of the second generation of the Holocaust.* London: Free Association Press.

Kohut, H. (1971). *The analysis of the self: A systematic approach to the psychoanalytic treatment of narcissistic personality disorders.* New York: International Universities Press.

Koziol, L. F. (2014). *The myth of executive functioning: Missing elements in conceptualization, evaluation and assessment.* New York: Springer.

Koziol, L. F. and Budding, D. E. (2010). *Subcortical structures and cognition: Implications for neuropsychological assessment.* New York: Springer.

Kuhl, P. K. (1998). Language, culture and intersubjectivity: The creation of shared perception. In S. Braten (ed.), *Intersubjective communication and emotion in early ontogeny* (pp. 297–315). Cambridge, UK: Cambridge University Press.

Kwong, M. J., Bartholomew, K., Henderson, A. J. Z., and Trinke, S. J. (2003). The intergenerational transmission of relationship violence. *Journal of Family Psychology*, 17, 288–301.

Lambert, J. E., Holzer, J., and Hasbun, A. (2014). Association between parents' PTSD severity and children's psychological distress: A meta-analysis. *Journal of Traumatic Stress*, 27, 9–17.

Lane, R. D. (2000). Neural correlates of conscious emotional experience. In R. D. Lane and L. Nadel (eds.), *Cognitive neuroscience of emotion* (pp. 345–70). New York: Oxford University Press.

Lane, R. D. (2008). Neural substrates of implicit and explicit emotional processes: A unifying framework for psychosomatic medicine. *Psychosomatic Medicine*, 70, 214–31.

Lane, R. D., Ryan, L., Nadel, L., and Greenberg, L. (2014). Memory reconsolidation, emotional arousal and the process of change in psychotherapy: New insights from brain science. *Behavioral Brain Sciences*, 15, 1–80.

Langer, L. L. (1991). *Holocaust testimonies: The ruins of memory.* New Haven, CT: Yale University Press.

Laub, B., and Auerhahn, N. (1993). Knowing and not knowing massive trauma: Forms of traumatic memory. *International Journal of Psychoanalysis*, 74, 287–99.

LeDoux, L. (2000). Cognitive-emotional interaction: Listen to the brain. In R. D. Lane and L. Nadel (eds.), *Cognitive neuroscience of emotion* (pp. 129–55). New York: Oxford University Press.

LeDoux. J. (2002). *Synaptic self: How our brains become who we are.* New York: Viking.

LeDoux, J. (2014). Coming to term with fear. *Proceedings of the National Academy of Science USA*, 111, 2871–78.

LeDoux, J. E., and Doyere, V. (2011). Emotional memory processing: Synaptic connectivity. In S. Nalbantian, P. M. Matthews, and J. A. McClelland (eds.), *The memory process: Neuroscientific and humanistic perspectives* (pp. 153–71) Cambridge, MA: MIT Press.

LeDoux, J., and Schiller, D. (2009). The human amygdala: Insight from other animals. In P. J. Whalen, and E. A. Phelps (eds.), *The human amygdala* (pp. 43–60). New York: Guilford Press.

Lenzi, D., Trentini, C., Pantano, E., Macaluso, E., Iacoboni, M., Lenzi, G. L., and Ammaniti, M. (2008). Neural basis of maternal communication and emotional expression processing during Infant preverbal stage. *Cerebral Cortex*, 19, 1124–33.

Lessem, P. A. (2005). *Self-psychology: An introduction*. Northvale, NJ: Jason Aronson.

Lev-Wiesel, R. (2007). Intergenerational transmission of trauma across three generations. *Qualitative Social Work*, 6, 75–94.

Levy, K. N., Meehan, K. B., and Yeoman, F. E. (2011). Transference-focused psychotherapy and other psychotherapies for borderline personality disorder. In R. A. Levy, J. C. Ablon, and H. K. Kachele (eds.), *Psychodynamic psychotherapy research: Evidence-based practice and practice-based evidence* (pp. 139-169). New York: Springer.

Lewis, M. D. (2005). Bridging emotion theory and neurobiology through dynamic system modeling. *Behavioral and Brain Science*, 28, 169–94.

Lewis, M. D. and Todd, R. (2004). Toward a neuropsychological model of internal dialogue: Implications for theory and clinical practice. In H. J. M. Hermans and G. Dimaggio (eds.), *The Dialogical self in psychotherapy* (pp. 43–59). New York: Brunner-Routledge.

Lewis, M. D., and Todd, M. (2007). The development of self regulation: Toward the integration of cognition and emotion. *Cognitive Development*, 22, 405–30.

Libet, B. (1985). Unconscious cerebral initiative and the role of conscious will in voluntary actions. *Behavioral and Brain Sciences*, 8, 529–66.

Libet, M., Alberts, W. W., Wright, E. W., and Feinstein, B. (1967). Responses of human somatosensory cortex to stimuli below threshold for conscious sensation. *Science*, 158, 1597–600.

Lieberman, A. F., and Knorr, K. (2007). The impact of trauma: A developmental framework for infancy and early childhood. *Psychiatric Annals*, 37, 416–22.

Lieberman, M. D. (2003). Reflective and reflexive judgment processes: A social cognitive neuroscience approach. In J. P. Forgas, K. Williams, and W. von Hippel (eds.), *Social judgment: Implicit and explicit processes* (pp. 44–67). Philadelphia: Psychology Press.

Linden, D. J. (2008). *The accidental mind: How evolution has given us love, memory, dreams, and God*. Cambridge MA: Harvard University Press.

Loftus, E. E. (1996). *Eyewitness testimony.* Cambridge, MA: Harvard University Press.

Luu, P., Tucker, D. M., and Stripling, R. (2007). Neural mechanisms for learning actions in context. *Brain Research,* 1179, 89–105.

Luyten, P., Blatt, S. J., and Mayes, L. C. (2011). Process and outcome in psychoanalytic psychotherapy research: The need for a (relatively) new paradigm. In R. A. Levy, J. C. Ablon, and H. K. Kachele (eds.), *Psychodynamic psychotherapy research: Evidence-based practice and practice-based evidence* (pp. 345–60). New York: Springer.

Lyons-Ruth, K. (1999). The two-person unconscious Intersunjective dialogue, enactive relational representation, and the emergence of new forms of relational organization. *Psychoanalytic Inquiry,* 19, 576–617.

Lyons-Ruth, K. (2003). Dissociation and the parent-infant dialogue: A longitudinal perspective from attachment research. *Journal of the American Psychoanalytic Association,* 51, 883–911.

Lyons-Ruth, K., and Block, D. (1996). The disturbed caregiving system: Relations among childhood trauma, maternal caregiving, and infant affect and attachment. *Infant Mental Health Journal,* 17, 257–75.

Lyons-Ruth, K., Yellin, C., Melnick, S., and Atwood, G. (2005). Expanding the concept of unresolved mental states: Hostile/helpless states of mind on the Adult Attachment Interview are associated with disrupted mother-infant communication and infant disorganization. *Development and Psychopathology,* 17, 1–23.

Macfie, J., McElwain, N. L., Houts, R.M,, and Cox, M. J. (2005). Intergenerational transmission of role reversal between parent and child: Dyadic and family systems internal working models. *Attachment and Human Development,* 7, 51–65.

Main, M. (1991). Metacognitive knowledge, metacognitive monitoring, and singular (coherent) vs. multiple (incoherent) models of attachment: Findings and directions for future research. In C. M. Parkes, J. Stevenson-Hinde, and P. Marris (eds.), *Attachment across the life cycle* (pp. 127–59). London: Routledge.

Main, M., and Hesse, E. (1990). Parents' unresolved traumatic experiences are related to infant disorganized attachment status: Is frightening and/or frightened parental behavior the linking mechanism? In M. Greenberg, D. Cicchtti, and E. M. Cummings (eds.), *Attachment in the preschool years: Theory, research and intervention* (pp. 161–82). Chicago: University of Chicago Press.

Main, M., Kaplan, N., and Cassidy, J. (1985). Security in infancy, childhood, and aduldthood: A move to the level of representation. *Monographs of the Society for the Research in Child Development,* 50, 66–104.

Mancia, M. (2006). Implicit memory and unrepressed unconscious: How they surface in the transference and in the dream. In M. Mancia (ed.), *Psychoanalysis and neuroscience* (pp. 97–123). Milan: Springer.

Mancia, M. (2007). *Feeling the words: Neuropsychoanalysis understanding of memory and the unconscious.* London: Routledge.

Mann, D. (2009). Enactments and trauma: the therapist's vulnerability as the theater for the patient's trauma. In D. Mann and V. Cunningham (eds.), *The past in the present: Therapy, enactments, and the return of trauma* (pp. 8–30). New York: Routledge.

Maroda, K. J. (1991). *The power of countertransference: Innovations in analytic techniques.* New York: Wiley.

McClelland, J. L. 2011. Memory as a constructive process: The parallel distributed processing approach. In S. Nalbantian, P. M. Matthews, and J. L. McClelland (eds.), *The memory process: Neuroscientific and humanistic perspectives* (pp. 129–52). Cambridge, MA: MIT Press.

McClosky, L. A., and Bailey, J. A. (2000). The intergenerational transmission of risk for child abuse. *Journal of Interpersonal Violence,* 15, 1019–35.

McGilchrist, I. (2009). *The master and his emissary. The divided brain and the making of the Western world.* New Haven, CT: Yale University Press.

McRae, K., Ochsner, K. N., and Gross, J. J. (2013). The reason in passion: A social cognitive neuroscience approach to emotion regulation. In K. D. Vohs and R. F. Baumeister (eds.), *Handbook of self-regulation: Research, theory, and applications* (pp. 186–203). New York: Guilford Press.

Mechelli, A. (2010). Psychoanalysis on the couch: Can neuroscience provide the answer? *Medical Hypotheses,* 75, 594–99..

Mesulam, M. M. (2000). *Principles of behavioral and cognitive neurology.* New York: Oxford University Presss.

Miller, B. L., Seeley, W. W., Mychack, P., Rosen, H. J., Mena, I., and Boone, K. (2001). Neuroanatomy and the self. Evidence from patients with frontotemporal dementia. *Neurology,* 57, 817–21.

Miller, M. L. (2008). The emotional engaged analyst I: Theories of affect and their influence on therapeutic action. *Psychoanalytic Psychology,* 25, 3–25.

Milner, B., Squire, L. R., and Kandel, E. R. (1998). Cognitive neuroscience and the study of memory. *Neuron,* 20, 445–68.

Mischel, W., and Ayduk, O. (2013). Willpower in a cognitive affective processing system: The dynamics of delay of gratification. In K. D. Vohs and R. F. Baumeister (eds.), *Handbook of self-regulation: Research, theory and applications* (pp. 83–105). New York: Guilford Press.

Mitchell, J. P. (2009). Inferences about mental states. *Philosophical Transactions of the Royal Society of London, Series B,* 364, 1309–16.

Mitchell, J. P., Banaji, M. R., and Macrae, C. N. (2005). General and specific contributions of the medial prefrontal cortex to knowledge about mental states. *Neuroimage*, 28, 757–62.

Mitchell, S. A. (1988). *Relational concepts in psychoanalysis.* New York: Basic Books.

Mitchell, S. A. (1993). *Hope and dread in psychoanalysis.* New York: Basic Books.

Mitchell, S. A. (1997*). Influence and autonomy in psychoanalysis.* Hillsdale, NJ: Analytic Press.

Mitchell, S. A. (2000). *Relationality: From attachment to intersubjectivity.* Hillsdale, NJ: Analytic Press.

Modell, A. H. (2008). Implicit or unconscious? Commentary on paper by the Boston Change Process Study Group. *Psychoanalytic Dialogues*, 18, 162–67.

Monk, C., S., Grillon, C., Baas, J. M., McClure, E. B., Nelson, E. E., Zarahn, E., et al. (2003a). A neuroimaging method for the study of threat in adolescents. *Developmental Psychobiology*, 43, 359–66.

Monk, C. S., McClure, E. B., Nelson, E. E., Zarahn, E., Bilder, R. M., Leibenluft, E., et al. (2003b). Adolescent immaturity in attention-related brain engagement to emotional facial expressions. *NeuroImage*, 20, 420–28.

Morris, J. S., Ohman, A., and Dolan, R. J. (1998). Conscious and unconscious emotional learning in the human amygdala. *Nature*, 393, 467–70.

Morris, J. S., Ohman, a., and Dolan, R. J. (1999). A subcortical pathway to the right amygdala mediating "unseen" fear. *Proceedings of the National Academy of Science USA*, 96, 1680–85.

Moses, R. (ed.) (1993). *Persistent shadows of the Holocaust: The meaning of those not directly affected.* Madison, CT: International Universities Press.

Moustafa, A., Sherman, S., and Frank, M. (2008). A dopaminergic basis for working memory, learning and attentional set shifting in parkinsonism. *Neueropsychologia*, 46, 3141–56.

Murray, S. L., Holmes, J. C., and Collins, N. L. (2006). Optimizing assurance: The risk regulating system in relationships. *Psychological Bulletin*, 132, 641–66.

Nadel, L. and Hardt, O. (2011). Update on memory systems and processes. *Neuropsychopharmacologia*, 36, 251–73.

Nader, K., and Einarsson, E. O. (2010). Memory reconsolidation: An update. *Annals of the New York Academy of Sciences*, 1191, 27–41.

Nalbantian, S. (2011). Autobiographical memory in modernist literature and neuroscience. In S. Nalbantian, P. M. Matthews, and J. A. McClelland (eds.), *The memory process: Neuroscientific and humanistic perspectives* (pp. 255–75) Cambridge, MA: MIT Press.

Niv, Y. (2007). Cost, benefit, tonic, phasic: What do response rates tell us about dopamine and motivation? *Annals of the New York Academy of Sciences*, 1104, 357–76.

Northoff, G., and Panksepp, J. (2008). The trans-species concepts of self and the subcortical-cortical midline system. *Trends in Cognitive Science*, 12, 259–64.

Ochsner, K. N., and Barrett, L. F. (2001). A multiprocess perspective on the neuroscience of emotion. In T. Mayne and G. Bonnano (eds.), *Emotion: Current issues and future directions.* New York: Guilford Press.

Ochsner, K., N., and Gross, J. J. (2005). The cognitive control of emotion. *Trends in Cognitive Science*, 9, 408–9.

Ogden, P. (2009). Emotion, mindfulness, and movement: Expanding the regulatory boundaries of the window of affect tolerance. In D. Fosha (ed.), *The healing power of emotion: Affective neuroscience, development and clinical practice* (pp. 204-232). New York: W. W. Norton.

Ogden, P., Minton, K., and Pain, C. (2006). *Trauma and the body.* New York: Norton.

Ogden, T. H. (1986). *The matrix of the mind: Object relations and the psychoanalytic dialogue.* Northvale, NJ: Aronson.

Ogden, T. H. (1994). *Subjects of analysis.* London: Karnac Books.

Ogden, T. H. (2004). The analytic third: Implications for psychoanalytic theory and technique. *Psychoanalytic Quarterly*, 73, 167–95.

Ohman, A. (2009). Human fear conditioning and the amygdala. In P. J. Whalen and E. A. Phelps (eds.), *The human amygdala* (pp. 118–54). New York: Guilford Press.

Ohman, A., Flykt, A., and Lundqvist, D. (2007). Unconscious emotion: Evolutionary perspectives, psychophysiological data and neuropsychological mechanisms. In S. Braten (ed.), *On being moved: From mirror neurons to empathy* (pp. 296–327). Amsterdam: Benjamins.

Olds, D. D. (2006). Identification: Biological and perspectives. *Journal of the American Psychoanalytic Association*, 54, 17–46.

Olds, D. D. (2012). Identification: The concept and the phenomenon. In A. Fotopoulo, D. Plaff, and M. A. Conway (eds.), *From the couch to the lab: Trends in psychodynamic neuroscience* (pp. 439–54). New York: Oxford University Press.

Pally, R. (2000). *The mind-brain relationship.* London: Karnac Books.

Pally, R. (2007). The predicting brain: Unconscious repetition, conscious reflection and therapeutic change. *International Journal of Psychoanalysis*, 88, 861–81.

Panksepp, (2003). At the interface of the affective, behavioral, and cognitive neuroscience: Decoding the emotional feelings of the brain. *Brain and Cognition*, 52, 4–14.

Panksepp, J. (2008). The power of word may reside in the power of affect. *Integrative Psychological and Behavioral Science*, 42, 47–55.

Panksepp, J. and Biven, L. (2012). *Archeology of mind: The neuroevolutionary origins of human emotion*. New York: Norton.

Papastathopoulos, S., and Kugiumutzakis, G. (2007). The Intersubjectivity of imagination: The special case of imaginary companions. In S. Braten (ed.), *On being moved: From mirror neurons to empathy* (pp. 219–36). Amsterdam: Benjamins.

Papie, E. K., and Aarts, H. (2013). Nonconscious self-regulation, or the automatic pilot of human behavior. In K. D. Vohs and R. F. Baumeister (eds.), *Handbook of self-regulation: Research, theory, and applications* (pp. 125–42). New York: Guilford Press.

Parnell, L. (2006). *A therapist's guide to EMDR: Tools and techniques for successful treatment*. New York: Norton.

Paul, E. J., and Ashby, F. G. (2013). A neurocomputational theory of how explicit learning bootstraps early procedural learning. *Frontiers in Computational Neuroscience*, 7, 1–17.

Perani, D., Cappa, S. F., Schnur, T., Tetamanti, M., Collins, S., Rosa, M. M., and Pazio, F. (1999). The neural correlates of verb and noun processing: A PET study. *Brain*, 122, 2337–44.

Petrosini, L. (2007). "Do what I do" and "do how I do": Different components of imitative learning are mediated by different neural structures. *Neuroscientist*, 13, 335–48.

Pezzulo, G., and Dindo, H. (2011). What should I do next? Using shared representations to solve interaction problems. *Experimental Brain Research*, 211, 613–30.

Pfeifer, J. H., and Dapretto, M. (2011). "Mirror, mirror, in my mind" : Empathy, interpersonal competence, and the mirror neuron system. In J. Decety and W. Ickes (eds.), *The social neuroscience of empathy* (pp. 183–98). Cambridge, MA: MIT Press.

Pfeifer, J. M., Iacoboni, M., Mazziotta, J. C., and Dapretto, M. (2008). Mirroring others' emotions relates to empathy and interpersonal competence in children. *Neuroimage*, 39, 2076–85.

Phelps, E. A. (2007). The interaction of emotion and cognition: The relation between the human amygdala and cognitive awareness. In R. R. Hassin, J. S. Uleman, and J. A. Bargh (eds.), *The new unconscious* (pp. 37–60). New York: Oxford University Press.

Phelps, E. A. (2009). The human amygdala and the control of fear. In P. J. Whalen and E. A. Phelps (eds.), *The human amygdala* (pp. 204–19). New York: Guilford Press.

Phelps, E. A., and LeDoux, J. E. (2005). Contributions of the amygdala to emotion processing: From animal models to human behavior. *Neueron*, 48, 175–87.

Pinker, S. (2007). *The stuff of thought: Language as a window into human nature*. New York: Penguin Books.

Pizer, B. (2003). When the crunch is a (k)not: A crimp in relational dialogue. *Psychoanalytic Dialogues*, 13, 171–92.

Pizzagalli, D. A., Evins, A. E., Schetter, E. C., Frank, M.J., Pajtas, P. E., Santesso, D. L., et al. (2008). Single dose of dopamine agonist impairs reinforcement learning in humans: Behavioral evidence from a laboratory-based measure of reward responsiveness. *Psychopharmacology*, 196, 221–32.

Pollack, A., Watt, D.F., and Panksepp, J. (2000). The feelings of what happens: Body and emotion in the making off consciousness (a review). *Neuro-Psychoanalysis*, 2, 81–88.

Prince, R. M. (1999). *The legacy of the Holocaust: Psychohistorical themes in the second generation*. Research in Clinical Psychology, book 12. New York: Other Press.

Prinz, W. (2003). How do we know about our actions? In S. Maasen, W. Prinz., and G. Roth (eds.), *Brains, minds and sociality* (pp. 21–33). New York: Oxford University Press.

Pulver, S. E. (2003). On the astonishing clinical irrelevance of neuroscience. *Journal of the American Psychoanalytic Association*, 51, 755–72.

Rabung, S., and Leichsenring, F. (2011). Effectiveness of long-term psychodynamic psychotherapy: First meta-analysis evidence and its discussion. In R. A. Levy, J. C. Ablon, and H. K. Kachele (eds.), *Psychodynamic psychotherapy research: Evidence-based practice and practice-based evidence* (pp. 27–50). New York: Springer.

Racker, H. (1991). *Transference and countertransference*. London: Karnac Books.

Radman, Z. (2012). The background: A tool of potentiality. In Z. Radman (ed.), *Knowing without thinking: Mind, action, cognition, and the phenomenon of the background* (pp. 224–42). New York: Palgrave Macmillan.

Raichle, M. E., MacLeod, A. M., Snyder, A. Z., Powers, W. J., Gusnard, D. A., et al. (2001). A default mode of brain function. *Proceedings of the National Academy of Science USA*, 98, 676–82.

Rall, J., and Harris, P. (2000). In Cinderella's slippers. Story comprehension from the protagonist point of view. *Developmental Psychology*, 36, 202–8.

Ramachandran, V. S. (2011). *The tell-tale brain: Unlocking the mystery of human nature*. New York: Norton.

Ranote, S., Elliott, R., Abel, K. M., Mitchell, R., Deakin, F. W., and Appleby, L. (2004). The neural basis of maternal responsiveness to infants: An fMRI study. *Brain Imaging*, 15, 1825–29.

Rashkin, E. (1999). The haunted child: Social catastrophe, phantom transmissions, and the aftermath of collective trauma. *Analytic Review*, 86, 433–54.

Renik, O. (1998). The role of countertransference enactment in a success-ful clinical psychoanalysis. In S. J. Ellman and M. Moskowitz (eds.), *Enactment: Toward a new approach to the therapeutic relationship.* Northvale, NJ: Aronson.

Renn, P. (2012). *The silent past and the invisible present: Memory, trauma, and representation in psychotherapy.* New York: Routledge.

Renner, L. M. (2009). Intimate partner violence victimization and par-enting stress: Assessing the mediating role of depressive symptoms. *Violence Against Women,* 15, 1380–401

Reznik, I., and Andersen, S. M. (2007). Agitation and despair in relation to parents: Activating emotional suffering in the transference. *Euro-pean Journal of Personality,* 21, 281–301.

Rizzolatti, G., Fogassi, L., and Gallese, V. (2002). Motor and cognitive functions of the ventral premotor cortex. *Current Opinion in Neuro-biology,* 12, 149–54.

Rizzolatti, G., and Luppino, G. (2001). The cortical motor system. *Neu-ron,* 31, 889–901.

Rogers, C. (1951). Client-centered therapy: Its current practice, implica-tions and theory. London: Constable and Robinson.

Roisman, G. I., Tsai, J. L., and Chiang, K.-H. S. (2004). The emotional integration of childhood experience: Physiological, facial expressive, and self-reported emotional response during the Adult Attachment Interview. *Developmental Psychology,* 40, 776–89.

Rolls, E. T. 2011. Functions of human emotional memory: The brain and emotion. In S. Nalbantian, P. M. Mathews, and J. L. McClelland (eds.), *The memory process: Neuroscientific and humanistic perspec-tives* (pp. 173–92). Cambridge, MA: MIT Press.

Rothman, A. J., Baldwin, A. S., Hertel, A. W., and Fuglestad, P. T. (2013). Self-regulation and behavior change: Disentangling behavioral initia-tion and behavioral maintenance. In K. D. Vohs and R. F. Baumeister (eds.), *Handbook of self-regulation: Research, theory and applications* (pp. 106–24). New York: Guilford Press.

Rowland-Klein, S. S., and Dunlop, R. (1998). The transmission of trauma across generations: Identification with parental trauma in children of Holocaust survivors. *Australian and New Zealand Journal of Psychi-atry,* 32, 358–69.

Rubin, D. C. (2006). The basic systems model of episodic memory. *Per-spectives on Psychological Science,* 1, 277–311.

Rubino, V., Blasi, G., Latorre, V., Fazio, L., d'Errico, I., Mazzola, V., et al. (2007). Activity in medial prefrontal cortex during cognitive evalua-tion of threatening stimuli as a function of personality style. *Brain Research Bulletin,* 74, 250–57.

Ruscio, A. M., Weathers, F. W., King, L. A., and King, D. W. (2002). Male war-zone veterans' perceived relationships with their children: The importance of emotional numbing. *Journal of Traumatic Stress*, 15, 351–57.

Rustin, J. and Sekael, C. (2004). From the neuroscience of memory to psychoanalytic interaction: Clinical implications. *Psychoanalytic Psychology*, 21, 70–82.

Safran, J. D., and Shaker, A. G. (2011). Commentary: Research on short- and long-term psychoanalytic treatment—the current state of the art. In R. A. Levy, J. C. Ablon, and H. K. Kachele (eds.), *Psychodynamic psychotherapy research: Evidence-based practice and practice-based evidence* (pp. 3–8). New York: Springer.

Sato, W., and Aoki, S. (2006). Right hemisphere dominance in processing unconscious emotion. *Brain and Cognition*, 62, 261–66.

Schmahmann, A. N., Weilburg, J. B., and Sherman J. C. (2007). The neuropsychiatry of the cerebellum—insights from the clinic. *Cerebellum*, 6, 254–67.

Schmahmann, J. D. (2004). Disorders of the cerebellum: Ataxia, dysmetria of thought, and the cerebellar cognitive affective syndrome. *Journal of Neuropsychiatry Clinical Neueroscience*, 16, 254–67.

Schore, A. N. (1994). *Affect regulation and the origin of the self: The neurobiology of emotional development*. Hillsdale, NJ: Erlbaum.

Schore, A. N. (2003). *Affect regulation and the repair of the self*. New York: Norton.

Schore, A. N. (2005). A neuropsychoanalytic viewpoint: Commentary on paper by Steven H. Knoblauch. *Psychoanalytic Dialogues*, 15, 829–54.

Schore, A. N. (2009). Right brain affect regulation: An essential mechanism of development, trauma, dissociation and psychotherapy. In D. Fosha, D. Siegel, and M. F. Solomon (eds.), *The healing power of emotion: Affective neuroscience, development and clinical practice* (pp. 112–44). New York: Norton.

Schore, A. N. (2011). The right brain implicit self lies at the core of psychoanalysis. *Psychoanalytic Dialogues*, 21, 75–100.

Schore A. N. (2012). *The science of the art of psychotherapy*. New York: Norton.

Schore, J. R., and Schore, A. N. (2008). Modern attachment theory: The central role of affect regulation in development and treatment. *Clinical Social Work Journal*, 36, 9–20.

Seligman, S. (2009). Anchoring intersubjective models in recent mental psychology, cognitive neuroscience and parenting studies: Introduction to papers by Trevatahn, Gallese, Ammantini and Trentini. *Psychoanalytic Dialogues*, 19, 503–6.

Seng, J. S., Speerlich, M., Low, L. K., Ronis, D. L., Muzik, M., and Liberzon, I. 2013. Childhood abuse history, posttraumatic stress disorder, postpartum mental health, and bonding: A prospective cohort study. *Journal of Midwifery Women Health*, 58, 57–68.

Sergerie, K., and Armony, J. L. (2006). Interactions between emotion and cognition: A neurobiological perspective. In M. Mancia (ed.), *Psychoanalysis and neuroscience* (pp. 125–50). Milan: Springer.

Shapira, M. (2013) The war inside: Psychoanalysis, total was and the making of the democratic self in postwar Britain (Studies in the social and cultural history of modern warfare. Cambridge: Cambridge University Press.

Shapiro, F. (2002). EMDR treatment: Overview and integration. In F. Shapiro (ed.), *EMDR as an integrative psychotherapy approach: Experts of diverse orientations explore the paradigm prism* (pp. 27–55). Washington, DC: American Psychological Association.

Sharpley, C. F. (2010). A review of neurobiological effects of psychotherapy for depression. *Psychotherapy Theory, Research, Practice, Training,* 47, 603–15.

Shedler, J. (2011). The efficacy of psychodynamic psychotherapy. In R. A. Levy, J. C. Ablon, and H. K. Kachele (eds.), *Psychodynamic psychotherapy research: Evidence-based practice and practice-based evidence* (pp. 9–26). New York: Springer.

Sheets-Johnstone, M. (2010). Thinking in movement: Further analysis and validations. In J. Stewart, O. Gapenne, and E. A. DiPaolo (eds.), *Enaction: Toward a new paradigm for cognitive science* (pp. 165–82). Cambridge, MA: MIT Press.

Sheets-Johnstone, M. (2012). Steps entailed in foregrounding the background: Taking the challenge of languaging seriously. In Z. Radman (ed.), *Knowing without thinking: Mind, action, cognition, and the phenomenon of the background* (pp. 187-205). New York: Palgrave Macmillan.

Sheya, A., and Smith, L. B. (2010). Development through sensorimotor coordination. In J. Stewart, O. Gapenne, and E. A. DiPaolo (eds.), *Enaction: Toward a new paradigm for cognitive science* (pp. 123–44). Cambridge, MA; MIT Press.

Siegel, D. L. (1999). *The developing mind: Toward a neurobiology of interpersonal experience.* New York: Guilford Press.

Siegel, D. J. (2007). *The mindful brain: Reflection and attunement in the cultivation of well-being.* New York: Norton.

Siegel, J. P. (2013). Breaking the links in intergenerational violence: An emotional regulation perspective. *Family Process,* 52, 163–78.

Sillitoe, R. V., and Vogel, M. W. (2008). Desire, disease, and the origins of the dopaminergic system. *Schizophrenia Bulletin, 34,* 212-219.

Slade, A. (2005). Parental reflective functioning: An introduction. *Attachment and Human Development,* 7, 269–81.

Slavin-Mulford, J., and Hilsenroth, M. J. (2011). Evidence-based psychodynamic treatment for anxiety disorders: A review. In R. A. Levy, J. C. Ablon, and H. K Kachele (eds.), *Psychodynamic psychotherapy research: Evidence-based practice and practice-based evidence* (pp. 117–38). New York: Springer.

Slochower, J. (1996). *Holding and psychoanalysis: A relational perspective.* Hillsdale NJ: Analytic Press.

Solms, M., and Zellner, M. R. (2012a). Freudian drive theory today. In A. Fotopoulo, D. Plaff and M. A. Conway (eds.), *From the couch to the lab: Trends in psychodynamic neuroscience* (pp. 49–63). New York: Oxford University Press.

Solms, M., and Zellner, M. R. (2012b). The Feudian unconscious today. In A. Fotopoulo, D. Plaff and M. A. Conway (eds.), *From the couch to the lab: Trends in psychodynamic neuroscience* (pp. 209–18). New York: Oxford University Press.

Solomon, Z., Debby-Aharon, S., Zerach, G., and Horesh, D. (2011). Marital adjustment, parental functioning, and emotional sharing in war veterans. *Journal of Family Issues, 32,* 127–47.

Steele, K., van der Hart, O., and Nijenhis, E. R. S. (2009). The theory of trauma-related structural dissociation of the personality. In P. F. Dell and J. A. O'Neil (eds.), *Dissociation and the dissociative disorders: DSM-V and beyond* (pp. 239–59). New York: Routledge.

Stern, D. B. (2010). *Partners in thought: Working with unformulated experience, dissociation, and enactment.* New York: Routledge.

Stern, D. N. (1985). *The interpersonal world of the infant: A view from psychoanalysis and developmental psychology.* New York: Basic Books.

Stern, D. N. (2004). *The present moment in psychotherapy and everyday life.* New York: Norton.

Stern, D. N., Sander, L. W., Nahum, J. P., Harrison, A. M., Lyons-Ruth, K., Morgan, S. C., Bruschweiler-Stern, N., and Tronick, E. Z. (1998). Non-interpretive mechanisms in psychoanalytic therapy: The "something more" than interpretation. *International Journal of Psychoanalysis, 79,* 903–21.

Stewart, L. (2010). Foundational issues in enaction as a paradigm for cognitive science: From the origin of life to consciousness and writing. In J. Stewart, O. Gapenne, and E. A. DiPaolo (eds.), *Enaction: Toward a new paradigm for cognitive science* (pp. 1–32). Cambridge, MA: MIT Press.

Stickgold, R., Hobson J. A., Fosse, R., and Fosse, M. (2001). Sleep, learning, and dreams: Off-line memory reprocessing. *Science, 294,* 1052–57.

Stolorow, R. D., Brandschaft, B., and Atwood, G. E. (1995). *Psychoanalytic treatment: An intersubjective approach.* Hillsdale NJ: Analytic Press.

Stoycheva, V., Weinberger, J., and Singer, E. (2014). The place of the normative unconscious in psychoanalytic theory and practice. *Psychoanalytic Psychology, 31,* 100–118.

Stueber, K. R. (2006). *Rediscovering empathy: Agency, folk psychology and the human sciences.* Cambridge, MA: MIT Press.

Sullivan, H. S. (1948). The meaning of anxiety in psychiatry and in life. *American Journal of Psychiatry*, 11, 1–13.

Surgulladze, S. A., Brammer, M. J., Young, A. W., Andrew, C., Travis, M. J., Williams, S. C., et al. (2003). A preferential increase in the extrastriate response to signals of danger. *NeurImage*, 19, 1317–28.

Suvic-Wrana, C., Beutel, M., Garfield. D. A., and Lane R. D. (2011). Levels of emotional awareness: A model for conceptualizing and measuring emotion-centered structural change. *International Journal of Psychoanalysis*, 92, 289–310.

Tamir, D. I., and Mitchell, J. P. (2011). The default network distinguishes construals of proximal versus distal events. *Journal of Cognitive Neuroscience*, 23, 2945–55.

Tammir, D. I., and Mitchell, J. P. (2013). Anchoring and adjusting during social inferences. *Journal of Experimental Psychology: General*, 142, 151–62.

Taylor, D. (2011). Psychoanalytic and psychodynamic therapies for depression: The evidence base. In R. A. Levy, J. C. Ablon, and H. K. Kachele (eds.), *Psychodynamic psychotherapy research: Evidence-based practice and practice-based evidence* (pp. 95–116). New York: Springer.

Testa, M., Hoffman, J. H., and Livingston, L A. (2009). Intergenerational transmission of sexual victimization vulnerability as mediated via parenting. *Child Abuse and Neglect*, 35, 363–71.

Thach, W. T. (1996). On the specific role of the cerebellum in motor learning and cognition: Clues from PET activation and lesion studies in man. *Behavioral and Brain Sciences*, 19, 411–31.

Thach, W. T. (2014). Does the cerebellum initiate movement? *Cerebellum*, 13, 139–50.

Toates, F. (2006). A model of the hierarchy of behavior, cognition, and consciousness. *Consciousness and Cognition*, 15, 75–118.

Tomasello, M. (2001). *The cultural origins of human cognition.* Cambridge, MA: Harvard University Press.

Toomey, B., and Ecker, E. (2009). Competing visions for the Implications of neuroscience for psychotherapy. *Journal of Constructivist Psychology*, 22, 95–140.

Tottenham, N., Hare, T. A., and Casey B. L. (2009). Developmental perspectives on human amygdala function. In P. J. Whalen and E. A. Phelps (eds.), *The human amygdala* (pp. 107–17). New York: Guilford Press.

Trevarthen, C. (1979). Communication and cooperation in early infancy. In M. Bullowa (ed.), *Before speech* (pp. 321–47). New York: Cambridge University Press.

Tronick, E. (2007). *The neurobehavioral and social-emotional development of infants and children.* New York: Norton.

Tzourio-Mazoyer, N., De Schonen, S., Crivello, F., Reutter, B., Aujard, Y., and Mazoyer, B. (2002). Neural correlates of women face processing by 2-months-old infants. *NeuroImage*, 15, 454–61.

Tsuchiya, N., and Adolphs, R. (2007). Emotion and consciousness. *Trends in Cognitive Science*, 11, 158–67.

Uddin, L. Q., Kaplan, J. T., Molnar-Szakacs, I., Zaidel, E., and Iacoboni, M. (2004). Self-face recognition activates a frontoparietal "mirror" network in the right hemisphere: An event related FMRI study. *Neuroimage*, 25, 926–35.

van der Kolk, B. A. (1987). *Psychological trauma*. Washington, DC: American Psychiatric Press.

van der Kolk, B. A. (1996). The body keeps the score: Approaches to the psychobiology of posttraumatic stress disorder. In B. A. Van der Kolk, A. C. McFarlane, and L. Weisaeeth (eds.), *Traumatic stress: The effects of overwhelming experience on mind, body and society* (pp. 214–41). New York: Guilford Press.

Van Ee, E., Kleber, R. J., and Mooren, T. T.M. (2012). War trauma lingers on: Associations between maternal posttraumatic stress disorder, parent-child interaction, and child development. *Infant Mental Health Journal*, 33, 459–68.

Van Ettinger-Veenstra, H. M., Ragneheld, M., Hallgren, M., Karlsson, T., Landiblom, A. M., Lundberg, P., and Engstrom, M. (2010). Right-hemisphere brain ctivation correlates to language performance. *Neuroimage*, 49, 3481–88.

Varela, F., Thompson, E., and Rosch, E. (1991). *The embodied mind.* Cambridge, MA: MIT Press.

Viamontes, G. J. 2011 The neurobiological foundations of psychotherapy. In R. A. Levy, J. C. Ablon, and H. K. Kachele (eds.), *Psychodynamic psychotherapy research: Evidence-based practice and practice-based evidence* (pp. 313–36). New York: Springer.

Vuilleumier, P. (2009). The role of the amygdala in perception and attention. In P. J. Whalen and E. A. Phelps (eds.), *The human amygdala* (pp. 204–19). New York: Guilford Press.

Wager, T. D., Davidson, m. L., Hughes, B. Ll., Lindquist, M. A., and Ochsner, K. N. (2008). Prefrontal-subcortical pathways mediating successful emotion regulation. *Neuron*, 59, 1037–50.

Waelde, L. C., Silvern, L., Carlson, E., Fairbank, J. A., and Kletter, H. (2009). In P. F. Dell and J. A. O'Neil (eds.), *Dissociation and the dissociative disorders: DSM-V and beyond* (pp. 447–69). New York: Routledge.

Wallin, W. J. (2007). *Attachment in psychotherapy*. New York: Guilford Press.

Wardi, D. (1992). *Memorial candles: Children of the Holocaust* (N. Goldblum, trans.). London: Routledge.

Watson, J. C., and Greeberg, L. S. (2011). Empathic resonance: A neuroscience perspective. In J. Decety and W. Ickes (eds.), *The social neuroscience of empathy* (pp. 125–38). Cambridge, MA: MIT Press.

Watt, D. F. (2003). Psychotherapy in an age of neuroscience: Bridges to affective neuroscience. In J. Corrigall and H. Wilkinson (eds.), *Revolutionary connections: Psychotherapy and neuroscience* (pp. 79–115). London: Karnac Books.

Watt, D. F. (2005). Social bonds and the nature of empathy. *Journal of Consciousness*, 12, 8–10.

Watt, D. F. (2012). Theoretical challenges in the conceptualization of motivation in neuroscience: Implications for the bridging of neuroscience and psychoanalysis. In A. Fotopoulo, D. Plaff and M. A. Conway (eds.), *From the couch to the lab: Trends in psychodynamic neuroscience* (pp. 85–108). New York: Oxford University Press.

Wegner, D. M. (2002). *The illusion of conscious will*. Cambridge, MA: MIT Press.

Wegner, D. M. (2007). Who is the controller of controlled processes? In R. R. Hassin, J. S. Uleman, and J. A. Bargh (eds.), *The new unconscious* (pp. 19–37). New York: Oxford University Press.

Westen, D. (1999). The scientific status of unconscious processes: Is Freud really dead? *Journal of the American Psychoanalytic Association*, 47, 1061–106.

Westen, D. (2006). Implications of research in cognitive neuroscience for psychodynamic psychotherapy. *Focus*, 4, 215–22.

Westen, D., and Gabbard, O. G. (2002). Cognitive neuroscience: Conflict and compromise. *Journal of the American Psychoanalytic Association*, 50, 53–98.

Winnicott, D. W. (1969). The use of an object. *International Journal of Psychoanalysis*, 50, 711–16.

Whalen, P. J., Davis, C., Oler, J. A., Kim, H., Kim, J., and Neta, M. (2009). Human amygdala responses to facial expressions of emotion. In J. P. Whalen and E. A. Phelps (eds.), *The human amygdala* (pp. 265–89). New York: Guilford Press.

Wilkinson, M. (2010). *Changing minds in therapy: Emotion, attachment, trauma and neuroscience*. New York: Norton.

Wilson, T. (2002). *Strangers to ourselves: Discovering the adaptive unconscious*. Cambridge, MA: Harvard University Press.

Wilson, T. (2003). Knowing when to ask: Introspection and the adaptive unconscious. *Journal of Conscious Studies*, 10, 9–10.

Wilson, T. D. (2011). *Redirect: The surprising new science of psychological change*. New York: Penguin Press.

Winnicott, D. W. (1967). Mirror-role of the mother and family in child development. In P. Lomas (ed.), *The predicament of the family: A psycho-analytic symposium* (pp. 26–33). London: Hogarth Press.

Winnicott, D. W. (1969). The use of an object. *International Journal of Psychoanalyis*, 50, 711–16.

Wittling, W., and Roschmann, R. (1993). Emotion-related hemisphere asymerty: Subjective emotional esponses to laterally presented films. *Cortex*, 24, 431–48.

Yehuda, R., Bell, A., Bierer, L. M., and Schmeidler, J. (2008). Maternal, not paternal, PTSD is related to increased risk for PTSD in offspring of Holocaust survivors. *Journal of Psychiatric Research*, 42, 1104–11.

Yehuda, R., Engel, S. M., Seckl., J., Maecus, S. M., and Berkowitz, G. S. (2005). Transgenerational effects of posttraumatic stress disorder in babies of mothers exposed to World Trade Center attacks. *Journal of Clinical Endocrinology and Metabolism*, 90, 4115–18.

Yehuda, R., Teicher, M. H., Trestman, R. L., Levengood, R. A., and Siever, L. J. (1996). Cortisol regulation in posttraumatic stress disorder and major depression: A chronological analysis. *Biological Psychiatry*, 40, 79–88.

Zachar, P., and Ellis, R. D. (2012). *Categorical versus dimensional models of affect: A seminar on the theories of Panksepp and Russell* (Consciousness and Emotion Series). Amsterdam: Benjamins.

Zaidan, H., Leshem, M., and Glaisler-Salomon, I. (2013). Prereproductive stree to female rats alters corticotropin releasing factor Type 1 expression In ova and behavior and brain corticotropin releasing factor Type 1 in offspring. *Biological Psychiatry*, 74, 680–87.

Zept, S., and Hartmann, S. (2008). Some thoughts on empathy and contertransference. *Journal of the American Psychoanalytic Association*, 56, 741–68.

Zwiebel, R. (2004). The third position: Reflection about internal analytic working process. *Psychoanalytic Quarterly*, 73, 215–65.

INDEX

empathetic reflection for, 161

holding for, 161

implications and treatment for, 161–62

interpersonal limitations of, 157

narcissistic personality structure costs to, 156, 155

injury and defense and, 143–62

narrative(s). *see also* self-narrative(s)

developing, 109–15

emotions conveyed through, 98

intersubjectivity and, 99–103

nature of, 97–99

roots of, 99–103

"negative" bias, 81

negative feedback

positive feedback *vs.,* 137–38

negative self-narratives, 176

negative self-systems, 106–7

negative spin

case example, 100–1, 118–21, 108–11

neuron(s)

mirror. *see* mirror neuron(s)

neural lessons

power of, 122–25

neural maps

unconscious, 9

neural self-systems

enaction of, 57

neural systems

interacting with environment, 8

neuroscience

in art of healing, 233–37

for clinicians, 178–81

to mental activity, 236

nondynamic unconscious, xxi–xxiii

nonverbal communication attunement and, 225–26

normative unconscious, xxi–xxiii

novelty–routinization dimension of brain/mind processes, 18

Oettinger, G., 177

Ogden, T.H., 234, 214

out-of-awareness learning process, 131

out-of-awareness patterns, 5

out-of-awareness route to amygdala, 47–48

PAG. *see* periaqueductal gray (PAG)

panic/grief system, 52

Panksepp, J., 9, 10, 18, 22, 36, 37, 41, 57, 58, 60, 153, 95–96, 109–10, xxiv

Papie, E.K., 177

parental attunement

in child's emotional development, 99–100

parental PTSD, 189–190

parental trauma

physio/affective marks on next generation of, 190

patient(s)

therapists and, 222–24

Perani, D., 84, 60–61

perception

action and, 59–60

amygdala's impact on, 51

perceptual processing, 8

in cerebellum, 13–15
defensive functions of, xix
dreams as voice of, 32–35
dynamic, xxi–xxiii
enacted, 56–60
fault of, 1–35
inclusive and comprehensive
nature of, 2
memory research on, 26–30
neuropsychological model
within existing clinical
knowledge, 31–32
new model in context of old
concepts, xx–xxi
nondynamic, xxi–xxiii
normative, xxi–xxiii
power of, xxii
scope of action and influence
of, 4–6
sexual urges and, xxiii
tackling of, xv–xxvi
"vast," xxiv
unconscious action
in cerebellum, 13–15
unconscious automaticity and
repetition, 8
unconscious brain/mind, 4–6
unconscious communication
shared, 84–87
unconscious convictions
case example, 138–42
power of, 138–42
unconscious defensive systems
personality traits and, 154–55
unconscious disturbing emotional state
"disconfirmation" of, 178
unconscious fears
consciously felt fears *vs.,* 48

unconscious identification
with therapist, 182
unconscious neural maps, 9
unconscious processes
connectedness of, 2
described, 2–4
function of, 55–75
as inferred or glimpsed, 56–57
neural connections underpinning, 5–6
revealed, 76–94
as silent but constant engines
behind most psychological
functions, 3–4
subcortical regions role in,
9–16. *see also* subcortical
regions
therapeutic implications of,
60–64
unconscious self-system(s), 8,
xxv
active self-system *vs.,* 66
embedded fears as part of,
45–48
in intergenerational enactment
of trauma, 189–210. *see also*
intergenerational
transmission of trauma
intersubjectivity and, 211–28
self-narratives as expression
of, 95–121
unconscious system(s)
either-or-responses and,
152–54
power of learning in shaping,
26
unconscious to conscious
therapeutic significance of,
70–73

17 Is K priming R?
    i.e. is enough "rejecting" causing him to blow?
    humiliation
    "decision to expel R".?
    R. never gets attunement?
       nor does K?
    love for children
    · self-love?
    love fr other

66 the P's
82·3

* 146 Defenses
√ 161-2 relational vs. self psych